american ships

american ships

ALEXANDER LAING

American Heritage Press [c1971] New York

Book design by Elaine Gongora
Typography and composition by University Graphics, Inc.

Library of Congress Catalog Card Number: 76-149727
07-035846-X

TITLE PAGE: Crowninshield's wharf, Salem, in 1806, as painted by George Ropes

To My First
and Best Shipmate
BILL GRIFFIN,
1903–1958

Contents

Foreword

My main theme is a talent for innovation developed by peoples of the Americas as they shaped materials at hand into watercraft answering to their specific needs and circumstances. We begin with evocative remnants of a marine activity perhaps 4,000 years old and approach a conclusion as twilight fades in the latter 1920's upon the raveled canvas of New Bedford's last working whaler: an arbitrary beginning but the actual end to the vast whale hunt that first made Yankee enterprise distinctive throughout the world of water and gave to our literature its largest epic tale. Dark follies of greed and ruthlessness mar the achievement throughout, as Herman Melville knew. There is not much to glorify. Ours is a mixed history of a generally violent people who have put their worst with their best into adventures upon the sea, and continue to do so.

A long row of volumes, a few of which have already been written by specialists, will be required for an adequate treatment of this theme. Here I attempt only to interweave a selection of representative marine developments into a pattern that may suggest many more, thus leaving myself room for some attention to the social and physical "specific needs and circumstances" to which several particular examples of innovative American watercraft were responses.

One thing will be found missing: the customary romantic sketch of an impulsive North American primate gripping a log with his knees while he makes the enormous technological discovery that the motion of hands in water will move it forward. Surely it must have happened? Most probably it has happened for the very first time over and over again in many places, but there is not the thinnest flicker of evidence that this really was the beginning of man's long adventure afloat. For maneuverable whaling craft of some sort, based four millenniums ago on the Pacific shores of Alaska, there is scientifically respectable evidence, although we as yet have no idea what they looked like. Where the record falters, between scraps of fact that have survived accident, I have tried to label with clear signs of warning the urge to suppose.

The point is often stressed that sudden inventions in the history of watercraft have been minor, and extremely few. No-one "invented" the schooner or the submarine or the steamer or the clipper ship. Improvement is the best that can be claimed for nearly all seeming novelties: improvement and the adaptation of well-known devices in novel combinations.

This book is concerned with performances only when they have stimulated the evolving shapes and controlling mechanisms of vessels afloat. A dramatic happening that called attention to the shortcomings or virtues of an unusual ship should have influenced the shape or equipment of others, but a slow accretion of experience seems to have produced most valid changes. What form of hull, under what rig, had the best success in biting its way around Cape Horn? What would a skipper hope to have under his heels next time, after a month-long tussle to gain fifty miles against the currents and the slamming westerlies in 56 degrees south latitude? The mounting experience of many such occasions forced particular changes in hull and rig to produce the Cape Horner. Yet there were famous shipmasters—some of them naval heroes—who did nothing significant to improve the kinds of ships in which they spent their lives. Many senior officers of the United States Navy, for two or three decades before the Civil War, ardently opposed any considerable change in the fighting ships to which they had become accustomed.

Shipmasters in the merchant marine had a much better record for enterprise. Some, like Robert Bennet Forbes, were notable experimenters in marine technology, but the valid theorists have been curiously few. Naval architecture, as a profession based in conceptual and experimental science, has existed for not much more than a century. The earlier eminent designers combined experience with inspiration, shaping vessels that sometimes were highly successful, but the rules of design by which they purported to work were akin to the mystical formulas of alchemy. The two Americans who probably did most to establish naval architecture as a scientific profession, John W. Griffiths and Samuel Hartt Pook, figure more largely in this book than in its predecessors. It has been the custom to mention Pook with the highest respect, while offering almost no information by which a reader may judge the opinion. I have made a start here toward putting the record of his work to rights.

Excepting the cod fishery and the coastwise hauling of passengers and freight, whaling was the earliest American marine activity to attain a highly developed technology worthy of endurance with little change. It is the cable of consistent experience that holds this book together, often submerged while other subjects are on the surface, but there all the way. The neglected career of Samuel Hartt Pook provides a similar ligature across the last half of the nineteenth century: a line of reference to the conditions that produced in the early 1850's the response of his incomparable wooden sailing ships but that soon thereafter turned him toward an increasing reliance upon metal and steam.

I have hoped to clear away some misconceptions of the interplay between these two structural materials and these two means of thrust, which emerged sometimes in curious combinations up to the days—within this century—when it became clear that metal, both for hulls and for propulsive mechanisms, had won out. The frustrated final voyage of the last United States whaler propelled only by canvas brings to a symbolic end the principal interplay of these forces. It is followed in this account by a brief inspection of the highly innovative recent whaling activity in the Antarctic, not because the two United States vessels that were marginally involved represent creative contributions to a much revised technology, but to demonstrate that technical innovation may in this field as in others be a menace if uncontrolled by a humane intention. The earlier kinds of vessels with which this account begins its consideration of whaling were wrought from natural materials found nearby—the skins of aquatic creatures, driftwood, birchbark—substances intimately suited to the regions of their use. This close interrelationship between man and his surroundings, now the belated subject of intense public concern, has been an overlooked factor in past considerations of the origins and evolution of watercraft. Archaeologists and anthropologists have given it sporadic attention, but since the remarkable treatises of Griffiths in the middle of the nineteenth century, technical discussions of naval architecture have avoided it as a rule.

For a rightness that blended continually into the lives of its developers, the kayak seems to me a much more admirable technological achievement than the nuclear-powered submarine: the kayak, as pure and uncluttered in conceptual form as a primary formula of basic scientific research. Its persistence in vital use over many centuries, as the best answer to needs and circumstances of its region, suggests a measurement of merit applicable when judging anything else that has been built by man, including whalers of a larger size. Nothing in this country's experience better exemplifies its intransigeant devotion to conflicting endeavors—the heroic as well as the idiotic aspects of an assault upon the natural world which for too long has assumed that the victim would cheerfully replace, for the advantage of man, anything he plundered from a bounty that seemed limitless.

The assault upon whales in particular, to meet pressing human needs, has come very close in the last decade or so to the elimination of this particular resource from all the oceans. By what standards, then, are we to judge the comparative merits of watercraft that have made possible so muddled an achievement? Has the development of devices by which to inflict prolonged and hideous cruelties upon other creatures, as a matter of routine, any part in such judgments? This question, which surfaces briefly in some classic accounts of whaling only to be evaded, may itself be evaluated by the reader as he proceeds. Whaling watercraft are convenient exemplars of a problem that appears even more intensely in the development of efficient slavers and in the more recent creation of oil tankers so large (a thousand times the capacity of a classical whaleship of a century ago) that any accident inflicts upon the life of sea and shore a colossal devastation. Have intricacy and largeness anything to do with basic merit? Such considerations are not the prerogative solely of specialists.

The problem of design as a meaningful reflection both of purpose and of physical surroundings, in a human context, has generally been exemplified throughout the following pages by an examination of the careers of specific ships. The movement toward a suitable rig for long-voyage whalers appears in what can be untangled from records of two contemporary Nantucket vessels named the *Leo*. The early career of the China packet *Race Horse* takes precedence over better-known contemporaries and their voyages, which have been considered at length in prior works. A number of vessels, such as the iron tug *R. B. Forbes,* emerge as having a greater importance than previous casual references would indicate. A few famous ships, typified by the early clipper *Sea Witch,* appear so frequently in contemporary comparisons that they should not be obscured by any routine desire to avoid what is well known.

While prowling like the princes of Serendip in search of something else, I have stumbled over information on some topics that makes the standard summaries or the habitual curt references to them seem seriously in error. These include David Bushnell's submarine of 1775 and the 90-day gunboats of 1861, which are here given, I hope, their belated due.

At the first mention of any particular vessel in the text following I have roughly indicated her size by her capacity tonnage. The repetitious phrasing, although it reads awkwardly, is justified further as one quick means of distinguishing between vessels christened with the same name. Capacity tonnage is a measurement of usable cubic space inside an arbitrarily curving container. It has nothing to do with the number of tons by weight that the vessel can carry; in the case of light or bulky cargo this often is irrelevant. It is not a measurement either of the water displaced. The concept originated with a count of the number of "tuns" a vessel could stow, each tun holding 252 old wine gallons. Formulas for determining tonnage have varied from time to time and at the same time in different places. Still, for most vessels of the great age of European exploration it is the only measurement that survives. In functional comparisons between more recent vessels their usable interior space makes for fairer judgments than their gross or displacement tonnages. It should be noted, however, for reasons given in Appendix A, that prior to the close of the American Civil War registered measurement tonnage reflected true capacity with an uncertainty flickering between the capricious and the bizarre. It may be helpful to remember that typical ships of the early European age of exploration measured less than 100 tons; that most whalers were registered at 300, more or less; that for the great early clippers the figure is around 1,000; and that in a few late instances a capacity of about 5,000 tons was found to be the limit for steel vessels driven by wind alone. Length, which was also variously measured—on the keel, on the water line, on deck—varied in the above cases from as little as 50 feet to something over 400. Within these limits, comparisons are more often indicative than precise.

Major aspects of a large subject that have been covered in standard works are here, as a rule, merely sketched in for continuity. I have aimed only to supplement what has been splendidly done by Carl C. Cutler, Howard I. Chapelle, and Robert G. Albion. My debt to many earlier students, who wrote before the kind of scholarship that steadily marks the contributions of these three came into fashion, is indicated in the text. The book for which I have most often felt a frustrated need is a comprehensive history of American whaling. Alexander Starbuck's basic work is a roughed-out monument, riddled with errors and unexplained anomalies. Its tabulations have been carried forward with admirable devotion by Reginald B. Hegarty, up to the last deep-sea voyage by harpooners of the United States; yet his work too has errors and omissions. Although scores of accounts help to fill in the chinks, questions dependent upon an orderly scanning of all early logbooks and port records remain to be answered. The last significant whaling activities of Americans, based at San Francisco, have been little noticed, perhaps because Starbuck's history ends just before they strongly began. Edouard A. Stackpole, Curator of Mystic Seaport, in his introduction to Lloyd C. M. Hare's somewhat fictionalized monograph, called San Francisco whaling in 1960 "this practically unknown chapter in American whaling." I have had space here only to sketch in the outlines. A book is called for.

My thanks to a representative few of those who have generously helped me with this undertaking will perhaps symbolize, at least, a variety of debts I owe to many others: thanks, then, to Miss Clara Beetle, for information concerning the most eminent builders of whaleboats; to Mrs. Linda Sykes, for tracking down pictures of the hardest sort to find, some of which I feared did not exist; to Alfred Mayor, editor, for maintaining his cool aplomb as the text relentlessly grew to five times the wordage stipulated in the original contract, and even more for his wise guidance in helping me to bring it down again to only four times that once-contemplated length; to Ramon Guthrie, who gave to a careful reading of both galleys and page proofs time that should have gone into the making of his own superb poems; and to Veronica, my wife, for all sorts of sustaining help, particularly with the fearsome discipline of indexing.

As on previous occasions, the reference services of Dartmouth College's Baker Library, directed by Professor Virginia Close, have helped me incomparably. The good-humored patience and insight with which she and her assistants have located strange titles afar, for use on interlibrary loan, has made the inland writing of this book possible, between infrequent visits to the seaport repositories. For the kind welcome I have learned to count upon at the Massachusetts Historical Society in Boston and at the Peabody Museum of Salem I want to thank Stephen T. Riley and Ernest S. Dodge, their directors, whose policies encourage the gracious impulses of their staffs. This book about the shaping of ships got the beginnings of its own shape in visits to the Smithsonian Institution in Washington, where Howard I. Chapelle, Curator of Transportation in the Museum of History and Technology, is generous of his learning.

A. L.

Hanover, New Hampshire,
February 17, 1971

american
ships

1 Shaping a Ship

EARLY AMERICAN WHALE HUNTERS

In the sands of a broad beach that has been building outward from Cape Krusenstern, on the northwest coast of Alaska, archaeologists have identified 114 strips of artifacts and other remains of the kind of culture that lives at the sea's edge, dependent upon products of the sea. The materials of a distinct culture, evidently the oldest, have been turned up in digs on higher slopes inland. All those along the beach define former waterfronts, which for a while were relatively stable between geological movements or periods of violent weather that put an inconvenient new stretch of sand between the homes of the people and the water that provided sustenance. The most recently inhabited strip, nearest to the present waterfront, and several more that run parallel with it nearby, contain evidence of fishermen and small-game hunters. Beach strip Number 53 differs suddenly and dramatically in its long-hidden contents, revealing activities that are not hinted at in any of the archaeological digs made nearer to the ocean, nor in any of those made beyond it, up to the higher ground. The people of beach strip 53 had left in the earth clear evidence, discovered by J. Louis Giddings, that they were whalers. Skeletal parts of whales entered somewhat into the structure of their collapsed houses. Whale skulls and other massive bones are concentrated in this beach strip to an extent that cannot be plausibly explained by the supposition that the animals had all been stranded when the beach was narrower.

The most telling evidence of this one whaling culture among many that came earlier and later was found by Giddings in their weapons. These, from layered deposits carbon dated at about 3,800 years ago, include the basic harpoon and lance: the harpoon to secure and hold on to a whale, the lance used to probe deep and accurately at last for the kill. Among the artifacts of beach 53 there was a harpoon blade; "its size," Giddings wrote, "was much greater than flint blades we knew to have been set into harpoon heads for walrus hunting." It was about four inches long and three wide, artfully chipped from chalcedony, with keen entering edges and a blunt base to prevent its being easily withdrawn. Heads of the same shape and dimensions were noted in use by the Eskimo whalers of Point Barrow, still farther north, about a century ago. The lance blade, likewise of chalcedony, was twice as long as the harpoon but only half as wide, suitable to thrust, withdraw, and thrust again.

Other weapons found in beach 53 were unlike those of the adjacent cultures but similar to some found in northern Greenland. Lance and harpoon forms in the Arctic are diverse, including many ancient examples of the toggle harpoon that was credited as an invention of New England blacksmiths of the early nineteenth century, but the basic forms for use in the most arduous hunting avoided complexities that might weaken them at a perilous moment. The simple, rugged harpoon and lance from the Cape Krusenstern whalers' house could hardly have been used to advantage upon lesser creatures.

These were the two weapons, translated from stone into metal, that became standard in the Bay of Biscay and northern Europe. Both, when earliest observed in use by the chroniclers, were flung or thrust from the bows of small watercraft. Other means of attack were in use elsewhere, but the presence of harpoons and lances in the spacious pit houses of Cape Krusenstern strongly suggests their use in whaling craft of some kind, in the very waters where whalers of the United States made their last dubious forays.

It is tempting to suppose that if weapons hold to so strict a pair of patterns, over thousands of years, then the vessels from which they were used should have been similarly standardized in the unchanging conditions of isolated subarctic life. No remains of ancient Eskimo vessels have been unearthed, but early observers from Europe reported upon the use of bidarkas in this region as whalers. These were a form of kayak. A French voyager, Auguste Bernard du Hautcilly, described a whale hunt observed in 1827. It was so different from European practices that the method appears to have been indigenous:

Frederick Martens published in Amsterdam, in 1685, his account of the manner in which whaling was practiced in the European Arctic. Its symbolic title page displays prominently the metal harpoon and lance that had long been the essential, supplementary weapons of the whale hunt. For how long? The broad harpoon and slim lance blades of chalcedony, reproduced at the left at about two-thirds of their actual size, were found a few years ago by J. Louis Giddings in the ruins of an Eskimo whaler's house on the northwestern Alaska coast. Carbon dating indicated that they had been used in the whale chase almost 4,000 years ago. (See pp. 1–2.)

DE
NOORDSCHE
WERELD.

. . . several hundred bidarkas . . . pursue the monster . . . every time it is obliged to appear above the water to breathe, they hurl at it all at once a plentiful rain of small harpoons to which bladders are attached . . . until the whale, bristling with harpoons, can no longer overcome the resistance of these bladders together . . . they finish it then with longer and stronger darts.

Harpoons and lances: this may have been the ancient method of their use off Cape Krusenstern. We do not know.

In the summer of 1892 Hartson H. Bodfish, mate of the steam whaler *Mary D. Hume,* came upon a recently abandoned Eskimo village at Warren Point, on the northern Canadian coast of the Beaufort Sea. Many pole graves suggested a flight from pestilence. "These natives must have been whalers," he wrote, "for there were bones of whales about the place and other indications of whaling. . . . the graves were filled with relics and native-made weapons." Some of the Eskimos he encountered in the region, who had never before seen white men, had harpoons and lances of forged copper, but most were of stone. This region lies a third of the way from Cape Krusenstern to Greenland.

For the very earliest contemporary written accounts of indigenous American seafarers the scene shifts down from the Arctic Circle to earth's next convenient hoop, the Tropic of Cancer, and eastward along this invisible line into another sea.

DUGOUTS OF THE CARIBBEAN

On Saturday, October 13, 1492, the ships of Columbus were visited by "small canoes, made out of the trunk of a tree like a long boat, and all of one piece, and wonderfully worked, considering the country. They are large, some of them holding 40 to 45 men, others smaller, and some only large enough to hold one man. They are propelled with a paddle like a baker's shovel, and go at a marvellous rate."

This report, written on the second day of the explorer's first visit to the island he mistook for Japan, is the earliest dated reference we have to watercraft made in America. It gives us at the outset some idea of the material, structure, range of sizes, builders' skill, and speed. The material, huge tree trunks, suits the locality. Nothing of the sort could have been used at Cape Krusenstern.

Thirteen days later, during his search for a place that some natives he had taken aboard called Cuba, Columbus was told by them as he anchored for the night that "thence to Cuba was a voyage in their canoes of a day and a half; these being small dug-outs without a sail. Such are their canoes." The Spaniards, logging about 8 knots part of the time, ran more than 130 miles by their reckoning to a Cuban river, which suggests that the canoes could reliably navigate in the open ocean, between the Bahamas and Cuba, at a rate of 80 or 90 miles a day, and without a sail.

A month later, detailing the virtues of his new-found land for the king, Columbus describes how "in some pleasant groves of trees, like a delightful orchard" he saw "a canoe, dug out of one tree, as big as a galley of twelve benches, fastened under a boat-house made of wood, and thatched with palm leaves, so that it could be neither injured by sun nor by water." Another, "dug out of a single tree, 95 palmos long, and capable of carrying 150 persons," is the largest he mentions. At 8¾ inches to the palmo, she would have been about 70 feet long.

There are other such references in the journals and in letters. Columbus tells the Chancellor of the Exchequer that most of the canoes are "larger than a barge of eighteen seats. They are not so wide, because they are made of one single piece of timber, but a barge could not keep up with them in rowing, because they go with incredible speed, and with these canoes they navigate among these islands, which are innumerable, and carry on their traffic. I have seen in some of these canoes seventy and eighty men, each with his oar."

These observations include no close descriptions of structure. Taken with other reports in the Columbus manuscripts, they do boldly reveal a skillful people in and near the Caribbean Sea, who had almost no interest in clothing and were content with modest houses for themselves, but gave loving attention to the construction, maintenance, and shelter of their water-craft. Columbus seems not to have observed their use as whale-boats, but other Spaniards, a bit later, did. They were swift enough. Some, which would have been unnecessarily large for the pursuit of whales, were longer than either of the Spaniards' two caravels and were designed to accommodate about as many men. All were limited in lateral dimensions by the thickness of a single available tree faired to shape, but this limitation brought with it the gift of great speed. A boat built of strakes upon a frame could be made of any width. The larger European boats were typically much more beamy than a canoe of similar length, safer no doubt, but slower. The brisk deep-water traffic described by Columbus is evidence of a well-developed model for voyaging, stable enough to be relied upon by large crews who understood its whims. The sheltered boathouses would have been necessary to keep these huge unit carvings from splitting if they dried out too quickly.

A single reference to sail, by Columbus, tells us that there was no sail. If, on the Atlantic coasts of the pre-Columbian Americas, sail was in use anywhere south of Greenland, the earliest European observers failed to report it. Second-generation evidence is regarded as dubious by most scholars.

From Greenland southward, all the primary reports of native American watercraft describe either bark canoes or dugouts similar to those seen by Columbus. Vespucci, who accidentally bestowed his given name upon two continents, chased a cannibal dugout canoe in the southern Caribbean for hours in what he described as his own "fast sailing caravel" before he could overtake the 70 paddlers. Vespucci's accuracy has at many points been questioned, but this episode has a melancholy circumstantial aspect. The cannibals jumped overboard near shore, leaving in the canoe four freshly castrated boys who were being brought home to be fattened.

The method of manufacturing such huge dugouts seems to have been the same everywhere, although the shapes differed. Here is the description given by Captains Amadas and Barlowe in their account of the 1584 voyage to Virginia:

The manner of making their boates is thus: they burne downe some great tree, or take such as are winde fallen, and putting gumme and rosen upon one side thereof, they set fire into it, and when it hath burnt it hollow, they cut out the coale with their shels, and ever where they would burne it deeper or wider they lay on gummes, which burne away the timber, and by this meanes they fashion very fine boates, and such as will transporte twentie men. Their oares are like scoopes, and many times they set with long pooles, as the depth serveth.

THE GUARA RAFT

The earliest report of a vessel of native design seen under sail by a primary European intruder into coastal waters of the

Americas was made by Bartolomeo Ruiz in 1526. To reach the locality of this occurrence we move due south from the subtropical Cuba of Columbus to another imaginary girdle, the equator, where a Spanish fleet under Francisco Pizarro and Diego de Almagro was probing southward from Panama toward the shining rumor of Peru.

Vasco Nuñez de Balboa and his scrupulous notary make no mention of any vessels seen under sail on the south side of the Isthmus of Panama until the conquistador himself built there from badly chosen wood some ships that were promptly sunk by ravenous worms. The calamity, if you wish, may be regarded as a well-earned retribution for the conquistador's indomitable viciousness in whipping Indian slaves through swamps and over mountains with timbers on their shoulders that had been shaped by Spanish shipwrights on the coast of the Caribbean. It has pertinence here as a reminder that there is a functional connection between the watercraft of any locality and its own available materials.

Balboa, and his successors on the Pacific coast for almost a decade after his head fell, had found nothing in limited probes toward the south to substantiate accounts of riches given them by the inhabitants of Panama. The Pizarro-Almagro expedition, more ambitiously planned, likewise had been disappointed so far when it paused near the equator for refreshment and sent Ruiz ahead in a small frigate. In latitude 3 degrees 30 minutes south, Ruiz captured a ship capable of carrying about 36 tons, by comparison with his own frigate's 40. The deck and hull were made of what he called "reeds as thick as posts," tied with a hemplike rope. The upper deck was made of "thinner reeds, tied with the said cords, whereupon the people and merchandise ride on brushwood because everything beneath gets wet. It carried masts and yards of very fine timber and sails of cotton of the same shape as with our ships, and very good rigging . . . like hemp, and some anchor stones similar to millstones."

Ruiz reported that he threw eleven of the crew overboard, seized the other nine, put six of these ashore, and kept three for interpreters. The available vocabulary of primary observers, confronted by strange objects, is often inadequate. It seems clear enough from the general description, forwarded to Spain five years before Pizarro went south again to the final conquest of Peru, that Ruiz was referring to soft, durable balsa logs when he

European engravers made their own kind of sense out of sketches brought home by travelers from the New World. Guara boards, the unique navigational controls of Peruvian sailing rafts, may have become paddles in a picture *(upper left)* from Benzoni's voyage of 1572. The manner of their use is faithfully if faintly shown in Spilbergen's *Speculum Orientalis* of 1619 *(lower left)*, as a close look at three seamen in the adjacent detail will show. Both pictures mismanage the biped masts drawn correctly by Humboldt *(top, above)* and Admiral Paris *(center)* early in the nineteenth century. (See pp. 7–10, 13.)

wrote of "reeds as thick as posts." It has sometimes been objected
that there is no evidence of aboriginal sail in any temperate
waters of the Americas until a period long enough after the first
Spanish conquest to make it seem that the natives were imitating
a device brought in by the invaders. This is probably the case
with canoes seen by Gonzalo Fernandez de Oviedo off Cartagena
in 1522 "with two sailes . . . which they make of very good
cotton." Many Spaniards had been on this coast over a period of
two or three decades without making any such observation.
There are, however, clear hints in the early chronicles of Panama
that the accounts of Peru given to the Spaniards by the cacique
Comogre and other eminent Indians included information that
the Incas had sailing vessels. Large fleets of balsa rafts under
sail, encountered by Pizarro himself not long afterward, can
hardly be explained by word drifting south from Panama in the
mouths of Indian travelers. That explanation becomes wholly
implausible in the light of experimental researches by Thor
Heyerdahl, who called to notice, after his *Kon Tiki* voyage from
Peru far into Polynesia, the fact that the guara boards in Peruvian
museums were surviving proof of an ancient method of navigation under sail.

The guara board is one of the major technological ingenuities
of the New World. The fact that its function was misapprehended
until 15 or 20 years ago, by scholars who neglected their home-
work, long cast an aura of dubiousness over the well-recorded
achievements of the nautical craftsmen and navigators of Peru.
Heyerdahl meant to build in the *Kon Tiki* a faithful duplicate
of the deep-water sailing vessels described by the first Spaniard
to encounter them. He assumed that she could reach Polynesia
only by riding a known western current in the belt of the southeast trade winds. The idea that a raft could possibly be made to
sail against the wind did not enter into his calculations, partly
because it was irrelevant to his first purpose: to present experimental proof that the islands of Polynesia could have been
peopled from South America. The dramatic wreck of the *Kon
Tiki*, on an atoll against which she was inevitably blown by
the following wind, could probably have been avoided if she had
been given the most significant item of an Incan craft's structure,
a set of guara boards.

The multitudinous small American craft called Sailfish and

Sunfish, flat as a dinner plate, have exactly the same device: a dagger board that can be thrust downward through a "trunk," or slot, amidships to reduce the tendency to slip sidewise, but so thin that it presents only a little resistance to forward motion. By a twist of the rudder the Sailfish can be made to swing upwind, pivoting on its dagger board. The test of a practical sailing vessel in most regions is this ability to turn into the wind—to tack—and make positive progress aslant toward the direction from which the wind is blowing.

As it turned out, there was an abundance of printed as well as manuscript evidence of the manner in which guara boards had been used in Peruvian navigation. It was only necessary for a researcher to have a reason for digging it out. The doom-struck hours that Heyerdahl had spent while his craft was blown toward a coral reef with nothing to be done about it were reason enough. In Sydney, Australia, he found an unpublished journal written in 1840 by Captain George Blaxland that described an encounter between a British naval vessel and a balsa raft at an island 60 miles off the Peruvian coast, to which the native skipper had sailed to catch and dry a cargo of fish. "The vessel I was in, a schooner of 40 tons sailed for the same place in company, and it was surprising to see the manner the raft held the Wind, going at the rate of four or five knots an hour; we kept together for some time and arrived the next day within a few hours of each other." The voyage was made against a contrary wind. Blaxland reported that even at this date the commerce of some parts of the coast was made "entirely by these balsas." Many carried salt between ports "two or three hundred miles apart, another proof they are trustworthy."

Some references to guara rafts in well-known works are confusing because of special terminology. William Dampier, the buccaneer-botanist, told of another buccaneer's report that he had captured in the "Bay of Guiaquil . . . a Bark-log, or pair of Bark-logs as we call it, laden chiefly with Flower. She had other Goods . . . he took out as much of each as he had occasion for, and then turned her away again. The Master of the Float told him, that the Kings ships were gone from Lima." The fact that the buccaneers had their own name—Bark-log—and that Dampier further describes her as a float confirm her identity as a guara raft freighter in common use at the end of the seventeenth century. She was captured about 800 miles north of Lima, from which she appears to have brought recent news.

The late assumption that the natives must have borrowed sail from the Spaniards seems to have diverted attention from such evidences. But sail alone, borrowed or not, failed to explain the remarkable, frequently observed handling qualities of balsa rafts in rugged weather. The first visual clue is a drawing published in 1619 by a Dutch circumnavigator, Joris van Spilbergen. It is crude, but it clearly shows the device for handling the small raft: three of the five crew members in the act of raising and lowering guara boards, one forward, two aft. There was no rudder or steering oar. None was needed.

Suppose a raft with the minimum of two boards—one forward, one aft—was sailing with the wind blowing against the starboard quarter, the rear right-hand corner, both boards down. If the board at the stern was lifted, that part of the vessel would present less resistance to being blown sidewise. With the board at the bow still down, the balsa would begin to pivot upon it and turn its head into the wind. When the desired direction had been attained, the board at the stern would be lowered again. The resistance to sideslip, fore and aft, would be equalized, and the raft would hold its new course, somewhat against the wind. The sail would have had to be trimmed at the same time.

To veer away from the wind, the forward board would be lifted, and the head of the raft would be blown around on the pivot of the board astern. In the larger rafts there were several guara boards, amidships as well as fore and aft. These divided the leverage pressures, which if only two large boards had been used might have pried the balsa logs apart. They also provided for the gradual adjustments that the steersman of a vessel with a rudder sometimes wishes he could make when the single controlling blade develops an ailment known as lee helm.

Several of the earliest historians of Peru received from independent sources substantially identical accounts of a yearlong voyage to distant Pacific islands made in about the year A.D. 1457 by the impetuous Inca Tupac Yupanqui. The event was recorded when survivors of the voyage could still have been alive. One informant was the guardian of sacred objects brought home by the Inca. A Spanish viceroy, a hundred years after the event, credited the story sufficiently to outfit a lavish expedition to search for the islands. He put his young nephew Alvaro de Mendaña in charge of it. Later, with the notion that the Peruvians must have borrowed sail from the Spaniards, the account drifted into fable. Yet its historical sources are as well verified as those of some accepted European voyages of the same century. Heyerdahl proved with the *Kon Tiki,* even though she lacked the vitally important guara boards, that the outward voyage in such a craft could have been made. With the addition of guara boards the homeward voyage should also have been possible. Indeed, the upwind sailing qualities of late commercial guara rafts, observed by Blaxland and others, indicate that they were more weatherly than the best vessels built by the Spaniards themselves on the Pacific coasts of the Americas in the first century or so after the conquest. The history of Pacific exploration is full of occasions when a navigator found it impossible to beat back to an island in plain view that had been passed in the darkness.

Heyerdahl, by a combination of research and adventurous experiment, has brought to the guara balsa sailing raft belated recognition as a practical device in which the physics of propulsion and of maneuver were uncommonly well applied. It held its own as a deep-water fisherman and freighter for four centuries after the introduction of planked vessels in the European style. His detractors, most of whom seem unwilling to forgive him for having done extraordinary field work without first undergoing their own tedious martyrdom of graduate study, have not shaken his main points: (1) that sailing craft of an utterly novel design were seen in large numbers by the first Europeans to arrive off the Peruvian coast, (2) that guara boards found in pre-Columbian graves had no usefulness except in connection with sails, (3) that early visitors observed and described this use. It is a mournful judgment upon some assumptions of archaeological scholarship that a function immediately perceived by many nautical men was quibbled over for years in professional journals until Dr. Clinton R. Edwards, in 1965, curtly announced that "the case for Ecuadorian and Peruvian aboriginal sailing is closed," thus completely supporting the heretic Heyerdahl.

THE NORTH AMERICAN BARK CANOE

None of the early reports of the guara balsa raft suggests that it was ever employed as a whaler, but another distinctive craft of American origin appears to have been in some respects the true parent of the final whaleboat. Jacques Cartier witnessed its use in 1534 for the pursuit of a smaller marine mammal. When off Newfoundland, on his first voyage of exploration, he noted: "They have canoes made of birchbark in which they go about and from which they catch many seals. . . . I have been informed . . . that they come from warmer countries to catch these seals."

Cartier's report was followed by many others to confirm the versatility of birchbark canoes, which represent a long technological leap ahead of the Caribbean dugout. It seems likely that the bark canoes were first developed on northerly inland rivers, but special variants were often observed on deep water. Settlers from Europe paid them the best of compliments, adopting them in preference to their own planked vessels for river travel and borrowing much from both model and method of manufacture for the cedar-planked whaleboats that they later carried all over the world.

It was a common practice of the sixteenth-century explorers to have a shallow-draft flyboat in company to investigate harbors and estuaries or to search for good holding ground for the anchors of larger ships. Still smaller vessels, with confusingly interchangeable names—shallop, frigate, pinnace, brigantine—were carried in frames, ready to be set up ashore and planked when needed. Sometimes these were built of green timber on the spot. But on inland rivers all such smaller vessels of exploration were promptly abandoned in favor of the light, excellently adapted native product, the birchbark canoe. Howard I. Chapelle says of them:

The great skill exhibited in their design and construction shows that a long period of development must have taken place before they became known to white men. . . . they were capable of being propelled easily with a single-bladed paddle. This allowed the paddler, unlike the oarsman, to face the direction of travel, a necessity in obstructed or shoal waters and in fast-moving streams. . . . The bark canoe . . . shares with the Eskimo kayak the distinction of being one of the few primitive craft of which the basic models are retained in the boats of civilized men.

The availability of a phenomenally light wood on the Peruvian coast was the principal factor in the development of a capacious, stable, oceanworthy sailing raft. There was no incentive, once the guara board had been developed, to employ intricate shaping and fastening processes like those of the Polynesians to produce a hollow vessel of similar capacity from wood much harder to work.

In North America the prevalence of a strong, light bark was the primary factor in the development of a craft particularly suitable for the special aspects of stream and river travel. These aspects included rapids and waterfalls. A light, narrow vessel, easily repairable, could shoot the rapids in one direction and be carried around them in the other, both choices prohibitively dangerous and irksome for even the smaller kinds of ships' boats. The resilient strength of frame of a bark canoe was one of its important qualities. This, too, came with the available materials. All who shape wooden ships hope for timber and planking in which the grain follows the final curvature, but even the best hand-sawing processes seldom provide it. The Indians of North America made a maximum use of round branches or small, tall-growing trees, split once and shaped in hot water. The result was a half round that was entirely straight-grained, with the least tendency to fracture after being fastened in place. Although some boring was done, most of the frame's members were fastened by overall lashing. The timbers of European boats were mutilated by their own fastenings, whether nails of metal or treenails of wood. The canoe's framing pieces were kept whole, bound together by thin, tough rootlets of black spruce—it too a straight-grained, unwounded substance having great strength.

Canoe design varied somewhat regionally, but the manner of construction did not. The shape was established by first building the gunwales and thwarts. This pattern was laid upon wet bark, which was bent upward around its edges and held so by many vertical stakes. The gunwale frame was then lifted and sewed to the bark. Ribs and stringers were inserted afterward, snug against the resulting envelope: the reverse of the European

Birchbark canoes made by local craftsmen were the freighters of the fur trade until early in the nineteenth century, largely because they struck a prudent bargain between lightness and strength. The pictures above emphasize a melancholy change that occurred when the Hudson's Bay Company began to substitute heavy planked boats. "Wearisome Portage" is the artist's title for the second picture. Pitched seams of a Chippewa canoe *(below)* hint at the ease with which damage could be repaired. (See pp. 15, 51.)

practice of building the frame first, to be planked afterward. Pitch sealed the seams and holes. Offshore canoes often had a keel-strip and gunwales humped upward amidships where the waves slopped in.

Use of the bark canoe as a whaleboat was observed on the coast of Florida by the *adelantado* Pedro Melendez, founder of Saint Augustine in 1565. The most detailed written account of what he saw appears in a natural history of the New World published in 1589 by Jose de Acosta, who also acknowledges as his informants "some expert men" well acquainted with the procedures involved. Acosta was an early missionary in Peru, where he says he encountered many witnesses who testified that "they sailed in the south sea before the Spaniards came." He begins his whaling passage in the Samuel Purchas translation with praise of his Creator for giving to "so base a Nation, as be the Indians, the industrie and courage to incounter the most fierce and deformed beast in the worlde." He continues:

The maner the Indians of Florida use . . . is, they put themselves into a canoe, which is like a barke of a tree, and in swimming approach neere the whales side, then with great dexteritie they leape to his necke, and there they ride as on horsebacke expecting his time, then hee thrusts a sharpe and strong stake, which hee carries with him, into the whales nosthrill, for so they call the hole or vent by which they breathe; presently he beates it in with an other stake as forcibly as hee can; in the meane space the Whale dooth furiously beate the sea, and raiseth mountaines of water, running into the deepe with great violence, and presently riseth againe, not knowing what to doe for paine; the Indian still sittes firme, and to give him full payment for his trouble, he beates another stake into the other vent or nosthrill, so as he stoppeth him quite, and takes away his breathing; then hee betakes him to his canoe, which he holds tied with a cord to the whales side, and goes to land, having first tied his corde to the whale, the which hee lettes run with the whale, who leapes from place to place whilest he finds water enough; being troubled with paine, in the end hee comes neere the land, and remaines on ground by the hugenesse of his body; then a great number of Indians come unto the conquered beast to gather his spoiles, they kill him, and cut his flesh in peeces, this do they drie and beate into powder, using it for meate, it dooth last them long. . . .

From its description of the tortured animal's behavior, much the same as that in later whaling narratives, Acosta's account seems to have been based in precise observation. An earlier brief description of essentially the same method appears in a work on West Indian medicines by Nicolás Monardes, published in Spain in 1574 and Englished in 1577 as *Joyfull Newes out of the Newe Found Worlde*. Acosta refers to it in corroboration of his own. The minor but distinct differences indicate information from different observers to strengthen the assumption of both accounts that the method was standard on the coast of Florida. Dr. Monardes studs his herbal with stories evidently picked up from voyagers who brought him his medicines, but he seldom identifies the source: in this case, "They that come from Florida." In his account the Indian, in "a little Boate," picks a young whale in company with its mother, lassos it, rides it down as it sounds, and plugs the nostril only when the animal comes up again in need of air: "surely a delicate and marveilous huntyng."

Theodore de Bry's engraving, widely distributed across Europe, gives us a dubious hint of the structure of a Floridian bark canoe. Although he was the first great visual publicist of the "newe founde worlde," his Indians resemble Flemings and he usually worked as best he could from verbal descriptions rather than from sketches. The important exception: his renderings on copper of the drawings made by John White.

White, who sailed on the several Virginia voyages promoted by Sir Walter Raleigh between 1584 and 1590—on the second as artist-cartographer and on the third as colonial governor—made the first sizable group of American drawings and paintings that have survived as finished originals. From some of these, probably made in 1585, we can check his precision as an observer against the known shapes of fish, insects, and birds that he drew. He took no notice of bark canoes of the Roanoke region, but his picture of "A Cannow" made from a tree trunk can still be compared with the engraving De Bry made from it in 1590. There is no known White original of the De Bry plate that immediately precedes it, detailing the method of manufacture of a dugout. The fact that there are three successive stages of the procedure in a single view is a hint that the engraver conceived his scene from a written account, and I assume that the

Theodore De Bry, illustrating in 1589 José de Acosta's report of the Indians of Florida, produced the engraving above of their method of whaling. The scene is probably reconstructed from a verbal account and tells us nothing reliable about the structure of the canoes. De Bry's method of using his sources can, however, be closely examined in his engravings based upon actual drawings made in Virginia by John White. White's canoe *(left, below)* is faithfully rendered, although the engraver elaborates the fish weir beyond it. (See pp. 17–22.)

The manner of makinge their boates. XII.

He manner of making their boates in Virginia is verye wonderfull. For wheras
they want Inſtruments of yron, or other like vnto ours, yet they knowe howe to
make them as handſomelye, to ſaile with whear they liſte in their Riuers, and to
fiſhe with all, as ours. Firſt they chooſe ſome longe, and thicke tree, according to
the bignes of the boate which they would frame, and make a fyre on the grownd
abowt the Roote therof, kindlinge the ſame by little, and little with drie moſſe of trees, and chipps
of woode that the flame ſhould not mounte opp to highe, and burne to muche of the lengte of the
tree. When yt is almoſt burnt thorough, and readye to fall they make a new fyre, which they ſuffer to
burne vntill the tree fall of yt owne accord. Then burninge of the topp, and bowghs of the tree in
ſuche wyſe that the bodie of theſame may Retayne his iuſt lengthe, they raiſe yt vppon potes laid
ouer croſſ wiſe vppon forked poſts, at ſuche a reaſonable heighte as rhey may handſomlye worke vp-
pó yt. Then take they of the barke with certayne ſhells: thy reſerue the, innermoſt parte of the lenn-
ke, for the nethermoſt parte of the boate. On the other ſide they make a fyre according to the
lengthe of the bodye of the tree, ſauinge at both the endes. That which they thinke is ſufficientlye
burned they quenche and ſcrape away with ſhells, and makinge a new fyre they burne yt agayne, and
ſoe they continne ſomtymes burninge and ſometymes ſcrapinge, vntill the boate haue ſufficient
bothowmes. This god indueth thiſe ſauage people with ſufficient reaſon to make thinges neceſſarie
to ſerue their turnes.

Theodore De Bry, engraver, the New World's diligent European publicist, elucidates in 1590 the manufacture of dugout canoes. (See p. 18.)

same is true of De Bry's picture of the Floridian whalers. In several respects he follows Acosta's account rather than that of Monardes, whose Indian plugs only one blowhole, using his fist for a hammer.

Indian whalers were noticed at the mouth of the St. Lawrence in 1603 by Samuel de Champlain, who passed "neere two hundred canowes" making for the ocean. "Though our shallop was well manned, yet they were more swift than we. There are but two that row, the man and the wife." In the same year, Martin Pring reported that the canoes of the Massachusetts coast,

whereof we brought one to Bristoll, *were in proportion like a Wherrie of the Riuer of* Thames, *seuenteene foot long and foure foot broad, made of the Barke of a Birchtree, farre exceeding in bignesse those of* England: *it was sowed together with strong and tough Oziers or twigs, and the seames couered ouer with Rozen . . . it was also open like a Wherrie, and sharpe at both ends, sauing that the beake was a little bending roundly vpward. And though it carried nine men standing vpright, yet it weighed not at the most aboue sixtie pounds. . . . Their Oares were flat at the end . . . made of Ash or Maple very light and strong, about two yards long, wherewith they row very swiftly.*

Off the coast of Maine, where ocean canoes of birchbark appear to have been standard for a long time, James Rosier in 1605 saw them in use as whaleboats. He briefly described the method of hunting, but also included details of the vessels' structure and performance.

One especial thing is their manner of killing the whale . . . they go in company of their king with a multitude of their boats, and strike him with a bone made in fashion of a harping iron fastened to a rope, which they make great and strong of the bark of trees, which they veer out after him: then all their boats come about him, and as he riseth above water, with their arrows they shoot him to death: when they have killed him and dragged him to shore, they call all their chief lords together, and sing a song of joy: and those chief lords . . . give to every man a share, . . . which pieces . . . when they boil them, they blow off the fat, and put to their pease, maize, and other pulse which they eat.

Rosier, whose name survives on a cape thrusting into Penobscot Bay, was the recorder of Captain George Waymouth's voyage, the first close English inspection of the coast of Maine. He wrote:

Their Canoas are made without any iron, of the bark of a birch tree, strengthened within with ribs and hoops of wood, in so good fashion, with such excellent ingenious art, as they are able to beare seven or eight persons, far exceeding any in the Indies.

Purchas, in reprinting this account 20 years later, tampered with it. He gave "beech" for "birch," a change that has evidently misled some students of Abnaki canoe structures. The heavier beech canoes were made only where birch was unavailable, farther south and inland.

THE WHALERS' SHALLOP

Rosier's descriptive comparison of the qualities of native and imported watercraft sketches at outset the elements that were soon to combine in the American whaleboat that would be superior to either of its ancestors: birchbark canoe and shallop. Our knowledge of the latter is sketchy. Newcomers from Europe took care to describe strange products of the New World. The canoe was one of them. They felt no need to write about their own familiar shallop, but the boat depicted in the midst of a fleet of kayaks on page 30 was probably a shallop, and we can pick up some structural hints from Rosier. On May 20, 1605, he says, "by three a clocke in the morning, our Captaine caused the Shalop to be carried ashoare. . . . This day our Pinnace was fitted together and launched."

Perhaps "fitted together" implies a vessel prefabricated in sections rather than a frame to be assembled and planked. It is unclear whether "pinnace" and "shallop" here refer to the same vessel. A pinnace should have been the larger, but several following references to the shallop indicate that this one was of a substantial size. What was usually called a pinnace should have taken more than a day to put together. On May 30 Rosier wrote, "the Captaine with thirteen departed in the Shallop," but its maximum capacity as well as its comparative efficiency can be gathered from a later passage: "Our Captaine manned the shallop, with as many men as he could well, which was about fifteen with the rowers." A direct comparison with the Indian craft followed:

. . . they in their Canoa with three oares, would at their will goe ahead of us and about us, when we rowed with eight oares strong; such was their swiftnesse, by reason of the lightnesse and artificiall composition of their Canoa and oares.

Here Purchas made a more justifiable change, which indicates the flux of descriptive language. "Artificiall" was becoming ambiguous; he substituted "exquisite."

The four vessels listed at outset of John Davis's second voyage toward the Northwest Passage, in 1586, included a "pinnesse of tenne tunnes named the North Starre," which was carried collapsed "in the Mermayd to be our scout for this discovery." She was taken ashore on June 30 in Davis Strait for assembly and launched four days later with 40 Eskimos helping. This ten-tonner was thought large enough to return alone to England, on a course intended to confirm existence of a passage between Iceland and Greenland. The *Mermayd* vanished, but she can serve us here in judging what was meant by "pinnace" and "shallop" about two decades later in the Rosier account. In many early seventeenth-century references the burden of a shallop is given as two tons, which appears to have been typical. Larger ones were referred to as double shallops; this too is ambiguous, sometimes merely meaning a double-ender rather than the common square-sterned model.

Davis had brought back bags of train oil to prove that the Eskimos practiced whaling, but the first eminent Englishman of the contentious Greenland whale fishery was William Baffin, who had got his schooling from the Basques off Spitsbergen. Baffin and his companions, in their writings, maintained a distinction between pinnace and shallop. The former was an explorer's auxiliary, the latter an all-purpose vessel used as a skiff, small freighter, whaleboat, blubber basin, and oil-cooling tank. Fotherby, of Baffin's 1613 voyage, wrote:

. . . the Basks, our whale strikers, went presentlie back againe to the Foreland with their shallops, ther to attend the coming-in of the whales . . . newes was brought us in the morning that the Basks had kil'd a whale; therefore we hasted to sett up our furnaces and coppers.

The improvised processing plant ashore was equipped with blubber tubs, mincing blocks, copper caldrons, and two shallops. Minced blubber was raked from the blocks into one of the shallops and scooped with big ladles, as needed, "into a great tubb which hangs upon the arme of a gibbet, that is made to tourne to and again between the blubber boat and the coppers. This tubb containeth as much blubber as will serve one of the coppers at one boiling . . . ready to be putt into the copper when the frittires ar taken out." The fibrous "frittires," soaked with oil, were ladled into a wicker basket hanging over another shallop to drain. "And this shallop, because it receaves the oile hott out of the two coppers, is kept continuallie half full of water, which is not onlie a meanes to coole the oile befor it runnes into a cask, but also to cleanse it from soot and drosse, which discends to the bottom of the boat. And out of this shallop the oile runneth into a long trough, or gutter of wood, and therby is conveyed into butts and hogsheads," which were knocked together by the cooper and his apprentices from staves shipped in bundles and hoops forged on the spot.

The Greenland fishery, like whaling in general for more than another century after this report of 1613, depended for its operation upon whales obliging enough to swim to their deaths within reasonable towing distance of the shore. As the whales in each succeeding fishery became more wary, or were simply exterminated, the practice arose of packing the blubber in casks to be shipped to the nearest shore station or even to be taken back to the whaling ship's home port. A whaler was not always a sweet-smelling object to windward. One with rotting blubber aboard was a horror.

Such were the conditions of the whaling industry when in December of 1620 the *Mayflower* bucked her way for protection inside the hook of Cape Cod, to be promptly inspected by an impressive flotilla of whales. She was backtracking from dangerous shoals encountered to the southward. Her people lamented their lack of harpoons. The sight of the whales is thought by some historians to have been decisive in causing the Pilgrim fathers to abandon their original intention of settling among the Dutch and to seek instead a harbor near at hand, which turned out to be "new" Plymouth.

There was more than whaling at issue. The land to the west was mostly forested. Years would be required to clear enough of it for the raising of adequate food crops. Herds of hoofed creatures were still to be propagated and given grazing room. Between frosts the growing season was short by comparison with England's. But alongshore food slid through the sea. When there was a choice between harvesting food later and catching it now, those fearsome hindrances confronting the farmer—

tall stands of ancient timber—were a joy at least to the ship-wright's eye.

Christopher Levett, in his 1624 inventory of good and awkward features—from a settler's standpoint—of the region around the mouth of the Piscataqua, notes:

. . . there may be Shippes as conueniently built there as in any place of the world . . . and better cheape. As for Plancke, crooked Timber, and all other sorts what so euer can be desired for such purpose, the world cannot afford better. Masts and Yeards of all sises, there be allso Trees growing, whereof Pitch and Tarre is made. . . . I dare say no place in England can afford better Timber for Pippe-staues, then foure seuerall places which I haue seene in that Countery.

Orthodox shipbuilding in Massachusetts Bay began, however, with the assembling of imported parts. The *Mayflower* carried a shallop "in quarters." High and dry historians have assumed that the phrase refers to her stowage in the "quarters" of the passengers. Professor William A. Baker of the Massachusetts Institute of Technology, who has built and sailed what he believes to be an approximation of this craft, says that she was merely "cut down" for stowage. It seems to me much likelier that she was shipped in sections, not necessarily four. *Mourt's Relation* of the *Mayflower's* voyage is Professor Baker's authority for saying that she had been "cut . . . down"—or diminished in height—but the warping that caused the carpenters trouble in putting her together again, the result of "people lying in her," would have been even more likely to occur if she had been shipped in sections. It is difficult to imagine the stowing of the Baker vessel—33 feet by 9 feet—between decks, even if somewhat cut down. William Parker, another mariner who left Plymouth 25 years earlier to hunt plunder in New Spain, makes the meaning of "quarters" clear. It was his intention "to have passed overland . . . with two companies of men, and to have carried a pinesse in six quarters to be set together with skrewes, and therein to have embarked ourselves in the South sea." Defeated by the mountains of Panama, Parker "put 56 of our men into a Peragio, or long Indian Canoa," and captured a Spanish treasure ship off Yucatán. From him we learn not only the elastic contemporary meaning of "quarters," but also that Caribbean Indians, a century after Columbus, were still making large seaworthy dugouts preferable in some combat situations to planked watercraft.

Whether Parker's "pinesse" would have been called a shallop by another adventurer we can only guess. The pinnace of about 1600 was at least partly decked over; the shallop was not. The pinnace had two masts and the shallop one. The necessities of local situations caused both distinctions soon to blur. Shallops decked over for long coastal voyages were still referred to by the same name. Some stepped two masts. The pinnace grew larger, toward mid-century, then dwindled and became an open boat. The shallop's many functions were taken over by a number of more specialized local craft, suited to different coasts and weathers, as well as by the ubiquitous sloops and schooners.

The mountains and swamps of the Isthmus were well enough known in Parker's day to make it seem wildly unlikely that he would have contemplated the carrying of a ten-ton pinnace over to the South Sea, even in six "quarters," but he regarded the craft he did have as adequate for piratical operations with no assured home port for a base. Fotherby, in the primary Hakluyt account, identifies one of Baffin's fleet as "a piniace of 60 tunnes, intended for further discoverye," perhaps a misprint. At any rate, the pinnace seems to have had less influence upon watercraft design in the Americas, at outset, than the smaller shallop did.

In 1602 Bartholomew Gosnold encountered off what was to be the New Hampshire coast a "Baske shallop, with mast and sayle," being deftly handled by an all-Indian crew of eight. John Brierton, "one of the voyage," describes the event as if it were not too far out of the ordinary. There is no inference that there was piracy or that the shallop was a prize of battle. The two crews found a means of conversing. Gabriel Archer, another witness, says that an Indian who drew for the English a map of the adjacent coast was familiar with a particular bay on the south shore of Newfoundland.

Robert Juet's account of Henry Hudson's voyage of 1609 mentions the taking of 71 lobsters in Penobscot Bay.

Then wee espied two French shallops full of the country people come into the harbour, but they offered us no wrong, seeing we stood upon our guard.

Four days later, "We kept good watch for fear of being betrayed by the people," and,

In the morning wee manned our scute with foure muskets and six men, and tooke one of their shallops and brought it aboorde. Then we manned our boat and scute with twelve men and muskets, and two stone pieces or murderers, and drave the savages from their houses, and took spoyle of them, as they would have done of us.

Half a dozen similar meetings at about that time suggest a considerable coastal trade by the native Americans in shallops acquired in the waters near the Grand Banks, where Basques probably had been fishing—with the usual secrecy of fishermen —long before the first formal voyages of exploration. If the Indians captured their shallops, the circumstance seems to have been regarded as no different from the constantly occurring seizures on European coasts: a vessel belonged to the taker, at least until a prize court decided otherwise.

The evolution of colonial American watercraft begins, then, with an exchange from both sides: Indians in shallops, Europeans in canoes; but I have come upon no evidence of Indians using a shallop as a whaler. For a quick and quiet approach to a whale their own bark canoes were much superior to the all-purpose shallop. Europeans regarded their shallops as comparatively light and swift, but they were no match for canoes on either count. The combination of man and vessel, as always, was important. In any kind of boat, Indians were the preferred harpooners for more than two centuries of New England whaling.

John Smith put a knocked-down shallop together in 1607 for the exploration of the James River in Virginia. A few others were built at Jamestown, but the colonists at the first permanent English settlement in the Americas seem to have relied for many years upon dugouts as lighters between their plantations and visiting ships. The development of new models for American reasons, to supplement excellent native craft, proceeded more noticeably in New England. The Plymouth colonists, after much prodding, received a reassurance concerning their most critical needs:

"We have now sent you, we hope. men & means, to setle these 3. things, viz. fishing, salt making, and boat making. . . . This

*ship carpenter is thought to be the fittest man for you in the
land. . . . Let him have an absolute comand over his servants &
such as you put to him. Let him build you 2. catches, a lighter,
and some 6. or 7. shalops. . . ."*

The Pilgrims' shipwright built two shallops, then died of
a fever. With one of his shallops the process of adaptation to
local need began: "They sende out a boats load of corne 40.
or 50. leagues to ye eastward, up a river called Kenibeck. . . .
They had laid a litle deck over her midships to keepe ye corne
drie. . . ." A few months later, another change:

*"Finding they ranne a great hazard to go so long viages in a
smale open boat, espetialy ye winter season, they begane to
thinke how they might gett a small pinass. . . . They had no
ship-carpenter amongst them . . . but they having an ingenious
man that was a house carpenter, who also had wrought with y^e
ship carpenter (that was dead) . . . he put forth him selfe to make
a triall that way of his skill; and tooke one of ye bigest of ther
shalops and sawed her in ye midle, and so lenthened her some
5. or 6. foote, and strengthened her with timbers, and so builte
her up, and laid a deck on her; and so made her a conveniente
and wholsom vessell, very fitt & comfortable for their use, which
did them servise 7. years after. . . ."*

We are told here that both shallops and pinnaces varied
in size, that a small pinnace might be five or six feet longer
than a big shallop, and that the former should have a deck.
Whales and fish were so plentiful still that standard shallops
would do for the fisheries. In 1624 Captain John Smith edited
an account that describes the bounty of the sea at "New-Plimoth":
"Cod also presseth in such plenty . . . three men oft loadeth a
Boat of two tuns in two houres." Again we can infer the burden
of a standard shallop. A few pictures on maps' edges and in
views of harbors confirm Smith's count of three as the crew of
a cod fisherman: foreshipman, midshipman, and helmsman.
Toward mid-century the standard rig in these vague portrayals
became two square sails, the larger a short distance aft of midsection, the smaller well out of the way in the bows. This arrangement gave a maximum of working room to the fishermen,
between the masts, and just enough space abaft the mainmast
for navigation.

Shipbuilding in the Massachusetts Bay Colony thus took its

first distinctive turns from the usual impulse—immediate need. After the arrival of ship carpenters who managed to survive local plagues—as a large proportion of the earliest ones did not—adequate freighters were slowly developed while shallops for fishing and for whaling began to take different directions. The cod boat became both larger and smaller, evolving two functionally interdependent types, sloop and dory. This greatly extended the range of their operations, in response to the finding that John Smith's abundant tumble of fish was a seasonal phenomenon. The flat-bottomed dory was a late end product in this evolution. Its predecessors had the continuous curvature of the shallop and were called—as often as not—just boat.

Within two years of the Pilgrim landing John Smith was urging the prompt establishment of British shipyards in America to build naval vessels for the defense of the new colonies:

We contend for New-Englands goods, but not Englands good. . . . I can finde them wood and halfe victuall . . . with what facility they may build and maintaine this little Navy Royall, both with honour, profit and content, and inhabit as good a Country as any in the world within that parallel. . . .

He was willing to back his proposal with a substantial personal investment, but it was an age of monopolies. British ship-builders, already extremely hard put to it to find suitable wood in England, were unwilling to tolerate colonial competition. The king's broad arrow was soon to appear on standing American pines, marking them for masts for the Royal Navy, but a British shipbuilding industry in the colonies was, in the politicians' evasive word, inexpedient. Those who take satisfaction in distinctively American achievements can thank the opponents of Smith's scheme for seeing to it that American shipwrights would be left for a century or so to work out their own problems apart from traditional practices evolved upon a very different kind of coast. The earliest highly distinctive response to local need was a whaleboat combining certain virtues of European structural carpentry with the lines, lightness, and framing principles of the Indian bark canoe. Before having a closer look at it we should examine two other native whaling craft of North America that express a remarkable technical triumph over the sparseness of natural materials suited to the purpose.

Viking vessels such as the bog-preserved Gokstad ship *(below)* could have influenced builders of Eskimo umiaks. Frobisher saw some under sail in 1576, although the picture of a sailing umiak at the lower left was made two centuries later. The method of framing appears above it. Whaling umiaks *(left, adjacent)* were observed by Hans Egede in the 1720's. Kayaks were a wholly native conceptual triumph. The kayak navigator in Lucas de Heere's picture *(upper right, opposite page)* was treacherously seized and taken to England by Frobisher on his first voyage. A member of his second voyage, perhaps John White, drew the picture of kayaks at lower right, opposite page. The 1577 woodcut *(upper left)* was the first of a kayak to be widely distributed in a book. (See pp. 29, 32–39.)

SKIN BOATS: THE KAYAK AND THE UMIAK

On his first probe toward a northwest passage in 1576, Martin Frobisher sailed westward past the southern tip of Greenland to the sound on Baffin Island that bears his name, in 63 degrees north by his reckoning. For this frigid journey the capacity of his entire fleet of three was about equal to that of the single smallest vessel of Columbus: they measured 25, 20, and 10 tons. Perhaps these were the best that could be risked for a dubious venture; on the other hand, the positive merits of smallness in craft employed for exploration had been well established. The estimate given by Ruiz in "toneles" for the burden of a guara raft was higher than the tonnage of Frobisher's largest vessel. His ten-ton pinnace sank in a storm not far from the spot where Davis's *Mermayd* of the same rating was to vanish a decade later. The famous perishing of Sir Humphrey Gilbert between these events, also in a ten-tonner listed as a frigate, is another indication that if the experience of Columbus proved a 100-tonner too large for exploration, pinnaces and frigates of one-tenth the size were too small to have a fair chance of getting home.

Near the headlands of Frobisher Sound, which the explorer mistook for a strait that would surely lead him to Cathay, he encountered a group of seven small boats carrying people that "bee like Tartars, with long blacke haire, broad faces, and flatte noses, tawnie in colour. . . . Their boates are made all of Seales skinnes, with a keele of wood within the skin: the proportion of them is like a Spanish shallop, save only they be flat in the bottome, and sharpe at both ends."

The quotation is from the first Hakluyt account, written by the master of the *Gabriel,* Christopher Hall. The lightness of the Eskimos' kayaks, and the care the Eskimos took not to be parted from a contrivance that for each assured life itself, were confirmed a few hours later when 19 came aboard the flagship, carrying their boats with them. Frobisher brought an Eskimo and his kayak back to England. The subterfuge that took him in is described by an anonymous adventurer in the voyage, probably Michael Lok. The Englishmen behaved themselves when the Eskimos were numerous, but on a later occasion one man was maneuvering warily alongside the *Gabriel,* darting back when he thought himself endangered. Frobisher pretended to hand him a bell, then dropped it into the sea as if by clumsiness. The man seemed "greatly sory for the los," and the captain thereupon offered him another bell "with a short arme, and in that reach caught holde on the man's hand, and with his other hand caught holde on his wrest; and suddenly by mayn force of strength plucked both the man and his light bote owt of the sea into the ship in a tryse and so kept him withowt any shew of enmity." The Eskimo's shirt was of course fastened to the coaming of his kayak.

George Beste, Frobisher's lieutenant for the second voyage and captain of a ship in the third one, was aboard the *Gabriel* during the first voyage as well. His, the longest account of it, reveals the Eskimo's own view of the matter of enmity: "Wherupon, when he founde himself in captivitie, for very choller and disdain, he bit his tong in twayne within his mouth: notwithstanding, he died not thereof, but lived untill he came in Englande, and then he died of colde which he had taken at sea."

By comparison with what Europeans had so far learned of dugouts, bark canoes, and balsas, Frobisher's uncivilized behavior toward his visitor provided a much more accurate knowledge of the technologically most remarkable native American watercraft. The records of Bristol reveal that on October 9, 1576, the captive made the first of several demonstrations of duck hunting in his kayak in nearby waters. On one of these occasions Lucas de Heere drew his portrait, showing the sealskin shirttail provided with a drawstring that made an almost watertight seal around the hatch, uniting man and craft in a functional unit. The seascape behind him shows the same Eskimo using his kayak offshore.

The evidence is good that in the following year John White—who was later to govern and depict the Roanoke colony—went to Frobisher Bay in the second attempt to find a northwest passage. Someone, anyhow, made a veracious sketch on the spot that resembles in style White's later work, with a detailed view of a kayak in use in the forewater and seven more in the distance. It probably was the drawing from which woodcuts were prepared to illustrate Dionyse Settle's narrative of the voyage, published in English before the year's end and in French in 1578. Both wood engravers let their fancies roam, as usual; they converted White's pup tents of sealskin to shapes more familiar to the

European eye, but the essential nature of the kayak is well enough observed in these first published views.

White's original is lost. The contemporary copy of it that came to light again only recently shows us an additional craft from which we perhaps can gather some hints of the construction of a shallop. The narratives of this voyage refer merely to the "ships' boates." The word "shallop" was new in English, first printed in the following year. Hall, in the quotation above from Hakluyt, thought it necessary to make the distinction "Spanish shallop" to indicate something very different from the heavier Basque variety, the *chaloupe*, from which the name was derived. The copy of White's drawing shows a double-ender, an aspect more characteristic of the smaller ships' boats of the time, and there is no evidence of mast or sail. The sturdy frame and heavy planking are in notable contrast with the delicacy of the Eskimo craft, developed to withstand upon a different principle extreme hazards of a cruel environment.

The most widely circulated account of Frobisher's first voyage —Hall's in Hakluyt—calls only kayaks to notice. The record of it, ascribed to Lok, which lay unpublished for nearly three centuries, adds that soon after the sighting of seven small craft like Spanish shallops, the Englishmen "espyed a great bote of that cuntry with men therin hard by them behynde a rok." Later it mentions "one of their great botes having xx men therein." These were umiaks, which have received much less notice than kayaks—probably because of their superficial resemblance to many other watercraft in use when they were first reported. Settle, whose terse record of the second Frobisher voyage was printed ahead of any that dealt with the first, gave a good basic account of both kayak and umiak:

They have two sorts of boats made of leather, set out on the inner side with quarters of wood, artificially tyed together with thongs of the same: the greater sort are not much unlike our wherries, wherein sixteene or twenty men may sit: they have for a sayle dressed the guts of such beasts as they kill very fine and thinne, which they sew together: the other boate is but for one man to sit and row in with one oare.

Although Europeans had been publishing accounts of the Atlantic and Gulf coasts of the Americas for more than 80 years, this is the first reference I have found that clearly implies that the use of sail was habitual before the intrusion of a known sailing vessel from Europe that might have provided the native Americans with a model. If sail was in use south of Hudson Strait, no startled observer of the New World bothered to say so. The size, shape, and rig of the sailing umiak, however, do raise the question of an unrecorded influence of the Vikings. Frobisher's men noticed some weapon tips of metal, which had probably originated in the Bygd settlement of western Greenland. This settlement had slipped out of history in 1410, after having existed as a Christian bishopric for three centuries.

I find it hard to credit the argument of some specialists that resemblances between the umiak and other skin boats around the world prove it to be older than the unique kayak. Chapelle points out that only the Irish used skin boats at an early period on deep water and that we know nothing of any ancient examples beyond references to their existence. Surviving umiaks and models all are recent, none made much longer ago than 1880. We have no close structural information about those seen in 1576. As a rule, umiaks studied by Chapelle were highly sophisticated in structure, with a large number of well-wrought ribs or framing members. Settle's phrase—"leather, set out on the inner side with quarters of wood"—suggests a contemporary use of "quarter" as a synonym for "frame," with many more than four pieces intended. In that case a shallop "shipped in quarters" could have referred to a compact bundle of frames, a score or more, ready to be assembled.

The scholars' wrangle over relative age of kayak and umiak is an intrusion of a more general problem from the happy academic category of the unsolvable: are cultural patterns spread by migration and trade or independently evolved as responses to particular needs and conditions? I assume here that skin boats were prevalent in the American and East Asian Arctic primarily because marine animals provided available materials, supplemented by driftwood from ocean currents and from northward-trending rivers. I infer also, from the many local forms of the kayak, that it is just as likely to have been the first of the two craft to have sent its essential concept east and west, producing local varieties that answered particular conditions. It is not surprising that kayaks used on the stormy ocean coasts were larger and sturdier than those that had to be more often transported to fissures in the great ice packs of the ultimate north.

Since we have no factual knowledge of construction of oceanic skin boats in the remote age of Irish exploration, not much can come of musings upon an Irish-Eskimo cultural contact as the point of origin of the umiak. The known structures of Viking ships, preserved in frigid bogs, are a likelier source of influence, which need not be dated as late as Eric's settlement of Greenland. Earlier adventurers who never came home may have left their long ships among the deft marine designers still farther west, and men who developed the astonishing kayak should have had no trouble in conceiving of the more commonplace larger vessel.

The first references to umiaks suggest a craft 30 or 35 feet long. Hans Egede, a century and a half after the Frobisher voyages, reported a length as great as 60 feet. The intervening period of contact with European whalers probably stimulated several changes. The Frobisher accounts of umiak crews mention only men, but Egede, a missionary who vainly searched in 1721 for descendants of the vanished Viking colonies in Greenland, wrote:

The other kind of Boats are large and open, like our Boats . . . and these are called Kone-Boats, that is, Women's Boats; because the Women commonly row them. For they think it unbecoming a man to row such a boat. . . . And when they first set out for the Whale-Fishing, the Men sit in a very negligent Posture, with their Faces turned toward the Prow, pulling with their little ordinary Paddle; but the Women sit in the ordinary Way, with their faces toward the Stern, rowing with long Oars. . . . In these Boats they transport their Baggage . . . they also carry sails, made of the Bowels and Entrails of Seals . . . and with these Sails they sail well enough with the Wind, not otherwise.

The long oars had almost certainly been borrowed from Europeans, but umiaks retained into the era of outboard motors their most distinctive feature: an intentionally loose skin. All Eskimo craft were built in the sequence preferred by Europeans, first the frame, then the covering—contrary to the tradition followed by North American Indians in making birchbark canoes. But whereas the bark itself in the latter became a fairly rigid part of the structure, in Arctic vessels the covering of walrus hide or seal-skin was not made fast to the ribs and keel. The leather was kept oiled and flexible. A shock against ice or stone that would shatter the plank of a European boat would simply stretch the skin of a umiak; if framing members broke, the chances were that no water would enter. Similarly, the distorting effect of violent waves, which would cause European joints and fastenings to "work" and the seams to open, would have no effect upon a umiak's resilient skin. The structure over which it was stretched would be able itself to flex with less strain.

Local forms of both umiak and kayak that evolved to meet the conditions of different regions included some that were flat bottomed, some V-shaped in cross section. The driftwood frames and stringers were fastened by lashings with very few treenails. Although close comparative examination of building practices came late, the similarity of method all across the Arctic suggests the persistence of ancient ways rather more than the transmittal of medieval European and equivalent Asian influences in framing. Chapelle, in pointing to some resemblances between the whaling umiak and the whaleboat, notes that the influence might have run either way. The Greenland whale fishery pursued by Europeans was a belated intrusion into whaling grounds long used by Eskimos. The whaleboat, which reached its ultimate refinement in the Nantucket and New Bedford models of the nineteenth century, was evolved by Yankee boatbuilders who discontentedly observed the virtues of bark canoes while they were struggling at the oars of their heavy shallops. But whaling was always an international affair in the fo'c's'le. Men who had chased whales in Davis Strait probably brought news of the umiak and its merits down to the waters off Cape Cod, to be an additional spur toward the replacement of the whalers' shallop with a sharper and more resilient craft.

Although Eskimos had an evident need to give far more attention to clothing than did the Indians of the Caribbean, early writers noted a patience characteristic of both peoples in the construction of their watercraft. Walrus hides for the covering of umiaks were sewn together by an exacting procedure of overlapping seams in which the needle that was thrust through the cut edge never quite pierced the leather against which it was being secured. The entire cover, when ready, was lapped over the gunwales and its inner edge laced to a horizontal framing member a few inches below. External lashings under the bottoms also are visible in early prints.

The smaller kayak, similar in its basic structural principles to the umiak, was in detail and in variation of shape much more complex. Having when normally loaded almost no free-

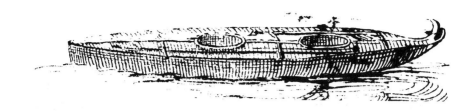

All kayaks observed the principle of uniting the boat's and the paddler's leather clothing into one watertight unit, but special shapes were evolved for different conditions. Two-man kayaks, like the one sketched by Thomas de Suria in 1791 *(top of the page)*, were used in Bering Strait. The bidarka of Unalaska *(upper left)* was drawn by a Russian in the 1760's. Where portages over rocks or ice packs were frequent, kayaks were made small and light *(above)* to be carried like baskets. Inflated sealskins *(left and below)* were attached to harpoon lines to tire the prey. A umiak may be seen in the backwater of the lower picture, with Y-shaped lashings to hold the resilient envelope of walrus hide snugly against the frame. (See pp. 29–37, 39.)

board—distance between gunwales and water—it had to be decked over completely except for the manhole to which the paddler's leather shirt could be snugly fastened to keep the deck wash out. The curved shirttail in De Heere's drawing was not a style note but a provision of flexible fullness to allow the paddler's body to bend forward and from side to side for balance. Eskimo skin clothing was in several ways a detachable extension of the skin of an Eskimo vessel, which in its turn was almost a part of the man. Chapelle points out that some kayaks were "capable of being carried like a large basket, by inserting one arm under the decking at the manhole. . . . In the majority of types the degree of seaworthiness obtained is very great. Some types are built very narrow and sharp-ended; these usually require a skillful paddler. Others are wide and more stable, requiring less skill to use."

The likeliest sort of influence of one regional building method upon another might be looked for where Indians came into contact with Eskimos in estuaries of rivers flowing into Hudson Bay and other parts of the northern coast. Yet each tradition kept its own integrity. Some Indian canoes on northern rivers were enveloped in skin instead of birchbark, but the Indian sequence in manufacture was preserved: a long leather bag was first prepared and the structural members were inserted into it. The covering was not, as in the Eskimo tradition, stretched over a previously completed frame. Ethnologists concede that this cultural contact in permafrost regions was ancient and continuous. That there was so small an exchange of influence between the boatbuilding methods of the Indians and the Eskimos suggests that Eskimo marine carpentry had attained a level of excellence long before transoceanic cultures began to impose changes at the eastern and western outposts of the vast Eskimo domain. It seems likely that the gut sails first reported to Europe in 1576 were imitations of the woolen sails of Vikings who entered Davis Strait five or six centuries earlier, but the sophisticated framing of kayaks cannot be confidently related to any external influence, and the structure of the umiak might have been a home-grown enlargement. It would be pleasant to discover proof, deep in the sands of Cape Krusenstern, of the particular vessel used as a whaler 4,000 years ago. The concurrence of harpoon and lance in the digs at Cape Krusenstern argues for some sort of vessel from which they would have been hurled and thrust—a umiak, a kayak, perhaps an ancestor of one or the other. The excellence of the unique kayak by itself, which had received its ultimate development before anything remotely like it was recorded anywhere else, proves that the Eskimos, as technical craftsmen, had no need of instruction in the framing of any other watercraft from mere Europeans.

EUROPEAN OBSERVERS

The earliest written accounts, some of them quoted above, place highly distinctive aboriginal sailing craft on the west coast of South America, near the equator, and off the northeastern islands that flank the coast of North America near the Arctic Circle. None between. They also give evidence of whaling off Florida and Maine, as well as in Davis Strait, west of Greenland. Such primary observers, alas, have a perverse way of noting things of interest to themselves rather than what we belated pokers into the past wish that they had put down. Later reports of observation are sometimes more satisfactory when they reinforce with clear detail the vaguer inferences of the first accounts that survive. An example is a note in Rear Admiral W. H. Smyth's translation, published in 1857, of Girolamo Benzoni's *History of the New World* (1565). Benzoni, one of the earliest of the Renaissance travelers who were primarily interested in learning what the New World was like, visited Peru a decade or so after the conquest. He gave a terse account of the sailing balsas he had seen, which tells us not much more than that they were sometimes made of as many as 11 logs, always with the longest in the middle. To this unsatisfactory glimpse the admiral adds his own evidence:

Every country seems to contrive embarcations adapted to the locality. So with the rafts or balzas here mentioned, which are admirably contrived for their duty. We used some of them which we took in 1807, and found them made, as Benzoni states, of logs of trees lashed together—catamaran fashion—with bejuccas, or ropes made of ox-hide thongs. The larger balzas carry sails on masts resembling shears; and they are steered by raising or lowering, as the occasion may require, some boards which enter vertically between the timbers at either end of this rude, but ingenious, floating vehicle.

"Rude but ingenious." Even so devoted a translator and editor as Smyth drops into the supercilious attitude of most European observers who have reported surviving evidence of different cultures, which they and their kind did so much to destroy—often in an uncomprehending exercise merely of a will to dominate and supersede. Smyth found it helpful to capture and use balsas in support of his own naval operations. But of their persistent suitability to marine tasks on the Peruvian coast, almost four centuries after the Spaniards established shipyards to produce a "superior" European kind of vessel, he took scant notice.

At the other geographical extreme, where native sail was early reported, the dolefully high-minded Danish missionary, Egede, was as little impressed by evidence that the Greenlanders had developed a more durable maritime culture than that of the heroic but vanished Vikings themselves. The disciplined miracle of swift, resilient watercraft, built entirely out of materials taken from the sea and excellently adapted for use in conditions of great peril, escaped his parochial eye. He saw "no fine Arts or Sciences or the like; but only a Number of mean, wretched, and ignorant Gentiles who live and improve the land according to their low capacity." This low capacity included the development by Greenland technologists of an "invention" usually thought of as belonging to the latter twentieth century: the wet suit. Egede at least gives us the information with some particularity. When a harpooned whale, hindered by having to drag an inflated sealskin,

grows tired, and loses Strength, they attack him again with their Spears and Lances, till he is killed, and then they put on their Spring Coats, made of dressed Seal Skin, all of one Piece, with Boots, Gloves, and Caps, sewed and laced so tight together that no Water can penetrate them. In this Garb they jump into the Sea, and begin to slice the Fat of him all round the Body, even under the Water: For in these Coats they cannot sink, as they are always full of Air; so that they can, like the Seal, stand upright in the Sea: Nay they are sometimes so daring, that they will get upon the Whale's Back, while there is yet Life in him, to make an End of him, and cut away his Fat.

One variant item about the kayak comes from an observation made in Europe itself. Isaac de la Peyrère's gathering of information on Greenland, published in 1647, includes a touching record of nine Eskimo captives in Denmark and of their attempts to evade their guards and paddle home. The compiler invites his readers to visit certain persons who have on view examples of the "machine" in which the captives thought they could make it to faraway Greenland:

> . . . picture to yourself, sir, a weaver's shuttle ten or twelve feet long, made of whalebone, broad, and about the thickness of a finger, covered over and made like the sticks of a parasol with skins of seals or walruses, sewn with sinew. This machine has a round opening in the middle about the size of a man round the flanks, going to a point at each end in proportion to its thickness in the middle. The strength and neatness of the structure depend on the two ends where these sticks are joined and fastened together; on the opening or circle above, to the circumference of which all the sticks must be brought; and on the half circle below, which is fastened to the upper circle like a basket-handle turned upside down. Picture to yourself that through this half circle pass or terminate both the ribs and the crossribs, and the whole is so well sewn and bound and so well stretched, that it is capable, from its lightness and the skill with which it is built, to bear the tossings of a storm in a high sea.

Observers of Frobisher's captured craft did not say what its frame was made of. Wood is frequently mentioned in descriptions of kayaks, but some, it is clear, were fashioned completely from animal parts.

The products of a region thus define the possibilities of its watercraft: tall trees on the Logwood coast, seasonal driftwood deliveries at the mouths of Arctic rivers, balsa logs in Peru, beech or paper birch throughout temperate North America. Amid its advantages and limitations, each region by trial and error shapes its "embarcations" to its particular needs. The imperfection of early reports by European observers becomes almost irrelevant before a realization that every one of them represents a chance moment in a process probably very old. The technological procedures observed by Egede in the 1720's may represent an intelligent adjustment to a severe nautical environment perfected thousands of years earlier, even before the times of the Cape Krusenstern whale hunters, whose weapons were so similar to those of the Greenlanders. Such a culture, in an isolated environment, could have become as stable as that of old Cathay, having passed beyond any evident need for change until obtrusive Europeans upset its balances at its eastern and western extremes.

Problems remain concerning these external influences. There is no clear evidence whether the two- and three-manhole kayaks reported only from the Alaskan Arctic preceded the arrival of the Russians. They may have been descendants of the ancient whaling craft of Cape Krusenstern. Such guesswork, however, is no more to be credited than the uncharitable theory that the two-holer was developed because a Russian could not keep a kayak right side up without an Eskimo aboard to steady it or that the three-holer followed because it proved desirable to have two Eskimos to transport one Russian, which could be done in safety if he would agree not to try to do anything helpful with a paddle.

Bernard du Hautcilly, whose description of a whale hunt off Alaska in the 1820's is quoted in the first chapter, claimed better success than the yarn grants to his predecessors from Russia:

This boat, made of sealskin, carried only two persons. . . . Great precautions were necessary to creep half-way into a round hole . . . in my quality as a sailor, I seized a paddle, and I dabbled with it in a way to satisfy the old pilot.

The significant question at the Eskimo world's eastern edge is concerned not so much with particulars of umiaks seen by chance in 1576 as with their parental ancestors in use when the first Vikings coasted past Cape Farewell. Unless a loitering ice process has obligingly kept one for us in deep freeze, like the still-edible Siberian mammoth, no answer is to be expected.

THE EXPLORER'S SHIP

Local habits of wind and current along gently sloping beaches or ironbound coasts of rock, prevalence of estuaries or a lack of them, wild or gentle rivers and streams—such factors shape available materials into local watercraft that can be relied upon, but they also have a decisive influence upon the ships of visitors from afar. The Europeans who set out to make a New England or a New France discovered vessels in some ways superior to their own, shaped by different weathers upon other shores. The contours of their European ships were also slowly altered by the environments of the New World. American conditions completed an evolutionary process begun when Europe's impetuous age of exploration first probed south and east before it turned toward the west. The explorer's ship in her fully developed form was an answer to failures and successes of tentative predecessors in waters of the Americas. European coasters, evolved to meet particular regional circumstances, developed into a vessel suited to all conditions in all places throughout the world.

The answer, in this sense partially an American product, was a three-master of modest dimensions and moderate draft, employing the separate virtues of some square with some fore-and-aft sails, using bonnets and bowlines and other devices to adjust the area and set of the canvas to all humors of the weather. Heavy carracks and galleons were useful only on routes already well explored; they were not to be risked in strange waters. But a number of smaller types, such as the Portuguese caravel, began to merge their qualities into a much less pretentious version of the carrack.

The resulting vessel could stay alive in heavy offshore storms. Her combination of sails was adaptable to trade winds and to westerlies. She could carry provisions for a voyage of several months and platform a few small guns without shaking herself apart or wallowing crankily from their weight. She could venture into moderately shallow waters. When she came from the yard of a good builder she could even claw her way into the wind somewhat. In a severe blow she could take in all canvas and proceed backward for days at a time, with a minimum of discomfort, as Sir Francis Drake did in the tremendous storms he survived west of Tierra del Fuego, the high poop of the *Golden Hind* acting as her only sail. Such vessels had a burden of between 60 and 100 tons—about one-tenth the capacity of the famous early China clippers.

The fact that these little ships could work somewhat to windward, but in a chancy manner, is illuminated at many points in the narratives of their navigators, such as the moment when Samuel Argall—bound for Bermuda from Virginia in 1610— "being to windward of our Admirall . . . bare up under his lee: who when I hayled him, told me that he would tack it up no longer, because he was not able to keep the sea any longer, for lack of road and water: but that hee would presently steere away North Northwest, to see if he could fetch Cape Cod." What Argall fetched, instead of either Bermuda or Cape Cod, appears to have been Matinicus Island, off Penobscot Bay.

Yet even the standard explorer's ship, refined by such vicissitudes until she could go literally to the ends of the earth and sometimes come home again, was ill adapted to employments that would sustain life in her people. She was of little use as a fisherman or whaler, perilous to manage in tidal rivers and helpless in swift ones. Amid the shifting sandbars and spits of any estuary such as Chesapeake Bay a shallower vessel would spend more of its time afloat. In regions where the set of the currents was constant, a sharper one, such as the felucca, was needed to work against them, at the sacrifice of other qualities. When "those grand wind muscles, her sails," and the lesser muscles of men were the only choices for a vessel's propulsion, the best decision could be a reliance upon both. Except where slaves were abundant, vessels intended mainly for rowing were made small on purpose. Since a sheltered anchorage was not always easy to find when most needed, a vessel of shallow draft had many more havens available to her than one with a deep keel.

For such reasons the primary advantages of the remarkable, recently evolved ship used by the world explorers ended—as Argyll's account emphasizes—at about the line where coastal shoals began. The very first well-recorded transatlantic voyage of exploration demonstrates the elements that have shaped marine evolution. Columbus set out in a conventional sizable trader, a nao, for his flagship, and two varieties of caravel as her auxiliaries. Both caravels got safely back to Spain, but the nao, *Santa Maria,* as has been hinted above, was wrecked at the mouth of what seemed a good harbor on the northern coast of Hispaniola. Frequently, during the outward voyage, the smaller and swifter caravels had had to shorten sail and wait for the flagship to catch up with them. Columbus in his own writings indicates that he was thoroughly satisfied at the outset with the deliberate balance of qualities he had chosen, represented in the three vessels. His nao was a comfortable early version of the ultimate sailing ship. Her keel was only twice as long as she was wide, but the slow upward curve of her stem gave her a length on deck

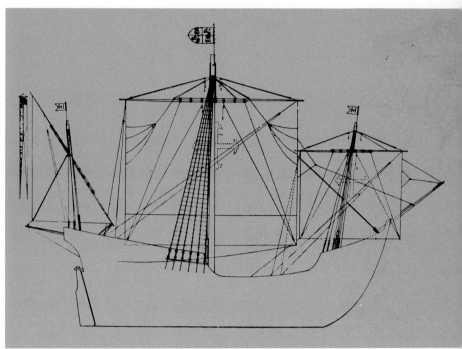

The all-purpose explorer's ship evolved experimentally from two hull forms and two sail plans of medieval Europe. "Long ships" were used for conflict and other occasions of state, "round ships" for trade *(right)*. Square sails pushed big merchantmen when the wind was right. Lateen sails made small coasters more maneuverable. Columbus tested the merits of these forms and sails. His "nao" *Santa Maria (model below, plan lower right)* was too large and slow. His caravel *Pinta (above)* was given unusual square sails at the outset. His *Niña (below, left)* was rerigged with them at the Canaries. See inset at left. These plans are plausible reconstructions by José Maria Martínez-Hidalgo. The model follows his plan. (See pp. 45, 48, 50, 187, 242, 244.)

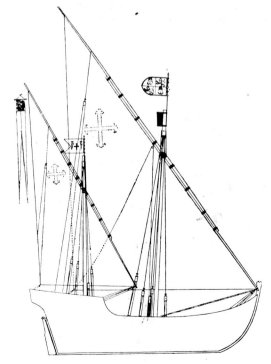

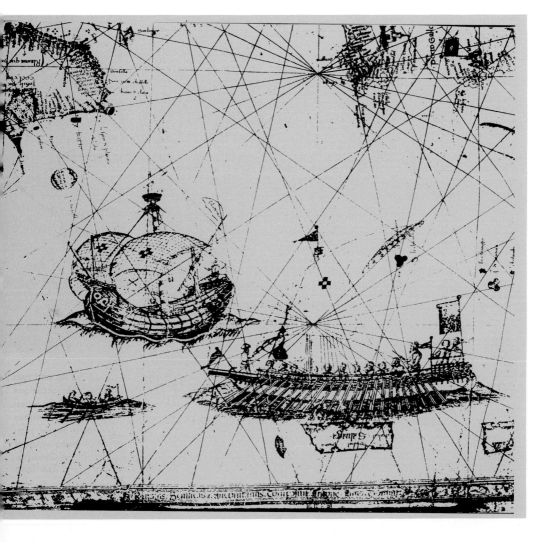

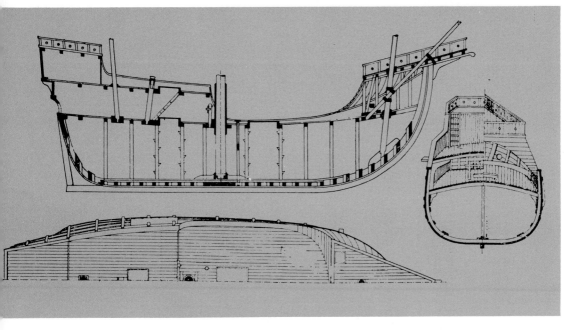

that was three times her breadth. She had the usual fore and after castles, developed in the Middle Ages for defense against boarders. Primarily a cargo carrier, with maximum capacity for her length, she stepped three masts with square sail on the fore and main and a triangular lateen on the mizzen. A small square topsail was set above the crow's nest on the main and another small square sail under the high-steeving bowsprit. Columbus mentions that the mainsail had two bonnets, either or both of which could be unlaced from the foot of the sail to "shorten" it in a strong wind.

The phrase "to shorten sail" persisted after the less complex practice came in of bunching the upper part of a square sail against its yard and tying it there with reef points.

At the outset the two caravels were differently rigged. The *Niña* began the voyage as a traditional lateener, with a large triangular sail on her mainmast amidships and a smaller one on the mizzen. Since the foot of the long, slanting main yard moved from side to side across the bow whenever she was put upon the opposite tack, there was no room for a forecastle; the after castle was modest in height.

The *Pinta,* following a recent innovation, was rerigged before she sailed to make her a "square caravel," with the same basic sail plan as that of the nao but without a topsail or spritsail. Her mainsail had only one bonnet. Since there was no lateen yard to interfere forward, her forecastle probably was built up a bit, if only to hold a bowsprit at the convenient angle to sustain her new square sails' bowlines.

The fleet that sailed from Palos westward for Asia thus had three substantially different vessels for the unknown conditions ahead: a standard square-rigged cargo carrier of about 100 tons burden, a standard lateen-rigged caravel on the Portuguese model of about 53 tons, and an experimental compromise of about 60 tons with the essential rig of a nao on the hull of a caravel.

For some years the Portuguese in their African explorations had been propagating a rumor that nothing but a caravel could make these distant voyages in both directions: the winds were such that square-riggers could not beat their way against them during some stages of the journey. On one occasion when they sent two heavy cargo ships to an African trading station, both were deliberately destroyed there either to make the difficulties

Two scenes inset upon a map celebrating Drake's circumnavigation, issued soon after its triumphant completion in 1580, are among the earliest portrayals of a specific "explorer's ship." They do not suggest that the map maker ever saw his subject, the *Golden Hind*. A standardized explorer's ship of the fifteenth century can be more plausibly perceived in the vessel that appears repeatedly, with little change, in many engravings made about 1590 by Theodore De Bry. Those at the bottom of this page are supposed to represent Goulaine de Laudonnière's ships off Florida in 1564. They are more probably like those De Bry often had actually in view 20 years or so later. (See pp. 43–45, 50, 187.)

evident to possible competitors or because the Portuguese really believed that they could not get home. Columbus would have considered all this as one factor in his experimentation. He soon discovered that the Portuguese inference was dubious, at least for Atlantic adventurers. A lateener sails comfortably with the wind abeam or ahead. When it comes from any point astern, she slues in every trough of the waves and requires a hero at the tiller to hold her to a course. As he approached the Canary Islands, his last known landfall, Columbus had decided to convert the *Niña,* his standard caravel, to the same novel rig worn by the *Pinta.* This he did at Las Palmas. She proved thereafter to be the handiest of the three vessels.

Still in the larger nao, where the comparison would appear most vexatious, Columbus found not only that she was slower than his converted caravels but also that with a beam wind she made about as much progress sidewise as she did ahead. When she ended her journey abruptly on a reef off Hispaniola, Columbus wrote that "the nao was too heavy and not adapted for discovery work." He transferred his flag to the *Niña,* the smallest of the original fleet, a move that symbolized the restraint put by hard experience upon a commander's usual impulse to make the largest available vessel his "admiral."

Each of the first two circumnavigations was begun with a fleet of five vessels, but only Magellan's *Vittoria* and Drake's *Golden Hind* completed their journeys. Eight that failed to do so dropped out for various reasons, including the inability of the smallest to endure the worst weathers. Thus the size of the explorer's ship was determined at both extremes. The commander's skill was a factor, but when the *Golden Hind,* bulging with Spanish plunder, re-entered the Thames, everyone knew what sort of vessel was needed to go anywhere and come home again. A harsh process, which had vetoed the *Santa Maria* of Columbus for one reason and Drake's little consorts for another, approved the size and structure of the *Golden Hind*—a vessel of about the same burden as the *Santa Maria,* 100 tons, but much handier in her sailing qualities.

Remarkable as she turned out to be, the usefulness of the explorer's ship still ended just off soundings. On shallow coasts, and in the estuaries, the Europeans who became Americans were content for many decades to acknowledge the superiority of native dugouts and bark canoes over their own shallops and pinnaces, few of which were locally built.

The most widespread and lucrative inland enterprise of the American colonists, after the first visits of Cartier, was the fur trade. In pursuing it, predecessors of the eventual Hudson's Bay Company relied for their vast fleets of river freighters entirely upon Indian manufacturers. A standard 26-foot canoe would carry 3,000 pounds of cargo and a crew of ten men—a number needed chiefly on the portages, where the lugging of shallops would have been an all but impossible horror, if only because they were much too broad for existing portage trails between large trees. It was not until about 1800 that French Canadian flat-bottomed bateaux began to outnumber canoes on the more easily navigable streams. A cocky new management of the Hudson's Bay Company, in the 1820's, imported York boats and Durham boats from the Middle Atlantic States, but the voyageurs hated the clumsy substitutes.

In the remote filaments of water that weave into major rivers, small freighters of birchbark upon a pre-Columbian model continued to give the safest and most economical transportation, at the sources of the fur trade, centuries after the remarkable explorer's ship had completed its task forever.

Whaling Craft

BEACH-BASED WHALING CRAFT AND THE CEDAR WHALEBOAT

It has been a characteristic of the major fisheries that enterprises of local scope have had to push farther and farther from their bases, either to pursue marine life in its seasonal migrations or to find new fishing grounds when the original ones have been diligently fished out. The Basque cod fishery off Newfoundland, preceding the explorers of record, is an instance. Basque whale strikers, when their Biscay waters were depleted, moved northward to Spitsbergen in vessels of their own and of other nations, then to Davis Strait, west of Greenland. For a number of reasons, including the political, but most probably for the better preservation of blubber in freezing weather, European whaleships left the leviathans that the Pilgrims noted in abundance to be fished for by local coast-dwellers. The general experience of the Basques was thus repeated by New Englanders from bases concentrated between Long Island and the coast of Maine. A local enterprise gradually expanded until it became worldwide.

The earliest consistent evidence of beach-based whaling appears in the elaborate provisions of many towns and districts to determine the ownership of drift carcasses, which sometimes contained identifiable harpoons. From ordinances and court decisions, it is apparent that Indians and newcomers participated with a decent harmony in the shore-based operations of eastern Long Island. It was not until about 1640, however, with the establishment of firm townships, that such records began. Most of the entries are concerned with ownership or with division of blubber. References to watercraft used by early hunters are rare and unhelpful: they are called boats. "Indians in their boats" may or may not mean "canoes."

In 1672 James Lopar agreed "to carry on a design of Whale

Citching on the Island of Nantuckket," and a little later John Savage made a similar contract with the town, the islanders having been previously concerned much more with agriculture than with the riches of the sea. In 1690 an expert from Cape Cod, Ichabod Paddock, reorganized the Nantucket fishery, posting lookouts on high spars at four points around the coast and making full use of the local Indian population in the boats—but there is still no good evidence of what the boats were. Whenever a whale was beached, an engine called a crab was used to help tear off its blubber, which was carried in carts to refining plants near the principal harbor. Later the logic of erecting "fry houses" on the beach was recognized, from which only the less weighty final product needed to be hauled in casks ready for shipment. Odors of the process also were kept by this arrangement farther from the clustered habitations.

What the boats in use at this period were is still mere speculation. The two chief qualities needed in a pursuing craft were quietness and agility, making possible an unobserved approach to within a yard or two of the whale, and a sternward leap out of range of a thrashing, tortured colossus. The birchbark canoe was ideal in both of these ways. Paddles were much quieter than oars, which might creak or rattle against their thole pins. At close quarters they could be thrust with a deft assurance into reverse, within inches of the canoe, where a shifting of the attacked animal's position might make it impossible to extend an oar at all. There was, however, a limitation in the Indian method of hunting, as there was in that of the Eskimos. Both fastened objects to their harpoons to tire the whale. That might take a long time and involve a very long pursuit after the first strike. The Indians used a wooden drogue, the Eskimos an inflated sealskin. The Basques had developed the procedure of using their boat itself as a drogue, but this was less than satisfactory because their shallops were too heavy. Accounts of the Greenland fishery include many reports of whales cut free, with the loss of much tackle, in order to save the shallop, or of harpoons tearing loose when all the line was payed out.

We can only guess at the timing and details of a process by which New England's boatbuilders evolved their compromise, a craft lighter than the shallop but sturdier than the canoe, following closely the lines and manufacturing procedures of the latter. The earliest description I know of appears in a report sent to England in 1725 by the chief justice of Massachusetts, who said that the boats were

made of Cedar Clapboards, and so very light that two Men can conveniently carry them, yet they are twenty Feet long, and carry Six Men, viz., the Harpooner . . . four Oar-men, and the Steersman. These boats by reason of their Lightness can be brought on and off, and so keep out of danger. Our People formerly used to kill the Whale near the Shore; but now they go off to Sea in Sloops and Whale boats, in the months of May, June, and July, between Cape Cod and Bermudas.

The British, for a number of sound and poor reasons, ignored the chief justice's hint that they might do well to look into the virtues of the native New England whaleboat. England for her own fishery made parallel improvements in the shape and structure of the original whaler's shallop until she had a boat superficially resembling that of the Yankees in its lines and general dimensions, but much heavier. As late as 1820 an experienced British whaleman recommended one-half- or three-quarter-inch oak planking. This would have weighed about twice as much as the standard American half-inch cedar, which was as strong as it needed to be. When a whale attacked, no boat was sturdy. Whalers' journals contain descriptions of oak being cut as cleanly as with a saw by a blow of the whale's flukes. What the American designers most aimed at was the agility that allowed their boats "to be brought on and off, and so keep out of danger," the maneuver more personally described by Captain William M. Davis on page 167, "the backward start of the boat. . . . A stroke or two astern, and we pant for breath in safety."

The early structural influence of the birchbark canoe appeared not only in the fine taper of the American whaleboat to almost identical ends but also in the method of construction. For as long as there are records, boats made by the famous Beetle firm of New Bedford were planked over a mold with the ribs sprung into place afterward in the Indian manner. The Americans developed and persisted in another significant peculiarity never adopted by other countries: oars of three different lengths. The practice reflected a careful calculation of efficient leverage in a boat that tapered from the midsection steadily toward the ends. In both the European and the American boats each oarsman sat close to the gunwale opposite from the one upon which his single oar pivoted. This gave him the full width of either boat for leverage. The heavier European whaleboat continued almost to the end of whaling to have a long, broad midsection, with benches, or thwarts, of approximately the same length, gunwale to gunwale. The resulting leverage was thus almost the same for all the oars. The much more pronounced tapering of the American boat produced a different leverage at each thwart—hence the oars of differing length, the two longer on one side balancing three shorter on the other.

If veterans of the northern fisheries were living in Nantucket, they would have had to adapt what they had learned in Davis Strait to the parsimonious resources of their island—a limitation that still forced ingenuity upon all New Englanders. The traditional whaling practices required a large capital investment. Competitive only within the limits of their own old habits, the French, Dutch, and English were vulnerable to an imaginative challenge, particularly to one from seafarers who, if they had accepted the orthodox practices, could not have competed at all. The challengers had to proceed with their own materials, which by one twist of good fortune happened to be excellent, adapting an Indian concept of construction to European carpentry. In these ways the New England cedar whaleboat was poverty's most fortunate child.

THE WHALING SLOOP

Before the name disappeared from common use, shallops had shrunk and expanded in two concurrent evolutionary processes that made them both much lighter and much heavier. When used in combination these were better, for the explicit purpose of whale hunting, than their single shore-based ancestor had been by itself. One offspring of the shallop became a light whaleboat of limited practicable range, the other its carrier, which could take it to fish in far distant waters. The change from the practice of towing whales ashore to be chopped up to that of cutting them up at sea to be brought back in pieces was gradual.

Hakluyt had published in 1600 a description of the ideal whaleship: a 200-tonner, diverted from some other use, carrying five stout shallops and a crew of 55 men, these to include five Basque harpooners and five coopers. From her size—twice that of the maximum explorer's ship—it is obvious that she was not intended for hunting in unknown waters. By contrast, the first whaling vessels employed by the New Englanders to carry their light whaleboats far offshore and lug home the blubber were ludicrously small.

For some time after Hakluyt broadcast his specifications, with a detailed list of equipment for the vessel, Davis Strait had been regarded as the monopolistic province of any nation that happened to have there the most powerful concentration of ships. Interlopers might be tolerated, but only if they turned over a portion of their catch. The New Englanders, until well into the eighteenth century, were not tempted to adventure northward into that cold puddle of risks.

When the offshore fishery began, the only vessels being built in the northern colonies that approached the dimensions of the smallest European whalers were intended for the lucrative carrying trade with the West Indies. It would not have been easy to divert them into a previously untried venture. To carry their cedar whaleboats to the vicinity of the retreating right whales, and to sleuth in the Gulf Stream for sperm whales of greater value, the Nantucketers acquired a modest fleet of vessels that they registered as sloops, a catchall category.

What kind of sloop was it that became a whaleboat carrier? The seeker after the comfort of exact truth finds himself awash in ambiguities. Thomas Riley Blanckley's *Naval Expositor,* a handsome marine dictionary published at about the right date to enlighten us—1750—tells us: "Sloops——Are sailed and masted as Mens Fancies lead them, sometimes with one Mast, with two, and with three, with Bermudoes, Shoulder of Mutton, Square, Lugg, and Smack Sails; they are in Figure either square or round Stern'd."

So now we know.

A consultant told Thomas Jefferson 69 years later that in 1715 Nantucket had six sail of whalers measuring between 30 and 40 tons. These had room for one active whaleboat and one spare. They had too little freeboard to carry the boats safely except by lashing them on deck. Both because of the cramped space and the need to hoist them in and out with primitive tackle, there were inducements to make the boats as light as possible. If both boats were badly damaged, the cruise was over. This difficulty was partly met by the practice of cruising in pairs. One could at least serve as freighter for the blubber casks of the other until both were full or all the boats were gone.

Some of the difficulty in describing a sloop was contrived on purpose. Britain's Navigation Acts, and other legal annoyances applied to blister the unruly colonists, included a regulation forbidding the use in the lumber trade on the Maine coast of any vessel larger than a sloop. Originally this was intended to prevent wily Yankees from carrying away tall pines marked with the king's broad arrow as masts for his fighting ships. The response might have been foreseen: large vessels were amiably entered as "sloops" on the registers. After the Revolution this muddle was sorted out. A sloop became a single-masted vessel, chiefly powered by a fore-and-aft gaff mainsail, with one or more fore-and-aft headsails. The larger examples carried a square topsail for more comfortable and efficient sailing when the seas ran high.

Several sloops' logbooks from the 1750's are preserved in the Nantucket Atheneum. They contain enough positive references to the sail being carried to show that some Nantucket whaling sloops conformed to the description above. The *Grampus*, on June 18, 1751, was kept on a course "N.W. under a balanc'd Mainsail and Gib." Several entries in the *Greyhound*'s cruise of 1753 indicate that she was rigged as an orthodox sloop. The Massachusetts Historical Society has recently acquired the manuscript *Journal of a Voyage from Cape Cod towards Davis's Streights in Sloop Seaflower.* "About Noon We came to sail from Billinsgate Bay, a fine Breeze at SW; being bound on a Waling Voyage." The log entries commence on May 6, 1754, at the port inside the hook of Cape Cod now called Wellfleet. Many references to the setting and taking in of canvas make it clear that the Cape Cod *Seaflower,* too, was an orthodox sloop with a mainsail, foresail, and jib. On July 15, while cruising westward toward Cape Farewell, her people "ab^t 10 aClock Saw a large Spermaceti nearing got out Boats & gave chase but she run off & it being (?) Calm could not follow her with the Vessell." She carried and could man at least two boats, with probably a spare.

The sloop *Seaflower* had her best luck on July 16 when a sperm whale spouted near her during a continuation of the previous day's calm. Selections from the log entries for a week afterward indicate the procedures and the problems when whale-hunting at that date from so small a vessel:

. . . we got our Boats & gave Chase, upon being Struck she made away to Windward it being almost calm the Vessel could not follow so that the Boats got almost out of sight of the Vessel, in Working upon her they hung 4 Lances & 4 Irons. She went down Several times & staid very long, an hour & an hour & quarter W^{ch} together wth her making from the Vessel made us fear losing her & a great deal of necessary Craft. . . .

"Craft" meant the four lances and four harpoons embedded in the whale, an indication that the *Seaflower* lacked the large reserve of weapons stipulated for a European whaleship. The entry continues:

however ab^t 6 aClock they took her in Tow & the wind breezing at ESE, I turn'd the Vessell up towards them, they bearing SE Ab^t Dark we got her Cabled & she appear to be a Exceeding large Fish lay a hull till ab^t 2 aClock Morning When the Wind blowing up Stormy Rain at SEbE, Ballanc'd M. Sail, head Northward, hawled up ye whale & Spaded off one Fluke could not come at'tother. . . .
July 17th 1754 Continued Stormy all the Afternoon, in Night Wind died almost away ab^t 8 aClock, we hawled up the Whale & began to work on her. Altho' there was a very great Swell going & very foggy & hard Rain which renderd it exceeding difficult working however by Noon We got off the Blubber from one side & the (?) Weather being so hard that we could not Scuttle her Head We veered her out. . . .

"Scuttle her head" was a reference to the baling out of the fluid wax, or spermaceti, concentrated in the whale's "case."

July 18th 1754 The weather continuing unfit for Cutting we proceeded to Hand the Blubber & to stow it away in H'hds (?) We filled Nine H'hds & topt up some of the other to the value of 1 H^{dd}. The Blubber proves to be exceeding good, & to our Joy we Saved all our Craft except one 1 Lance which Broke. . . .

For more than a day following, a great swell made work on the whale impossible. On the twentieth they "rowled & tumbled much & carried away the chop of the Larboard Crotch," a minor calamity worth pausing over because it was a kind of damage to which all fore-and-afters equipped with booms and gaffs were subject when "rowling" in big rollers offshore. Square-riggers had the advantage of yards held firmly by ropes at both ends,

They place 2 or 3. coppers on a ro~ and y̆ chopping
boat on the one side and the cooling boate on the other si~
to receive y̆ oyle of y̆ coppers, the chapt blubber being
hoyled is taken out of the coppers, and put in wiker
baskets or barowes, throw̆gh wch the oyle is d~reane~
and runes into — y̆ cooler wch is ½ full of water, out of
wch it is con~ ~veg'd by troughs into bu~ or
hogshead

The sturdy and versatile shallop that was employed by Arctic whalers for more than a century, before the development of a better substitute in New England, was used (right) as a hunting vessel and a tug, and also (above) as a large blubber tub and as an oil cooler in improvised refineries. The sketch (below) of the *Sea Flower* may be the earliest we have of a specific New England whaling sloop. It flanks her log entry for May 29, 1754. Cod fishermen drying their catches (lower right) resented the intrusion of such whalers. (See pp. 23, 58–59, 62–64.)

but the free-swinging spars of a fore-and-after chafed constantly even in a pleasant breeze and slammed back and forth in light winds when there was a swell.

At last, toward dawn of the twenty-first, a fresh wind "laid the swell & made Smooth Water."

ab^t 4 aClock we hawled up the Whale & went to work on her head & dip't out 14 B^{lls}. . . .

July 22 1754. continued cutting the Whale & got off all her Blubber & got our Vessell clean. . . .

July 23 1754. at Noon we began to Hand our Blubber & stow it in H^{ds} & B^{lls} & by Dark We got all done & clear'd the Vessell We fill'd this day 5 H^{dds} & 35 B^{lls} with Blubber, so that in Whole this Whale has fill'd 14 H^{dds} Blubber & 35 B^{lls} D^o mark'd 0 & 15 B^{lls} Spermaceti mark'd P.

On the day following, as he was making ready to sail for home, Captain Robert Treat of the *Seaflower* went aboard a Dutch ship, but found that her people "spoke so bad English I could not learn much of them but that whales was scarce." By the evidence of his journal, he was an uncommonly literate seaman, but he displayed the testy provincialism that already was strongly appearing in the New England character.

Earlier journals may come to light. Alexander Starbuck, author of the classic *History of the American Whale Fishery from its Earliest Inception to the Year 1876*, seems not to have known of any as early as the three mentioned above. His work, published as an appendix to an enormous United States Senate document of that year on the state of the various fisheries, has long been the primary fishing ground of authors concerned with whaling: sturdy proof that official reports do not have to be as lugubrious as the Government Printing Office still tries hard to make them look. But even Starbuck is skimpy for the period of beach-based whaling and for the mid-century activities of the whaling sloops, which preceded an astonishing surge of activity, based on one small island.

TRYWORKS OFFSHORE

When the *Seaflower,* in the spring of 1754, was three weeks out from Cape Cod, an event occurred at the confluence of the Allegheny and Monongahela rivers that announced a grave new element of risk for any such voyage into northern waters. George

Washington was victorious in a small skirmish that triggered the French and Indian War. The French wanted to possess the enormous inland region reached by the St. Lawrence gateway and leave the English in possession of their well-settled coastal strip to the south. The British colonists thought themselves entitled to both regions, and the inland contest was promptly supplemented by privateering at sea. New England's whalers consequently suffered the first and by far the smallest of four wartime erasures of their fleets. Some vessels were captured. More were outfitted as privateers for the time being. A few continued to fish safely in the Gulf Stream when the weather was cold enough to keep blubber from turning into a seething mass of worms.

The fall of Montreal in September of 1760 marked the end of effective French resistance, and whaling was resumed. A change had occurred. Shipbuilding, pressed vigorously during the conflict, left the Massachusetts Bay region with a surplus of tonnage and with shipyards ready to build more. The ten whalers registered in the province during the following year were dramatically larger than the prewar whaling sloops. They ranged from 70 to 90 tons. Only two years later the Massachusetts fleet, including Nantucket's, had zoomed to 80 vessels. If we can trust a contemporary list composed in dreadful doggerel by Thomas Worth, nearly all of these, whatever their hailing ports, were skippered by Nantucketers; the island at this date had already assumed its character as the dominant training point for experts. Northern waters were again attractive, but a new hindrance arose in the regulations of colonial governors of Labrador and Newfoundland. It had been the thrifty Yankee practice to fish for whales and cod in the same voyage. This was forbidden under pain of confiscation of the vessel, but while it was being practiced by New Englanders, they began also to try out blubber on shores adjacent to the hunting grounds. Blubber might survive a cold homeward voyage, but fish had to be dried promptly. Thus there was an encouragement to render blubber into oil on the same coasts.

In July of 1765 the whalers were met by new posted regulations against fouling the environment. They were required "to carry the useless Parts of such Whales as they may catch to at least Three Leagues from the Shore" of Labrador, and they could not come ashore at all on the coast of Newfoundland. Local residents, as well as competing fishermen who had come all the way from England, had a point of view in such a situation. If the behavior of the whalers is truly reported in the preamble to the new regulations, it was often abominable. Whatever the facts may have been, such prohibitions sent the interlopers farther north to the fishery off Disco Island in Baffin Bay, which they had tried tentatively before, in 1751. This much more distant enterprise encouraged the prompt further development of vessels having a longer range.

Clifford W. Ashley, the artist-author and experienced whaleman who wrote *The Yankee Whaler* (c. 1926), says, "The first record of try-works on shipboard is in the logbook of the ship *Betsey* of Dartmouth in 1762." This date corresponds with the several pressures, political and pragmatic, that spurred the New Englanders to convert their whaling vessels into processing plants afloat. The dead whale would then no longer have to be tediously towed ashore, often for many backbreaking miles, to temporary tryworks set up on a barren coast. By comparison with the British practice of carrying the blubber home in casks, trying it out aboard ship had multiple advantages. Instead of filling, emptying, and refilling the casks, they were headed up at once. Newly rendered oil was of far better quality than that made months later from rancid or wormy blubber. Fresh blubber, put promptly into the try-pots, was much less unpleasant to work with: men handling rotten blubber developed serious ailments, particularly of the eyes, throat, and skin. Finally, a ship loaded to capacity with blubber casks was carrying home a considerable proportion of waste matter. It made sense to use all her space for clean oil.

Ashley implies that the trying out of oil on shipboard was a Yankee idea. If this were true, his date for the first trial of it would need revision. He cites the *Betsey*'s voyage of 1762, but the 1753 log of the *Greyhound*, cited above, mentions her tryworks with no indication that they were at that time a novelty. The claim is wrong anyhow. There is some evidence that the practice was originated by the Basque captain François Sopite Zaburu around the year 1600. Friedrich Martens, in his account of a whaling voyage to Spitsbergen made in 1671, contrasts the methods of the Dutch and the French on that coast. The Dutch had erected two principal factories on shore, but "the *Frenchmen* try up their Train-oyl in their Ships, and by that means many ships are burnt at *Spitsbergen* and this was the occasion of the burning of two Ships in my time."

A previous book of mine, *American Sail* (1961), reproduces a "pleasantly inaccurate engraving" of whale strikers off Spitsbergen from an English translation of Martens' work, published in 1719. It depicts harpooners poised to hurl their irons over the flat sterns of their boats. I have since noticed that this is the error of a copyist, who enlarged a small area of a wide seascape included in the original German edition of 1675. Martens made the drawings from which the first engraver worked. The 1719 re-engraver mistook shadows under the bows of the whaleboats for flat transoms. The point is worth raising here because the descendants of Elizabethan shallops, which were being used as whaleboats a century later, appear not to have been significantly improved. The bows were so blunt that they could be mistaken in this case for a square stern, and so they still appear in many other pictures of the late seventeenth century.

Since there is surprisingly little record of early Yankee whalers burned by accident at sea, it may be that the French ships with tryworks aboard lacked the big water pan over which Americans built their brick furnaces. This may have been the improvement that freed them from the old practice of bringing blubber home in casks to the "fry-houses" on the beach. There would not have been room enough for an adequate furnace in the first small whaling sloops. Nine Nantucket-owned vessels listed by Starbuck as registered between 1698 and 1714 had an average tonnage of 23. The largest was only 40 tons. These figures reflect those earlier given by Thomas Jefferson. The habits developed in shorebased whaleboats changed slowly; the men who still operated from the sands of Nantucket had their best year in 1726, when they beached 86 whales. At that time the sloops, which had been in use for more than a quarter-century, were hunting off Newfoundland, bringing all their blubber back in casks to Nantucket.

The trying out of blubber ashore, even in the primitive plant described by Fotherby of Baffin's 1613 voyage, called for a good deal of movable equipment. The more permanent shore establishments used cranes, windlasses, and sometimes the specialized large wheel called a crab, for all of which a ship's existing yards, blocks, and tackle could largely serve, if supplemented by one

big masthead block for hoisting the "blanket piece"—a long strip
of blubber unrolled from a whale slowly turning alongside. The
brick furnace, over its protective water tray, which the whalers
came eventually to call the duck pen, was sometimes built during the voyage to the whaling grounds and was knocked down
again as a rule when the casks were full of oil. The Nantucketers
do appear to have originated the practice of using the still-oily
"fritters," fibrous fleshy matter from which most of the oil had
been cooked out, as fuel—a great economy over the early practice of including a heavy load of firewood in the outward-bound
cargo. It was the sum total of such practices, exemplified chiefly
by the tryworks on deck and by its economical fueling, that en-
abled the New England whalers to compete profitably along the
edges of monopoly's realm, where habitual fixed costs and
perquisites of a caste system of investment and ownership added
considerably to the market price of oil.

Resistance to innovation in the British fishery can be noticed
at many points in the remarkable career of William Scoresby.
Beginning in the latter eighteenth century, he made 30 Greenland voyages, which earned him an average return of 30 per cent
on his investments. A seaman of great competence, he deserved
his success, but it should be noted that the continuity of his
career as a whaler depended upon his government's provision of
bounties and its ruinous taxation of foreigners' oil whenever
the market slumped. An account written by his son of the same
name, who tells us most of what we know of the northern fishery,
does not suggest that there was any attempt, in the much larger
British Greenland whalers, to imitate the tryworks on the decks
of the earlier American sloops. In an appendix to his stout two-
volume work published in 1820, the younger Scoresby describes
cautiously, as if it were an innovation for which he did not want
to be held responsible, the tryworks used in the southern fishery
in which he had not himself sailed; but all his inferences are that
blubber was still being brought home in casks to Britain from the
back side of Greenland, at the expense of about one-quarter to
one-third of each ship's carrying capacity.

To some degree it was a question of feasible distance. There
are accounts, even in the cold northern fishery, of blubber seething noisily on the way home, like beer in a brewer's vat. But the
port of Hull, where most British whalers were based, had exten-

sive manufacturing plants that supported, and were in turn supported by, its shipping. Some were devoted to the processing of blubber into oil. The usual interlocking pattern of investments made it difficult to cut off their supplies for the sake of a more efficient operation. The mutual back-scratchers of finance have seldom been notably interested in efficiency. Perhaps the most curious example of this attitude was the ship's husband who owned ships solely for the purpose of renting them to the East India Company, which by law was not allowed to own any. The ship's husband did nothing whatever but live comfortably on his rentier's profit, which was arranged for by his solicitor.

Such practices, in a society based largely upon hereditary privilege, gave the Yankees their opportunity to substitute ingenuity for insufficient capital. If the fur trade was the first extensive financial enterprise of the northern colonists, whaling was the first in which they created their own capital and proceeded to outmaneuver the entire world in a swift rise to eminence. The important turn came with a shift from emphasis upon pursuit of the northern right whale to the even farther-ranging quest for the sperm whale, in or beyond the tropic seas. This itself had been made possible only by the equipping of Nantucket's whalers with tryworks, after the French and Indian War. Necessity gave ingenuity no other option. The more valuable sperm whale blubber could not be brought home in casks from an extended voyage. Tryworks on board, the most efficient choice anywhere, were indispensable in the warmer seas. Whether the idea of tryworks was independently conceived of in Nantucket, about 1750, or was picked up from the Basques —the Frenchmen of Martens's account—it seems clear that Nantucketers were the first to make it both foolproof and standard in their ships. When the migrations of whales and the conditions of markets began to extend the typical voyage beyond a single season, American whalemen had perfected the one device that made this possible. In 1767, largely from forays southward along the Gulf Stream, Nantucket's efficient whalers pocketed £ 70,000.

It was still customary to charter, for any sort of voyage, the most suitable vessel that could be found—her owner receiving shares in the adventure as a part of his fee. In 1768 the merchants of Nantucket, aided by their profits of the preceding year, had the means to fit out 80 vessels as whalers, more than the combined whaling fleets of all other North American ports of registry. Their average measurement had risen to 75 tons. When the long-simmering Revolution flamed up, the tiny island had 150 whalers at sea, most of them in distant waters, where news of their danger from British men-of-war and privateers on the way home would be slow in reaching them. The Boston *News-Letter* lists separately the vessels "fitted" for the northern and the southern fisheries, 65 for the former, 85 for the latter. Those for the southern fishery already were substantially larger: 120 tons on the average, compared with the steady figure of 75 tons for those sent northward. All were still a long way below Hakluyt's recommendation of nearly two centuries earlier, but what was much more important, all were equipped with tryworks, a device that gave the Nantucketers at this period a long head start on the rest of the world, in an endeavor that was to be suddenly terminated.

3 Screw Propulsion –American Forerunners

DAVID BUSHNELL'S SCREW-DRIVEN SUBMARINE

The chief instrument by which Great Britain's privileged orders enforced their will in exploiting their American colonies was the Royal Navy. It transported with impressive style and ceremony the colonial administrators who were the visible symbols of taxation without representation and of exasperating inequities frequently expressed in new and harsher variants of the Navigation Acts. The harshest measure of all, introduced in February of 1775, prohibited the colonies from "carrying on any fishery on the Banks of Newfoundland or on any other part of the North American coast." British sea power thereupon scoured New England's whalers from the ocean within a few months, but this and other harassments exasperated the colonists into subtle ingenuities. One of these, based in experiments begun when the first tremors of revolution were felt four or five years earlier, was nothing more modest than a machine for the destruction of Britain's major fighting ships.

Thomas Jefferson has been credited above with some of the scanty surviving information about early Nantucket whaling vessels. It is largely as a result of Jefferson's practice of perceiving relationships between separate phenomena that we have enough information from the inventor himself to make sense out of other fragmentary testimony concerning David Bushnell's screw-propelled submersible of 1775. The evidence has been misread with a curious persistence. Close re-examination reveals that Bushnell's turtle—as the nameless craft was commonly called—did work, because in theoretical planning and in technical detail it deserved to work.

When Charles Griswold, almost 50 years after the event, published in the foremost American scientific journal an interview with old Ezra Lee, the turtle's first heroic combat navigator, the inquirer declared that "the whole merit of this invention is unanimously agreed to belong" to the revolutionary Bushnell: a judgment written when Robert Fulton's more recent triumphs and his treatise on torpedoes made his own submarine experiments better known. Yet unanimous agreement upon Bushnell's pre-eminence, so confidently alluded to in 1820, had dissipated about a century later when a prominent English nautical technologist published an otherwise well-documented life of Fulton in which the part of a page given to Bushnell is full of strange bloopers, such as, "The vessel . . . had practically no manoeuvring power, and was really intended to drift just awash with the tide."

That quotation is the evident basis for a curt dismissal of Bushnell in the principal American study devoted wholly to Fulton's submarine endeavors, published in 1922 by a scholarly university press: "His boat . . . was scarcely a submarine as it was not intended to plunge, but to float just 'awash' or almost submerged." Bushnell's boat was intended to plunge; it did so many times and came up again reliably. The quoted statement at least recognizes the forerunner's existence. When his name appears at all in works on the American Revolution, it is embedded as a rule in confident inaccuracies lifted from book to book.

Fulton's rightful repute as a submarine experimenter has no need of a boost got by diminishing Bushnell, who a generation earlier designed the most subtle technological mechanism of the age and built it under conditions of extreme difficulty. The distinguished array of witnesses and consultants whose testimony enters into that judgment includes not only Jefferson, but two other Founding Fathers, George Washington and Benjamin Franklin; General Israel Putnam and his aide the soldier-poet Colonel David Humphreys; the logistical diplomat Silas Deane; Yale's most distinguished early president, Ezra Stiles; the ardent revolutionary physician Benjamin Gale; and assorted others, including the Tory governor of New York and a spy he planted in the Continental Congress.

Simply as a lurking threat that it might be imprudent to

laugh off, the turtle had an important strategic effect upon the disposition of British fighting ships. But Bushnell's submarine, despite its remarkable advances in technology, was not the first thing of its kind, any more than Fulton's was. Even if recent historians have treated its deviser badly, an adequate knowledge of the turtle's mechanisms has been preserved.

Fair recognition of earlier submarine navigation is hampered because such possibly valid accomplishments as those of Cornelius Drebbel in the 1620's did not tickle the curiosity of any such devoted inquirer as Thomas Jefferson. Drebbel, a respectable engineer employed in great projects of water supply and drainage during the reign of James I, contrived some sort of submarine of which the reports are hazy and conflicting. One of them expresses amazement that the rowers sat on benches over open water that was calm when there were waves above. This suggests the possibility of an elongated diving bell paddled through the water from within. It was also reported that Drebbel renewed vitiated air with an alchemical mixture. Conceivably he anticipated Lavoisier's production of oxygen by a century and a half, but for this and several other reportedly workable submarines we have uncertain witness.

If we had to rely upon nothing but the surviving reports of persons who similarly saw Bushnell's turtle in operation, we would be little better off than we are in the cases of Drebbel and of several intervening experimenters, some of whom went down to be seen no more. It takes a scientific sort of curiosity to prod out technical information. The interest of Jefferson in Bushnell's turtle was fortunately aroused less than ten years after its hazardous first mission, and in a particularly Jeffersonian way. As United States representative in Paris in the 1780's, he was moved by private fascination and public duty to inspect many of the contraptions fostered by a growing interest in the physical sciences. On February 6, 1785, in a letter to Congressman Hugh Williamson, Jefferson described a test he had witnessed on the Seine of a catamaran propelled by an air screw about four feet in diameter and eight feet long. At first he wrote "spiral thread," then crossed out the latter word and substituted "vane" as a better indication of the broad, thin kind of screw he was describing, activated by a belt and pulley. He thought that if the screw were "made to work in water it's effect will still be greater"—and added, "I suspect the Connecticut turtle must have been navigated in this way. If so, I wish we knew it, the precise construction of the Connecticut turtle and it's actual performance."

Jefferson carried the matter in mind and wrote again five months later to Ezra Stiles, president of Yale College, who was better located to get in touch with the Connecticut mechanic David Bushnell. Noting that the French operator of the air screw "did not know himself the principle of his own invention," Jefferson now provided a more functional description:

a thin plate with it's edge applied spirally round an axis. This being turned operates on the air as a screw does, and may be literally said to screw the vessel along. . . . I very much suspect that a countryman of ours, Mr. Bushnel of Connecticut is entitled to the merit of a prior discovery of this use of the screw. I remember to have heard of his submarine navigation during the war, and . . . I conjecture that the screw was the power he used.

Jefferson thought it "too great a liberty for a stranger" to seek from Bushnell the information upon which we now primarily depend. The inquiry does not suggest any awareness either that the intermediary, Stiles, had long ago received a confidential report of the turtle's earliest trials. Jefferson did pledge himself "never to disclose" Bushnell's secrets except for the inventor's own benefit. On the same day an inquiry went to George Washington, who promptly replied that he had "wanted faith" in the turtle: "A combination of too many things were requisite, to expect much success . . . against an enemy, who are always upon guard." He said, however, that he had supplied the inventor liberally with funds. Washington suggested that Colonel David Humphreys, Bushnell's chief advocate among the military, should have a better memory than his own, but Humphreys replied that he could give Jefferson only "a general idea" of the turtle. As for screw propulsion, he had no memory at all of the "means contrived to produce" its maneuvers.

In a letter dated "Oct.   th 1787," the exact day left blank, Bushnell at last reported that almost two years earlier he had heard from both Humphreys and Stiles. Referring to Jefferson's promise not to disclose any secrets, the inventor acknowledged that he had been concealing his "principles and experiments" and that a severe illness had delayed his response. He enclosed a description of his craft so detailed that it should be "clear without drawings, which I cannot easily execute or obtain." His primary working plans probably were destroyed as a security measure. Pictures, in encyclopedias and a few popular histories of technology, all are arbitrary reconstructions based upon the description sent by Bushnell to Jefferson. The visual source of these, drawn to illustrate a centennial lecture delivered in 1875 at the Newport Torpedo Station, was made anachronistic by a navigator wearing a neat Victorian jacket with pantaloons. Some later artists have substituted more plausible revolutionary attire while faithfully swiping the shape and the mechanisms referred to by the lecturer as giving only "a tolerably correct idea of its general appearance."

Although the turtle's first foray against His Majesty's 64-gun ship *Eagle* had become a standard legend of the Revolution, arousing much more ridicule than pride, the multitudinously busy Jefferson kept for more than a decade his pledge of secrecy. In the meanwhile the beginnings of accurate public information appeared in a small book written by one of Jefferson's correspondents and advertised on September 1, 1788, in the Connecticut *Courant* as "published this day" in Hartford: *An Essay on the Life of the Honorable Major-General Israel Putnam . . .* , by Col. David Humphreys. Its author asked "indulgence for its venial errors, as it is the first effort in biography, that has been made on this continent." He was forgetting Cotton Mather — a hard thing to do. Most of the six or seven pages devoted to Bushnell and his "wonderful machine . . . not less ingenious than novel" probably were fished up from his own memories as a witness, but there is enough technical detail to make it seem likely that the author's letter to Bushnell, sent as a result of Jefferson's prodding, had elicited some further information:

General Putnam . . . afforded his patronage to a project for destroying the enemy's shipping by explosion. A Machine, altogether different from any thing hitherto devised by the art of man, had been invented by Mr. David Bushnell, for submarine navigation, which was found to answer the purpose perfectly of rowing horizontally at any given depth under water, and of rising or sinking at pleasure. To this Machine, (called the American Turtle) was attached a Magazine of Powder, . . . to

*be fastened under the bottom of a ship with a driving screw; . . .
the same stroke which disengaged it from the Machine should
put the internal clock-work in motion. This being done, . . . a
gun-lock (at the distance of half an hour, an hour, or any deter-
minate time) would cause the powder to explode and leave the
effects to the common laws of nature.*

A description follows of the first use of the machine in August,
1776, against Lord Howe's flagship, anchored near Manhattan
Island. The inventor, not sturdy enough to sustain the effort
of propelling his submersible over long distances, had trained
his brother "to manage it with perfect dexterity." This is the
judgment of a sponsor whose own repute was involved, reporting
at a later time when mockery over the failure to sink a major
enemy vessel was probably the dominant layman's attitude;
"but unfortunately his brother fell sick of a fever." Sergeant
Ezra Lee, a volunteer, therefore "received whatever instructions
could be communicated to him in a short time, went (too late
in the night) . . . under the bottom of the Eagle. . . . In coming
up, the screw, which had been calculated to perforate the copper
sheathing, unluckily struck against some iron plates, where the
rudder is connected with the stern." The sergeant, with dawn
breaking, prudently disengaged his vessel. General Putnam,
who had been watching from the wharf, sent a whaleboat to
rescue the turtle and saw the cast-off magazine explode.

*As the whole business had been kept an inviolable secret, he
was not a little diverted with the various conjectures, whether
this stupendous noise was produced by a bomb, a meteor, a
water-spout or an earthquake. Other operations of a most serious
nature rapidly succeeded and prevented a repetition of the
experiment.*

Soon after he confided his description to Jefferson, David
Bushnell vanished. The financially calamitous last years of the
original Confederation of Britain's former colonies were a bad
season for naval advocates. A promoter of submarines would
have got the least sympathetic hearing. Some think that Bushnell
sailed to France and may there have influenced Fulton, but if
the two did meet, it would have had to be elsewhere. Fulton
went to live in France in 1796—and the fact was belatedly
disclosed that Bushnell, not later than 1795, had moved to
Georgia, where he sought severance from his past under a short-

ened form of his name as the schoolteacher and physician Dr. Bush. Whether mockery of his achievements was a factor is unclear, nor have I been able to find out if he ever saw the evidence published before his death in 1824 of a new respect for what had been ignorantly ridiculed. The rehabilitation of his repute began in the American Philosophical Society, founded by Franklin in 1743 and concerned much more with "Useful Knowledge" than with speculative thought. Jefferson and Stiles had both been elected councilors to the society before the Revolution ended; Jefferson, as its president, was in the chair on June 15, 1798, when the minutes mention the presentation of a "'Description of a submarine vessel, calculated to effect the firing of vessels under water,' by D. Bushnell, of Stamford, Connecticut, read and referred to Mr. Patterson." The author's place of residence, thus given at a time when he had been living for three years in Georgia, indicates that Bushnell himself did not authorize release of the document, and the roster of those present does not include his name.

Six months earlier, Fulton had submitted well-developed plans for a submarine to the French Directory and had reported in a letter to an English scientific associate the results of actual tests of a four-bladed screw with which he proposed to drive it through the water. At this time Fulton was living in the Paris home of Jefferson's friend, the poet and land promoter Joel Barlow. In an era when a great deal of scientific information was propagated internationally by quill and ink, it might be inferred that the current president of the chief American organization concerned with such matters would have got some news of Fulton's project. As guardian of an important addition to the history of technology, written by a man presumably dead, Jefferson may have considered it his duty to release the evidence of Bushnell's quarter-century priority over Fulton with a screw-propelled submersible. The fact should also be taken into account that the United States had sidled into its quasi-war at sea with France, thought by Jefferson to be the wrong enemy when England was still the great offender against neutral shipping. He, among the Founding Fathers, had been the only strong advocate of a defensive force of frigates soon after the Revolution ended. Some 13 years later, with frigates at last slipping into the water, he was unhappy over their probable uses by the government from which he had dissociated himself. This, too, may have moved him to put on public record the details of an unarguably defensive naval device.

For whatever reason, Jefferson released the Bushnell account, and at the next meeting of the philosophers Robert Patterson, the mathematician to whom it had been referred for routine study, pronounced it "worthy of publication." It appeared at last in Volume IV of the society's *Transactions* in 1799. Technologists who now reread the inventor's own description ought to be impressed by Bushnell's handling of factors closely similar to those that shaped the first Mercury space capsule almost two centuries later. Each provided a compact environment for one navigator, insulated from the machine's surroundings and seated within arms' reach of all essential instruments and controls. The differences between them also are significant. The Mercury capsule was multitudinously instrumented, for control as a rule by external operators. The turtle's controls and instruments expressed the sophistication of exact simplicity, operated entirely from within.

The external shape of the sub-marine vessel bore some resemblance to two upper tortoise shells of equal size, joined together; the place of entrance into the vessel being represented by the opening made by the swell of the shells, at the head of the animal.

It is this first sentence of Bushnell's own description that has misled nearly all who have tried to draw pictures of the revolutionary submersible. Reinforced by its contemporary nickname—turtle—this statement produces the image of two tortoises, belly to belly, standing on their tails. Bushnell, however, claimed only "some" resemblance in a passage stressing the upper part of the resulting image, the opening for access.

The earliest dimensional description of the machine makes the synthetic pictures seem clearly wrong. This is a letter sent on August 7, 1775, to Benjamin Franklin by Benjamin Gale, a physician who was the inventor's first serious sponsor. Gale wrote, "It doth not Exceed 7 feet in Length, and the Depth not more than 5½ feet." Writing two months later to Silas Deane, who at this point was one of Connecticut's delegates to the Continental Congress, Gale gave approximately the same proportions: 7½ feet long, 6 feet in "heighth." Ezra Lee, the man with the most intimate reasons for knowing exactly what the turtle was like, told Humphreys in 1815 that the submarine "was most like a round clam, but longer, and set up on its square side . . . its extreme length was not more than 7 feet." Griswold, in his interview with Lee five years later, reported that the old man again used the simile of a "round clam." It is unclear whether "heighth" included the conning tower. One way or the other, the vessel appears to have been about one-quarter or one-third longer than it was deep, with a flat keel long enough to suggest to Sergeant Lee the straight hinge of an elongated clam.

Later writers, elaborating upon the imaginary pictures, have likened the submarine to a "top," as if it were everywhere circular in cross section——a double distortion of the evidence. Bushnell wrote:

The internal shape of the vessel, in every possible section, verged toward an ellipsis, as near as the design would allow, but every horizontal section, although elliptical, yet as near to a circle, as could be admitted. . . . a firm piece of wood was framed, parallel to the conjugate diameter, to prevent the sides from yielding to the great pressure . . . in a deep immersion. This piece of wood was also a seat for the operator.

How "near to a circle"? Enough of an ellipse, evidently, to make the designer aware of maximum pressure on the sides. "Conjugate diameter" likewise expresses a meaningful distinction between length and breadth, reinforced by Bushnell's first reference to the propulsive and steering mechanisms:

At one edge which was directly before the operator, who sat upright, was an oar for rowing forward or backward. At the other edge, was a rudder for steering. An aperture at the bottom, with its valve, was designed to admit water, for the purpose of descending; and two brass forcing-pumps served to eject the water within, when necessary for ascending. At the top there was likewise an oar, for ascending or descending, or continuing at any particular depth—

Jefferson wanted to credit Bushnell with the invention of screw propulsion. What did the inventor himself mean by "oar," as used in this passage? Precise technical vocabularies are developed from the devices they describe. When Jefferson, in his letter to a congressman, scratched out "thread" and substituted "vane," he was laboring to create a new, precise scientific usage. President Stiles, recording in his journal the gist of what Jefferson had written him, tried another phrase—"spiral sail on an axis which screws the vessel along." The idea of screw propulsion was not new—James Watt was among those who had previously suggested it—but in practical application Bushnell may have been the first to rely upon it for a profoundly serious venture. It is clear from other evidence that his "oars" were what we would now call "propellers," a word for which compilers of the *Oxford English Dictionary* found no example, in this specialized sense, before 1809.

The same problem of vocabulary appears in a description dispatched by Dr. Gale to Franklin on August 7, 1775, when he reported on a night test of the "machine" in Long Island Sound:

He then sunk under Water, where he Continued about 45 Minutes without any inconveniency as to Breathing, he Can Row it either Backward or forward Under water about 3 Miles an Hour . . . he has allso another Pair of Oars by whi [tear] can Rowe it either up or Down—

Here "another pair" implies that there was a pair for each function. The much-copied centennial picture has two continuous threads, or vanes, each making one complete circuit of the hub, but Gale's closer description, in his following letter to Deane of November 9, 1775, did not emerge into scholars' print from its archival bundle until 1870, and the artist-lecturer evidently had not read it:

In the bow, he has a pair of oars fixed like the two opposite arms of a wind mill, with which he can row forward, and turning them the opposite way, row the machine backward; another pair fixed upon the same model, with which he can row the machine round, either to the right or left; and a third, by which he can row the machine either up or down: all which are turned by foot, like a spinning wheel.

Lee's letter of 1815 to Humphreys is even more closely descriptive:

. . . the navigator rows with one hand and steers with the other. It had two oars of about 12 inches in length, and 4 or 5 in width, shaped like the arms of a windmill which led also inside through

water joints, in front of the person steering, and were worked by means of a wench (or crank); and with hard labour, the machine might be impelled at the rate of 3 nots an hour for a short time.

The discrepancies in these letters do not necessarily reflect faulty observation. The machine was not, as most accounts imply, slammed hastily together in the spring of 1776 to help lift the siege of New York. Dr. Gale's letters to Franklin and Deane reveal it as fully operative more than a year before it was first put to the test of actual battle, and Bushnell said it had been "projected" in 1771. There were many trial runs and at least one delay for the replacement of faulty equipment. Gale had encouraged Deane to spread the news in the Continental Congress that the machine would be "in the camp" near New York when his letter of November 9, 1775, reached Philadelphia. On the twenty-second he wrote again to explain: "The forcing pump . . . not being made according to order given, did not answer; which has delayed him." Gale's report of a foot treadle to turn the propellers, when compared with Lee's phrase "rows with one hand," is not a discrepancy: the inventor's own description tells us explicitly that the "oar" for horizontal motion "was made to be turned by hand or foot" and that it was "formed upon the principle of the screw." Here, too, Bushnell's own words misled the maker of the first synthetic drawing, since Gale's and Lee's references to arms of a windmill, and the latter's explicit dimensions for the size of the blades, were evidently not before him.

That there were ever three "pairs of oars," the second pair for steering, does seem dubious. Mention of it is made only in Gale's second descriptive letter, to Deane. The explanation probably appears in Bushnell's reference to the rudder, which was "made very elastic, and might be used for rowing forward"—the common fishtail practice of sculling by wagging the tiller back and forth.

Griswold in 1820 quoted Lee as saying:

. . . two oars or paddles . . . revolved perpendicularly upon an axletree that . . . passed into the machine at a water joint and was furnished with a crank. . . .

These paddles were about twelve inches long, and about four wide. Two smaller paddles of the same description, also pro-

*jected near the head . . . by which the ascent of the machine
could be assisted.*

Bushnell thus relied upon a propeller with two slim blades,
which would have measured a little more than two feet from tip
to tip, with allowance for the unspecified diameter of the axletree. Fulton used a four-bladed propeller a generation later; but
in 1802, four years after his first trials, he reported that a two-
bladed one, given the same power, was more efficient. John
Ericsson, 70 years after the construction of the turtle, produced
extreme, multibladed elaborations of the screw propeller before
he arrived at last at Bushnell's efficient simplicity. Engineers
in the middle part of the nineteenth century advocated three or
four blades—with the admission that they were less efficient
than two—only because at high speeds they imparted less
vibration to the vessel.

Many other aspects of the turtle raise questions of its builder's
priority in technology. He wrote:

*Wherever the external apparatus passed through the body of the
vessel, the joints were round, and formed by brass pipes, which
were driven into the wood of the vessel, the holes through the
pipes were very exactly made, and the iron rods, which passed
through them, were turned in a lathe to fit them; the joints were
also kept full of oil, to prevent rust and leaking.*

As late as the 1850's a search was continuing for satisfactory
propeller-shaft bearings. Steel turning in wood was then thought
by some to be the best combination, but iron or steel shafts in
oiled brass bearings are still preferred in a great many machines.

The notion of a tricky gadget, put quickly together in an emergency, lurks in most recent descriptions of the turtle. It has
centered upon the device developed by Bushnell to affix his
case of explosive to a ship's bottom. All the intervening ridicule,
however, did not deter Fulton, about 25 years later, from employing exactly the same means: one of the reasons for supposing
that the two men had met. The drawings on pages 82–83 follow
Bushnell's own description. In one of his brass "water joints"
a hollow iron tube, or sleeve, could slide vertically up or down,
six inches. An iron rod, or bolt, threaded at the upper end, fitted
snugly in the tube and was screwed into an orifice in the head
of a very sharp wood screw, pointing straight upward above the
vessel. Thus the wood screw, the rod, and the tube became a firm

unit that could be turned or could slide up and down in its brass bushing; "by pushing the wood-screw up against the bottom of a ship, and turning it at the same time," Bushnell explained, "it would enter the planks; driving would also answer the same purpose." The rod could then be unscrewed and withdrawn from the head of the embedded wood screw, freeing the turtle to drift or be "rowed" away. Another screw, which similarly held the magazine of powder, could be turned to free it. The act of withdrawing this second screw tripped the preset clockwork, which, at the end of a chosen period of time, tripped in its turn a gunlock to explode 150 pounds of powder. The magazine, affixed to the wood screw by a short length of strong rope, was a little lighter than water and would thus float upward into close contact with the ship's bottom until it exploded.

Some commentators have doubted Sergeant Lee's explanation that he struck a bar of iron—a gudgeon strap—near the *Eagle*'s rudder, which prevented the screw from entering; they suggest that it was only at this time that its inability to pierce copper sheathing was discovered. But Humphreys, in the first published technical description of the turtle (1788), said that the screw "had been calculated to perforate the copper sheathing"— which at the time was a recent development and therefore much discussed. It seems unlikely, in view of Bushnell's account of the training of his brother, that the trials would have failed to include tests on copper. The inventor wrote:

I made him descend and continue at particular depths, without rising or sinking, row by the compass, approach a vessel, go under her, and fix the wood-screw *. . . into her bottom, &c. until I thought him sufficiently expert to put my design into execution.*

. . . it required many trials to make a person of common ingenuity, a skilful operator: the first I employed was very ingenious, and made himself master of the business, but was taken sick . . . before he had an opportunity to make use of his skill. . . .

Bushnell, furthermore, had provided a second expedient: if the turning screw did not take hold in the ship's bottom, "driving would also answer." A smart whack would have pierced the soft copper of the period. The brave but hastily trained Lee may have forgotten this option in the excitement of the first submarine attack.

The turtle had other supplementary devices, such as the ver-

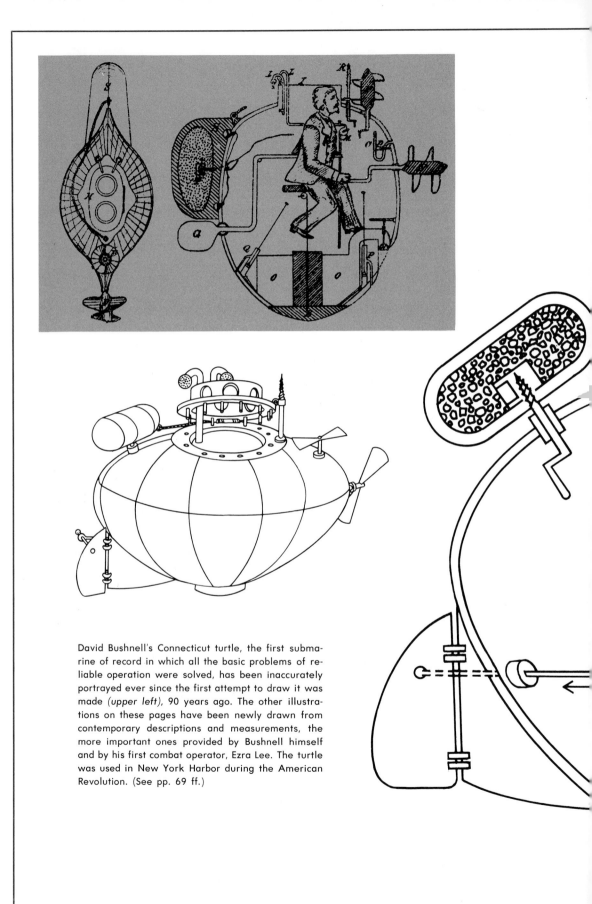

David Bushnell's Connecticut turtle, the first submarine of record in which all the basic problems of reliable operation were solved, has been inaccurately portrayed ever since the first attempt to draw it was made *(upper left)*, 90 years ago. The other illustrations on these pages have been newly drawn from contemporary descriptions and measurements, the more important ones provided by Bushnell himself and by his first combat operator, Ezra Lee. The turtle was used in New York Harbor during the American Revolution. (See pp. 69 ff.)

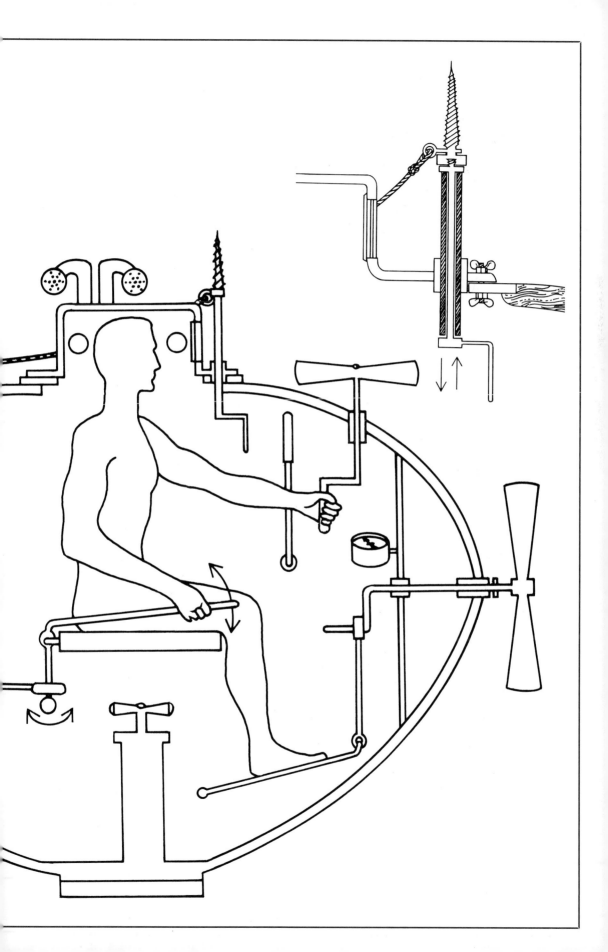

tical screw propeller that provided a finer depth adjustment than the taking in of water and expelling it with force pumps. This mutual relationship of different means to the same purpose, one more powerful, the other more subtle, has become standard practice in submersibles. Another example appears in Bushnell's arrangements for ventilation, which are not as satisfactorily described in any of the documents. The inventor himself wrote:

There were two air pipes in the crown. A ventilator within drew fresh air through one of the air pipes, and discharged it into the lower part of the vessel; the fresh air introduced by the ventilator, expelled the impure light air through the other air pipe.

I assume that the "ventilator within" was an air pump, since it had the force to draw, to discharge, and to expel—but there was some sort of automatic safety provision:

Both pipes were so constructed, that they shut themselves whenever the water rose near their tops, so that no water could enter through them, and opened themselves immediately after they rose above the water.

Sergeant Lee reported that at two fathoms depth the "corked" seams of the turtle's hull leaked, but he mentioned no trouble at all with the more subtle mechanical arrangements for propulsion and ventilation. The air tubes were protected from injury and from clogging at the outer ends by perforated spheres; each pipe had also a manually operated emergency valve or shutter inside the vessel that could be closed if the automatic one outside should jam.

Bushnell's simile for his conning tower, "resembling a hat with its crown and brim," is helpful. "The entrance into the vessel was elliptical, and so small as barely to admit a person." It was surrounded by an iron band, above which "a brass crown, or cover, . . . shut water tight" upon it and could be screwed snugly down either from within or from without. The two ventilating tubes were in the hat's crown and the screw mechanism for affixing the powder magazine to a ship was in the forward part of its brim. There were three air ports in the crown, one facing forward, one at each side, "large enough to put the hand through . . . their shutters were ground perfectly tight into their places with emery." Bushnell in his paper emphasizes the structural importance of his elliptical iron band as reinforcement of the oak into which it was "let." The conning tower, hinged at one side, had in addition to the air ports six glass windows "for looking through, and for admitting light in the day time, with covers to secure them." Sergeant Lee said they admitted enough light in clear water for reading at a depth of 18 feet. In view of many such particularities in the primary testimony it is disconcerting that in this century scholars of some repute should have spread the myth that the turtle was intended only to voyage "awash."

So far as I have been able to discover, Bushnell was the originator of self-illuminated instruments for navigation by night: a compass and a depth gauge. The latter, which mystified Sergeant Lee, was an 18-inch vertical glass tube, closed at the top and fastened at the lower end into a brass pipe thrust through the side of the vessel. As the depth increased, a head of air inside the tube was compressed. The water column rose about an inch for each fathom that the turtle descended below the surface. The problem, both with the depth gauge and the compass, was to make them visible during dives after dark. On December 7, 1775, Gale wrote to Deane at Philadelphia, telling him that the replacement pump worked well but that a more puzzling difficulty had arisen:

He proposes to go in the night, on account of safety. He always depended upon fox-wood, which gives light in the dark, to fix on the points of the needle of his compass, and in his barometer . . . both which are of absolute necessity for personal safety of the navigator: but he now finds that the frost wholly destroys that quality in that wood.

Urging the continental congressmen to believe that he had not been telling them "an idle story" about the phenomenal machine, Gale asked Deane if Dr. Franklin knew "of any kind of phosphorus which will give light in the dark and not consume the air." A candle had been tried, but it rapidly diminished the oxygen.

The person, the inventor of this machine, now makes all his affairs a secret even to his best friends, and I have liberty to communicate this much from him only with a view to know if Dr. Franklin knows of any kind of phosphorus that will answer his purpose; otherwise the execution must be omitted until next spring, after the frosts are past. I am therefore to request your strictest silence in that matter.

Deane—on January 13 in a letter now lost—evidently named two substances because Gale, on February 1, wrote again to ask "if the Philosopher's Lanthorn may be attained, and will give a better light than what is proposed, should be glad you would get what knowledge you can from Dr. Franklin respecting it."

Foxwood was the ordinary rotting wood that glows from life processes of tiny luminescent fungi that are helping to decompose it; as Bushnell had discovered too late, they become dormant in cool weather. The "Philosopher's Lanthorn" probably was yellow phosphorus, which had been derived from urine about a century earlier by the alchemists. At the time of the turtle's development, yellow phosphorus was just beginning to be a commercial product of bone. In his 1787 letter to Jefferson, Bushnell said of his "water gauge or barometer":

There was a piece of cork with phosphorus on it, put into the water-gauge. When the vessel descended the water rose in the water-gauge, condensing the air within, and bearing the cork, with its phosphorus, on its surface. By the light of the phosphorus, the ascent of the water in the gauge was rendered visible, and the depth of the vessel under water ascertained by a graduated line. . . .

A compass marked with phosphorus directed the course, above and under the water; and a line and lead sounded the depth when necessary.

On the morning of February 2, 1776, while a search for the Philosopher's Lanthorn was being projected, Bushnell appeared by invitation before the governor of Connecticut and the colony's Council of Safety to explain what he was up to. The council voted, when he had left, that "we hold ourselves under obligations of secrecy about it" and that he should "proceed to make every necessary preparation and experiment about it, with expectation of proper public notice and reward." On the day following, the council eased itself a bit beyond its first caution and voted the sum of £60 to the deputy governor, authorizing him to spend some of it to aid Bushnell "to carry forward the plan &c.&c., it appearing to be a work of great ingenuity &c, and a prospect that it may be attended with success. . . ."

BUSHNELL AT WAR

Committees of Correspondence, channels for subversive communication among conspirators against the king's peace, had reached the height of their activity when the Connecticut turtle was being readied for battle. The earliest surviving description of it appears to be a letter written by a tutor at Yale to Ezra Stiles, who was soon to be the college's ardently rebellious president. Stiles, at odds with orthodoxy in church and state, was still practicing his in-and-out profession of clergyman at Newport, Rhode Island, when Tutor John Lewis wrote him a letter that began:

Newhaven Aug 3 1775.

Rev'd Sir

*I have this moment parted with M*ʳ*. Bushnel; hic homo est machinæ Inventor. . . .*

The description that follows in late Church Latin was meant to bewilder Tory snoops; it is still a bit bewildering to some of my helpful Latinist friends, but Lewis was doing his own inventive best with equivalents for terms missing from the Latin lexicons, such as "gunpowder."

This letter—which preceded by four days Gale's first on the subject, to Franklin—incautiously named the inventor, whom Gale always called "the person" or "the man." But the rumor was out. An inquiry from Deane to Gale, dated a week later than Tutor Lewis' Latin dispatch to Stiles, wanted to know "what ground is there for the report of a certain new invention for destroying Ships." The subsequent exchanges dispose of much of the diligent confusion about the turtle, such as the assertion that it was first employed against His Majesty's ship *Asia* in 1775, rather than against the *Eagle* a year later. This error comes from someone's too credulous glance over an intelligence report given by Royal Governor of New York William Tryon to Captain George Vandeput, commander of the *Asia*, when she was anchored in the harbor off the tip of Manhattan as the Revolution got under way. Tryon had prudently withdrawn from his executive mansion to the safety of the ship of the line, but he had managed to plant a former body servant as valet to one of New York's representatives to the Continental Congress.

On November 16, 1775, when Gale's second letter descriptive of the turtle should have reached Philadelphia, the spy wrote from that city:

The great news of the day with us is now to Destroy the Navy, a certain Mr Bushnel has compleated his Machine, and has been missing four weeks, returned this day week.

It is conjectur'd that an attempt was made on the Asia, *but proved unsuccessful—Return'd to New Haven in order to get a Pump of a new Construction which will soon be completed,— When you may expect to see the Ships in Smoke.*

Bushnell was being competently tailed; both he and Gale knew it. The British at the time took him much more seriously than his own countrymen did a few years later: the blockading vessels, soon after the report from Tryon's spy, dropped down into the Lower Bay to await reinforcements. There is some information in the spy's report that he could not have picked up from Gale's known letters. Evidently there were other sources from which he got the notion of an attack against the *Asia,* alleged to have been made when the turtle was still in Connecticut.

Detailed information from the Gale-Deane-Franklin correspondence lapses when the two latter were designated to hunt munitions and other aid in France. The turtle—ready at last, luminescent instruments and all—probably underwent the standard fate of strategic new weapons and was held in reserve for the best moment, when it could have a maximum effect of surprise. During the skirmishes and battles around New York in the spring and summer of 1776 the problem of bringing the vessel to a prudent point of use without risking its capture above water would have been difficult. Putnam finally got it carted over to the Hudson, where Sergeant Lee was hastily trained for an attack upon the British flagship.

A second attack, attempted on another vessel in the Hudson, above the city, was unsuccessful. Bushnell, in his report to Jefferson, wrote:

In going toward the ship, he lost sight of her, and went a great distance beyond her: when he at length found her, the tide ran so strong, that as he descended under water, for the ship's bottom—it swept him away.

The operator himself, in 1815, gave Humphreys a different explanation. It had been decided that he should approach the British vessel submerged, come up under the overhanging stern, and drive the screw just above the surface. It is likely that British intelligence had spread an alert, because the watch on board promptly discovered the emerging conning tower:

. . . shutting my doors I dove under her, but my cork in the tube (by which I ascertained my depth) got obstructed and deceived

me, and I descended too deep and did not touch the ship; I then left her.

The two accounts are not really in conflict. Washington may have been right when he wrote that too many factors had to coincide in the use of the new device. In the waters around Manhattan the tide at times runs more rapidly than the three-knot maximum speed of the craft. Darkness also was requisite. Bushnell says that Lee, on this second attempt, lost sight of his target and spent so much time in getting back into range that the tide was running strongly when he did so. Evidently the attack had been calculated for a turn of tide shortly before dawn.

It is no part of this book's purpose to celebrate naval victories or to excuse defeats, but sometimes rather to examine such encounters for their revelation of qualities of certain vessels that were engaged. Testimony surviving from Lee's two forays makes the point that Bushnell designed a submarine capable of all necessary maneuvers within the limits of its propulsive force of one manpower. It could surface promptly and reliably from dives to a recorded depth of at least three fathoms. It had the two essential instruments for subsurface navigation by day or night, although one according to Lee failed him at an awkward moment. It had secondary provisions for all its vital functions: water tanks and pumps supplemented by a vertical screw and by lead ballast that could be jettisoned in a crisis, ventilators with automatic and manual controls, propulsion by hand or foot power, screens to protect the intake orifices for both air and water. By contrast with many earlier and later submersibles that fatally failed to respond when the time came to surface, there is no indication in the record that the turtle ever hesitated.

It is just as clear that Bushnell, making his lonely advance into sophisticated technology, was creating the need for precise, matching skill in the operator. Management of the less sophisticated but much more intricate contemporary machine, the sailing ship, with its hundreds of controlling ropes and lines, called for an apprenticeship of many years in a considerable number of men who divided a multitude of functions. Ezra Lee, as the almost successful original pigboat warrior, can hardly be overpraised, but he did need more training than he got in the use of a device that competently announced, for better or worse, the assured beginnings of safe submarine navigation.

The only detailed account of the turtle's third foray was not published until almost 70 years after the occurrence. It has some of the flavor of romantic fiction and adds nothing to our knowledge of the craft. Bushnell himself merely mentions it as having, like the second one, "effected nothing." He concludes:

I found it absolutely necessary, that the operators should acquire more skill . . . which would have taken some time, and made no small additional expense. I therefore gave over the pursuit at that time, and waited for a more favorable opportunity, which never arrived.

The first attack, on the *Eagle,* dissipated any supposititious advantage in secrecy. James Thatcher, an army surgeon stationed at Fort Ticonderoga, wrote in his diary a few weeks after the event:

By some gentlemen from head quarters, near New York, we are amused with an account of a singular machine, invented by a Mr. D. Bushnell of Connecticut, for the purpose of destroying the British shipping by explosion.

A description that follows was evidently interpolated in the first edition of the diary, published in 1823, from other works that had come out in the meanwhile—but the explosion in New York harbor of the magazine cut loose by Sergeant Lee made a noise that echoed well beyond Ticonderoga, significantly altering the tactical disposition of British ships.

The memoirs of General William Heath, issued in 1798, the year when Jefferson released the first full technical description of the turtle, give us in the entry for October 9, 1776, a last glimpse of it in a combat situation:

The enemy . . . sunk a sloop, which had on board the machine, invented by, and under the direction of, a Mr. Bushnell, intended to blow up the British ships. This machine was worked under water. It conveyed a magazine of powder, which was to be fixed under the keel of a ship, when freed from the machine, and left with clockwork going, which was to produce fire when the machine got out of the way. Mr. Bushnell had great confidence in its success, and had made several experiments which seemed to give him countenance; but its fate was truly a contrast to its design.

Referring to this event in his report to Jefferson, Bushnell added, "Though I afterwards recovered the vessel, I found it impossible, at that time, to prosecute the design any farther." He was unwell. Most of his experimentation had been conducted at his own expense. "I despaired of obtaining the public attention, and the assistance necessary. I was unable to support myself, and the persons I must have employed, had I proceeded."

The inference often drawn from these words, that discouragement and ridicule caused Bushnell to hide from the public at about this time, is not supported by the records of the Revolutionary Army. It was after the failures in New York waters that Major General James Wadsworth wrote to Governor Trumbull proposing that Bushnell be dispatched to Kingston, farther up the Hudson, to attack the British ships stationed there. The idea was not implemented, perhaps because Bushnell himself was developing other and simpler procedures, based in his own experiments that preceded the construction of the turtle. Here again the vagueness of earlier records makes it difficult to determine the extent to which Bushnell was an innovator in his demonstrations of the nature and effect of underwater explosions. In the British Calendar of State Papers for the year 1626 (O.S. 1627) there is a Navy Office document that provided for the manufacture of "watermines, water petards, forged cases to be shot with fireworks, and boats to goe under water." The records of one expedition for which they were prepared by Drebbel, contain, however, no evidence of their use; on a second occasion, when Drebbel himself sailed with the offensive fleet, it did not get near enough to the enemy to use them.

The various Bushnell documents, on the other hand, reveal a careful sequential experimentation, begun in 1771, when the inventor was a Yale freshman, and conducted before credible witnesses, to prove the possibility of underwater explosions and to show their particularly devastating effect upon nearby objects, far greater than that of explosions in air. The idea for some reason had great difficulty in pounding its way through orthodox nautical brain cases. Three decades after Bushnell made his conclusive demonstrations, Fulton persuaded the British Admiralty to provide him with an old vessel, the brig *Dorothea,* for an actual test of a torpedo. More than a hundred officers of the Royal Navy were on hand on October 15, 1805, as observers. One, a Captain Kingston, told Fulton 20 minutes before the test that "if a torpedo were placed under his cabin while he was at dinner, he should feel no concern for the consequence." A torpedo carry-

When Robert Fulton was working in Paris on his submersible *Nautilus*, John Vanderlyn made the pencil drawing of him at the right. Fulton's preliminary plan of the craft, now in the French archives, appears below. The vessel he launched and successfully tested in 1800 seems to have been a compromise between this plan of 1797 and the revised drawings at the lower right, dated 1804, from which he was turned by the luck of politics. In 1805 he demonstrated for the British Admiralty the effect *(upper right)* of his submarine torpedo on an old brig. (See pp. 91, 94, 96–103.)

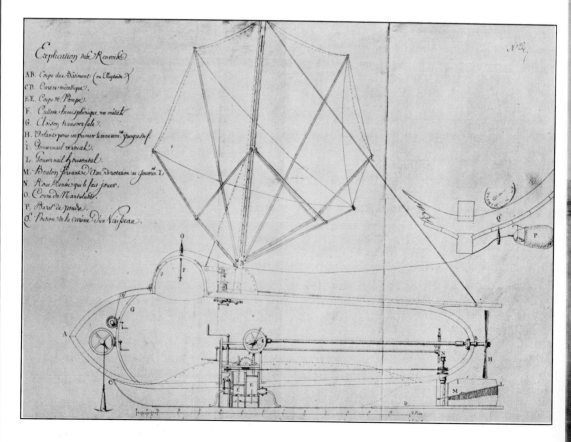

ing 180 pounds of powder thereupon broke the *Dorothea* into two pieces, just forward of her mainmast. Until that moment the delusion had persisted among otherwise competent officers that water would "dissipate" the shock. Bushnell had long ago proved, to the contrary, that water would contain the explosive force almost as if it were a solid wall, and direct toward any yielding object in the vicinity most of that part of the shock that would in fact be dissipated in air.

In Fulton's hasty treatise entitled *Torpedo War and Submarine Explosions* (1810), although it consists chiefly of elaborations upon a method of torpedo attack developed by Bushnell, there is no mention of the originator. This method was the towing of surface mines on a curving course that would drag them into contact with an anchored vessel—or, alternatively, the release of mines coupled together in such a fashion that the current would drift the rope that joined them across the bows of a vessel and press the mines against her on both sides to be exploded by contact triggers.

In 1777, using a whaleboat, Bushnell attacked the frigate *Cerberus* at her anchorage near New London "by drawing a machine against her side, by means of a line." Approaching in the darkness, he was unable to make out the shape of a schooner anchored just astern of the larger vessel. His machine demolished only the schooner, but in so doing lifted the British blockade on the Connecticut coast. The *Cerberus* went romping promptly off to New York to report upon unprecedented perils to the eastward.

In December of the same year Bushnell loosed upon the Delaware, above Philadelphia, a small flock of contact mines to drift against the British ships off the port. His recurrent problem, lack of trained or reliable staff, followed him again. His local river pilot grossly misjudged the distance at night. The mines did not reach the ships until daylight and were fended off. This event called forth Francis Hopkinson's satiric jingle "The Battle of the Kegs," which was intended to mock the British but had the sad sidelong effect of linking Bushnell's endeavors with humor.

The extent to which Bushnell's services as a civilian warrior were valued appears in an episode marked by the failure of British intelligence to maintain its usual alertness. Early in May of 1779, in a dispatch to General Washington—reporting the seizure of several civilians, including Bushnell—General Putnam wrote:

As the last-mentioned gentleman, who was there in the prosecution of his unremitting endeavors to destroy the enemy's shipping, is personally known to very few people, it is possible he may not be discovered by his real name or character, and may be considered of less consequence than he actually is.

On May 10, 1779, Bushnell was traded back to the rebels in an exchange of civilians. When the Corps of Sappers and Miners was organized in the Continental Army, he at last received a formal post as Captain-Lieutenant, on August 2, 1779. Less than two years later, as a full captain, he directed operations against the enemy's defenses around Yorktown and was present when the siege ended in the surrender that brought the active conflict practically to an end. For the next two years he was with the ring of troops that kept British occupiers of New York from misbehaving while the peace treaty was under discussion. When his corps was disbanded at West Point in December, 1783, he was its commanding officer.

These records, and the testimony of General Putnam, leave no basis for the careless canard that Bushnell, depressed by his failures, dropped out of sight early in the war. The very secrecy that he appears to have maintained so successfully as a civilian combatant prevents an accurate assessment of his value, but Putnam's references to his endeavors as "unremitting" and to his "consequence" are hints that he accomplished more than is on record.

What caused him, at last, truly to drop out of sight and to alter his name? The explanations, if they survive, are still in hiding. What we do have amply on the record is his remarkable achievement in designing and building, almost unaided, the first submersible about which we can be sure, both in its design and in its behavior. With his turtle, Bushnell foresaw and overcame all the major problems of submarine navigation, with a controlled adaptation of means to purpose that is hardly ever found in a prototype. The device for attaching a torpedo to its victim, while tricky, should with a well-trained operator have worked. Whether the world would have been better for that is a question upon which the reader may wish to meditate.

ROBERT FULTON'S SCREW-DRIVEN SUBMARINE

Robert Fulton, who was 18 when the American Revolution ended, experienced the average Yankee's multiplied exasperations as the great cyclic struggle between England and France rose toward its climax, marked by a worldwide use and desperate misuse of naval might. The misuse included impressment of American seamen into foreign fighting ships—into British ships particularly. The Royal Navy harassed American traders in waters where it had formerly had the explicit function of protecting them. Fulton as a consequence developed the conviction that a reliable device for the destruction of major fighting ships would be an incomparable blessing. If all naval nations acquired short-range defensive weapons such as submarines, splendid. It did not matter which began to use them to eliminate ships of the line from all coasts. The complete lack of a naval force in his own country between 1783 and 1797 must have shaped his thinking. It was a demonstrated possibility, despite humiliations, to live without one.

Fulton, a competent graphic artist with a visionary view of mechanical contrivances as friends to man, had spent almost two decades abroad when he came home in 1806 to begin the development of river steamers that got him his principal fame. He had passed about half of his self-exile in England, first as an apprentice portrait painter, then as an experimenter in the construction of incline planes to replace the slow and cumbersome locks in canals. After moving to Paris in 1796, he continued to use both of his chief conceptual talents, for the visual arts and for mechanics. He initiated in France a kind of mechanistic public art that had become suddenly popular during his stay in England: the panorama. His huge circular oil, "Fire of Moscow," went on display in 1800 in a building designed to contain it.

We are not likely ever to know just what Bushnell's turtle was supposed to look like, but Fulton's own cross section of his *Nautilus,* as he originally conceived of it, survives in the Archives Nationales in Paris. It turns out to be Bushnell's machine elongated to accommodate a crew of three, with a number of consequent modifications. It was a little more than 21 feet long and about 6½ feet in diameter. The descriptions of the turtle do not make it clear whether water for ballast was simply admitted into the bottom (there was always some bilge water in a wooden ship) or whether there was a built-in tank. Fulton's *Nautilus* had a tank of metal, rather like a false keel, under the main wooden hull. It was propelled by a single four-bladed screw with its shaft in the center of the main hull, the blades turning above a conventional rudder hinged upon the after end of the ballast tank, which was faired to a vertical edge about 2½ feet forward of the main hull's rounded stern.

As originally conceived, Fulton's submersible was to be assisted in diving and ascending by a horizontal rudder hinged to the vertical one. Sprockets and a chain brought the controls of the rudders to a point under the conning tower forward where two tillers were provided for the navigator. When the French Directory's experts, assigned to study Fulton's request for backing, objected to the horizontal rudder, the inventor offered to replace it with a vertical screw resembling Bushnell's —one of several hints at a possible contact between the two men. H. W. Dickinson, the British engineer who about 60 years ago published the first accurate description of Fulton's *Nautilus* in English along with a thoroughly erroneous one of the Connecticut turtle, suggested that Fulton had been influenced by a description of Bushnell's "invention . . . published in 1795." This is evidently a reference to a passage in John Lendrum's *Concise and Impartial History of the American Revolution*, where the author has merely inserted phrases from the Putnam biography of seven years earlier. Fulton would probably have found the biography on the shelves of his well-to-do Parisian host, Joel Barlow. Putnam's biographer Humphreys, and Barlow, had both attended Yale when their fellow undergraduate Bushnell was at work on his submarine: a reason for Humphreys's confidence soon afterward in sponsoring the machine. Both were involved in the sprawling battle of Long Island when the turtle was being readied for its first foray. Both later joined in the impudent enterprises of the Hartford Wits. Barlow probably had a copy of his friend's book on the commander under whom they both served.

Close resemblances between the first two successful submersibles may thus be explainable without assuming a personal contact between their builders. Fulton did provide the perilous innovation for his vessel of a long lanyard attached to his torpedo, which would be payed out as the submarine retreated from its victim and yanked at some distance to trip a flint lock and cause an immediate explosion. All very well if it happened not to foul during the process.

Another novelty in Fulton's design was a sail that opened rather like an umbrella and folded under the twin covers of a long hatch, much as the fragile wings of a beetle disappear beneath its hard elytra. There was also a sealed-off compartment in the nose containing a kind of windlass for the anchor rode and a smaller one for the torpedo lanyard. Fulton is sometimes credited with the first use of a fish's name, "torpedo," in this connection. Bushnell used the term "magazine." There are allusive references to explosive devices as torpedoes before Fulton, but he had sufficiently fixed the meaning by 1807 for it to appear in an Admiralty report: *A Description of the Machine Invented by Mr. Robert Fulton for Exploding under Ships' Bottoms and by Him Called the Torpedo.* A letter of transmittal accompanying the report consistently refers to it as "the Weapon"—again an instance of the period of uncertainty when technological terminology is being created. In this case the subject was a towed torpedo like Bushnell's, to be dragged by a surface vessel into contact with the enemy.

Arguing nine years earlier for his proposed submarine, against a friend's warning that the idea of secret underwater attacks was "not liked," Fulton wrote:

. . . a free Ocean is particularly Important to America. I would ask anyone if all the American difficulties during this war is not owing to the Naval systems of Europe and a Licensed Robbery on the ocean? How then is America to prevent this? Certainly not by attempting to build a fleet to cope with the fleets of Europe but if possible by rendering the European fleets useless.

This he expected to do by interesting any nation in his submarine, trying France first as the likeliest to succeed with it against the worst naval tyrant. But, in the confidence that it, like all other naval weapons, would be copied, he later offered it to the Dutch, the English, and the Americans.

Fulton's frustrations with changing personnel in the Directory have been covered in earlier books. It is enough here to point out that amid the shilly-shallying politicians there was one

exception, Pierre Forfait, who steadily favored Fulton's proposition. When Bonaparte's counterrevolution of November, 1799,
toppled the Directory, Forfait magically survived and became
the new minister of marine. Work on the *Nautilus* actually
began at about that time; but in April, 1800, Forfait took care
to warn Fulton that his machine, significantly referred to as
"not yet in use," infringed the laws of war. This had not bothered
inheritors of sans-culottic attitudes in the Directory, although
the previous negotiations had been hung up over refusal to
grant Fulton a naval commission as commander of the *Nautilus.*
There was still a difficulty in the prospect that a successful
submarine might bring reprisals against the large number of
French prisoners held by the English.

Documentation in the French archives is sketchy at this point,
which may reflect Forfait's legal qualms; at least there is no
surviving written authorization for Fulton to go ahead with
the construction of the *Nautilus.* Since it was an expensive
contraption, with machinery and controls much more elaborate
than those of the turtle, and since his panorama had not yet
begun to make the pleasant profits it eventually brought in,
it seems likely that Fulton received ministerial financing by
some backdoor route. The submarine at any rate was launched
on July 24, 1800, having in the last phase of its construction
been altered to include a deck that gave it the general appearance
when awash of a small sailboat, although the peculiar rig
would have revealed its identity to the knowing.

The British intelligence was, as usual, knowing. Observers
seem to have been posted for the tests made in the Seine estuary
at Le Havre during the week or two following the launch. The
screw propeller, which Fulton called a fly, was tried out, as was
the horizontal rudder for plunging and rising. This latter device
had survived earlier objections. It constitutes one of his contributions to submarine technology. The longest dive lasted an hour
and two minutes. At this time Fulton also rediscovered Bushnell's finding that the compass worked satisfactorily when
submerged. His craft was large enough to justify the placing of
a candle near the instruments, despite its extravagant appetite
for oxygen. Bushnell's account of his use of phosphorus should
have reached Paris in the *Transactions* some months before
this date. If Fulton knew of it he may have felt the need of some

general illumination for an enlarged crew. On November 7 he gave two French friends a report of additional trials, one showing that the same manpower, using oars on the surface, could move the *Nautilus* only half as fast as when she was driven by her propeller while submerged. The report included trial of a torpedo, so called in Fulton's letter, towed Bushnell-fashion against a target barrel. The inventor made a 70-mile voyage in his small craft, trying at one point to approach a couple of British blockaders, who hastily got out of his way. They had received a specific warning of his trials.

The following year was marked by a return to bureaucratic normality, which is to say, frustration for the inventor. The practicality of his submarine had been shown in every reasonable test except the most important. Like Bushnell's, Fulton's workable submarine had not demonstrated its ability to sink a major vessel by the means provided: the same means in both. The two French scientists to whom the inventor had made a report asked Forfait to sacrifice an old hulk for an experiment, but the minister was suddenly vacillating in a fashion that suggests pressures from the top:

I have always been the most ardent defender of the plunging boat, and it is with pain that I see it abandoned; for it is abandoned in the new system. . . .

Forfait objected that the initial expense of the requested hulk would be too great and that the cost of raising it if it should sink would be excessive as well. Fulton's scientific friends were spurred by this to an appeal to the First Consul, which resulted in a reversal of Forfait's stand and the provision at last of a formal agreement that approximately repaid the cost of building the submersible. It also authorized a version of Fulton's original request that he be finally recompensed in accordance with the value of the enemy vessels sunk by him: 400,000 francs for a vessel of more than 30 guns, lesser amounts for smaller ones. The document is dated March 28, 1801.

All that followed is anticlimax. The *Nautilus* was moved, probably overland, to Brest, where she was repaired. During the process Fulton experimented with screw propulsion in a surface craft, a specially built 36-foot pinnace powered through four cranks, each operated by six men. He hoped for a speed of 12 knots but achieved only 4. The pinnace was supposed to drag a torpedo into contact with an enemy ship. The maritime prefect of the port, who had been ordered to construct the pinnace for him, reported later that this use of torpedoes was a fine idea but that neither a submersible nor a propeller-driven pinnace was needed. One or two light canoes would be faster and better because machinery was much too noisy for the necessary surprise attack. The prefect had scruples about submarine warfare. Those who tried it and failed would not be dying "a gallant death."

Fulton's experiments in his repaired *Nautilus* during the summer of 1801 included a dive with three companions but without candles, in which a copper globe of one cubic foot capacity, pumped full of ordinary air to 200 atmospheres, was taken down as an aid to breathing. This provision of 200 extra sea-level cubic feet, released gradually, made possible a dive for the four-man crew of 4 hours 20 minutes.

In September the inventor learned to his embarrassment that Bonaparte himself wanted to see the submersible. The reply explains:

I am sorry I had not earlier information of the Consul's desire to see the Plunging Boat. When I finished my experiments, She leaked very much, and being but an imperfect engine, I did not think her further useful,—hence I took her to pieces, Sold her Ironwork, lead and cylinders, and was necessitated to break the greater part of her movements in taking them to pieces. You will be so good as to excuse me to the Premier Consul when I refuse to exhibit my drawings to a Committee of Engineers.

Fulton gave two reasons for the refusal: security against a possible leakage of this information to an enemy of France and his own belief that his invention was private property. He said that anyone who wished to cultivate the useful arts must have the means "to put a succession of Ideas to immediate proof." That took money, which his invention was supposed to supply.

Whether dismantling of the *Nautilus* to make way for an improved model caused Bonaparte to think it a failure is unclear. It probably would have made no difference because Fulton's best champion, Forfait, resigned a week or two after the letter above was written, and the officer who replaced him at the top of the French Navy was a traditionalist. Nothing more is heard of Fulton's plunging boat in France. Three Frenchmen, three Englishmen, and a German contrived in the next 33 years to produce submersibles that came up again, but none of them made any substantial addition to the several principles worked out by Bushnell and Fulton. The enterprise awaited a means of propulsion more concentrated than human muscle.

Submarines were advocated for reasons other than the destruction of capital ships; salvage was the persistent one. Yet the happy fact that for a long time after 1815 there were no major international conflicts muted further experimentation. It began again in the 1850's, but for 88 years after Ezra Lee first tried it, no vessel described as a submarine succeeded in sinking a ship of war. On February 17, 1864, the U.S.S. *Housatonic* was sent to the bottom by a screw-driven Confederate submersible, which on this occasion made a surface attack, successful but suicidal. Bushnell's objective—the sinking of an enemy from under water, attacker surviving—was not attained until September 7, 1914, when the U-21 sank the British light cruiser *Pathfinder* in the North Sea.

Frustrated in his efforts to interest governments in submarine navigation, Fulton turned his efforts toward surface devices for the delivery of submarine torpedoes. His destruction on October 15, 1805, of the 200-ton brig *Dorothea*, in the view of a hundred British naval officers, again employed Bushnell's method. It was witnessed also by Colonel Sir William Congreve, who thoughtfully gave the world in that year the Congreve military rocket, soon to turn up in the first stanza of "The Star-Spangled Banner."

Fulton seized for his purposes upon many devices. Whaling provided him with one: a gun-fired harpoon, to be driven into the bow of an anchored or moving vessel. In either case the movement of water along its sides would tow the attached torpedo into contact. "Should the harpooner miss the ship, he can save his torpedo and return to the attack." Fulton's description of the best boat to use, with which he said he had had some experience while a visitor in the British blockading fleet off Boulogne in 1804 and 1805, was quite clearly a clinker-built whaleboat, 27 feet long.

Having tried both sides in Europe, he shifted his talents at home to the swift development of practical river steamers. It was after the success of his *North River Steamboat* of 1807 and the bay steamer *Rariton* of 1808 that he proposed the harpooning of enemy ships. His chief promotional journey took him to the elegant waterside residence of his friend Joel Barlow, in January, 1810, to explain and demonstrate his devices to President Madison and to former President Jefferson. Senators and representatives also were present. In a pamphlet printed soon afterward, addressed to Madison and to "both Houses of Congress," Fulton epitomized his own philosophy of torpedo warfare by quoting a remark made to him by Earl St. Vincent over the shattered *Dorothea*: "Pitt was the greatest fool that ever existed, to encourage a mode of war which they who commanded the seas did not want, and which, if successful, would deprive them of it."

For America, I consider it a fortunate circumstance that this experiment was made in England, and witnessed by more than a hundred respectable and brave officers of the Royal Navy; for, should Congress adopt Torpedoes as a part of our means of defence, lords Melville, Castlereagh, and Mulgrave, have a good knowledge of their combination and effect.

Congress did about as little as it possibly could to prepare for the looming trial of strength with the naval giant, but when war came two years later British strategy on the coasts of the United States was such as to suggest a prudent respect for the possibility that American whalemen would be attaching torpedoes instead of drogues to their harpoons. Anchored blockaders were a rarity. Nearly all the naval actions were fought far from shore.

SCREW PROPELLERS OR PADDLE WHEELS?

The last years of the eighteenth century seethed with experiments for translating the thrust of steam into kicks against the water surrounding a vessel. Franklin favored jet propulsion, which James Rumsey employed in his modestly successful experiments of 1788, near the site of the impending city of Washington. John Fitch set up in 1787 a remarkably uncomplicated mechanism for conveying the movement of a piston into the alternate dipping and lifting of paddles like those of a canoe—four groups of three. The forward group on each side lifted as the aft group dipped, and vice versa. Between 1787 and 1790 his boat and a speedier successor with stern oars made many successful voyages on the Delaware, but Fitch was defeated by a problem that nobody was to solve for almost two decades. Too much of his boat's space was

By a lack of training in conceptual science, the ingenious mechanic John Fitch was doomed to fulfill, in the development of steamships, the sort of peripheral task that eliminates by demonstration the less fruitful possibilities. His first steamer *(below)* of 1787 worked, but it was inefficient because energy was wasted in imitation of human paddlers. His third *(bottom)* similarly imitated the rearward kick of waterfowl. His second, with conventional paddle wheels, operated commercially on the Delaware but steadily lost money. (See pp. 103, 105, 109.)

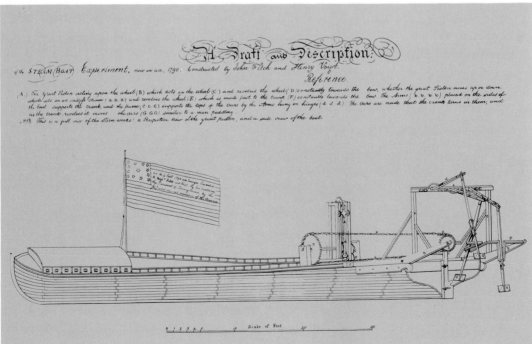

occupied by fuel and machinery. His backers lost money. Several experimenters, including Fitch and Fulton, tinkered with blades attached to belts or chains resembling those of caterpillar tractors. The common recourse was to fall back, as Fulton eventually did, on some form of the ancient paddle wheel.

Tentative steamboats were numerous on both sides of the Atlantic, but Americans seem to have tried the greater variety of devices to achieve thrust. The inventors and entrepreneurs were a mixed lot: some, like Fitch, poverty-stricken and driven by misfortune to a deepening eccentricity; others, like Robert R. Livingston, rich amateurs. It was Livingston, sent as minister to France in 1801, who lifted Fulton from the ruins of his submarine enterprise and turned him toward the development of surface navigation, which made him wrongly famous as an inventor. Despite his dependence upon the prior work of Bushnell—details of which must have reached him roundabout if not directly—Fulton as an experimental technician is much more impressive in his work with the *Nautilus* and with his floating mines or torpedoes than in his anticlimax with steam on the surface of the Hudson. For the latter he has a secure place in the history of enterprise and management, a place that he could not have attained so quickly if he had not been an excellent practical mechanic as well. In the history of nautical innovation, nevertheless, his steam-propelled catamaran the *Demologos* of 1813 has a stronger claim to importance than the river steamer usually miscalled the *Clermont.* By placing a paddle wheel between the hulls of this floating battery he solved the problem of steam propulsion for warships thirty years in advance of the first intelligently designed naval steamers. Fulton left a sickbed in midwinter to oversee installation of machinery in the *Demologos* and died a few days later, on February 24, 1815, at the height of his fame. The war for which she was intended already was dwindling away. With the Second Peace of Paris under its belt, Europe lapsed from its world-buffeting quarrels, and the impulse toward naval innovation everywhere got little response for many years from keepers of the public purse. A half-million-dollar appropriation for more floating steam batteries on the model of the still-unfinished *Demologos* lapsed in Congress when hostilities ended. Fulton's last major effort consequently had no lasting influence upon the design of steam-driven fighting ships, which reappeared a generation later as dreadfully vulnerable side-wheelers. These, a transient aberration of the strategists, were quickly superseded by screw-propelled naval craft, although a few paddlers were still in operation as late as the Civil War.

America's energetic forerunner in the development of steam-powered screw propulsion was John Stevens, a name that crops up frequently in the records of maritime achievement without always meaning the same man. John Stevens of Hoboken, born in 1749 and known best for his advocacy of steam railroads, took out in 1791 the first patent for a multitubular boiler, providing for a much more rapid transference of heat than had been possible in the oversize cooking pots previously in use. He was in that year experimenting also with jet propulsion. Under the recent patent act, for which he had been the principal lobbyist, he registered in 1792 the plans for two sorts of steam engines. Fulton's success on the Hudson, fifteen years later, was made possible chiefly by a James Watt engine, which he brought with him upon his return from Europe: almost the first for which an export permit was issued. Stevens designed his own engines and had them built in primitive shops. Boulton and Watt had begun the manufacture of sophisticated steam engines in Scotland at about the time when Bushnell was perfecting his man-driven screw propellers, but engine building as a specialized enterprise was not attempted in the United States until about the turn of the century. The Scottish mechanics maintained their lead for some time after that.

Stevens was experimenting with screw propulsion not later than 1801, influenced at first probably by William Lyttleton's British patent of 1794 for a device resembling the reel of a lawn mower, but the American soon turned to something closer to Bushnell's prophetically simple design of 1776. Lyttleton's water screw resembled the air screw that Jefferson had seen on the Seine, but with three blades all starting in the same cross section 120 degrees apart, each making a complete circuit of the hub. His experiments with it were made with manpower. Stevens seems, despite dubious claims of an attempt by Fitch, to have been the first to drive a screw efficiently with a steam engine. The date was 1802. In a letter published ten years later, he described both engine and propeller:

A cylinder of brass, about 8 inches in diameter, and 4 inches long, was placed horizontally on the bottom of the boat; and by the alternate pressure of the steam on two sliding wings, an axis passing through its center was made to revolve. On one end of this axis, which passed through the stern of the boat, wings, like those on the arms of a windmill, were fixed, adjusted to the most advantageous angle for operating on the water. . . . This simple little steam engine was, in the summer of 1802, placed on board a flat-bottomed boat . . . 25 feet long, and about 5 or 6 feet wide. She was occasionally kept going until the cold weather stopped us. When the engine was in the best order, her velocity was about 4 miles an hour.

A reciprocating engine of the commoner sort gave the same boat, the *Little Juliana,* "somewhat more velocity than the rotary engine." In 1804 John Stevens developed for her his own variant of an engine on Watt's principle, omitting the beam. Describing it long afterward, Francis B. Stevens wrote:

Colonel Stevens' plan for working twin screws by a single cylinder is the most simple one that could be devised. The reaction of the connecting rods against each other at their junction with the piston rods acting as a parallel motion, or as slides would do, to keep the rod in alignment.

If this is not perfectly lucid, the reader can inspect the original in the Smithsonian Institution.

Stevens had noted the tendency of a single screw to slue his vessel. His use of one cylinder to drive two shafts, a highly efficient device in itself, corrected the tendency and greatly improved the effectiveness of the rudder. About 40 years later, one of his original propeller blades was an exhibit in a lawsuit against John Ericsson, who had the further annoyance of seeing the complex propeller with which he had equipped his U.S.S. *Princeton* replaced by "the Stevens Scull."

In a letter dated November 16, 1805, Stevens gives this description of his screw:

To the extremity of an axis passing nearly in a horizontal direction through the stern of the boat, is fixed a number of arms with wings like those of a windmill or smoke jack. These arms, are made capable of ready adjustment, so as that the most advantageous obliquity of their angle may be attained. . . .

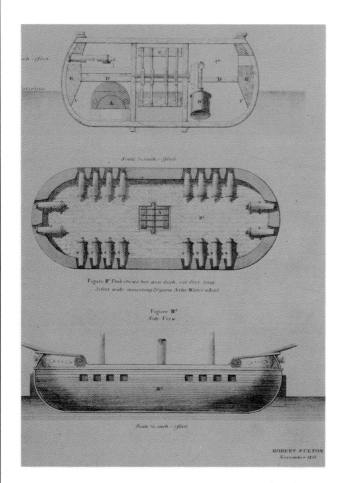

Scale ½ inch = 1 foot

Figure II This shews her gun deck 156 feet long
24 feet wide mounting 20 guns X the Water wheel

Figure III
Side View

Scale ⅛ inch = 1 foot

ROBERT FULTON
November 1815

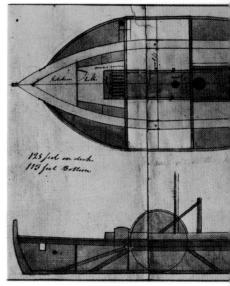

125 feet on deck
115 feet Bottom

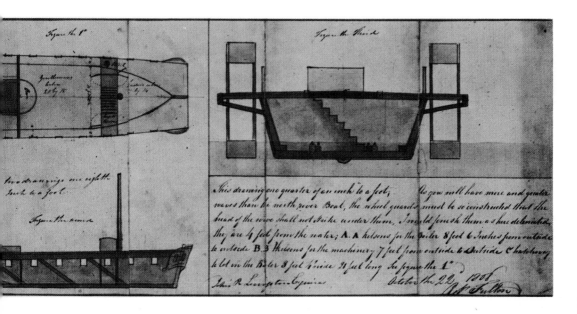

A variety of devices for converting steam into thrust were tried with some success in America before Robert Fulton established paddle wheels as the best means, with available engines, for commercial success. In 1787, the year of John Fitch's first workable boat, James Rumsey had some luck with one propelled by water jets. *(Smithsonian model, lower right.)* Fulton's plans for his improved second steamer, the *Rariton* of 1808, appear above. A little later he reverted to torpedoes. One of his proposals was to affix them to ships with a harpoon gun *(left)*. His steam frigate *Demologos (far left and below, left)*, built during the War of 1812, was in concept the most sophisticated naval vessel of the first half of the nineteenth century, with all its machinery well protected. (See pp. 102–6.)

Here too language is formative. Stevens in the same letter contrasts his "wheels" with the "sculls" he had first tried, to kick the water astern in the fashion of ducks' feet. Although he carefully differentiates between scull and wheel, stressing the advantages of the latter, somewhere in the long period of paddle wheels superseding both devices his own terminology was reversed by others, and his screw propellers re-emerged in the 1840's as "sculls."

The commercial persistence of paddle wheels well into the twentieth century was largely a response to conditions on rivers of the United States. Screws, for continuous efficiency, had to operate at a considerable depth. Paddles could be designed for their own kind of maximum thrust when they dipped only a foot or two. Screws soon fouled where there was weed. When a blade was bent by a submerged object, its repair was more difficult than the replacing of a bashed paddle, which could be done by merely turning the wheel to bring it up to deck level. At a time, however, when Fulton's decisive demonstration in favor of paddle wheels still lay a year or two in the future, Stevens had foreseen the shape of the choice between paddles and screws. On November 16, 1805, he wrote to the Philadelphia chemist Robert Hare:

The consideration which determined me . . . to make a trial of the paddles, was merely to avoid the necessity of giving the boat a draft of water too great for passing the overslough near Albany; but this objection to the use of wheels, I expect to obviate by an increase of the number of them, and consequent diminution of their diameter.

Again, "wheels" means screw propellers. Stevens at the time was looking forward to a larger river steamer for the run soon pre-empted by the Livingston-Fulton legal monopoly secured by the former for operations on the Hudson. In the same letter Stevens reported upon manpower tests between oars and a screw, which resulted in stopwatch readings "a few seconds in favor of the wheel," even with machinery "put up in a very coarse manner." An evidently hasty sketch, made on the letter paper, illustrates the way in which he considered propellers could be placed so that they would "be defended from all external injury." It locates only one wheel, but earlier in the letter he had said that "it is absolutely necessary to have at least two, revolving in opposite directions."

Stevens, then, before the nineteenth century was five years old, had successfully demonstrated all the major aspects of screw propulsion under steam: propellers with two and four blades having adjustable pitch and an efficient curvature, operating in pairs with contrary rotations. When Ericsson defended his British patent in 1850, the testimony included this exchange between the attorney general and an expert witness:

Q. Did not Captain Ericsson first introduce a fixed shaft, or a shaft running horizontally below the water-line?
A. Yes, Captain Ericsson did.
Q. He was the first that introduced the shaft running below the line of the water through the stuffing-box outside the stern?
A. Yes.

Despite the reappearance of the Stevens scull on the U.S.S. *Princeton* in the trials of March, 1845, the pioneering of Stevens had been so far forgotten that the witness in London probably believed what he was saying. It was better known that Stevens had settled for paddle wheels in his first full-size steamer, the *Phoenix*, built at Hoboken and launched in 1808. The Fulton-Livingston monopoly kept her off the Hudson, but by so doing forced upon her the fame of being the first steamship to navigate the open ocean, which she did with some difficulty on a voyage to Philadelphia, where she was based during about six years of service on the Delaware. The *Phoenix* was the first steamer of practical dimensions built entirely in the United States and powered by domestic machinery.

Whether Stevens chose paddle wheels as a result of the informal race that shaped up between the builders of the first two American steamers is unclear. The *Phoenix* was laid down in advance of the *North River Steamboat,* but Fulton's having a complete engine ready to install gave him the advantage, and his demonstration got him the monopoly from the New York legislature. Stevens was probably aware that the engine that drove the twin screws of his *Little Juliana* at 4 knots could not be simply enlarged to provide a competitive thrust in a hundred-footer. He had produced a small engine that operated successfully in a small craft at a relatively high pressure, but more than three

"CLARION"

Late in the eighteenth century John Stevens of Hoboken, New Jersey, experimented with steam engines. By 1804 he had developed a reciprocating engine for twin screws. His original *(left)* is preserved in the Smithsonian Institution, where a recent model *(below)* shows its installation. Stevens's *Phoenix* of 1808 *(bottom)* was the first steamer to adventure upon the open ocean, the first commercially successful one built wholly of American materials. With her Stevens reverted to the paddle wheels that drove all steamers for about three decades. Then new experiments with screws began, such as the conversion of the *Clarion* in 1841 to a novel arrangement *(lower left)* of twin screws on external shafts. (See pp. 106–11, 114.)

decades were to pass before large high-pressure engines would be reliable. To give screw propellers an adequate rate of spin, a low-pressure engine would have had to be geared up in a fashion wasteful of energy.

John Stevens of Hoboken died in 1838, a few months after Ericsson had demonstrated on the Thames an engine capable of driving a screw at a rate of ten miles an hour. Ericsson thereupon became the leading contender in an often bitter controversy to identify the legal inventor of the screw steamer, but it was his engine rather than his complicated and inefficient propeller that renewed the development that had come to a pause when John Stevens shifted his attention from the *Little Juliana* to the *Phoenix.* Stevens's son John Cox Stevens, one of the original skippers of the *Little Juliana,* so far abandoned steam propulsion as to become a founder of the New York Yacht Club and the guiding spirit of the group that turned up at Cowes in 1851 to make another kind of nautical history in the utterly engineless yacht *America.*

4 Whalers to the World

DETACHABLE HAMLETS OF NANTUCKET

American forerunners such as Bushnell and Fulton, who tinkered with belligerent devices for the destruction of other men's engines of destruction, had some remarkably different contemporaries. Many inhabitants of a sea-rimmed town on a hook-shaped hump of clay and sand —some hours' sail to the southward from Cape Cod— practiced a religion that repressed their hostility toward human beings. They found their different release for it through the development of a peculiar excellence in hunting to their anguished deaths the huge submersible mammals of another species. Quakers and other residents of Nantucket evolved a complex social contrivance that by the test of worldwide influence is unexampled in maritime history. In the seminal latter years of the eighteenth century, when American inventors almost perfected screw propulsion and submarines and the happy blessing of torpedoes, the internationalists of Nantucket chartered orthodox sailing vessels and developed them into a system of detachable hamlets that wandered all over the Atlantic oceans. A concentration of uniquely purposeful skills and talents, in a population that never reached 10,000, spilled beyond a sandy perimeter enclosing less than 50 barren square miles until, eventually, there were scores of small Nantuckets dotting the Atlantic and Indian oceans, as well as the huge Pacific, from ice to ice. European countries sent even more vessels annually into the trade, but these were based upon large populations at home and did not adventure very far, nibbling the edges of the adjacent Arctic for round voyages of four or five thousand miles at the most. The detachable hamlets of Nantucket often came home with distances equivalent to circumnavigations entered in their logs.

After whaling out of Nantucket reached its apex, the

nearby city of New Bedford sent to sea, each year, the largest number of whalers that had ever sailed from any port. The difference was that Nantucket, for almost a century, manned its whaleships with its own people. New Bedford agents went into the back country to pick up sturdy, discontented farm boys; its waterfront had the usual international mixture of seamen willing to give whaling a try. Nantucket nourished whalemen almost exclusively, along with such technicians as coopers, and smiths specializing in manufacture of the weapons and implements that whalemen called craft. The system eventually had to change, but whaling as a great worldwide adventure was evolved in one small isolated port that manned the ships which brought its own people home again to maintain an extraordinary efficiency and homogeneity in the enterprise.

It is a primary oddity of this great maritime episode that the island itself had no shipbuilding timber. The first nine whaling sloops listed by Starbuck as belonging to Nantucket all were built at identifiable places "off island," which is still the native Nantucketer's phrase for the other part of the world. At the height of its triumphs, the island put together a few whalers from imported materials, but in the early years of far voyaging the Nantucketers followed what was standard practice at the time. A vessel was found and "taken up" by joint stockholders to spread the risk of each voyage. At its conclusion the owners sold both ship and cargo, closing out the accounts with a division of the receipts. In an expanding economy the ship itself sometimes brought more than it had cost at the outset, despite wear and tear of the voyage. A form of insurance was thus provided that required no separate accounting if an owner bought a one-eighth share in each of eight voyages, instead of hazarding the same amount in the sole ownership of one vessel.

The next form of self-insurance came with individual American fortunes sufficiently large to allow the ownership of a considerable number of vessels by a single man or family. Nantucket, prior to the Revolution, produced far more than a normal share of such owners, who held on to good ships and sent them out again and again. But in general, American shipwrights in the decade or two before the Declaration of

Independence were hammering together an export product. The northern colonies for that reason confronted their Revolution with shipyards and skilled mechanics as their most important economic assets. It turned out that they could afford to lose almost their entire original fleet, naval and merchant, by maintaining their capacity to replace it during the conflict. Off the mainland coast, American privateers also were busy, helping to balance losses with captures of British ships. These private fighting vessels, on models developed for local conditions alongshore, were adept at evading more powerful blockaders. The usual count puts their number above 2,000, of which 200 belonged to the tiny port of Salem alone.

In such circumstances, however, the situation of Nantucket was calamitous: far enough offshore to be indefensible by Continental foot soldiers and too vulnerable to blockade to be garrisoned. When commercial or naval fleets based at mainland ports were destroyed, there were shipyards beyond the first bend of every river and sizable stream. Construction of ships as an export product had expanded the capacity of the industry far beyond local needs, which made quick replacement of losses possible. This, however, was no help to Nantucket, which lost in the war years 134 whalers by capture and 15 more wrecked. None could be replaced during the conflict.

When the war began, *Lloyd's Register of Shipping* for 1775–76 listed 2,343 vessels built in North America, about one-third of the Empire's total, an indication of the extent to which shipbuilding had become the dominant American enterprise. But at Nantucket, at the close of the war—as Obed Macy reported —"there remained only two or three old hulks." A population much influenced by Quakers had tried to continue peacefully: their town-meeting government declared the community's neutrality. In 1780 it even petitioned for licenses to go whaling under the protection of the Royal Navy. American privateers captured some of the 24 vessels sent out with British papers, but the Continental Congress knew of the acute privations brought by war to an isolated community its armed forces had been unable to protect; the whalers were all released.

When peace was made, a remarkable community starved by the conflict faced novel difficulties. Forty years earlier, Nantucketers had begun to carry their oil directly to England as soon as their casks were full, saving the costs of transshipment and middlemen's fees. As free Americans they now were met in England by the kind of political protection that helped the elder Scoresby to prosper so steadily for so long: a ruinous tax on all oil imported in foreign bottoms. Efforts to sell it elsewhere glutted the world market and brought prices below cost. Petitions for a United States bounty, similar to that which the British had intermittently provided for their own subjects, at first were fruitless. In consequence, the small island community, which had always been curiously international, began to negotiate for migration.

The British needed their skills and their product. Some Nantucketers were induced to move to Dartmouth in Nova Scotia, and thence to a better prospect in Milford Haven, Wales. Others founded a new whaling port far up the Hudson River, near Kingston, which reflected Nantucket in its commercial and social arrangements, with the added advantage of a shipyard. A third group sent William Rotch to negotiate with the dilatory British Ministry. Patience stretched to the twanging point, he stipulated the hour at which he would sail from his anchorage in the Thames, inviting Lord Hawkesbury to come aboard, if he chose, to sign an agreement, which his lordship neglected to do. Such, at least, is the traditional story. Rotch next turned to the protean Thomas Jefferson, who aided him in establishing a Nantucket fleet to sail out of the French port of Dunkirk.

For several years after the successful conclusion of a revolution that had ruined their enterprise and had held them at the literal edge of starvation, the Nantucketers pressed for recognition as a free port, under conditions that would have made of them a tiny independent nation in the sea. In direct negotiations with at least three sovereign governments, the town clerk of Nantucket and his emissaries were unable to achieve the contemplated arrangement: complete migration. Many left, some returned, and those who remained went ahead with their Nantucket conquest of the oceans in a manner implying that the little island could easily afford to supply experts to the rest of the world without diminishing its own phenomenal primacy.

A large accumulation of capital, from the prosperous decade prior to the Revolution, had been kept on deposit by merchants of the island, who for seven years had been unable to spend it even for food. Those who established themselves in Nova Scotia, in Wales, in France, and at Claverack Landing on the Hudson had somehow hoarded money enough to equip sizable fleets. Only two of the four ventures lasted, but there were others closer to home. New Bedford as a whaling port was Nantucket's child, destined to grow taller than its parent. Many of the island's merchants moved to other ports, where specializing shipwrights could be closely overseen, to establish competitive fleets. John Adams mentioned to Jefferson in 1785 that the Portuguese "had now a very pretty sperma Ceati Whale Fishery which they had learn'd of the New Englanders." The other New Englanders had learned this deep-water kind of whaling from Nantucket. Merchants, retired captains as a rule, gave direction to the industry, but skilled six-man crews in a thousand whaleboats were the true explanation of a phenomenal enterprise. When negotiations for a removal of the population to Europe were at a chancy point, Jefferson wrote to John Jay that the French government "saw the danger of permitting five or six thousand of the best seamen existing to be transferred by a single stroke to the marine strength of their enemy, and to carry over with them an art which they possessed almost exclusively."

This recognition of the overwhelming pre-eminence of Nantucket as a sort of isolated, geologically anchored training ship for the perfecting of special skills had been earned in the decade before the Revolution. It had impressively survived a destructive interlude. The dependence of an entire population upon one enterprise left no doubt of the manner in which its talents should be applied after each of a sequence of calamities— up to the last one, the discovery in Pennsylvania of something that manufacturers who sailed their floating oil refineries to the ends of the earth contemptuously called earth oil. Nantucket became one of the best-known seaports of the world in spite of its notably poor harbor and its failure to launch a single whaleship before 1832. Even so, about 40 years earlier than that, when its emigrants had established its own flourishing colonies elsewhere, Nantucket had settled down again to the task of developing, in shipyards off island, an ultimate whaleship suited to its specific purposes.

The ship was a social as well as a mechanistic contrivance. Separate engines turned by steam, such as those newly patented

by John Stevens, were destined before long to remove men from
their close harmony with wood, hemp, and canvas, which made
rigging and sails an extension of human muscle in a shrewd
compromise between man's will and the will of the wind. In
the whaleship specifically, on long voyages, a purposeful concurrence had to be established—not only between the intricate
crisscross of rigging and sweeping lines of the hull—but also
between man and man. This was largely accomplished by the
lay system of investment and profit sharing, which guaranteed
at the outset to each member of the crew an exact proportion of
the profits—if any. If there were none, the master would go
ashore no better off than any foremasthand. The lay system was
older than Nantucket. Buccaneers were using a variety of it in
the Caribbean long before the first offshore whaling sloop sailed
between Brant Point and Coatue. Thus, using off-island vessels
that happened to be available for charter or purchase, and a
borrowed system of investing time as a part of the capital of the
voyage, the Nantucketers settled down in the 1790's to develop
a whaleship that could be an independent dwelling place for a
small community of hunters, sailors, manufacturers, mechanics,
and traders—a detachable hamlet that could gather its raw
material in all the oceans, process and package it on the spot,
and carry it for sale to the most advantageous port while sustaining itself independently in voyages of as much as four years
"from home."

THE ADAPTED NANTUCKET WHALESHIP

Almost any vessel measuring 30 tons or more could carry whaleboats and their skilled crews to the nearer whaling grounds.
Prior to 1835, ships previously used for other purposes made
up a large preponderance of the whaling fleets. But in the
whaleship, as in other competitive devices, subtle aspects might
make the difference between success and failure in a difficult
year. In large ports, shipowners could haggle afar for equipment
that converted a wooden shell into a complex mechanism, but
the Nantucket community was an intense concentration of
trades involved in preparing a ship for the whale hunt. A
cooper had a son at sea, setting up casks from staves split by
his father. The smith who forged harpoons on Water Street had
sailed his own voyages as smith in whalers, answerable to the

men whose lives hung upon his product. Investment centered in merchants whose prudently handsome houses still dot the slope with a view above the shallow harbor. But every voyage was in some measure also an investment of every man who sailed in it.

As a rule, several "owners" shared the cost of ship and outfit for the entire voyage, which, soon after the sperm fishery moved into the Pacific, customarily lasted two or three years. If there was a profit it was divided on a prearranged ratio among the owners and the ship's people. The latter, from master on down, each had his allotted lay. The captain's might be one-twelfth, the first mate's one thirty-sixth, the cooper's one-sixtieth, and so on. When there was no profit, the group of neighbors in a whaler had at least been sustained for three years or so by the owners, but the lay system guaranteed every man's interest in a better outcome. His performance affected his shipmate's profit, and he knew that his shipmate knew it. Again and again, six men in a frail boat were inches from snapping death. A brief lapse on the part of one could cost the lives of the others. Most of them had grown up together, in a compact community of about two thousand to which they felt answerable for qualities of endurance, courage, and skill taken for granted in an extraordinary calling. On the rapacious, cosmopolitan waterfronts where most hands were recruited, a returning seaman could lose himself amid strangers. The Nantucketer sailed with part of a community he knew well, and returned to all of it. In the years that were bad for profits, everyone was busy equipping ships for years that should be better. The very fact that it took three years, more or less, to find out whether there would be a profit brought stability to the tasks of workers ashore. On the little island that wanted to be an independent nation and usually behaved like one, there was no balance-of-payments problem. The product was sold abroad. Raw material was bought off island, as were nearly all the empty ships; but an unusually large part of the investment, which represented specializing, skilled labor in preparing the whalers for sea, went into local wages, and the returning mariners were paid on the island.

The possibility that any vessel of an appropriate size might be diverted to whaling influenced ship design. Whatever was taken up by Nantucket owners at about the turn of the century,

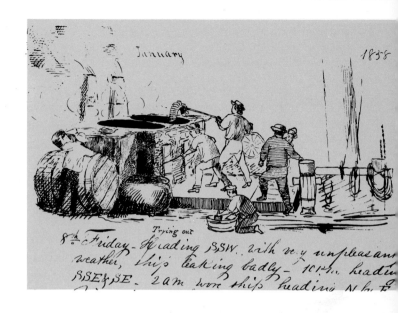

Tryworks afloat (above), as sketched in the Weir Journal at Mystic Seaport. The
Alice Knowles (right) of New Bedford, built in 1879, showing disposition of boats
and stowage of casks. Bentwood davits (lower extreme right) identified American
whalers. They can be seen in the Improvement (below) of 1817 or earlier, and
in the A. R. Tucker (lower right) of 1851. (See pp. 120–21, 124–25, 163–64, 474.)

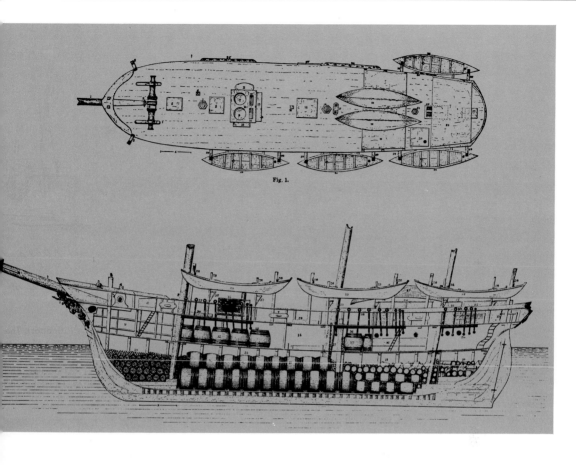

Fig. 1.

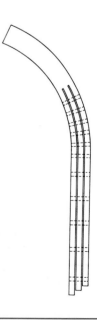

to be sent on fishing expeditions of twenty or thirty thousand miles, set the pattern for other Yankee ports, as well as for the older nations. A typical ship for some time thereafter could be described as a 200-tonner, 85 feet long on deck, 23 feet broad, and 11 feet deep. She had two decks without much vertical space between them, a square stern, and a minimum of decoration. Quakers were uneasy about images, even figureheads: a billet-head would do. She was ship-rigged, carrying square sail on each of three masts, with a fore-and-aft spanker, or driver, on the mizzen, the mast farthest aft. Fore-and-aft staysails were set between the masts when the weather warranted, and also forward of the foremast. Farthest forward was a jib. Between the fore- and mainmasts there was an oblong brick structure, the tryworks.

A distinctive feature of the vessel, probably developed to Nantucket specifications soon after the turn of the century, was a new kind of davit upon which to carry the whaleboats in readiness for instant lowering. The davit described in marine dictionaries and manuals of the latter eighteenth century was a movable spar, one end of which could be slipped into an iron ring in the middle of the deck, while the other extended outboard on one side or the other with a block attached to it for hoisting operations. "Fishing the anchor" was its usual function. Early British whalers are depicted with massive davit beams permanently supported across the after part of the deck, thrust outboard on both sides, for handling the boats. Their heavy oak shallops made such structures necessary, particularly since sometimes two whaleboats are to be seen suspended one above the other.

The Yankee answer to the problem of keeping very light cedar whaleboats ready for instant lowering was the bentwood davit. Four davits supported the two boats on the starboard side, and there were six for the three hung over the port side. Usually they were made from the root ends of oak trees of a size that could be quartered to produce four timbers eight inches square. The butt end of each, which would be uppermost, was hewn to a gentle curve. Two parallel saw cuts were made from the opposite end, leaving about a yard solid. The split timber was then steamed and clamped to a massive form having the proper final curvature. The outer and inner sections slid somewhat against the middle one to make the new form, which was maintained by driving treenails through the three sections. Three slots were mortised into the unsawn butt section—now the upper end—for sheaves for the boat tackles.

These distinctive white-painted davits were for many years a sure sign of an American whaleship. They endured past the "improvement" of steel davits for the purpose of sustaining a structure, the whaleboat, that was itself a deft compromise between lightness and strength. As Ashley puts it, "The bent davits were both stronger and springier. It was particularly for the latter quality that they were adopted, since it was essential that boats ride easily." Later in the century an old whaler could often be identified as such by stiff-knee davits, resembling gallows, used as cheap replacements for some of its graceful originals.

THE WHALEBOAT OF THE 1790'S

The Nantucket whaleship was primarily a carrier of whaleboats and their expert crews to a point within sight of whales: everything that the ship's people could do for themselves and the owners depended upon the remarkable New England whaleboat which in the 1790's was approaching its optimum dimensions. The 20-foot boat of 1725 had grown to 26 feet. It weighed about 500 pounds and had adequate freeboard when carrying half a ton of equipment and a little more than that of humanity. When a whaleboat was afloat, this weight was distributed over its immersed bottom; but when it was hanging from both ends at the davits, a whaleboat was imperiled by any large concentration of weight in one place, particularly amidships. The single item of equipment that represented the maximum concentration of weight was one-third of a mile of heavy whale line, which had to be so arranged that it could run out smoothly when a harpooned monster plunged straight for the antipodes at high speed. A flying loop of it could decapitate a seaman: hard experience led to the devising of line tubs, in which Flemish coils —layer upon layer of neat spirals—kept the line compact, ready, and safe. During the chase the two tubs were stowed fore and aft of the oarsman's bench just aft of amidships, which was called consequently the tub thwart. Line tubs made it feasible to keep the coiled line on the ship's deck, whence it could be quickly lifted into the whaleboat. Other equipment—spars with their furled sail, oars, harpoons, lances—could be kept ready in a davited boat with their weight distributed fore and aft.

A valid average figure for the tonnage of whaleships that carried such boats out past Brant Point is lost in the ashes of periodic waterfront fires, which destroyed many registers. Starbuck recovered enough figures from newspapers and personal letters to present representative information on 124 voyages out of Nantucket, between 1788 and 1800, made in vessels that were referred to as "ships." Of these only 18 have figures for tonnage, and they average 209 tons. The description "ship" would probably not have been entered in this period for a vessel of much less than 150 tons. The smallest Nantucket whaleship of the eighteenth century for which a figure actually is given measured 160 tons.

It is doubtful if there was enough difference between standard ships converted into whalers on the two sides of the Atlantic to explain the sudden rise of the New England whale fishery to world prominence. The remarkable Nantucket whaleboat does offer an explanation. It was ignored by the British for some 50 years after its merits were disclosed to them by an anxious chief justice of Massachusetts. Then, with the outbreak of the American Revolution, nearly all New England whalers were captured at sea and their crews given the choice of whaling as before under British officers or of being impressed into British fighting ships. The former choice was the obvious one for many internationalist Quakers. Their influence upon British whaling habits appears in skillfully drawn and painted whaling scenes made soon after the Revolution by British and French artists. These reveal a European boat unmistakably influenced by the Nantucket model. One certain bit of evidence is the location of the loggerhead, a post for snubbing the line attached to the harpoon. Everywhere outside New England the loggerhead had been placed in the bows, an inconvenience to the harpooner, who had troubles enough. The Nantucketers ran the line aft between the oarsmen to be snubbed around a loggerhead in the stern, where the crew learned to cluster to balance their light craft during a Nantucket sleighride.

A letter written by Alexander Coffin in 1785 reveals something of the tension that developed in Nantucket when many of his neighbors were preparing to transfer their enterprises to places where they would not be hampered so severely by their new status as citizens of a free but almost bankrupt country. Coffin informed his correspondent that his wealthy neighbor William Rotch, in arranging for his departure, was "taking on board a double stock of materials, such as Cedar boards, (commonly called boat-boards) of which they have none in England." That foremost trading nation, which imported so much, could have supplied itself with cedar boat-boards too. It may not have done so for a standard strategic reason: a people engaged in constant warfare does well to avoid dependence upon important materials that can be cut off by an adversary. Perhaps it had something to do with hearts of oak and an ancient reliance upon this symbolic tree in British shipbuilding. For whatever reason, the British whaleboat continued to be decidedly heavier than the American, in which cedar was an important contributor to final efficiency.

Some Distinctive American Sailing Vessels

THE UNFAIR FRIGATES

The effort to keep some sort of American enterprise afloat during the Revolution, when whalers were quickly gathered up by the world's most numerous navy, put American shipbuilders to a hard and exacting test. The problem was to design naval vessels that could be of some help in protecting merchantmen while they would also have sailing qualities adequate for keeping clear of British cruisers. The Continental Navy, starting at zero, could not possibly challenge scores of major ships and hundreds of lesser ones available to the enemy. One by one, almost as soon as they got to sea, newly built American naval vessels were captured or destroyed. Those of any importance that survived were taken into the French service, in which they could get support in kind. The situation was saved from calamity by 2,000 privateers, which made no pretense of fighting naval actions as such and were deftly designed to keep away from them to windward, out of reach of vessels more heavily armed.

Joshua Humphreys of Philadelphia was one of the most imaginative students in this harsh school. At the head of his own firm when only 24 years old, he built in 1776 the *Randolph,* one of the first group of five Continental frigates. Howard I. Chapelle argues that her plans were not drawn by Humphreys himself, a point of less importance here than his responsibility as constructor for the performance of his product. Of greater interest is the fact that her lines, which are preserved in the Smithsonian Institution, "differed a good deal," in Chapelle's judgment, "from the hull forms found in the majority of contemporary British and French frigates." He perceived "no evidence of any attempt to copy a foreign model of naval vessel . . . rather the natural development of a previous search for speed under sail in craft smaller than frigates."

In some measure certainly as a consequence of her fine lines under water, the *Randolph* saw more useful service than any of the four other frigates of the original group. One was burned on the stocks, another in the water. Two were captured, having accomplished little. After six months at sea, the *Randolph* was blown to splinters by a hot shot that reached her magazine during a spirited action with one of His Majesty's Third Rates, in the West Indies, on March 17, 1778.

An eighteenth-century Third Rate was not at all what the name of her category might imply nowadays. William Falconer's *An Universal Dictionary of the Marine* in 1769 defined a Third Rate as a ship carrying "from 64 to 80 cannon, which are 32, 18, and 9 pounders." The *Randolph,* in the British usage a small Fifth Rate, had half as many guns with a main battery of 18-pounders. She could probably have avoided the fight, but only by abandoning the convoy under her protection. The incident epitomizes the problem of a small country wanting some kind of naval force to pit somehow against a huge one. Its only valid recourse, as the builder of the *Randolph* came to see, lay in a vulnerable aspect of the system of Rates itself, defined by William Falconer as "the orders or classes into which the ships of war are divided, according to their force or magnitude. . . . The British fleet is accordingly distributed into six rates, exclusive of the inferior vessels."

Earlier methods of arranging fleets into Rates were different, but when Falconer propounded his definitions shortly before the Revolution, a First Rate carried at least 100 guns, in four tiers. Those on the lower deck, 42-pounders, threw a solid ball of that weight. First Rates carried 24-pounders on the middle deck, 12-pounders on the upper deck, and 6-pounders on quarter-deck and fo'c's'le.

Second, Third, and Fourth Rates carried from 90 to 50 guns. All of these were grouped, along with the First Rates, as Ships of the Line; they were designed for fleet actions, based upon a system of tactics that depended upon the maintenance of a "line of battle" in an orderly offshore chess game with intricate rules studied by all commanders and well understood by some of them. The important first objective was to break the opposing line and to inflict heavy damage on single ships before others could maneuver to their effective support. In this contest the pawns were the Fifth and Sixth Rates, which as Falconer says "are usually comprehended under the general name of frigates, and never appear in the line of battle."

Frigates were scouts. They tried to cut out supply ships. They nipped in to help smash partly disabled larger vessels, counting upon their quickness of maneuver to keep them out of close range of batteries that had to be aimed by aiming the whole ship sidewise. They fought one another on the fringes of the ponderous central action of Ships of the Line. Sea power in Europe was calculated in these terms. It shifted from country to country with the humbling of any large fleet.

Between such confrontations of great power, single vessels had separate employments. A Second Rate might blockade a harbor or loiter in a channel to frighten competitors out of it. Third and Fourth Rates often convoyed fleets of merchantmen. Fifth and Sixth Rates, frigates, did such jobs too—and many others. They were the most flexibly useful of wooden men-of-war. The loss of a frigate was a routine gambit, expected in all navies but the British. The loss of a major Ship of the Line, in any navy, was a catastrophe. Larger ships consequently stayed close to their bases except when they fared forth in clusters or when, in times of relative tranquillity, their presence off some distant coast might reduce the impulse toward fractious behavior in a minor power.

After the end of hostilities in 1783, remnants of the loosely organized Continental Navy reverted to the jealously sovereign states that had produced them, or were sold. For 14 years, despite the urgings of Thomas Jefferson, the country had no naval force afloat. Nautical historians, men generally of a Federalist temper, have monotonously failed to point to the fact that Jefferson was the first of the Founding Fathers to argue, as he did with eloquence in 1785, for a naval force adequate to protect American commerce. For a decade thereafter, a share in the lucrative Mediterranean trade was effectively denied to American vessels by the harsh fact that 119 American seamen were ill-treated slaves awaiting ransom in Algiers.

In 1791, when the Second Congress convened in Philadelphia, public agitation for a naval remedy was increasing, but three more years were spent in wrangling over ways to avoid it. A few small and smartly handled American fighting ships, as Jefferson had advocated, could have dealt with the Barbary nuisance when the first merchantmen were piratically seized. Two or three Algerian corsairs were showpieces of considerable force, given to the dey as bribes by European countries that were well pleased to have Yankee competitors scared out of their sea; but the Turkish officers of the regency seldom even tried to train their tough Moorish crews in gunnery. It was their favorite tactic, in swift and weatherly lateens, to carry a victim by boarding.

When Congress at last was coaxed into painful political action by embarrassment over the failure of diplomacy to free the enslaved seamen, the legislators had no permanent navy in mind. This fact is revealed quite plainly in an annex to the act of authorization passed in 1794: if a treaty of peace should be concluded with Algiers before the completion of the six frigates provided for, all work on them must stop immediately. This amendment was needed to secure any naval appropriation at a time when most legislators wanted the United States to stay out of all foreign contests. Their general view was that a token navy would be an absurdity, utterly ineffectual against any major power, yet a source of potential quarrels that could not be sustained.

The most important private document surviving from the debate that caused the country to sidle into establishment of a permanent naval force makes it evident, nevertheless, that one faction was thinking hardly at all of the problem of the pestiferous Algerian corsairs. This is the famous argument sent by the shipbuilder Joshua Humphreys to one of his senators, Robert Morris, 15 months before passage of the Navy Act of March 27, 1794. It is the pivotal letter of several, to and from Humphreys, which reveal his use of the Barbary agitation to get a grip on a much larger matter. He referred explicitly to an eventual conflict with Britain and to the consequent problem of confronting standardized double- or triple-decked enemy ships. Two decades in advance of the occasion, he discussed strategy for a specific war against an immensely greater sea power. For this war that Humphreys foresaw and expected, he advocated one special kind of ship that should be able to demolish any vessel in its own seeming category, yet could make its way into the wind rapidly enough to keep its distance from larger enemies.

Humphreys's plan for a United States Navy was one of the lucid simplicities that stagger history with the question, "Why was this not thought of before?" It involved no fundamental newness in lines of the hull, in rig, or in armament. Humphreys argued for an exemplary fighting ship somewhat larger and more heavily armed than a standard Fifth Rate, but mistakable for one in her rig and structure. She was to be as strongly built as a Fourth Rate, without a Fourth Rate's cumbersome upper works, which dulled her sailing qualities: an in-betweener, a Fifth-Rate-and-a-Half. In the weight of metal her broadside could deliver, she was to be decisively superior to any standard frigate afloat, but in her intended employment she would have no need of some features that made a Fourth Rate particularly vulnerable to raking fire when she was not protected by her deployment in a line of battle.

A Ship of the Line had one lamentable handicap: she made a superb target. Multiple decks were required for her extra tiers of guns, which pressed the largest ones, in her lowest tier, close to the water. Constant desire for heavier broadsides, to give a fighting edge to one's own ship—and of course responded to by the opposing navies within their own systems of rates—had forced the only significant modification of the rating system in the quarter century between Falconer's extensive explanation of it and Humphreys's concept of a way to outwit the entire scheme. Falconer noted that "the 80-gun ships however begin to grow out of repute, and to give way to those of 74, 70, &c. which have only two whole batteries; whereas the former have three." Fewer tiers of somewhat heavier guns thereafter became the fashion, but this change did not remove the most awkward handicap experienced by the captain of a Ship of the Line in brisk weather. Even with only two tiers of guns, those on the lower, or main, gun deck could not be used when the waves were of any considerable height. The gunports had to be fastened shut to keep the water out of the hold—and, what was more important, to prevent it from slopping the powder cartridges and the touchholes of the guns. Thus deprived of the use of her main-deck battery, the principal concentration of her total force, a 74 or 64 was left with about the same armament normally carried in a frigate, but with a lot more ship showing for an enemy to aim at. With stronger structure and a larger crew, she could more than hold her own in blowing weather against a standard Fifth Rate; but the novel frigate that Humphreys argued for, as he pointed out, would in these circumstances throw a heavier broadside than that available to the handicapped larger vessel and would be built just as strongly.

The degree of superiority of a Humphreys frigate over the standard one is suggested by a comparison of the actual force and dimensions of the *Constitution* and the *Constellation* with H.M.S. *Phoenix* and *Venus,* selected by Falconer as examples of the larger and smaller standard Fifth Rates. The dimensions of the *Constitution* were 175 feet by 43 feet 6 inches by 14 feet 3 inches. Those of the *Phoenix* were 140 feet 9 inches by 37 feet 1 inch by 16 feet—shorter, narrower, but drawing more water. The *Constitution* measured 1,576 tons, the *Phoenix* 856 tons. Yet both were rated as 44-gun frigates. Discrepancies in measurement between the *Constellation* and the *Venus,* both 36's, were even greater.

A more telling difference appears in the sizes of the guns. The *Constitution* was designed to carry 24-pounders on her gun deck and long 12's on the quarter-deck. The *Phoenix* mounted a main battery of 18-pounders and an upper battery of 9's. Guns above the main battery, in the Second and Third Rates of Falconer's day, were never larger than 18's. Thus in blowing weather, with a big ship's lower ports sealed, the *Constitution* could stay out of range of a 74's best remaining guns while reaching her with a main battery of 24's.

These numerical distinctions merely indicate differences in two concepts of what a frigate should be. Most of the ships afloat when Falconer selected several to be his exemplars had been replaced when the new United States Navy first was contemplated, but standardization of sizes within the Rates had become even more rigid. Third Rates were 74's or 64's, with few exceptions, leaving wider gaps between the Rates, and it was at the gaps that Humphreys was aiming. Industrious Falconer, author also of a popular long poem called *The Shipwreck,* lived only long enough to record the beginning of these rigidities; he perished in the wreck of H.B.M. Frigate *Aurora* in the year when his dictionary appeared.

Controversy has swirled around Humphreys and the extent of his responsibility for the six famous original frigates. As is often the case with remote historical figures, when fire and carelessness have had their way with the records, his defenders and those who would shave him down to size tend to concentrate upon different aspects of achievement. Josiah Fox, a skillful young naval architect from England and a tourist in America who was persuaded to stay, contributed notably to the drafting of plans that expressed the concept enunciated before his arrival by Humphreys. Fox should probably be credited with refinements of design that make the difference between ordinary ships and exceptional ones. Specialists have called him much the better draftsman. What matters here is the strategical concept, and Humphreys wrote of it, apparently unchallenged, as if it were all his own. His primacy was acknowledged by contemporaries who had to make critical decisions in response to his views. On June 28, 1794, in a letter appointing him "Constructor & Master builder" of one of the larger frigates that had been authorized by Congress three months earlier, Secretary of War Henry Knox said that his pay would be retroactive to May 1 "in consideration of your incessant application to the public interest in adjusting the principles of the Ship." On July 24, 1794, Knox ordered Humphreys to have moulds of the five other frigates sent from Philadelphia to the constructors at Baltimore, Boston, New York, Norfolk, and Portsmouth. He was to use "all possible dispatch," and to be aided by "Mr Fox who is under your direction." The moulds were thin wooden patterns by which to shape the massive ribs and other framing timbers. Thus, whatever proper credit may be allotted to the subordinate, Humphreys was clearly in charge of the essential designs for all six frigates.

When Joshua Humphreys conceived this new kind of naval force, British frigates were chiefly used as errand-runners upon tasks to which Ships of the Line could not prudently be committed. Everything to be accomplished by the show or use of American force would have to be attempted in the complete absence of Ships of the Line, for many perilous years. It was hard enough to convince the Congress that a few frigates were needed, though 74's were spoken of. Humphreys had probably made in his youth the draft for one built during the Revolution and promptly given to France. He assumed that they would be political impossibilities in the nineties. As the Quasi War with France—of which Jefferson disapproved—became heated in 1799, advocates of a strong navy grew more persuasive, and Humphreys was asked to draft plans for a dozen contemplated 74's, but diplomacy supervened and none of them was ever started.

A few passages from Humphreys's early letter to Senator Morris will best show the individual quality of his argument:

SIR

From the present appearance of affairs, I believe it is time this country was possessed of a Navy . . . I have ventured a few Ideas on that subject.

Ships that compose the European navys are generally distinguished by their rates . . . & as our Navy must for a considerable time be inferior in numbers we are to consider what size Ships will be . . . an over match for those of an Enemy, such Frigates as in blowing weather would be an over match for double deck Ships, & in light winds, to evade coming to action. . . . Ships built on these principles will render those of an Enemy in a degree useless. . . .

Frigates built to carry 12, 18 pounders in my opinion will not answer the expectation contemplated from them, for if . . . at a future day, we should be dragged into a war with any powers of the old continent, especially great Britain they having such a number of Ships of that Size, that it would be an equal chance by equal combat that we loose our Ships. . . .

Here Humphreys tactfully remembers to refer to the Algerian navy. He exaggerates its force, perhaps in deference to the views of those who advocated a navy only to combat the Algerians. Then he asks:

whether will one large or two small Frigates contribute most to the protection of our trade. . . . or whether two small ones are as able to engage a double deck ship as one large one. For my part I am decidedly of opinion, the large ones will answer best.

For a long while it was the fashion to exult over American naval victories in the War of 1812 on the assumption that superbly trained and high-spirited American gunners, outraged by the impressment of their friends into the British Navy, had defeated equivalent ships whose crews had less reason to fight as well. Good gunnery and high morale were factors, but Joshua Humphreys had carefully seen to it two decades earlier that the ships would not be equivalent. In the only instance when luck pitted two approximately equal frigates against each other, the British ship was victor.

In most frigate actions of the early nineteenth century both sides used carronades to supplement the main batteries. These were short guns with a powder chamber of small bore backing up a barrel with a diameter, in the case of 42-pounder carronades, as great as that of the heaviest guns in a First Rate. Their range was much more limited than that of the standard 42-pounders, which were twice as long, but at close quarters they were just as damaging.

Humphreys was authorized to design four 44-gun frigates and two 36's. The former he planned as firing platforms for a main battery of 28 long 24-pounders on the gun deck and 10 long 12-pounders on the quarter-deck, with ports provided for bow chases and stern chases of unspecified size to make up the complement of 44. Both the 24's and the 12's were a little under 10 feet in length; this fact dictated for Humphreys another prudent but novel aspect of design. Hatches of a British Sixth Rate left operating room for only small guns in the main battery amidships. The same fault to a lesser degree reduced the effective armament of the Fifth Rates. Humphreys gave his frigates sufficient width, and narrow enough hatches, to permit the use of the largest practicable guns from one end of the deck to the other. This fact was objected to by the British historian William James as giving the American frigates an unfair advantage in the War of 1812. Humphreys did not take fairness into consideration, in the European sense of pitting equal chessmen against each other within established categories. He was working within a system of absolute unfairness: six ships to confront more than a thousand. By his own calculation, against equal opponents, six standard frigates would all be eliminated in nine encounters.

As it actually worked out, the *Chesapeake* 36 was lost to the *Shannon* 38, and the *President* 44 was captured by a fleet. The other four Humphreys frigates won all their battles and lived, with the aid of much rebuilding, to an average age of 80 years. Their victories at sea, over the smaller British frigates which they were designed to vanquish, provided the United States with enough prestige to conclude the Treaty of Ghent as a sensible compromise: the best basis for any enduring peace.

Some have argued that the actual shape of the Humphreys frigates reflects French influence; others say Danish. Fox, who probably drew the final drafts under Humphreys's direction,

Michele Felice Cornè, painter of the liveliest early American marines, produced a remarkable squall scene *(below)* of the frigate *Constitution* in the year of her triumph over the *Guerrière:* 1812. In order to circumvent conventional naval tactics based upon the line of battle *(top, center)*, as in this action of September 5, 1781, between British and French fleets off the Virginia Capes, Joshua Humphreys had made the *Constitution* larger and stronger than standard frigates, which thitherto had been relegated to minor functions. Her maneuvers in her victory over the smaller *Java* are shown on a page of the journal *(upper right)* of a British participant in the fight. The frigate *President (lower right)*, designed by Humphreys at about the same time as the *Constitution*, and equally powerful, was caught alone and captured by a British fleet. (See pp. 130–31, 134, 137.)

surely contributed the results of his apprenticeship in British yards, but his ideas must have been modified by his travels of inspection on the Continent. The contours of a remarkably successful group of ships were advanced for the time, although not unprecedented. It was the idea behind their dimensions, their strength for sustaining an unusual armament, that expressed an American spirit in shipbuilding: a spirit that makes its distinctive emergence again and again—a willingness to examine tradition in search of room for the adaptation of existing forms and devices to novel needs of a quickly evolving society.

In this instance the force of one man's argument may actually have been the salvation of his country. Our second war with Britain was a small side show in the vast Napoleonic conflict. Sentiment was very strong, in maritime New England, for rejoining the mother country. The principal land campaigns ended disastrously for American forces, except the last one at New Orleans, fought after terms of peace had been settled. Two naval triumphs of small fleets on inland waters, and the victories in the Atlantic of Humphreys's frigates, restored a bedraggled public spirit, checkmated Federalists of the Hartford Convention who were ready to sue for a merchants' peace, and gave the commissioners at Ghent a much-needed element of dignity.

England in 1814 had the power to retake her former colonies, with their important shipbuilding facilities and vital timber reserves. Her decision not to do so was a minor aspect of major territorial problems under discussion at the Congress of Vienna. Amid these interweaving and worldwide considerations the fame of the Humphreys frigates may have been the last deciding factor in favor of a peace of mutual reasonableness.

THE PILOT SCHOONERS

Quakers produced a disproportionate number of contributors to American eminence on the sea. Their Nantucket contribution was appropriately peaceful, except from the point of view of the abominably tortured whales. As an employment better suited than frigate design to his continuing membership in the Society of Friends, Joshua Humphreys gave attention to the concept of an ideal pilot schooner. His draft of 1798, as was the case with his frigates, calls for a vessel large in its particular service, but the reason this time is not self-evident. Influences that shaped the optimum American pilot schooner were nevertheless peculiarly American, as were the circumstances favoring outsize frigates. The rating system in European navies had as traditional a counterpart in the often hereditary organization of pilotage. It was the European practice for any entrepreneur to make his best bargain with central authority; what he usually sought was monopoly, paid for with a contribution that assured the suppression of upstart rivals. In some measure this was a survival of the guild system that flourished in the thirteenth century, which guaranteed competence and saw to it that employment was equitably shared.

Off the large ports of Europe pilots waited their turn. In heavy weather an incoming ship would lie to and signal for a pilot, who might prefer to let the storm subside before sailing out of the harbor. In good weather the pilots cruised off the main channel, one boat on the pilot station being usually sufficient. When she had put her last pilot into an incoming vessel, another boatload of pilots would replace her. There was no contest for business.

Little of the guild spirit had survived the westward Atlantic crossing of the colonists. British attempts to enforce monopolistic practices through the Navigation Acts had left the colonists scratched and angry. The dangerous edge of the wilderness promoted measures for the general defense while it rewarded individualism in most other enterprises. Individualism so far emerged as the dominant American spirit that a decade was needed after the end of the Revolution for the discovery that the external discipline of the king had to be replaced in some aspects by an internal substitute.

Pilotage, on the outer edge of commercial activity, continued to express individualism in the extreme. There were associations of pilots, but within the associations the members were competitive: the first pilot boat alongside an incoming ship got the job. Pilots did not wait for the ship to approach. They sailed to a meeting that might be far offshore.

Under these conditions, fast and weatherly vessels of modest size were requisite. The designers could ignore cargo space, except for the stores for a week or two at sea. But the racing lines had to be combined with sea-keeping qualities. In foul weather, American boats snugged down as a rule and kept their stations, prepared for the looming of tall masts through the murk as the storm diminished.

Two other aspects notably affected the primary American pilot boat design, which began to shape up in the years when the Humphreys frigates were building. Having placed her pilots aboard other vessels, the boat had to make port herself, or in really bad weather seek shelter in a shallow haven. One seaman brought her home; size and rig therefore were limited to the management of a single skillful man. The second aspect was related to a peculiarity of the American Atlantic coast—the extensive estuaries to be traversed between many ports and the open sea. Special craft for pilots probably originated in Chesapeake Bay, where a 200-mile pattern of channels tends to wander a bit in the night. Sandbars shift disconcertingly between Capes Charles and Henry. Any incoming ship might be bound for the home port of pilots—Norfolk, inside the Cape Henry corner— but more likely was headed for Baltimore, 200 miles up the bay. Pilots had to be ready for either assignment as they hovered outside the capes, with an occasional critical need to slide into a shallow haven on the East Shore.

These influences produced the shallow-draft Virginia pilot schooner, 50 or 60 feet long, shaped under water for speed and steadiness, wearing a simple baldheaded rig. With only one hand aboard, the separate gaff sails of a schooner provided options that the fewer sails of a sloop did not. On a hull of the same size, a sloop rig would have offered one excessively large mainsail and two or three headsails. The mainsail could not have been used in a sudden squall unless close reefed, a task perilous for a single hand to attempt with his tiller in a becket. Headsails alone are an unsafe alternative on a lee shore.

The schooner, with her main canvas area divided between two gaff-headed sails, gave a single hand the option of setting only one of them. Pictures from the period often show a loose-footed foresail carrying the schooner's name and port in large letters above the close-reef band. The loose foot of this sail appears to have been twice as long as would have been possible if it had been attached to a boom swinging in the space limited by the mainmast. Chesapeake pilot schooners avoided the square yards aloft that were at the time customary in merchant and privateer schooners.

Delaware Bay also had its principal port city farthest from the ocean. Storms played the same tricks with its channels and sandbars. The refuges from violent weather were shallow in both estuaries. Consequently the Delaware pilot schooners, shaped for the same conditions, differed only in minor quirks from the Chesapeake model.

The next marked development, which produced along the way a famous, if aberrant, example of pilot schooner design, occurred at New York port. Here, before steam dredging became feasible, storm-altered channels offered near Sandy Hook the same problems found at the mouths of larger estuaries. The area where expert knowledge mattered most was smaller, but just as perilous. Havens inside the bay were deeper than those of the estuaries and could be reached about as easily as some hazardous little inlets of the northern New Jersey coast. For these reasons the New York model became larger and deeper than the Virginian, with the option of a sharper bottom. Moreover, the vast increase of shipping at New York port intensified competition among pilots. The flow of incoming vessels was almost constant, storm or no storm. In these conditions, pilot schooners tended to range far offshore, sometimes to Nantucket shoals. Ability to ride a storm out became a primary aim in design. The New York pilot schooner was for a while the most versatile craft on the seas, unexcelled for her size in all aspects but cargo capacity, in which she had no reason to compete. She was swift, as weatherly as any working vessel ever has been, stable—and about 70 or 75 feet long.

These are generalizations. No single standard model replaced all others. New York designers were intensively experimental. Because of the longer sea races off their port, stretching from Cape Cod to Cape May, they elaborated the baldheaded Virginia rig with square sails, and various fore-and-aft oddities aloft. The *Anna Maria* of 1812 set a deep square forecourse on occasion, as well as a square foretopsail; no novelty—the same rig appears on the *Baltick*, built about 50 years earlier as a general trading schooner. The lines under water show a considerable "after drag" in the earlier models, a feature supposed at the time to contribute to stability and weatherliness. A vessel with after drag was designed to draw more water at the sternpost than under the forefoot, the hull fairing away into a narrow fin to meet the rudder. Toward mid-century, after drag was abandoned in pilot schooners as in other classes of vessels. Adjustments of the lines produced greater speed without it, and as much stability.

The most famous outgrowth of the New York pilot boat contest in design, the yacht *America,* fostered a re-examination of assumptions in naval architecture throughout the world. Too large for a pilot boat herself, she was intended as an outsize example of American manufacturing skill to be exhibited off the British coast when more compact American products were on view at the Great Exhibition in London, the first world's fair. More of her later.

THE LINER PACKETS

When six unfair frigates designed by the Quaker Joshua Humphreys had done their notable part in bringing a dubious war to the balance of a sensible peace, when the Quaker-dominated enterprise of Nantucket was swiftly rebuilding itself a second time from almost complete devastation, two groups of Quakers in New York and in Liverpool were moving toward the establishment of a revolutionary notion in the concept of common carriers. On Friday, October 24, 1817, Isaac Wright & Son and Francis Thompson, whose principals were members of the Society of Friends, placed an advertisement in the New York papers announcing that a "Line of American Packets" would begin in January a schedule of regular sailings to Liverpool "on a certain day in every month throughout the year." Over the weekend the notice was amended to add the names of Thompson's brother, Jeremiah, and of Benjamin Marshall, the only member of the group who was not a Quaker. The Wrights were native Long Islanders; the other three, naturalized Americans from Yorkshire.

The New York *Evening Post* first printed the epoch-making advertisement, as amended, on Monday, October 27, and carried it every day thereafter through January 9, 1818. It was a giant among marine notices, almost four inches high, and in one other respect an eye-catcher. Newspapers for more than a century had drawn attention to a shipping item with a tiny woodcut in its upper left corner. Careful compositors chose from separate cuts of ships, brigs, schooners, and sloops. The first advertisements for the Line of American Packets smashed precedent by sending four cuts of ships sailing right across the head of the column, to match the four ships named below.

Despite typographical innovation, "the rail-road route to Europe"—as it came to be called only after railroads themselves began to operate on reliable schedules—was as much an evolutionary emergence as the idea of the ideal pilot schooner had been. Conditions shaped it in several phases. The steamboat, which had become a feasible means of public transport around the turn of the century, had helped to set aside the assumption that travelers upon the sea were inevitably at the mercy of adverse weather. When an otherwise usable gale of wind blew straight in between the chops of a harbor, nothing could get out by sail alone. Steam tugs were early envisioned, as in the Jonathan Hulls concept of 1736, but none was powerful enough to help in a real blow until almost a century later. What the little steamboats of America did do, as they greatly increased in number during and after the War of 1812, was to turn the absolute idea of dependence upon the weather into a relative one. When the scheduled packets began to operate, New York steamers for some years had been keeping to a regular daily schedule in runs from Manhattan to Peekskill and other places. The daily Brunswick steamboat from New York connected with a stagecoach, which in turn connected with another steamer on the Delaware, which made scheduled passages to Philadelphia.

Thus the idea of regularity was extending from mail coaches, with which it had long been a practice, to watercraft, in which it was made feasible by steam. British blockades of the War of 1812 stimulated activities on inland waterways. Fulton's catamaran *Jersey* of 1812 was probably the first steam ferry to be put into service in the United States. He built a similar catamaran, the *York,* in 1813, before proposing his warship in this form to the Navy. His third catamaran steam ferry, the *Nassau,* was built before the war ended.

These and other ferries became links in intricate transportation schemes, which included the wartime shipment of cotton from the fields of South Carolina to the mills of Rhode Island by inland waterways and wagons, a journey of three or four months. Regular sailings in such hampering circumstances were not meaningful, but they were tried before the war's end. Early in 1814 the "New Line for Albany" was advertised in the New York *Gazette.* The entrepreneurs purchased three Hudson River sloops—the *Gold Hunter,* the *George,* and the *Hardware*—one to head under canvas every Saturday northward from New York while another sailed southward from Albany. One sloop thus would "be in New York ready to receive freight at all times, as she will arrive before the other leaves." There was still a dependence upon the weather: "N B. The *Gold Hunter* will sail for Albany as soon as it is ascertained that the River is open." Ice persisted into March.

Vessels advertised "for immediate dispatch" to distant ports continued so to advertise week after week, waiting for cargo—or for passengers to sign up. Delays of as much as two months in the winter season were frequent. But with the beginning of a scheduled transatlantic packet service the advertisements for other sailings began to change too. The *Maria,* Latham, for Charleston, was advertised to sail on March 8, and she actually did clear on March 12, 1818. Captain Latham at least made an effort.

The famous phrase of the Atlantic packet line announcement originated in the Liverpool papers, which declared on December 5, 1817, that "the American Ships, COURIER, PACIFIC, JAMES MUNROE, AND AMITY . . . will *positively sail, full or not full,* from Liverpool on the 1st, and from New York on the 5th of every month, throughout the year."

The concept *"full or not full,"* appropriately italicized in these promises, was not entirely new either. It had been used more than a year earlier in at least one New York advertisement for a ship in the Liverpool trade, but in spite of the drastic determination, she had missed her announced sailing date "cargo or no cargo" by 18 days. What can surely be claimed for the New Yorkers who established the first scheduled transatlantic packet line is that they coordinated a number of existing practices and ideas into a novel pattern, recognized a risk, persevered under that risk, and kept with a remarkable fidelity to their undertaking. The result, after a brief delay, was a genuine revolution in shipping, and consequently in ship design.

The *James Monroe,* 424 tons, largest of the four original liners, was provided at sailing hour with the right circumstances for her first test of her owners' resolution. At 10:00 A.M. on January 5, 1818, the visibility was close to zero in a gusting snowstorm. Captain James Watkinson ordered his sails shaken out nevertheless, and when the foretopsail was sheeted home, a symbol was visible through the snow that was to make the line both famous and notorious, a large black disc painted on the canvas. The *James Monroe* averaged only three miles an hour down the bay to Sandy Hook, but she got to sea on the fifth, as promised. She was "not full." Her cargo included 400 barrels of ashes, some hops, some cranberries, but chiefly apples and flour. It could not have been profitable, but her owners were investing in something less immediate: repute.

A winter sailing was itself unusual. Two round voyages a year had been the rule for Liverpool traders, with a long layover during the worst weather. But if there was to be a sailing from each side once a month, each ship in a fleet of four would have to make three round voyages to maintain the schedule. Each would have about 55 days to make the easterly crossing and take in a cargo in time for the scheduled return sailing. For the westbound crossings, 65 days were provided. The different times reflected allowances for prevailing westerly winds. The actual average difference between "downhill" and "uphill" Atlantic passages was somewhat greater.

Despite planning and promises, the first westward sailing was three days late. It has been suggested that the British agents did not at first believe that the schedule was seriously intended, but seasonal weather in the Mersey probably made it impossible to get out. The river at its mouth runs northwest. A northwest gale, the typical winter wind, used to bottle up the sailing ships beyond remedy, until powerful tugs were provided. If Captain Bowne was a bit tardy in getting to sea, by comparison with the perfect punctuality that the *James Monroe* was to show at New York on the day following, his *Courier*, of 381 tons, improved the line's prospects with a full hold. Her mixed cargo reflected a widespread interest aroused by the first Liverpool advertisement's promises: "The dependance which may be placed upon the periods of their departure, afford to these conveyances advantages of so much importance to the Manufacturing Houses, and to the Shippers of Goods generally as it is hoped will secure to them general support."

And so it did, in westward sailings. The *Courier* carried about

80 separate consignments on her invoice, a much more remuner-
ative kind of freight than bulk cargo. British manufactures
constituted most of the 1,330 parcels of "quality freight" in her
hold. About one-quarter of them consisted of woolen cloth and
calico belonging to various owners of the ship—another clue
to the maturing circumstances that had brought the original
packet line into operation. Isaac Wright and his son William,
Benjamin Marshall, the brothers Francis and William Thompson—all were resident New Yorkers specializing in the importa-
tion of British fabrics. As naturalized Americans the Thompsons
and Marshall retained close family ties with operators of looms
in the British midlands.

The four ships with which these men set up the first scheduled
Atlantic packet line had been built for them previously to serve
as independent Liverpool traders. Their owners as a group exemplify an early phase of the American commercial tendency to
establish informal protective monopolies but to compete somewhat within them. There was a measure of joint ownership in
each of the four vessels, the usual risk-spreading device, before
a full partnership was arranged.

When assessing changes in American ship design that emerged
from close competition in the scheduled packet services, it should
be noticed that the majority of the Black Ball Line's founders
were transplanted Englishmen. In the early days of our republic
the emerging American character was importantly shaped by
men who had become Americans on purpose, and to a purpose
as clearly perceived as that of their predecessor immigrants in
the *Mayflower.* Tom Paine, John Paul Jones, Alexander Hamil-
ton, Josiah Fox, and many others can be cited. The Quaker
Thompsons, like the Nantucket Friends, would have put national allegiance below fidelity to their faith; as members of an
eminent commercial family they saw, however, an important
advantage in United States citizenship: foreigners could be
resident traders in America, but they could not be shipowners.
Thus it was American conditions, rather than a mystical quality
derived from native birth, that fostered the shaping of an idea in
New York port which soon would alter the shapes and employments of ships.

The ships that forced these great changes were products of
native American industry. The first Liverpool announcement

was emphatic: these four "American Ships . . . were all built in New York, of the best materials, and are coppered and copper fastened; they are all remarkably fast sailers. . . ." This was only three years after the initialing of the Treaty of Ghent, closing a small war chiefly marked in the British consciousness by controversy over the performances of a few American frigates and a swarm of swift American privateers. Whether the single-ship actions had been fair or unfair (the point apparently of steadiest interest to sporting Englishmen), there was no argument over the impressive quality of ships built in America: British commercial agents thought the nativity of the first four liner packets would be a lure for English shippers.

The advertisement's stress upon New York products was a portent. In four decades of sailing ship supremacy on the Atlantic shuttle, a heavy majority of all scheduled liners came from shipyards on the shores of New York port. Three New York yards built among them almost half of the 300 or so ocean and coastal packets launched at identifiable places.

The pioneer packet line that brought four ships from a complex pattern of shared investment into a closely timed system of use began its adventure during the downward cycle of a depression. No other shipowners cared, for four years, to compete in sending ships to sea "not full." The financial reserves of the original adventurers are revealed in their shrewd use of the business cycle, a recourse of merchants who can afford to take the long view. If their packets were too large for available cargoes during the postwar readjustment, they would be too small when business picked up again. It would be prudent to replace them while costs were low. Isaac Wright and his partners prepared to retire the *Pacific,* of 384 tons, and placed an order for her successor, the new *Albion,* 50 tons larger. The *Pacific* had been in service for eleven years as a general Liverpool trader before she spent a year or two helping to originate the Black Ball Line. Sold to New Bedford for a whaler, this vessel crafted to confront the growling Western Ocean took Cape Horn in her stride, again and again, in a profitable afterlife of 63 additional years.

As competition among proliferating packet lines called persistently for larger ships, many of the earlier ones became whalers. They helped in doing so to establish standards of size, shape, and sailing qualities for the successful whaleship as a separate kind of vessel. In 1821 the *Courier,* built only a few months before the Black Ball Line began operations, was retired in favor of the *Nestor,* exactly 100 tons larger in measurement. There was nothing wrong with the *Courier* other than her limited capacity for an expanding enterprise. Sold to Newport as a whaler, she was soon transferred to the growing port of New Bedford. On her first voyage out of that place—as Starbuck reports laconically—"Second mate Jeremiah Borden, and boats crew taken down by a whale and lost." No fault of the ship. When she returned on July 2, 1861, from her final voyage to the Pacific of almost five years, she was sold into the first stone fleet, to be sunk in an attempt to block the ship channel off Charleston, South Carolina. Whether she would have matched the *Pacific's* 75 years of varied service if there had been no war we can only guess.

The four-year-old *James Monroe,* superseded in 1821 by the *James Cropper* of 495 tons, was sold for a Cuban trader, but she too became a whaler 11 years later in the fleet sailing out of Hudson, New York, operated by Nantucket exiles. In 1849, while on a Pacific voyage, she put in at the newly booming town of San Francisco, where she was purchased for further services unrecorded.

Starbuck identifies 37 Western Ocean packets that became whalers as well as 10 more that were built originally for the coastal lines. Half of these were still out whaling in 1860, when the impending Civil War soon would catch whalers unnotified of their danger from enemy raiders. The date also marks the end of a quarter century after the building of the last packet that became a whaler. Of the 47 packet-whalers that sail in the pages of Starbuck, only 6 were built after 1831, none after 1835. The early liner packets were conceived of as speedy freighters. When whalers began to fish the Pacific, speed coming and going became an important economic factor, as capacity had always been for freighting the product home. In the 1830's packets developed increasingly into passenger ships, with a sacrifice of capacity to speed. The first Black Ballers, of about 350 tons, were as large as whalers needed to be. As the whales retreated into more distant reaches of the Pacific it often took four years to fill up a vessel of that size. There was no inducement to even longer absences from home.

The first packet liners could accommodate about 15 passengers in what for the time was unusual comfort. Two decades later, newly built ships carried 80 in staterooms described as elegant. Consequently, after transfers to the whaling service became impractical, the superseded Western Ocean packets went into the coastal lines. A few became "Canton packets," notably influencing the structure of the ultimate tea clippers.

The later emigrant packets carried several hundred steerage passengers apiece in accommodations anything but elegant. Each passenger was allotted merely a chalked rectangle of space on a lower deck—by law not less than two feet by seven—that could as well be laden with more inert kinds of cargo. When haulers of human beings in bulk came into use—as responses to famines and revolutions of the late 1840's in Ireland and Europe—about 70 deep-water American packet lines had been founded, and many had already gone out of business. Thomas Byrnes and George Trimble, two more Quakers, had given the imaginative Quaker originators of scheduled Atlantic packets their first formal competition in kind when they formed the Red Star Line, to operate by scheduled sailings four fine Liverpool traders that they had had built within the past five years. One, the *Hercules*, of 334 tons, later became an exceptionally long-lived whaler.

There was something of heroism in the challenge. The two young newcomers must have been aware, at the outset of the year 1822, that their well-established competitors were preparing to follow their replacement of three ships by the outright addition of four more—a total of eight in service, which would make two sailings a month in each direction possible. Moreover, all but one of the Black Ballers would be larger than the largest vessel in the competing Red Star Line. Even so, the predicted business expansion absorbed the capacity of all 12 liners; before the year was half over, the Swallowtail Line was advertised, to begin regular sailings to Liverpool on August 8. New York and Liverpool merchants then could count on four scheduled sailings a month all year long.

The year 1822, one of erupting activity, saw the beginnings of regular packet service to Liverpool from Boston and Philadelphia. New York lines were soon established to Le Havre and to London. By 1825 there were 32 deep-ocean packets sailing out of New York port and 26 coastal packets were also in less regular

lot schooners were among the earliest distinctive specializing American vessels, developed chiefly
or estuary conditions, such as those that lay between the Grey's Inn Creek Shipyard *(above)* and the
cean. The *Mary of Norfolk (below)*, drawn in 1795 by a British visitor, was typical. The scheduled
ankee packet lines were organized soon after the War of 1812. The famous first advertisement of
hat became the Black Ball Line appeared in 1817. The *Hercules (left, center)*, built in 1816, became
Red Star liner in 1821. The durable Black Baller *Isaac Webb (lower left)*, launched in 1849, was one
f the most famous. (See pp. 117, 141–51, 154–56.)

LINE OF AMERICAN PACKETS
BETWEEN N. YORK & LIVERPOOL

IN order to furnish frequent and regular conveyances for GOODS and PASSENGERS, the
subscribers have undertaken to establish a line
of vessels between NEW-YORK and LIVER-
POOL, to sail from each place on a certain day
in every month throughout the year

The following vessels, each about four hundred
tons burthen, have been fitted out for this purpose :

Ship AMITY, John Stanton, master,
" COURIER, Wm. Bowne, "
" PACIFIC, Jno. Williams, "
" JAMES MONROE, —— "

And it is the intention of the owners that one
of these vessels shall sail from New-York on the
5th, and one from Liverpool on the 1st of every
month.

These ships have all been built in New-York,
of the best materials, and are coppered and copper fastened. They are known to be remarkably fast sailers, and their accommodations for
passengers are uncommonly extensive and com-
modious. They are all nearly new except the
Pacific; she has been some years in the trade,
but has been recently thoroughly examined, and
is found to be perfectly sound in every respect.

The commanders of them are all men of great
experience and activity ; and they will do all in
their power to render these Packets eligible conveyances for passengers. It is also thought, that
the regularity of their times of sailing, and the excellent condition in which they deliver their cargoes, will make them very desirable opportuni-
ies for the conveyance of goods.

It is intended that this establishment shall commence by the departure of the JAMES MON-
ROE, from NEW-YORK on the 5th, and the
COURIER from LIVERPOOL on the 1st, of
First Month (January) next ; and one of the vessels will sail at the same periods from each place
in every succeeding month.

ISAAC WRIGHT & SON,
FRANCIS THOMPSON,
BENJAMIN MARSHALL,
JEREMIAH THOMPSON.

10m▫24

MARY
– of –
NORFOLK

operation to Charleston, Savannah, and New Orleans.

Rapid replacement, in a highly competitive business, provided chances and reasons for experimentation in design. A packet, crowded with sail, needed a buoyant stability when running to Europe, mostly before the wind, but also a weatherly stiffness to beat into the wind on her way home. Weatherliness and speed had been taken for granted as desirable in colonial America. In the 1740's, when the Admiralty for once found a way around the objections of British constructors and placed orders for a few minor naval vessels in the colonies, those produced were sharper, longer, and narrower than the standard specifications for their Rates. The group was greatly objected to in British dockyards, perhaps because of their comparative virtues as fighting ships. The virtues of speed and weatherliness were being stressed as American revolutionary frigates crept beyond the 3.5 to 1 figure in length-to-breadth ratio; Humphreys's designs of the nineties hovered around 4 to 1.

Most liner packets built between 1807 and 1822 had a trifle less than that ratio. Beginning with the second *Pacific* of 1824, a length-to-breadth ratio distinctly above 4 to 1 was regarded as normal by the packet builders. The *Isaac Webb,* a fast and famous Black Baller of 1,359 tons, launched in 1850, had a ratio of 4.73 to 1. The competing Red Star Line had ordered five years earlier the unusually slender *John R. Skiddy,* Donald McKay's first big liner packet, with a ratio of more than 4.9 to 1; and the largest Red Star ship, the *Constellation,* of 1,560 tons, added in 1849, had about the same ratio. Only one or two early clippers, by this date, had reached the magical 5 to 1 mark, and few of those to come would exceed it.

Before the great days of the packets, many classes of ships had been designed as seasonal carriers, adapted to make the best use of moderate weather, but unable to carry much sail in a hard blow, or to claw upwind off a lee shore. Except for certain kinds of fighting ships, the packets as a group were the first vessels, since the sixteenth-century ships employed in exploration, that were developed with the need foreseen to do well under all conditions, all year long. Their superiority over tough and admirable little vessels like Drake's *Golden Hind* came largely from a persistent extension of the length-to-breadth ratio, but this in turn was made more feasible by increasing size.

A new willingness, under competition, to set more sail per ton of burden than ever before in any merchant service influenced the vessel's architecture. The hull had to be designed to sustain unusually heavy spars, with an inherent stiffness that would keep the masts pointed closer to the zenith than to the horizon in a black squall. The liner packets were a national enterprise, with which foreigners did not care to compete until they had developed adequate steamers. The design of ships that could sustain merciless driving under unprecedented amounts of sail thus became an American specialty, a corollary of the bucko mate. Logbooks, memoirs, and news items confirm a steady movement away from the early conditions in the packet liners, when passengers often commended the amiability of the officers, to the times that produced a famous shanty with the line "For kicking Jack Williams commands that Black Ball." As Albion points out, there is something wrong here, since the only Captain John Williams of the Black Ball Line was an uncommonly humane commander. Cutler says he was the first to provide his crew with a library. He behaved nobly when he was drowned with his ship on the rocky Irish coast in 1822, long before the line developed its repute as a haven for the toughest officers. Williams's command, the *Albion,* was the first Black Baller of many to be wrecked. The ones that went whaling were luckier.

Conditions of the service are suggested by the fact that of the 35 ships built for the line between 1819 and 1855, two-fifths met violent ends by accident, not counting the packet-whalers scuttled with the stone fleet. Five were wrecked on the shores near New York harbor, two elsewhere. Three went down in collisions, one foundered, and one was burned. Two went missing without a trace. As those transferred to the whale fishery demonstrated, practically all were so well built that they would last for many decades of normal sailing, even after hard initial service on the Atlantic Shuttle. It took a tremendous shock to destroy one, as when the *Liverpool,* of 476 tons, walloped an iceberg on her maiden voyage in 1822, just three months after the dismasted *Albion* was smashed against the sheer cliffs of Kinsale. Advancement in ship design depended somewhat upon such random destruction and the consequent need to replace ships ahead of schedule.

Reliable railway service was established over considerable

distances in the 1840's. Coastal rail lines offered shorter routes and faster service than those of any vessel. Offshore, domestic coastal steamers were a financial challenge to the sailing packets a decade ahead of the success of ocean steamers, which still had to carry inordinate amounts of fuel. Thus the number of coastal packets shrank in the forties, when the deep-water packets were having their greatest success.

Although scheduled sailing packets were still in use in 1880, the packet era is commonly regarded as having ended in 1855, when the state of the economy made replacements too costly. A skimming of tonnage figures for new ships, up to that date, confirms a steady trend. There was a little seesawing, but in most cases each newly added ship was the line's largest to date.

The four original Black Ball packets averaged 401 tons in capacity, 110 feet in length, 28 feet in breadth, and 14 feet 3 inches in depth of hold. The six vessels added by the same line early in the 1830's averaged 636 tons, with equivalent dimensions of 136 by 32 by 16. The last six vessels added before 1855 had an average tonnage of 1,383, and average measurements of 185 by 40 by 26.6.

These figures show an increase, over about four decades, of 43 per cent in breadth, 68 per cent in length, and 86 per cent in depth. The first two figures accord with what we already knew: the length-to-breadth ratio was increasing throughout the packet period. The third percentage is more surprising. It indicates that as the ships grew larger it became feasible to compensate with greater depth for the relative loss in ideal capacity suffered when a floating cargo container was elongated. The ultimate—in some judgments the excessive—refinement of the sailing cargo carrier was the clipper, which achieved a parallel and more swift development in the last decade of packet construction.

6 Development of the Whaleship

BRIG INTO WHALESHIP—THE *LEO*

Starbuck's generalized records of pre-Revolutionary whalers out of Nantucket give an average measurement of 75 tons in the years between 1756 and 1775 whenever the capacity of the vessels is indicated at all. There is one exception: in 1770, a peak year, Nantucket sent out 125 vessels with an average tonnage of 93. What was their rig? A large sampling appears in a list of 42 whalers that were bonded at Boston early in the Revolution, between August of 1775 and the January following: 19 brigantines, ten schooners, eight sloops, five brigs. No ships. A similar variety appears among those on the same Boston list that were bonded from other ports—less altogether than half the Nantucket number, but including one ship, the *Africa,* hailing from Newport. After the British destruction of Nantucket's fleet, whaling began again from Massachusetts coastal ports, chiefly from Boston, and mostly in schooners of 50 or 60 tons. The largest vessels in use for several years were a couple of 90-ton brigs and a schooner of the same measurement.

When Nantucket had sent forth its postwar colonists to instruct the Nova Scotians, Welsh, French, Portuguese, and New Yorkers in higher mysteries of the whale chase, those who remained undertook to change their practices abruptly. Starbuck found no report of sailings from the island in the years 1784 through 1787, when the impulse to migrate was dominant, although he thought that "beyond a doubt several sailed each year." The change in 1788 was dramatic: Nantucket sent out one brig and six ships. From other ports no ships at all in that year are listed. One ship from Gloucester and one from Boston made Africa voyages in the following year, when Nantucket dispatched twelve ships and eight brigs.

There is also a 1789 report of six "ships" sailing from Cape
Cod to fish for whales in the Straits of Belle Isle, but with no
record of names or tonnage. Since their average catch was very
small, they probably were sloops or schooners. Starbuck noted
that records for 1790 were not "accessible," but by 1791 the
shift at Nantucket was complete: all eight departures were
in ships, of which four rounded the Horn into the Pacific. The
Beaver was the first American whaler in that ocean, and the
Washington the first vessel to carry the American flag into a
Spanish port on the Pacific: Callao. They had been preceded
offshore by two Boston traders that conquered the Horn in
1788, headed for Nootka Sound, and by the Nantucket commander of the British whaler *Amelia* in 1789. Archilaus Ham-
mond, the *Amelia*'s Nantucket mate, struck the first whale
taken by a New Englander west of South America.

New Bedford's only recorded whaler of that year, the ship
Rebecca, of 175 tons, was the first North American whaler to
come home from the Pacific, arriving on February 21, 1793.
Throughout the first decade of whaling in the Pacific, Nantucket
with 26 recorded voyages maintained a lead over all other
American ports combined. New Bedford dispatched 18, Hudson
3, New York 2, Boston and Norwich 1 apiece. For all these voyages, ship capacity and ship rig were deemed essential.

In 1789, the strong second year of Nantucket's postwar revival,
what were her twenty ships and brigs like? With the custom-
house records long since consumed by fire, Starbuck found
tonnage figures for only three of them: two ships measuring 172
and 200 tons, and the surprising *Leo,* credited in his tabulation
with 17 voyages to the Brazils, Africa, Patagonia, and the
Pacific. Her given tonnage—217—never varies; her rig does. In
her first three whaling voyages, from a departure in 1789 to her
return in 1794, she is a brig. For the next three, 1796–1803, she
seems to have been given an extra mast and rerigged as a ship.
Then, while her tonnage measurement holds steady at 217
throughout, the *Leo* is a brig for her seventh, ninth, eleventh,
and thirteenth voyages, a ship for her eighth, tenth, twelfth, and
fourteenth. No more changes after that until she was broken up
in 1823 for her metal and for that scarce commodity on Nantucket: firewood. Such, anyhow, is the *Leo*'s essential career as
it wanders across 48 pages of columnar records in Starbuck.

Between 1794 and 1802 Nantucketers dispatched 79 ships as whalers but not a single brig, a fact seeming to indicate that in their opinion, as voyages lengthened, the relative merits of the two rigs had been settled. A brig was notoriously "tall." She got from two towers of canvas the effort that a hull of the same size under ship rig could derive from three somewhat shorter ones. It was the custom "to send the topmasts down" as any vessel neared stormy high latitudes in the South Atlantic. A brig was underpowered in these circumstances, and might find herself quite unable to bite her way into the prevailing wester-lies, against a yearlong adverse current. A ship of the same tonnage could set about 50 per cent more canvas on her lower masts. At this period she would have been carrying about five more sails than a brig, making more variations possible for any sort of weather in the elastic area between too much risk and in-efficient prudence.

A ship was not necessarily preferable to a brig for shorter voyages. Modest investors, off-island, used brigs intermittently as whalers throughout the nineteenth century. In the expansive year 1803 Nantucket herself tried them again, sending the brig-rigged *Leo* and two other brigs to fish off Patagonia while a fourth Nantucket brig tried the Cape of Good Hope. Starbuck's records, noted above, of changes in the *Leo's* rig seem upon a closer examination to support the view that a definite experi-mentation was under way. She appears, after two Pacific voyages as a ship, to have been restored to her original brig rig in 1803 for a relatively short voyage in the Atlantic. A hiatus follows, in which she may have sailed upon ventures unrecorded, but when next she turns up in Starbuck's columns she is headed for the Pacific again, in 1807, and is once more a ship. Upon her next voyage in 1808 she is a brig again; what is more curious, she is the first brig-rigged whaler from the North Atlantic ports to attempt a voyage around Cape Horn. During these changes, and more to come, she is apparently the same vessel of 217 tons measurement, sailing out of the same port, Nantucket. And yet—?

Something is evidently askew in these diligent records: according to Starbuck, the ship *Leo* that sailed in 1807 did not return into port until May 17, 1809. How could she have been rerigged as a brig again for an 1808 departure? Clearly, from

1808 to 1813, there were two *Leos*, one a ship, the other a brig, both sailing out of Nantucket in alternate years on two-year voyages. But it puts a hard stretch upon credulity to suppose that a ship and a brig of the same name, owned in the same port at the same time, would both have had exactly the same measurement. Few American brigs of the eighteenth century measured as much as 100 tons. It was not until around 1820, when carriers of all categories were sharply increasing their dimensions, that brigs of 200 tons and over began to be common. I fear that Starbuck, having found a consistent tonnage figure for the well-documented voyages of the eventual ship *Leo,* after the War of 1812, went back over his lists and supplied the same figure—217 tons—wherever the name appeared earlier in his compilation. Although he must have had clerical help in his enormous task, he was not aided by the now customary covey of nit-pursuing graduate students. A few such, with access to a kindly computer, well might program his skeletal ship biographies into it to reveal by internal evidence other confusions. I have chanced upon several. This one, over the two (possibly three) Nantucket *Leos,* has a particular importance here only because it occurs within the turn-of-century period when Nantucket owners were evidently experimenting to determine the size and rig of a whaler best suited for distant voyages in all weathers. To say this is not to suggest that a vessel of any one description was the invariable answer. Some large brigs went whaling out of New Bedford in the second decade of the twentieth century, more than twenty years after the last ship-rigged American whaler, the *James Arnold,* was sold abroad.

An opportunistic flexibility is notable. The first three of the ship *Leo's* last four voyages, all made after the peace of 1815, were spent fishing mostly off the Brazils in repopulated whaling grounds that had not been exploited during the years of hostilities. But the old foolishness—unregulated plunder of the sea's resources—repeated its effect. Her catch dwindled from 1,310 barrels in 15 months to 804 in the same period—then to 600 in 19 months. For her final adventure the *Leo* returned to the Pacific, from which, after 32 months away, she brought home 1,108 barrels of sperm. That, for Nantucket vessels, was the standard experience. Upon news of unusual prospects, schooners and brigs were taken up from time to time for short voyages of

Small vessels used as whalers by New Englanders before the Revolution probably resembled the sloop *(right)*, schooner *(lower woodcut)*, and brig *(top)* as portrayed in Falconer's contemporary marine dictionary. The brig rig evolved several variations identified in the Boston registers by the catchall term "brigantine." Together they soon superseded the sloop rig in this employment, although schooners persisted to a minor extent as whalers until the 1920's. Brigs also were popular as privateers. The *Grand Turk (below)*, a Wiscasset brig, became a famous privateer in the War of 1812. She is generally identified as the third of at least eight well-known vessels of the name. Watercolor by Anton Roux, painted at Marseilles in 1815. (See pp. 157–60.)

limited risk. But throughout the first three or four decades of the nineteenth century the small island town put most of its energies into the refining of a particular kind of full-rigged ship, intended for Pacific voyages—at first refitting the best that it could find, but toward mid-century supervising the construction of exactly what it wanted.

As it turned out, the full-rigged ship that was Nantucket's clear preference from 1788 to the end of her whaling days, and during extended periods the only kind of vessel she would consider using, was not to be preferred in the ultimate New England fleets that ranged the farthest of all. Ship rig was first chosen for driving the kind of hull that was more or less standard in commercial employments at the end of the eighteenth century. When the rush into the Pacific began, a ship was a tremendous help both in getting rapidly to and handily around Old Cape Stiff. The need for more cargo space to make extensive voyages profitable is sufficient explanation of a shift from modest brigantines to stout brigs, but for long Pacific voyages something even larger and more handy was needed, with the driving capacity to reach high southern latitudes in a hurry and the versatility to nibble its way against furious opposition around the world's most unkindly headland. The decision in favor of ship rig seems sudden in the record, but the shaping forces of wind and current that refined the Nantucket whaler began in the nearby Gulf Stream, which lured the first little sloops out past Brant Point, and extended at last into the most distant icy crannies of the earth.

For some time after the Revolution, most whalers out of New England fished off the West Indies and the Brazils, but in the last years of the 1780's their coming lunge into the Pacific was preceded by about a dozen relatively distant voyages to Woolwich Bay. No such place is indexed in John Malham's marine gazetteer, the first American edition of which was published in two volumes at about the right place and time: Boston, 1797. The name does not appear in any other such compilation that I know of, but sailors spell as they please. Under what other name might it be located? When I put the problem to Professor Virginia Close of the Dartmouth College Library, she came up after a few days with the suggestion that I glance over the October 15, 1789, issue of the Boston *Independent Chronicle*. Its marine notes include this passage:

On Saturday the 4th inst. arrived at Cape-Ann, the Brig Sea-Horse, Capt. E. Mayo, from the coast of Africa, with 800 barrels Oil. — The Captain informs, that just before he left the bay of Wilwich, in lat. 23 deg. south, a large point of land sunk more than six fathoms under water in sight of the fleet then catching Whales in that Bay; and that a number of British and American seamen who had been on shore at the same place, had very fortunately embarked on board their boats a few minutes before the land disappeared.

Woolwich and Wilwich easily convert, upon a glance at a map of the west African coast, into Walvis or Walfish Bay in 22 degrees 56 minutes south. However the skipper might spell it in his log, the harpooners with a nicer sense of etymology called it Whalefish Bay. Starbuck consistently writes Woolwich when listing 51 voyages toward that destination between 1789 and 1811. There were 14 others during the same years, cleared simply for Africa or for the Cape of Good Hope, that may have tried Walvis Bay during the voyage, and about as many more that announced an intention of rounding the cape to fish at Delago, a reference to Delagoa Bay on the Indian Ocean shore. The point of chief interest is that the number of voyages to the nearer west-coast bay dwindled as the longer ones to the cape and the Indian Ocean became more frequent. There were none to Woolwich between 1802 and 1809, and only four are listed thereafter. A new, productive ground obviously was being fished out in a hurry, forcing the whalers to move on into even more distant waters and to evolve ships suited to journeys of two years or longer.

It was best to head for the South Seas in August. The risk of a hurricane in the North Atlantic was offset by a good prospect of emerging from the southeast trades and crossing the Calms of Capricorn into the westerlies of the South Atlantic at the onset of southern spring. November weather might be merely bad, rather than ferocious, off the Horn. When the ship *Leo* returned in February, 1803, with 1,000 barrels of sperm and 500 of whale oil, she had been 18 months away and had aimed for kindly November to get into the Pacific, but had come out in the easier direction somewhat earlier than that. This is to be presumed because the third of her cargo that is listed as whale oil probably was secured off Patagonia on the way home. It early became a practice of Nantucket captains to take on a lading of sperm oil, the more valuable sort, in the Pacific—enough to trim the ship at her most comfortable stiff level in the water for driving without having her decks constantly awash in the long combers of the Southern Ocean. They would then fill up in the Atlantic with oil from right whales for the less exhilarating part of the run home.

We do not know what the *Leo's* 1,500-barrel cargo measured in gallons because "barrels" was a loose description of casks that varied in capacity. There often was an assortment of sizes in the same vessel. At outset, everything was shipped headed up in casks, including staves, heads, and rushes needed to set up somewhat smaller casks as required. These and their original containers both came home carrying the refined product. As big casks of salt horse were emptied into the smaller harness cask on deck for distribution to the messes, they too were rinsed and became available for oil. There was no foreseeable waste of material or space. The *Leo's* pumps were used not only for clearing the bilges of unwanted leakage but also for pumping water into the hold on purpose to keep the oil casks from drying out and leaking at the rush-caulked seams. The lowest tier of outward-bound empties was shipped full of Nantucket harbor water, partly for ballast, but also to keep them tight.

In the early days there was an argument over the relative merits of iron and wooden hoops. Iron made a tougher container, but it did not shrink, as the staves did, in dry air. The weaker wooden hoops shrank with the staves. Some inventories show both kinds of casks provided for the same voyage.

No oil from the Pacific entered Nantucket during 1815. Warfare for a third time had almost erased her fleet, but the town scrabbled together an unprecedented number of bottoms from somewhere and sent them whaling to make up for lost time, beginning in May. Two or three sloops had been in use shortly before and early in the conflict; 11 were rushed to the once more profitable nearer whaling grounds when peace came. Nine brigs joined them and four schooners. Nearly all of these were back in port with good cargoes before the calendar year ended. A few ships, including the *Leo,* that went as far as the Brazils, came home in the following year. In 1817 the number of ships entering was up to 25, one more than in the previous banner year—1806. Over the next five years the number of returning vessels was stable: about 18 whaleships and 10 smaller vessels a year.

THE PERFECTED WHALEBOAT

When the ship *Leo* was broken up in 1823 an elastic partnership between the carrier and its whaleboat was coming close to its climax. Reginald B. Hegarty, whose description of the building of a whaleboat in *Birth of a Whaleship* (1964) is the most lucid I have so far come upon, remarks:

Although, for their size and usefulness, whaleboats were the lightest, weakest and cheapest to build, they never the less were the most efficient boats ever built. . . . These boats seemed to have attained their degree of perfection very early in the history of New England whaling since they remained practically the same for generations. While they were perfect for whaling, they were almost useless for anything else—

The opinion was earned. Hegarty served as a very young boy in a working whaler. His father, Captain William Hegarty, between 1905 and 1913 took the big whaling brig *Sullivan,* of 344 tons, out of New England ports on three voyages that filled up between them a total of 9,690 barrels of sperm.

Scattered references to the size and structure of whaleboats suggest that the principal development had occurred before the heroic age of Nantucket's worldwide eminence began. As was true of the whaleship itself, larger sizes were later tried and abandoned. Several minor refinements were agreed upon in the middle part of the nineteenth century. But whaleboats in use when the last *Leo*'s career ended in 1823 had already reached the high level of development mentioned in Hegarty's assessment. One description of a whaleboat in action in the 1820's became well known because it appeared belatedly in print just in time for Starbuck to seize upon it as a magnificent page-long footnote for the edification of the Senate.

In 1872 a publisher invited Captain William M. Davis to "overhaul" his whaling journal and to write "of that strange life as you saw it from the forecastle and the mast-head, from the boats and the quarterdeck." In the resulting volume, *Nimrod of the Sea; or the American Whaleman,* Davis says that he has opened the "old oil-stained pages" at October 10 in the year "18—," the date of his signing articles in the bark *Chelsea* of New London for his first voyage. The story is largely told from the standpoint of a foremasthand, but there is nothing by which the intended year can be certainly pinpointed. The bark *Chelsea* made seven voyages out of New London between 1827 and 1843, the first two with a Captain Davis in command. The seeming inconsistency between his being both foremasthand and skipper on the bark's first voyage is well enough resolved in later passages: the author is concerned throughout with the general truth of an activity for which his experience provided high authority. He is not even pretending to stick to routine facts of his actual first voyage, made earlier than 1827 in another ship. Instead, he has chosen events of either the first or second *Chelsea* voyage as a unifying sequence, if only because the "old, oil-stained pages" of his journal as her skipper conveniently jogged his memory.

It is our good fortune that he also interpolated some first-voyage recollections of hazardous experiences inside the whaleboat, supplying dimensions and describing appurtenances that extend more sketchy accounts published early in the century. One or two late changes, which had come into common acceptance before his book went to press, are not mentioned, a fact that stresses the likelihood that he was epitomizing the craft brought almost as near its own perfection in the 1820's as it was ever going to come. Almost a century later it was still the choice of William Hegarty's generation, the last to go whaling in canvas-driven vessels of wood. They preferred to risk their lives in the frail, classic whaleboat long after motor-driven launches had become available and when the harpoon guns that had intrigued Fulton were not yet regarded as certainly better for their purpose than a skillful human arm.

Davis's method in this excerpt is typical of his book, a mixture of narrative event and precise description. I quote it more extensively than Starbuck did.

. . . At two miles' distance from what seemed a good whale, the boats were lowered. The activity of the men, as they sprang barefooted into the boats and cast off the davit-tackles; the readiness

with which they handled the long, heavy oar, and dropped them silently into the well-thrummed thole-mats, and the ease with which they fell into the stroke, were wonderful. Four boats were down and heading to leeward, their course divergent, so that at two miles from the ship we peaked our oars with a space of about one-third of a mile between the boats, thus commanding a reach of nearly two miles' front.

As the boats thus ride the long, rolling swell of the sea lightly and gracefully as an albatross (and I know nothing more graceful than that), let us glance at the whale-boat and its fittings. It is the fruit of a century's experience, and the sharpened sense and ingenuity of an inventive people, urged by the peril of the chase and the value of the prize. For lightness and form; for carrying capacity as compared with its weight and sea-going qualities; for speed and facility of movement at the word of command; for the placing of the men at the best advantage in the exercise of their power; by the nicest adaptation of the varying length of the oar to its position in the boat; and, lastly, for a simplicity of construction which renders repairs practicable on board the ship, the whale-boat is simply as perfect as the combined skill of the million men who have risked life and limb in service could make it. This paragon of a boat is twenty-eight feet long, sharp and clean cut as a dolphin, bow and stern swelling amidships to six feet, with a bottom round and buoyant. The gunwale amidships, twenty-two inches above the keel, rises with an accelerated curve to thirty-seven inches at each end, and this rise of bow and stern, with the clipper-like upper form, gives it a duck-like capacity to top the oncoming waves, so that it will dryly ride when ordinary boats would fill. The gunwales and keel, of the best timber, are her heaviest parts, and give stiffness to the whole; the timbers, sprung to shape, are a half-inch or three-quarters in depth, and the planking is half-inch white cedar. Her thwarts are inch pine, supported by knees of greater strength than the other timbers. The bow-oar thwart is pierced by a three-inch hole for the mast, and is double-kneed. Through the cuddy-board projects a silk hat-shaped loggerhead, for snubbing and managing the running line; the stem of the boat is deeply grooved on top, the bottom of the groove being bushed with a block of lead, or sometimes a bronze roller, and over this the line passes from the boat. Four feet of the length of the bow is covered in by a depressed box, in which the spare line, attached to harpoons, lies in carefully adjusted coils. Immediately back of the box is a thick pine plank, in which the "clumsy cleet," or knee-brace, is cut. The gunwale is pierced at proper distances for thole pins, of wood, and all sound of the working oars are muffled by well-thrummed mats, kept carefully greased, so that we can steal on our prey silent as the cavalry of the poor badgered

Lear. The planking is carefully smoothed with sand-paper, and painted. Here we have a boat which two men may lift, and which will make ten miles an hour in dead chase by the oars alone.

The equipment of the boat consists of a line-tub, in which are coiled three hundred fathoms of hemp line, with every possible precaution against kinking in the outrun; a mast and sprit-sail; five oars; the harpoon and after-oar, fourteen feet; the tub and bow-oar, sixteen feet; and the midship, eighteen feet long; so placed that the two shortest and one longest pull against the two sixteen-feet oars, which arrangement preserves the balance in the encounter when the boat is worked by four oars, the harpoon-oar being apeak. The boat is steered by an oar twenty-two feet long, which works through a grummet on the stern-post. The gear of the boat consists of two live harpoons, or those in use, and two or three span-irons, i.e., harpoons secured to the side of the boat above the thwarts, and two or three lances, secured by cords in like position, the sharp heads of all these being guarded by well-fitted, soft-wood sheaths. The harpoon is a barbed, triangular iron, very sharp on the edges, or it is a long, narrow piece of iron, sharpened only on one end, and affixed on the shank by a rivet, so placed that before use the cutting edge is on a line with the shank, but after penetrating the whale, and, on being drawn back, the movable piece drops at right angles to the shank, and forms a square toggle about six inches across the narrow wound caused by its entrance. The porpoise iron is preferred among the Arctic whalemen, as, owing to the softness of their blubber, the fluked harpoon is apt to cut its way out. The upper end of a shank, thirty inches long, terminates in a socket, into which a heavy oak or hickory sapling pole six feet long is introduced. A short piece of whale line with an eye-splice at one end is then wrapped twice around the shank below the socket and close spliced. This line is stretched with great strain, and secured to the pole with a slight seizing of rope-yarn, intended to pay away and loose the pole in a long fight. The tub-line is secured to the eye of the short line after the boat is lowered. The lance is simply an oval-headed instrument, with a cutting edge, a shank five or six feet long, and a handle as long, with a light warp to recover it. A hatchet and a sharp knife are placed in the bow-box, convenient for cutting the line, and a water-keg, fire apparatus, candles, lantern, compass, and bandages for wounds, with waif flags on poles, a fluke-spade, a boat-hook, and a "drug," or dragging float, complete the equipment of a whale-boat. Among this crowd of dangerous lines and threatening cutting gear, are six pair of legs, belonging to six skilled boatmen. Such a whale-boat is ours as she floats two miles from the ship, each man in the crew watching under the blade of his peaked oar for the rising whale, and the captain and boat-steerer standing on the highest point, carefully sweeping the horizon with trained eye to catch the first spout, and secure the chance of "getting on."

At this moment of rest, when on the point of entering a contest in which the chances of mishap seem wonderfully provided for, I found that a green hand is apt to run back over his life with something of regret always, or forward, with a half-vow that from then and there, for ever and ever, he will be a better boy. The Frenchwoman found goodness possible when she was well dressed. I found evil hateful when I was near a sperm-whale. But how one wakes up from such moralizing as the captain lightly drops from his perch, runs out his steering-oar, and lays the boat around, with the words, "Take your oars, and spring; the whale's half a mile off!" That means that we are just four minutes from the whale, provided he is not running.

It would cheer a club man's heart to watch the movements of the crew, the splendid stroke and time, the perfect feather of the oars, their silent dip on entering the foaming whirl of the lifted water, the ashen shaft working silently in the oiled mat, the poise of the crew, as the five trained athletes urge their perfect structure through the waves. Long and careful training under danger breeds a unity in the men. The five work as a single hand under the direction of him who is steering and throwing his whole standing force in the push on the after-oar. Every energy of my soul and body is centred in that bow-oar, and I do not differ from four others who share in the excitement. An occasional glance at my springing ash, the leaping little waves, and the resolute face of the captain, tell me to a fathom the position of the chase. His eyes are fixed on the rising and sinking whale; color has left his features; his pale lips are drawn tight as he sways back and forth to the stroke of the oar. He, too, is straining on, and jerks out words of command, exhortation, and promise, to urge our energies to fiercer effort.

We are coming up at killing pace. The captain, eloquent, unconscious of his words, yet with method in his frenzy, still urges us on. Now the puff of a spout joins the splash of the bow, and the old man's voice sinks to a fierce whisper as he promises all his tobacco, a share in his little farm at home, and his "lay" in the whale, as he adjures us to put him on. Human muscle can not stand the strain much longer; the boat seems as lead; boiling foam curls and bubbles around the boat's head. The old man glances almost as low as the head of the boat; a puff is heard just under the bows; my oar-blade dips in the eddying wake of the whale's last upward stroke, and right under its blade I see the broad half-moon of his flukes as we shoot across the corner of *them. Now the odor of the whale, like a bank of seaweed, comes over us. "Stand up, Ben! Pull, pull for life! Good, good! Now again! Goody Lord, give it to him!" The backward start of the boat and the upward fling of the flukes tell the rest of that story. A stroke or two astern, and we pant for breath in safety.*

There is a hint in Captain Davis's description that he is remembering the batten boat developed in the 1830's—the first considerable change in a century. James Beetle, forerunner in the family enterprise most notably associated with the manufacture of whaleboats, claimed late in life that he had "invented" the batten boat in 1833. Beetle was born in New Bedford in 1812 and grew up halfway to Nantucket, on Martha's Vineyard. He was apprenticed to William Cranston at New Bedford in 1827, where he worked in the shops of other boatbuilders until he was able to establish his own there ten years later. The traditional American boat had been of lapstrake construction, each strake of cedar slightly overlapping the one below it, fastenings driven through both. The British boat had been carvel-built, with each strake snug against the edge of the strake below. If damaged, the former was harder to repair. The latter, because it was caulked between the seams, was harder to keep in repair. Beetle solved both difficulties by producing a carvel boat that, instead of caulking, was kept watertight by battens nailed over the seams on the inside. This produced a perfectly smooth outer surface, which made less noise as it passed through the water and was easy to maintain.

Nautical conservatism worked against the acceptance of Beetle's "invention," but he reported that it was popular by 1840 and at mid-century in general use. He claimed also the invention in 1837 of a hinged mast that could be folded flat and quickly raised. Small-boat sailors who have tried to step a mast in jumpy water will appreciate the importance of this simple innovation both for getting the mast up and for getting it down again out of the way in the tense moments of the whale chase. The first Beetle whaleboat with a hinged mast was produced by another member of the family in 1840, also the year in which— according to James Beetle—an unidentified New Yorker "invented" the centerboard. This means of giving a light boat a deep keel for working smartly to windward, retractable for sailing downwind, was of course a special application of the guara boards "invented" by Peruvians long before the incursions of the Spaniards. Chapelle states that the centerboard was in use in Chesapeake Bay soon after the War of 1812. Centerboarders were not liked by the first whalemen who reported upon their use because they interfered with the traditional placing of the line tubs. A later change that provided one large and one small line tub, with the single line divided between them, solved the difficulty. Centerboards were installed in all whaleboats before 1880.

There were two other mid-century modifications. Men thrown out of capsizing whaleboats had been accustomed to seek a fingerhold on a lapped strake of the inverted boat, near the keel, while awaiting rescue. The more efficient carvel boat offered no such comfort. James Beetle consequently built the first couple of strakes, outward from the keel, in this fashion, the rest in the smooth carvel finish. A final, gradual change turned the classical round-bottomed boat, which had a midships contour that was almost the arc of a circle, into one with a flatter bottom and straighter sides. In this the whaleboat followed a change of shape that was occurring in fast larger vessels.

Late experiments were made with whaleboats almost twice the length of the 20-footer carried in the early whaling sloops, but the optimum length continued to be 28 feet, settled for around 1830. It was roomy enough to hold the increasingly intricate gear, yet light enough to be rowed with great speed by a standard six-man crew. Additional hands, in larger boats, seem, at greater expense, to have accomplished no more.

The question of weight was raised not long ago by skeptics who doubted Davis's story, commonly repeated in books on whaling, that the traditional nineteenth-century whaleboat could be lifted by two men. One of the 28-foot boats preserved on the davits of the *Charles W. Morgan* was weighed and found, dry and empty, to bring the scale needle close to 1,000 pounds. If she had absorbed the normal amount of water of a boat in use, it would have been nearer to 1,100 pounds. The yarn probably originated with the 20-foot shore-whaling prototype, which should have weighed about half as much.

In the latter 1800's, on the Alameda waterfront, across the bay from San Francisco, a neat building with lines suggesting the wharf structures of New England displayed the sign "J. C. BEETLE,

"A brig was notoriously 'tall.'" The *Laura* (*above*), built at Salem in 1818, had deep topsails and carried skysails on both masts. Such brigs, in the fair-weather belts of the Atlantic, made satisfactory whalers, but when topmasts had to be sent down for safety near Cape Horn, a brig surrendered too much of her canvas. Ship rig was safer for bucking into the Pacific. Logs kept by whalemen often have illustrations, but not many were as skillful as those drawn by Robert Weir (*below*), during his 1855–58 voyage. The best-known designers and builders of nineteenth-century whaleboats were members of the Beetle family of New Bedford. After the center of the industry had shifted to San Francisco, J. C. Beetle set up his shop (*upper right*) at Alameda. The fully developed American whaleboat (*lower right*) could be identified by three rowlocks in the starboard gunwale, balanced by two for longer oars to port. Room for a centerboard was made by dividing the whale line between a small tub and a large one. The loggerhead which snubbed it was placed aft in American boats, leaving a less cumbered bow for harpooner and lancer. (See pp. 158–59, 170–71, 174.)

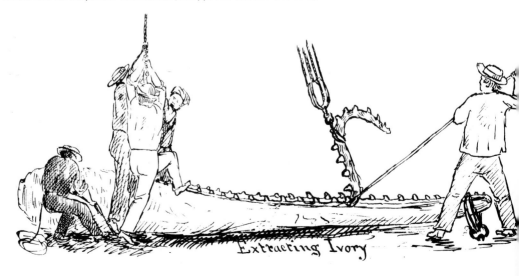

Extracting Ivory

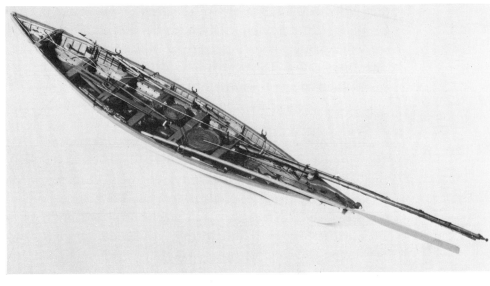

BOAT BUILDER.'' Recognizing the portent of tied-up whalers
with scores of good boats in evidence, James Clarence Beetle
had retired from the family business in 1887 and had set up
shop a couple of years later in the new center of American whaling. When the phenomenon of tied-up whalers repeated itself
in the backwaters of San Francisco Bay, the western shop wound
up its business for good, but the New England Beetles continued
to build small working craft and pleasure boats.

NANTUCKET YIELDS TO
NEW BEDFORD AND THE BARK RIG

Nantucket, complex focus of trades that maintained a vast worldwide adventure, was approaching maximum capacity as a ship-
fitting and chandlery center soon after New Bedford, in 1823,
drew even with her in both the number and the total tonnage of
her whalers. According to the usual economic wisdom, the larger
place with a better harbor, near many markets of an extensive
hinterland, should have forced a quick decline thereafter in the
isolated community's ability to compete, but the event was postponed for almost three decades. There is something bizarre about
Nantucket's persistence with her own kind of optimum whaleship because the shallowness of her harbor, and a constantly
rebuilding sandbar two miles offshore, forced the discharge of
oil casks into lighters at an exposed location where the task could
be attempted only when the winds favored it. Small brigs and
schooners could have continued to negotiate the bar, but the
town that called her chief financial institution the Pacific National Bank made little use of them.

Defying probability, the smaller isolated port from early in
the 1820's to mid-century kept about 75 whaleships at sea. About
one-third of these returned each year from lengthening voyages.
The number arriving in the relatively late year 1845 was the
highest ever, 29, and this was two decades after New Bedford
had begun to pull ahead of her island mentor. The fleet of whaleships owned in Nantucket had reached its maximum of 86 a
little earlier, in 1842; but in that year booming New Bedford
was home port to more than 200 miscellaneous whalers. In the
latter 1840's, as the New Bedford fleet continued to grow, Nantucket's declined steadily. By 1856 it had fallen to half its size
of 15 years earlier. At that point 329 whalers were registered

at New Bedford, the unsurpassed record number for any port. The Civil War was still five years away, but the little island that had invented worldwide whaling seemed to be quietly putting an end to its phenomenal adventure before being told by the large rush of history that it had to.

The 1830's in Nantucket, despite the panic of 1837, were an era of confidence and fulfillment. This was evidenced by the establishment of a marine railway and a shipyard on Brant Point capable of producing the first large whaleships. Between 1832 and 1838 four were constructed—the *Charles Carroll*, of 376 tons; the *Lexington*, of 399; the *Nantucket*, of 350; and the *Joseph Starbuck*, of 410. The first three had fairly long lives. In 1856, at age 24, the *Charles Carroll* was still whaling out of San Francisco. The careers of the others were ended by shipwreck at ages 23, 21, and 7. The fate of the largest reveals Nantucket's own fatal problem. Deep-laden with oil from her second Pacific voyage, the *Joseph Starbuck* was lost on the bar just outside her home harbor. She could have been brought safely in by the use of a novel device, "the camels," which at last had been got into readiness for just such occasions—but the storm would not wait.

In 1828, when the enterprising Nantucket *Inquirer* took up the question of hoisting laden whaleships over the shallow bar, its editor referred to something that the Dutch called camels as a proven device for the purpose: clear enough proof that at the time they were not regarded as a Nantucket invention. During more than a decade of diligent promotion, as the average size of whaleships crept closer to 400 tons, there was insufficient backing. In 1842 the camels at last were launched. William C. Macy, when he brought his grandfather Obed's 1835 history of the island up to the year 1880, described them from memory:

They resembled two immense blocks of wood . . . each block with a concave side the size of a ship . . . connected at the bottom by 15 chains, capable of bearing 800 tons. . . . These huge arrangements were easily filled with water and sunk to any required depth. The ship then sailed between the two and . . . was clasped in the embrace of the camels whose concave sides just fitted the shape of the ship. . . . fifteen chains . . . being drawn together and secured tightly, the pumping out of the 12,000 barrels of water each held, commenced. . . . as the water left, the ship and camels rose together, the whole drawing so little water that . . . a ship could be taken over the bar fully loaded.

On September 23, 1842, the *Constitution*, of 318 tons, was the first whaleship to enjoy the cozy embrace of the camels, outward bound. Some were apprehensive, but it seemed to do her no harm. She had come of age that year, having been built in 1821 for Nantucket account, designed specifically for long Pacific voyages. She brought a capacity load of sperm back to Nantucket four and a half years after her pioneer camel ride across the bar, and in 1856 was still whaling.

Three weeks after the camels had carried their first outward-bound passenger, "bells were rung, guns fired, and a great concourse of citizens greeted" the arrival of the *Peru*, 257 tons, the first whaler to be brought into their harbor by the huge catamaran. She discharged 1,340 barrels of sperm directly onto the wharf. The *Peru*, too, appears to have survived the experience unhurt. Three years older than the *Constitution*, her pioneer predecessor, she was returning from her tenth voyage out of Nantucket, her life so far having been divided about equally between the Atlantic and the Pacific fisheries. She had four Nantucket-Pacific voyages still to sail, and others out of New London and New Bedford. When Starbuck published his history in 1876, she was still at sea. It is on record in New Bedford that she again entered that port on September 1, 1881, with 1,410 barrels of sperm. She was then 62 years old.

It was the *Peru's* prophetic distinction that she had adopted, while still under Nantucket ownership, the bark rig that was to be New Bedford's principal contribution to the structure of the ultimate whaler. To a layman's eye, barks do not differ significantly from ships. Both are three-masted square-riggers. Stripped of their topmasts, for a go at Cape Horn, they become identical in the number, kind, and disposition of their remaining available sails. In the belts of friendly weather a ship could set two or three square sails above the spanker on her mizzen. A bark had no yards for mizzen square canvas, none of the numerous, intricate controlling ropes. She carried instead a triangular fore-and-aft topsail that swung with the spanker gaff and needed no attention. The area of canvas was thus reduced, by perhaps 10 per cent, but there were strong advantages. A route that would keep the trade winds astern as much as possible was important for a Pacific voyage. When studdingsails extended the mainmast's plain canvas, little thrust was gained anyhow by setting square sails on the mizzen. With the boats away, hunting, a bark would lie to, heading into the breeze. A ship was not so docile. It required fewer hands to manage a bark if a squall struck, or if it was necessary to work upwind to a distant boat to secure its catch before nightfall. The canvas on a bark's mizzen had a knack for taking care of itself.

An important change in the larger vessels' companion boats also argued for the bark rig. Prior to 1850, whaleboats used their sails mostly to return to their ship, all hands exhausted. The innovation of centerboards made it possible for them to sail part way in pursuit of distant whales. This change, with the increasing wariness of the prey, made the hunt's perimeter larger. Boats might have to be looked for in several directions, many miles apart. In doing so, the small crew left aboard could use a bark to best advantage.

The first trial of bark rig on a whaler seems to have been made out of New Bedford in 1803 for an Atlantic voyage of the *Hero.* Since the name was popular she may not have been the same *Hero* that took her departures from the same port in 1806 and 1808, rigged as a ship and listed as "belonging to Westport." In 1811 it was definitely the Westport *Hero* that sailed from her home port, rerigged as a bark.

The next voyage of a whaling bark noticed by Starbuck was that of the *Gideon,* 204 tons, which cleared from Nantucket in 1819 to fish off the Brazils; but when her owners sent her around the Horn two years later, they rerigged her as a ship. The *Gideon's* voyage of 1819 seems to be the only use of a bark out of Nantucket prior to 1832.

Beginning in 1828, and skipping only one year, New Bedford sent at least one bark out whaling every year until the First World War presented its ultimate whale-shaped peril to all merchant vessels. The number of annual sailings rose steadily: four barks in 1830, eleven in 1835, sixteen in 1840. When New Bedford owned its maximum number of assorted whalers, in 1856, 40 barks were included among the 91 whalers that put to sea. After the destruction of most of the fleet in the Civil War, 60 barks, 20 ships, and 1 schooner sailed from New Bedford in the short year following news of impending Southern surrender.

New Bedford's second bark, which took her departure 25 years after the first one, was the *Hesper,* of 261 tons. Her career em-

ntucket's problem, as one of the world's most famous ports, is dramatized in the two pictures
ove. The top one is of the shallow harbor in 1810, still barely able to accommodate modest ships
the period. The other is of the "camels" of 1842, two huge pontoons that could raise fully laden,
ger whaleships high enough to get them over the bar. The photograph at the upper left is of a
all part of New Bedford's waterfront—where there was no such problem—taken about 1880, when
ntucket whaling had ceased completely, but when booming New Bedford was about to give way
San Francisco. The perfected whaleboats celebrated by Captain William M. Davis are shown *(lower
)* off Hawaii in 1833. Our knowledge of whaling a decade later is enriched by J. Ross Browne,
ose *Etchings of a Whaling Cruise* includes the one below of the unwinding of the "blanket piece."
e pp. 158, 166–70, 175–77, 180.)

phasizes the experimentation in rigs best suited to increasingly distant whaling voyages while it displays at the same time the interchanges of management that were usual, both within and between ports. Those who held shares in any vessel for a particular voyage assigned one of their number to act as managing owner. In the brig *Hesper*'s case, the managing owner was a partnership, G. and J. J. Barney of Nantucket. In 1820 they gave her a third mast, rerigged her as a ship, and sent her out around the Horn. In 1823 J. J. Barney, without the aid of G. in her management, again sent her to the Pacific as a ship. When she returned in the spring of 1825 Peter Barney of New Bedford took over. Still as a ship, she made a short Pacific voyage—less than a year—and returned for reasons not noted with a disappointing catch. Barney transferred her to Charles W. Morgan, whose name is perpetuated at Mystic Seaport on the stern of the last existing whaleship. It was young Mr. Morgan who, after one more Pacific voyage, transformed her into a bark in 1828. He managed the *Hesper* for 12 years altogether, in which she completed four Pacific voyages for him. She made five more voyages as a bark, for three other managing owners. Dexter Jenney, her final owner, turned her into a ship again in 1859. She was condemned at Paita, Peru, in 1864, as unseaworthy.

Brig to ship to bark to ship again, but for the longest period, 31 years, the *Hesper* sailed under bark rig. The final change might mark nothing more significant than a particular captain's insistence upon having the rig to which he was accustomed. But evidence after the Civil War ran strongly against him. Nantucket had no ships left at all. Departures from New Bedford in the postwar decade attest the final triumph of the bark rig as the most adaptable for conditions in all waters, everywhere. Forty-six whaling barks but only three ships departed from New Bedford in 1875. During the decade that followed, the average for ships fell below one a year.

TRADITION AND EXPERIMENT
AT THE WHALING PORTS

In the 1830's the practice of buying sound ships for conversion into whalers was giving way before the realization that any specializing vessel should be built on purpose for its particular task. The experience of hundreds of whalers probing the Pacific resulted in refinements of both hull and rig. The islanders clung somewhat more firmly than the mainlanders to tradition, but a few Nantucketers were vigorously experimental. David Joy, managing owner of the *Peru,* was more innovative than most. He sent his schooner *Primrose* in 1834 to see if whales could profitably be taken off the coast of Mexico. In 1836 he commissioned the construction of one of the four large Brant Point whaleships, the *Charles Carroll.* He had the 32-year-old *Ganges* hauled out on Nantucket's new marine railway for a rebuilding that increased her capacity from 265 to 315 tons. The *Ganges* then went on for 17 more years as a whaler. Joy's willingness to be the first to hazard a deeply loaded ship, the *Peru,* in the new camels likewise marks the temper of the man.

The *Ganges* in 1825 had been one of three Nantucket whalers subjected to the experiment of partial sheathing in leather. All made good voyages. The only other whaleship mentioned in Starbuck as "leathered" was the *Atlas,* so treated in 1826 at New York. Copper sheathing was standard; whalers were the vessels most in need of it because of their long loitering in tropical seas.

Several works on whaling have copied Starbuck's assertion that Captain Barzillai Folger, in the same *Ganges,* struck in 1835 the "first" right whale taken off the northwest coast, opening the "Kodiah ground." As is customary, the evident priority of Eskimo whalers has been overlooked, but the claim is further in error since Starbuck himself states that the *Ganges* returned from a cruise in the Pacific under Captain Russell S. Bodfish on August 24, 1835, and sailed again under Captain Folger on October 26. She could not have approached the northwest coast until spring of the following year.

Nantucket's continuing preference for the ship rig, when most New Bedford whalers had become barks, may indicate that marginal economies were not yet crucial during two or three decades of optimum operations at the offshore port because of the self-contained organization of its crafts and trades. Joy's *Peru,* anyhow, was the only whaling bark recorded as sailing out of Nantucket prior to mid-century, with the one-voyage exception of the *Gideon* in 1819. Other specializing whaling ports throughout most of the nineteenth century sent out a variety of vessels year after year. The 1824 Nantucket fleet had been the first large one—19 in all—to be composed entirely of full-rigged ships. In the three-year period 1829–31, and again in 1840, nothing less than a ship went whaling from the island.

In this context of firm preference, David Joy made his experiments with the *Peru* in two phases. He surely knew of the seven New Bedford barks that by 1832 had sailed for the Pacific. When Joy rerigged his *Peru* as a bark, two of the seven barks out of New Bedford had already completed good voyages and were off for the Pacific again. In spite of these encouragements, Joy first tried the novel rig in two Atlantic voyages, but in each the supplies ran out long before the *Peru* had taken in a profitable quantity of oil. Joy then decided to send her to the Pacific, in 1835, but he first restored her ship rig.

Before her departure, two of New Bedford's barks had returned safely from their second Pacific voyages. Even so, Joy kept the *Peru* rigged as a ship until 1843, when, in Starbuck's phrase, she was the first homing ship "brought over the bar by the 'camels.'" It was for her outward voyage to the Pacific later in that year that David Joy again converted her into Nantucket's only bark. In the 20 years that followed she made five more Nantucket-Pacific voyages under bark rig. Joy sold her to New London in 1863. She made three voyages from that port, and two from New Bedford, all as a bark, before we come to her vanishing point upon the registry.

Even Nantucket, in the pinching years beyond mid-century, acknowledged the trend. She had a new bark of 309 tons built at Medford in 1850. Between that year and 1869 the island town dispatched 13 barks on 19 voyages. The small bark *Oak*, of 167 tons, was the last of all. She sent home 60 casks of sperm, 450 of whale, but she never came back herself. On her third year away, the last record of the *Oak* is also the last record of Nantucket whaling: "Sold at Panama 1872."

The fact that the island's whale chase, as a profitable enterprise, ended with the Civil War had no connection with the two "stone fleets" of old whalers sunk to block the channel into Charleston harbor. The 20-year-old *Potomac* was the only Nantucket ship bought for the first stone fleet, and there was none in the second. Most of the 45 whalers in the two fleets had been retired as unseaworthy in mainland ports. One had been a British store ship, captured by Yankees in the Revolution. If the stone fleets had any effect upon the future of New England whaling, it was helpful. The government paid about $135,000 for the hulks, money that should have been available for new ship-building when the war was over.

A century ago, when Nantucket's last whaler was making her final cruise, the shipowners of the island had not merely faded away. They had recognized the limitations of their shallow port and for some years had been diversifying their holdings. Many whalers sailing out of New Bedford were partly or wholly owned at Nantucket. In 1869, the year of the island port's last whaling voyage, New Bedford still was operating about half of her maximum prewar fleet: she sent out in that year 5 ships and 39 barks. Thereafter the departures of ships averaged one a year until 1892, when her last full-rigged whaler, the ship *James Arnold,* of 346 tons, headed for the Pacific.

The Origins of the Clippers

HABIT AND CONCEPT IN THE SHAPING OF SHIPS

The intermingling development of whalers and liner packets was marked by an adaptation of fast, tough ships meant only for the stormy North Atlantic to the needs of an often leisurely enterprise that voyaged all over the world. A similar but less extensive relationship was one factor in the origins of the most famous American marine product, the clipper ship. In this case also the imperative and abrupt demands of new trades put some North Atlantic liners to work, not in long, slow whaling voyages, but upon errands to waters even more distant and in an unprecedented hurry all the way. The clippers took something of their shape, along with a great deal of their characteristic manner of use, from the pilot schooners and the packets. They met superbly, if at undue cost, the imperious demands of a brief period in which steam was still only a tentative answer upon the oceans.

The vast concurrent development of steamers on the rivers of America was a response to different problems—a reminder of the extent to which the place and the circumstances of a vessel's use may warp it away from any abstract concept of hydrostatic efficiency. There is no perfect ship; there is only the best that an able builder can devise for a specific service. The men who in the same year, 1852, launched the *Eclipse* on the Mississippi and the *Sovereign of the Seas* on the Atlantic would have had to try hard to find more different forms for their purposes: the 300-foot-long saloon of the former, topped with Gothic arches, suited the desires of the river traveler of the time. There would have been no room for it in the 258-foot-long clipper, although her tonnage measurement was more than twice that of the shallow river palace.

Such bizarre divergences among contemporaries provide occasion for a glance at fundamentals of ship design and at Old World assumptions that still prevailed during much of the long period when Britain's colonies were teaching themselves the art of being independent upon the sea.

An ideal cargo carrier, defined as the least skin embracing the most space, would be a sphere—except for the fact that snugly fitting packages of freight are often rectangular. Thus, for the most efficiently stowable space within the least skin, we might select a cube. But neither sphere nor cube would be manageable when immersed partly in water and driven by wind. Our rectangular envelope for snug cargo should be elongated and reshaped so as to offer the least resistance at its forward end and create the least disturbance, or drag, aft.

Solutions to these problems, worked out in the ancient bathtub of Europe, the Mediterranean, may have been based in deliberate scientific inquiry. There is not much to go on except actual wrecks examined by underwater archaeologists. Pictorial evidence is almost useless because of deliberate conventions of stylistic distortion. Literary references distinguish "long ships" for military employments from "round ships" for trade. The problem of length-to-breadth ratio was recognized in a marked distinction between these types. Recently discovered sunken round ships, crowded with wine jars, have the lines of a bisected watermelon. They were evidently meant to sail on soundings as much as possible, where they could anchor as soon as the wind hauled against their intentions, and wait until Aeolus deigned to open a different bag.

For long ships of the Mediterranean, evidence is confused by a primary reliance upon oars: slaves were cheaper than seamen. Consequently the Viking ships, crafted with a capability for long deep-water voyages under sail, may be the best representatives of the early long ships. The lines of those recovered from Viking burials are superb, but their alleged Mediterranean origin rests upon thin conjecture. The Viking ship dug up at Gokstad, Norway, probably built about A.D. 900, is 79 feet long, 16 feet 8 inches broad, and 6 feet 8 inches deep; length-to-breadth ratio, 4.7 to 1. That is about the same as for extreme packets and early clippers. The lines of the recovered Viking ships all are similar, closely comparable to those of an 1830 whaleboat. One ancient slipway, in the harbor of Zea, suggests that the Greek galley for which it was intended had a length-to-breadth ratio of 9 to 1, but, unlike the Viking ships, it would have been chiefly dependent upon long oars.

The Portuguese, midway in the fifteenth century, joined the qualities and capacities of long and round ships into their carrack—not a weatherly vessel but one well armed for defense and capable of far voyages. Then the clumsy carrack gave way to the admirable all-purpose explorer's ship, which in the sixteenth century pierced the edges of Europe's dogmatic ignorance and opened the world to general knowledge. With a combination of square and lateen sail on three masts, she could work to windward somewhat. As Drake demonstrated, she could spend three years whacking her way around the world, endure spells of appalling weather for weeks at a time, and arrive home again in a state fit for the ceremonial visit of a monarch. Many succumbed to hazards of the sea, but so did many of the best Yankee packets. The underwater shape of such vessels as Drake's *Golden Hind* contented the average sailor so well that little was done to alter it for almost two centuries. Changes above the water line were substantial.

Long before the earliest speculative treatises on marine architecture were written, designers of ships seem to have taken it for granted that their underwater shape should resemble that of creatures living in the sea. There were important exceptions, such as the guara-balsa raft and the slab-sided flying proa of expert designers in the pre-Magellanic Pacific: products of a vivid perceptive sophistication not attained by Europeans until much later. But the close resemblance of most ship shapes to marine creatures is evident. Following custom, American colonists argued for "a codfish head and a mackerel tail." Reared in fresh circumstances, they appear to have been untouched by some remarkable advances in conceptual mathematics achieved in England in the latter seventeenth century, or by early stirrings of the scientific method. If they ever heard of Sir Isaac Newton's "solid of least resistance," the great mathematician probably bewildered them as much as he did his nearer neighbors. In Proposition 34 of his *Principia*'s Book II he noted that its demonstration "may be of use in the building of ships," but standard treatises on shipbuilding reflect Newton's solid as little as they do the rectangular theoretical cargo box discussed above. For reasons unexplained, they said that every line of a ship's hull must be an arc; wherever the radii of two adjacent arcs of the structure differed, a third arc must blend one harmoniously into the other.

Newton's solid, in the drawing that accompanies the scholium, begins as a stout ellipse. A geometrical calculation justifies the flattening of one end. A twirl of the two-dimensional figure on its axis will then describe a three-dimensional one that —the mathematician assures his readers—"will be less resisted than any other circular solid whatsoever," provided it is of "the same length and breadth." The solid in his diagram has a length-to-breadth ratio of about 4 to 3. Its flat nose is unlike that of any codfish. Its tail, far from resembling a mackerel's, is more like a codfish's face. The actual computation by which Newton proved what an early editor called "these curious Theorems" (intending something different from what we now mean by curious) is not supplied in the *Principia* at all. Some mathematicians who have since wrestled to reconstruct it conclude that it was in error. The shipbuilders seem to have agreed.

There were a few concerned theorists at the time. Sir William Petty, an ecological statistician who fizzed with ideas about America and other subjects, wrote the sketchy little *Treatise of Naval Philosophy*, which was not published until 1691, four years after his death. He argues in it for more observation of actual models to determine the best shape of a ship's bow for parting the water cleanly and of its after portion, which must bring it smoothly together at the rudder. In one of his lists of proposed experiments he includes the drawing of various objects through water "upon pullyes" to determine relative resistance. In 1662 and 1663 Petty built two modest catamarans, which he called *Invention* and *Invention II*. On December 22, 1664, he launched the more ambitious *Experiment*, a "double bottom'd" vessel designed for deep water, which he is said to have rigged as a sloop. Returning to England from Portugal in the following year, she went down in a Biscay howler that swallowed many other vessels without a trace; but the loss of a catamaran was particularly remembered and Petty did not try again until 1684, when he launched a large, double-decked catamaran, which he named *St. Michael the Archangel*. She

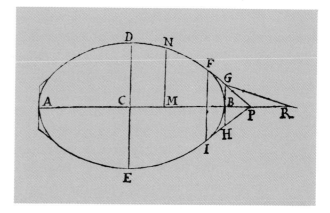

Seventeenth-century shipbuilders justified a naval architecture largely based in common sense by likening ships' lines to marine creatures *(top)*. In the 1680's Sir Isaac Newton pointedly offered them mathematical assistance with his "solid of least resistance" *(right)*, which for another century merely baffled them until 14-year-old Mark Beaufoy began a series of physical experiments that proved Newton for once in error. Beaufoy's model tank is shown below. (See pp. 187–88, 190.)

proved unmanageable. Petty's death in 1687 appears to have quelled catamaran experimentation except in the Pacific.

Newton's fame was so great that his puzzling theorem went untested for about a century. Then young Mark Beaufoy, the fourteen-year-old son of a British brewer, presumed to challenge a distinguished lecturer who had asked him to believe that a cone pulled through the water with its flat bottom forward would be met by less resistance than if it had its pointed end ahead. Using a brewhouse vat for his tank, young Mark rove a string over a "pullye," tied a cone to one end of it, with a heavy bunch of keys at the other for a counterweight to provide propulsion, and proved his authoritative elder wrong.

Some years later, chiefly between 1793 and 1798, Beaufoy methodically tested the resistance of many arbitrary forms. For a while he used a huge pendulum to swing his objects through the water, noting the diminution of its normal swing. Then he built, beside one of the basins in Greenland Dock, a tall frame within which heavy weights suspended from pulleys provided a constant lateral force for the dragging of larger models over longer distances than his pendulum could manage. Several of his "shapes" were based upon the Newtonian formula, with calculated variations. He evolved a number that were less resistant than Newton's "least" resistant proved, under the same conditions, to be.

It is a melancholy comment upon the division between the searcher for truth and the practical man of affairs in this period that Beaufoy's records were not gathered up for publication until after his death. His more important findings had been presented as papers before scientific organizations, but it was not until 1834 that his son Henry produced a sumptuous volume on his private press and distributed it without charge to institutions of higher learning, many of them in the United States.

It was by this chancy occurrence—the filial piety and benevolence of a wealthy brewer—that a scientific work of considerable consequence came within reach of American naval architects in the midst of the packet ship period. Eli Whitney Blake, an inventor who worked with the more famous uncle from whom he got part of his name, wrote a notice of the book for a leading scientific journal published at Yale College in which he characterized it as the first thorough and orderly contribution of its sort, all previous reports of such experiments having been fragmentary and intended to prove one narrow assumption—therefore dubious.

Beaufoy's tank experiments were not the only ones prior to 1800. Other experimenters, around the turn of the century, carried forward his work and began to apply some of its inferences in practical construction, chiefly of small British coasters. It was the impact of a massive publication that stirred things up: more than 9,000 experiments faithfully recorded.

JOHN WILLIS GRIFFITHS AND HIS COMPLICATED ART

If the British had been dilatory in making practical use of Mark Beaufoy's experimental method, America's even more belated shift from habitual to theoretical shipshaping seems to have been a prompt response to the generous distribution of the handsome quarto. John Willis Griffiths, a New York draftsman, was 25 years old in 1834, when Beaufoy's book became available. Within a year or two the young man began to publish articles of his own on problems of ship design. In 1841 he exhibited in New York a model embodying innovations that, taken together, constituted one of the two major influences upon the development of American clipper ships.

A practical shipowner's hunch for the solution of a local problem, about a decade earlier, provided the other strong influence. It was first tried out in five cotton packets built in 1831 for the New Orleans trade. Although they were closely similar in model, their odd differences of performance, in the uncontrollable big model tanks of the Atlantic and the Gulf of Mexico, postponed comprehension of the reason why the best of them performed so remarkably well. The reasoned challenge to conventional thought in naval architecture offered by Griffiths was greeted with willful misunderstanding, but its effects were much more promptly understood. Griffiths offered his manifesto as a radical marine architect in a long lecture delivered on September 20, 1844. It epitomized some of his previous talks, which had served mainly to demonstrate that parts of a coherent scheme can be brusquely demolished by those who do not comprehend the whole. This difficulty was referred to at the outset: "In connecting science with practice in this complicated art, my theorems must of necessity come in collision with the practice of the age. . . . The science of ship building has long been shackled with deep rooted prejudices." He then built a case concerning "the miserable failures in ship building," saying that they were "but the *index* of destiny, and will continue so to be until *guess* work is abolished from the art."

Griffiths gave himself room for some florid rhetoric. Even so, his lecture, which would have required about three hours for its delivery, is tightly constructed as a summary. I must not resubject him to the original trap of partial explication, but he made a number of points to be noted. He applauded the utility of a builder's model in solving questions of displacement and "comparative gravity" more quickly and more accurately than by pure Newtonian mathematics. "The model," he claimed, "is an American invention and a proud emblem of American genius."

Here, curiously, the challenger of "*guess* work" praises a genuine triumph of rule-of-thumb design, the Yankee "lift model," probably first used in Salem or Newburyport at about the time when Beaufoy was beginning his intensive tank experiments. The lift model, made of several longitudinal slabs of wood doweled or screwed together, could be carved to please the eye in a commonsensical way, then could be taken apart to show, by the shape of the edges of each "lift," the exact water lines of the hull at various depths. From it the dimensions could be transferred to full-size chalked lines on the mould loft floor. The usual mechanical drawings might even be dispensed with. Relatively few such American plans on paper survive from the early decades of the nineteenth century. One reason was hinted at by Griffiths when he returned to the subject in his elaborate *Treatise on Marine and Naval Architecture*, published in 1850: the lift model's "advantages were soon appreciated, and the draught was laid aside, and has at length grown obsolete."

In a magazine he later edited Griffiths published the opinion that Orlando B. Merrill (1763–1854) had invented the lift model or "slip model" at some time between 1794 and 1796, the first example being then in the possession of David Ogden of 97 Wall Street. Some assign the idea to Enos Briggs, whose model for the ketch *Eliza,* laid down at Salem in April, 1794, is preserved in the Peabody Museum of that port. Other existing models, undated, may be even older. Isaac Webb, the packet builder, was using lift models in New York around 1820. Griffiths, praising their convenience at mid-century, suggested some intricate longitudinal slicings of the lifts to facilitate more subtle calculations and comparisons, but his particular kind of genius, a rare blend of the aesthetic and the practical, could not reproduce itself. Upon a surer basis, which he did more than anyone else to construct, the mathematicians again took over. For us, the lift model retains its historical interest at least as an assured example of American priority in innovation.

Entitling one of his books, Lewis Mumford called the 1840's in America *The Golden Day.* It was a decade of expansive energies in which the profound division that resulted in the Civil War was confronted by only a few lucid moralists. Wealth increased abundantly, and with it the outward reach of commerce. An economic revolution in Britain suddenly invited the American competition it had been for so long the devoted purpose of British legislators to suppress. The consequent tussle for the world's carrying trade intensified the stress on speed, which earlier had given America's merchant marine its only chance of competing successfully against monopoly. This was the problem to which John W. Griffiths chiefly addressed himself: how to reshape the most convenient and capacious cargo box into a solid of least resistance—and how, at the same time, to translate the unpredictable energies of wind into the swiftest forward motion.

One should not look to this self-made scientific artist for a coherent technological system. In his remarkable writings he employed what he had taught himself of mathematics and hydrodynamics to justify his primary reliance upon beauty. His almost unprecedented contribution was the sense of complication in his art: a newly reasoned, concurrent reassessment of many interdependent aspects of a problem that customarily had been approached piecemeal. He has been credited with "inventing" hollow bows, but hollow lines, under water, were proposed as early as 1670 in England, on the basis of experimental evidence. They are perceivable in the plans of many

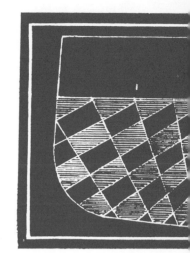

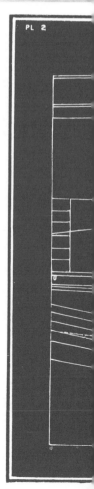

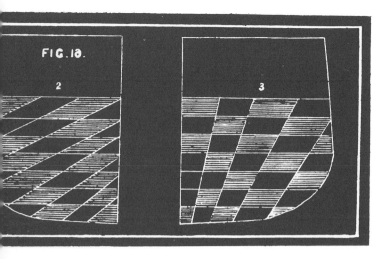

John Willis Griffiths *(below, left)* worked with devotion to establish naval architecture in the United States as a profession based in theoretical hydrostatics. He applauded the "lift model," such as the very early one of the ketch *Eliza (left)* of Salem, built in 1794, calling it an American invention that made draftsman's plans unnecessary; but he tried subtle variations *(above)* in its structure. Instead of a few flat slabs, or lifts, as in the *Eliza* model, he proposed complex cuts to aid in solving special problems. He and others continued to use plans, such as those below that demonstrate the clipper bow, an advancement in marine form for which he was chiefly responsible. (See pp. 191–93, 196–97.)

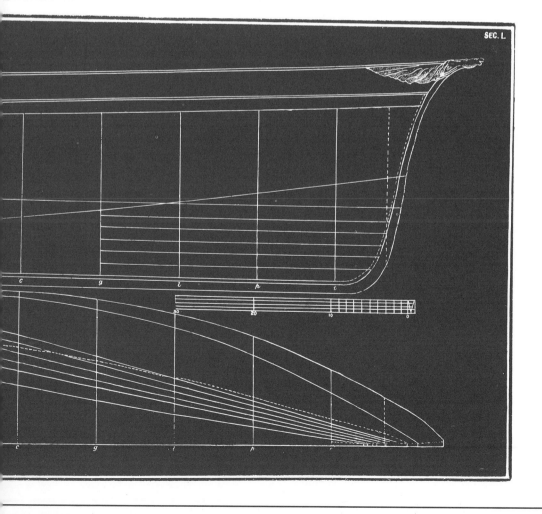

ships designed before Griffiths wrote his seminal lecture. He argued not merely for sharp, hollow water lines forward but for carrying them upward with an outward flare to join a concave stem or cutwater. This was the clipper bow—about as much of an innovation as can be claimed for any shape in the gradual evolution of shipping. His first clipper of 1844–45, the *Rainbow*, 752 tons, retained "trail boards" at her bows, timbers that formerly had helped to support a depressed structure built under the bowsprit of most ships. The last vestiges of it were eliminated in his *Sea Witch*, of 908 tons, launched December 8, 1846, the most famous ship of a phenomenal decade. In this vessel the spare, conceptual beauty upon which Griffiths insisted in his treatises (how wary we are of the word nowadays, especially the poets!) was revealed without any flourishes except a figurehead.

Griffiths's purpose, in this reshaping of the bows, was to reduce buoyancy at a point where it helped to pitch the forward end of the ship up in the air as it encountered a wave, but the outward-flaring wedge above water added more and more buoyancy as the crest of the wave rose toward deck level. Before the advent of Griffiths's clipper bow, even ships that were sharp or hollow well under the water's surface tended to smash against moderate waves. The clipper bow cut through them, keeping the vessel more nearly level, reducing the resistance.

With this change made forward, the designer realized that there must be a compensation aft. He provided it by carrying the full breadth of his cargo box somewhat farther toward the stern and by shifting the point of greatest breadth from forward of center to the actual midpoint. Having achieved in these ways greater stability, less tendency to pitch, he followed contemporary theory in giving his early ships the sharply wedge-shaped bottoms that had characterized the fast Baltimore clipper schooners.

These grown-up cousins of the little pilot schooners were prized in the nastier traffics—slaving and opium smuggling—in which a little extra speed made the difference between large profits and total loss. They were characterized by "after drag": their keels sloped downward toward the stern, the larger examples drawing as much as four feet more aft than forward.

Intended for trades in which carrying capacity was less important than velocity, the Baltimore clipper schooners (a few were ship-rigged) could afford their V-shaped bottoms if that was what made them fast. Their heyday was the 1830's, although they probably had emerged as a class, distinct from the similar pilot boats, around 1800. Their performances as privateers in the War of 1812 had given them a worldwide reputation for providing speed where speed was the primary objective. It was therefore logical enough for Griffiths to assume that a V-shaped cross section was desirable in a "Canton packet," intended as the *Rainbow* and the *Sea Witch* were to race home from China with expensive and perishable teas. The idea of after drag, however, did not comport with his carefully rationalized theories of buoyancy; Griffiths eliminated it.

His third major, interrelated alteration was in the sparring of his ships. Having revised the bow structure to slice rather than smash through a wave, he inferred that it was no longer necessary to provide so much downward leverage from the canvas on the foremast, which had helped to mute the old bluff-bowed tendency to bounce. He moved all three masts a few feet toward the stern.

When the *Rainbow* vanished, on her fifth outward voyage to China, it was easy for the wiseacres to assume that her skipper had driven her under water for want of buoyancy forward. Perhaps he did. She had been almost constantly under sail for more than three years, with the briefest pauses to discharge and stow cargo. If there was anything basically wrong with her balance, it should have shown up earlier. Other ships went missing every season, without a trace. The performance of the *Sea Witch*, built upon the same principles, was in constant evidence to offset such speculations. She made the best time ever, over segments of the ocean chosen by contemporary merchant-sportsmen for race courses: on the voyage ending March 25, 1849, she circled the world in 194 sailing days, having made the fastest direct passages from New York to Valparaiso, from Callao to China, and from China to New York. The last of these, in 74 days 14 hours was, as Carl C. Cutler remarks, "the world's first permanent sailing record."

ROBERT H. WATERMAN AND THE COTTON CARRIER

The first commander of the *Sea Witch,* Captain Robert H. Waterman, drove her as few ships have ever been driven, but even his talents could not have done anything so extraordinary in a mediocre ship. Captain Waterman had proved, in an earlier voyage home from China in 1845, that he could get phenomenal speed out of an old cotton packet, the *Natchez.* But she too was uncommonly well designed; both ships contributed importantly to the shaping of the ultimate clippers.

A deliberate change in design of five coastal packets, built concurrently in 1831 for the Louisiana and New York Line, produced the virtuous accident of marine development referred to above. Just as the bar two miles outside Nantucket harbor limited the size of vessels that could discharge their oil at the town's wharves, so the ungovernable bar at the mouth of the Mississippi had limited the size of New Orleans packet ships to about 400 tons. Of all raw materials, cotton offered the best reasons for using capacious carriers, but the ridge of particles that reestablished itself off the delta after every storm—always with a disastrous difference—dictated the maximum depth of a vessel of orthodox hull structure.

It was the traditional assumption that a ship in cross section should be somewhat kettle-shaped, to provide the best compromise between carrying capacity and stability under sail, but baled cotton—fairly light even when compressed, and rectangular—could be stowed most economically in a hull shaped like a cotton bale. With a flat bottom and vertical sides there need be no waste space. That, roughly, was the shape decided upon for the experimental cotton carriers of 1831. Their owners decided to sacrifice speed in order to lift about 30 per cent more cotton in each hull over the implacable Mississippi bar. It was a curiously confident experiment: five ships built at the same time, all more nearly like the theoretical rectangular cargo box than any sizable previous ships of which the lines are known.

The *Natchez,* which Captain Waterman would eventually take out to China, measured 130 feet 3 inches long, 29 feet 9 inches broad, and 14 feet 10 inches deep. The other four varied by only a foot or two in length, six inches or less in breadth, and three inches or less in depth. Their unusual shape was marked not only by their bale-shaped flat bottoms but also by their length-to-breadth ratio of about 4.4 to 1, which made them proportionally narrower than any other packets in existence. Their average tonnage was 523, which was the exact measurement of the *Natchez*. Extra capacity was achieved by abandoning the old kettle shape of the cross section in favor of a squat rectangle. Moreover, the flatness of the floor amidships was carried farther fore and aft than even the rounded fullness was carried in the seven more orthodox packets, all considerably smaller in measurement, built in the same year.

The risk in judging any design under uncontrollable conditions is emphasized in the performance of these closely similar flat-floored cotton packets. The largest, the first *Creole*, made a few slow passages and was promptly sold. The *Huntsville* for many years was the fastest packet on the New Orleans run, making her best passages between 1834 and 1836 under Captain Nathaniel B. Palmer, a name to remember. Only the *Sultana*, a larger vessel built 13 years later, ever turned in a better average, and that was after the *Huntsville* had become a whaler. The latter's average passage, over 13 years, was 15 days. The *Louisville* and *Nashville*, over a like period, averaged 19 and 18 days.

The *Natchez* spent only two years on the New Orleans run. Her 17-day average included a 13-day passage. It is noteworthy that the only two of these five vessels built in the same yard, thus having the best chance to be identical, stand first and fourth in average speed. These are the two that remained longest in possession of the original owners—from 1831 until 1844 and 1847.

The expansion in New York shipping had resulted in complex patterns of ownership. Length of service in a particular packet line is consequently an uncertain measure of a ship's qualities. When the owners of the *Natchez* diverted her from their cotton fleet for a voyage in the suddenly important Chilean trade, it was probably in recognition of her speed. Captain Robert H. Waterman, already a famous shipmaster in the Liverpool service, left Boston in her for Valparaiso in November, 1837, and continued as her skipper until 1846—a high compliment indeed to her merits because he could probably have had almost any ship to command that sailed out of New York in any direction.

The highly competitive packet services had dramatized the abilities of skillful officers. Passengers in a hurry chose the man together with the ship, partly because an aggressive shipmaster could be trusted to have got command of the best available ship for his own reputation's sake. Waterman would not have remained in the *Natchez* for nine years, as she shifted from one trade to another, if he had not had a very high regard for her sailing qualities. Nor would the firm of Howland and Aspinwall, her owners, have shifted her to the newly expanded China trade, in which swiftness was of first importance, if she had not been in their view an exceptional sailer. What made her exceptional was not well understood until later.

THE CHINA PACKETS

In 1842 the *Natchez* and Captain Waterman went out together on their first voyage to Canton. Trading to Valparaiso, they had had to negotiate the whaler's worst corner, Cape Horn, no place for a logy vessel to win the affection of an impetuous skipper. The China trade, rounding the Cape of Good Hope, both outward-bound and homing, offered a different kind of test. Much of the route lay in the trade-wind belts of moderate breezes that maintained a foreseeable direction all year long. A hull that could claw to windward in heavy weather was needed off the Horn. One that was responsive to light breezes was better as a Canton packet. The *Natchez*, slender for a packet but bluff in appearance, did unusually well in both environments. On their first China voyage Waterman brought her back in 92 days, next to the fastest homeward passage so far.

The following spring produced a meaningful comparison. The *Helena*, of 598 tons, built in 1841 by William H. Webb specifically for the China trade, came home in 90 days, while Waterman in the *Natchez* took four days longer. The lines of the *Helena* were a modest refinement of those of successful Liverpool packets of the thirties. Her length and breadth were within an inch of those of the *North America*, a Black Baller of about the same tonnage built a decade earlier, but the fact that the *Helena* was 4 feet 4 inches deeper was compensated for by her moderately sharp bottom and ends. Griffiths, who had had several months to consider the significance of these two performances when he went before the public, meant it when he said that even the most successful of existing ships could be substantially improved. In his first book, published six years later, he was to discuss the virtues and deficiencies of particular, named vessels. The 1844 lecture deals only with categories. For example, he doubted that any packet ship then afloat had been so shaped that she would have water lines of the same length, on the starboard and port sides, when she heeled over. He alludes to one unnamed but famous packet in which the leeward water line became eight feet longer than the windward one when she tipped at a moderate angle, with a calamitous effect upon her steering and a serious increase in friction. This was the sort of flaw that the simplest inspection of a lift model should have revealed.

Authoritative confidence is mixed with exasperation in Griffiths's lecture, perhaps because his firmly held theories could have been undergoing practical demonstration, even as he spoke, against such vessels as the *Helena* and the *Natchez*. This was not happening only because the first vessel in which he had been allowed a reasonably free hand as designer had been dawdling for many months on the stocks. Arthur H. Clark, author of *The Clipper Ship Era* (1910), suggests that this delay reflected the extreme care exercised by the builders, Smith & Dimon, over such an unusual design. Captain Clark, acquainted in his youth with builders and shipmasters who had been active in the forties, tells another story. The owners had sent to England to get the judgment of experts on the very latest concept for her spar plan. This would have ground Griffiths into the dust because abnormally long yards on masts placed well aft of the usual positions were integral features of his concept. But Clark adds that the owners, who later took great pride in the fact that the expensive English sail plan worked so well, never knew that the builders had completely ignored it.

For whatever reason, the vessel christened *Rainbow* at her launch on January 22, 1845, was delayed long enough to miss the favorable sailing season on her first voyage. The monsoons of the China Sea reverse their directions twice a year. She had to buck them both going out and coming home. Her time, 108 days to China, 102 days returning, was impressive in the circumstances, but small comfort to the impatient young ship designer. Her second voyage, however, from which she arrived home on April 18, 1846, was the fastest in elapsed time, New York to New York, ever made: 6 months 14 days. The homeward run of 84 days, in ordinary times, would have been phenomenal. But while she was making her first outward voyage against the monsoon, Captain Waterman, helped by the same wind that hindered the *Rainbow*, was driving the flat-floored old *Natchez* home, to arrive in New York on April 3, 1845, in the precedent-shattering time of 78 days: still, in the following April, the record.

These events bring together for us the two men, designer and shipmaster, who with the *Sea Witch* were to establish the clipper ship era beyond question and to define its meaning. There has been much argument over the *Rainbow*—whether she was a true clipper, a fast packet, or a transitional type. There is no argument over the *Sea Witch* as the first of the great clippers. Carl C. Cutler, a scholar who published in 1930 what is still the best history of the clippers, *Greyhounds of the Sea*, says of her:

Before her brief life had ended, the Sea Witch *had broken more records than a ship of her inches had ever broken. . . . She was the first vessel to go round the Horn to California in less than one hundred days. Twice she broke the record for speed from Canton to the United States, and neither of these passages has ever been equalled by any ship under sail.*

At the time of her launch the *Sea Witch*, of 908 tons, was the finest ship in the world for long voyages. She was the first to display a fully developed clipper bow, the visible mark of a new era. She had in moderation the V-shaped bottom that had characterized early fast-sailing design, but with much more fullness aft—both for balance and for capacity—than had been customary. Her water lines were markedly hollow. She was heavily sparred. In these aspects she represented the climax of Griffiths's early concept of form, judiciously balanced for all foreseen circumstances of the world of water. Howland and Aspinwall, the firm for which Waterman had done such wonders in the now 15-year-old *Natchez*, had ordered the *Sea Witch* particularly for him. Smith & Dimon had lavished on her their best workmanship. Her first voyage, like that of the *Rainbow*, had to be sailed against the monsoon. Waterman, who had set the bizarre 78-day in-season record as his last gesture in the *Natchez*, brought his new command home despite the opposing monsoon

American trade with China was confined for many years to transactions managed by Hong merchants at the island of Whampoa in the Pearl River, close to Canton. The system originated in an elaborate pretense that all foreigners were bringing tribute to the emperor, who graciously gave them gifts in return. After the opium wars commercial transactions were made to conform more closely to Western expectations. The picture below is of the Canton waterfront and Pearl River shipping in 1855. The *Sea Witch*, designed by John Willis Griffiths, was by far the most famous and successful of the China packets launched in the 1840's. She set records, from Hong Kong and from Canton to New York, that have not since been equaled under sail. (See pp. 196 ff.)

in almost as good time, 81 days, the quickest passage ever made in the off season.

Again the question: in the *Sea Witch* as in the *Natchez,* was the brilliant performance a measure more of the man than of the ship? We have to settle for them in combination, but the *Sea Witch* was not a mere extension of the genius of Waterman. Under later commanders she performed remarkably in contest with larger, newer clippers whose builders had profited from the example of her shape.

NATHANIEL B. PALMER AND THE FLAT FLOOR

While Griffiths, primarily a theorist, was working out ideas that culminated in the *Sea Witch,* the only feature that might explain the phenomenal performance of the old *Natchez*—even under Waterman—was being independently advocated by Captain Nathaniel B. Palmer, one of the nineteenth century's most remarkable men of action. At age 21, Palmer took a 44-ton Connecticut sloop far enough south, in search of seals, to get what was probably the first close, certain look at the long-fabled continent of Antarctica. In the *Huntsville,* a sister ship of the *Natchez,* Palmer consistently made the fastest sort of New Orleans passages. When he switched to the Dramatic Line of Liverpool packets, commanding the *Garrick* in 1837 and the *Siddons* in the two years following, he advised their owner, Edward K. Collins, to build his future ships on the flat-floored principle. One reason may have been Palmer's discovery that he could make only average transatlantic passages in the two Dramatic liners, by contrast with the very fast coastal ones he had become accustomed to in the much smaller *Huntsville.*

In 1842 Palmer made the fashionable shift to the China trade. On his homeward run of 1843 in the *Paul Jones* he took as passenger a wealthy shipowner, William H. Low, who was impressed by a model for an improved tea ship that Palmer had whittled. It turned out to be a happy concurrence of interests. Throughout the rest of his active seafaring Palmer commanded ships owned by Low, who built for him, to his whittled pattern, the 583-ton *Houqua,* launched on May 3, 1844. Her floors were not as flat as legend alleges, but they did not come together as sharply at the keel as those that Griffiths gave in the following year to his *Rainbow.* The next China packet built by Low for

Palmer was the *Samuel Russell,* said to have been rushed to completion to beat the *Sea Witch.* In all her dimensions the *Samuel Russell* was a little larger, giving her a measurement of 49 additional tons: 957. She partook a bit more of the lines of a fast Liverpool packet than her rival did, fore and aft, but there was no great difference in their degree of sharpness along the keel. Palmer had to wait a while longer for a forthright application of his chief specification for fast sailing ship design. Over the courses for which both were intended, the *Samuel Russell* did not beat the *Sea Witch,* but she made consistently fast passages during the 23 years of her operation by A. A. Low & Brother.

The convergence of these trends in naval architecture, in the latter 1840's, to produce at about the same time the not dissimilar *Sea Witch* and *Samuel Russell,* raises a temptation to look for their prompt merging thereafter in the ultimate sailing ship. But there is no ultimate model. Every altered watercraft is a hopeful response to conditions prevailing where it is to be used. We may argue from her performance that the *Sea Witch* was unsurpassed for the tea trade of mid-century, which followed a fair-weather route most of the way, yet one in which the reversing monsoons of the Indian Ocean and the South China Sea made weatherliness of great importance. If Adamastor was likely to whip up the water off the Cape of Good Hope, he almost never was as ferocious as the unnamed weather spirit who worked so malevolently off Cape Horn. A desirable tea ship, therefore, was one that could derive the best propulsion from the happy trade winds, but also do well in pounding weather farther north and south, and ride out a typhoon or a hurricane. The Atlantic packets had represented the best heavy-weather ships that could be created for the elite trade of the twenties and thirties. The newly expanded China trade made a different sort of demand upon designers of the forties. They had developed their two answers, concurrently exemplified in the *Sea Witch* and the *Samuel Russell,* when the dominant need shifted again at the wild yell "Gold!"—echoing from California.

SHIPS FOR THE GOLD RUSH: THE *CHALLENGE*

Speed, which had been highly desirable in the Canton packets, became more an imperative than ever in the rush to reach the

Nathaniel Brown Palmer (right) was one of the nineteenth century's most eminent seamen. At age 19 he was probably the first man to sight Antarctica. He championed flat-floored packets when Griffiths was advocating V-shaped bottoms. Griffiths came around to his view, as may be seen in the Griffiths design (center). At bottom, in a hurricane, is the Houqua, built by A. A. Low & Brother in 1844 for Palmer to command. (See pp. 204–5, 213.)

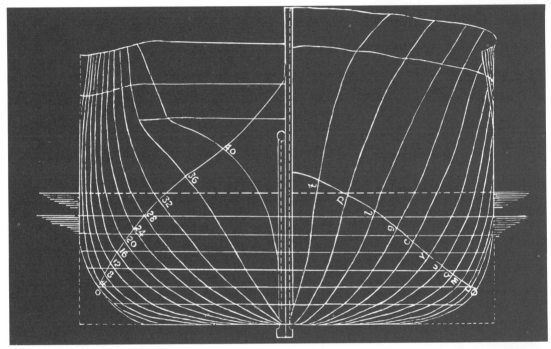

diggings before all the best claims were staked out. The shrewder merchants knew, moreover, that the richest trade would follow in goods with which to relieve the Argonauts of their new wealth.

Everything that seemed able to stay afloat pushed off for California in '49, crowded with passengers. Many regular trades were stripped of their vessels, requiring replacements. The California trade invited the prompt development of new and larger ships specifically for its own conditions—and these conditions included a shape that would not be hung up for weeks in the westerly gales and currents off the Horn. Thus the ultimate merging that might have occurred between Griffiths's and Palmer's concepts of an ideal tea clipper was never concluded because the tea voyages suddenly took on an extra dimension calling for a new modification of design. Instead of sailing out and home past Cape Town, many China packets became west-bound circumnavigators, first rounding Cape Horn into the Pacific to deliver cargoes at San Francisco, thence heading for China probably in ballast, and home again. Just at this season, changes in the British Navigation Acts provided a new option. Free trade meant that American ships could compete in the carrying traffic from China to England, which might be more profitable than the direct run home.

In 1850 the *Oriental*, of 1,003 tons, varied the gold rush habit by taking the old route eastward to China. She went out in 81 days, a new record. It so impressed British merchants on the Pearl River that they chartered her to carry their teas to London at about $10 a ton above the standard rate. Meanwhile, shipyards of the northeastern United States had responded to needs of the gold rush with unprecedented production. The California clipper as a purposeful type soon emerged. Early tea clippers had prob-ably reached their optimum size with the *Sea Witch* and the *Oriental*—900 or 1,000 tons—just as the whalers had leveled off between 300 and 400. The hungry maw of the Golden Gate called insistently for larger shipments than tea ships were designed to carry. Tea was a light cargo; California wanted heavy manu-factures. Even assembled steamboats of considerable size went out in sailing ships. The new need was for vessels at once more capacious and more weatherly to buck their way at maximum velocity over a route that included the howling unfriendliness of the Horn.

It can be mathematically demonstrated that the speed of ships of the same model increases with their size. Inertia of a larger mass irons out somewhat the pitch and wobble of heavy seas. Such factors prompted a sudden doubling in the size of fast ships for California. The *Challenge,* the second ship built to be commanded by Robert H. Waterman, measured 2,006 tons, exactly twice the tonnage of the *Oriental.*

William H. Webb has been praised for building more notably fine ships than any mid-century competitor. Most of Webb's models went a little beyond the sound orthodoxy of their day, but in the *Challenge* he seems to have lunged suddenly to outdo Griffiths, pushing to their farthest extreme the principles that had governed the great tea ship *Sea Witch.* Perhaps Waterman himself was to blame. He may have insisted upon aspects that in the smaller ship had harmonized so successfully with his personal genius as a hard-driving commander. The *Challenge* had an excessively sharp entrance. Her bottom along the keel was much more emphatically V-shaped. Her length-to-breadth ratio, 5.3 to 1, also outdid the 5 to 1 of her famous predecessor. In these aspects of her hull she was, however, the final expression of an early theory for the development of small fast ships rather than an example of a form well-suited to increasingly larger vessels.

Aloft the new ship was sparred to her commander's daring taste. He had stipulated a breadth of canvas, across her lower stu'n's'ls, of 160 feet: the sails, set for a stern wind, extended more than 58 feet on each side beyond the hull. The head of the loftiest sail was more than 200 feet above water. It was a far more heroic spread of canvas than even the most competent of Waterman's contemporaries of the quarter-deck could approve of. Each of the first three who succeeded him in command reduced the spar plan still further.

Just how sharp she was is dramatically revealed in the discrepancy between her tonnage measurement under the old and new rules. The tax law in effect when she was built assumed that all vessels of the same length, breadth, and depth could have the same number of cubic tons of cargo squeezed into them. Fine lines fore and aft consequently eliminated cargo space that was taxed anyhow. The original tonnage measurement of the *Challenge* was 46 per cent higher than the later figure based upon a close calculation of actual space available in her hold.

A Boston newspaper, sensitive to a growing rivalry between the two ports, sent its nautical specialist to New York to write what turned out to be a descriptive article conveying unrestrained enthusiasm, and more than 4,000 words long: "She is the sharpest as well as the longest sailing vessel in the world. . . . Her bow rises nobly, and although its lines are concave below, yet as they ascend they become gently modified, still preserving their angular form; and, on the rail, blend in perfect harmony with her general outline."

Between its lyrical moments the article provides scores of precise details that must have been received from the builder. Some scholars have argued that so extreme a vessel could hardly have expressed Webb's own shrewd judgment, but the Boston interviewer at the time had this to say:

The model and all the other details were left to the builder's skill, without reference to cost, the owners contracting only for the results. The Challenge, *therefore, is the embodyment of her builder's idea of the perfect in naval architecture, and his reputation is thus practically pledged for her success. That nothing might be wanting on the part of the owners, they obtained the services of the first of sailors to command her. Capt. Robt. H. Waterman, whose name is associated with the shortest passages on record from China, superintended her construction and equipment, and to his skill as a sailor, without trenching upon the province of the builder, may be attributed her completeness aloft.*

In view of this testimony, the most consistently successful American shipbuilder of the period may perhaps be granted one act of excessive experimentation amid the mad extravagances of the gold rush. Many factors outside the shipyards were knocked helter skelter by its effects. When the *Challenge* was being prepared for departure, New York was drained of experienced mariners. Crimps, brutal middlemen of the waterfront, delivered drunken crews on board at the last moment, in no condition to be judged for their competence. Most had been recruited by settling unpaid bills at their boarding houses with an advance against wages. The *Challenge* sailed with one of the worst crews ever. The tale of her mutinous first voyage has been wrangled over for more than a century. Captain Arthur H. Clark, who discussed it with Waterman himself, reports it in a fashion highly favorable to the famous commander, while admitting that he killed two mutineers with an iron belaying pin. Waterman had intended it as his last voyage before retirement in California; it proved to be the disastrous one too many. Average time for the huge fleet of forty-niners had been about 200 days. In spite of his difficulties Waterman made a very good but not great voyage in 109 days. His former command, the *Sea Witch*, under Captain George Frazer, had made it in the preceding year in 97 days—setting, as was her practice, another record, one equaled but not bettered in the following 13 months. A pilot boat, the *Fanny*, had come out from Boston in 106 days, beating the *Samuel Russell's* 109. Two months before Waterman's arrival, the *Flying Cloud* had set the 89-day mark, which has never been bettered under sail.

The first California voyage of the *Sea Witch* under a different captain largely answers any contention that her China records were a measure more of Robert H. Waterman than of his ship. Three weeks after the *Challenge* made port, the *Sea Witch* soared for a second time through the Golden Gate, still under Frazer, 111 days from Manhattan. On December 8, 1852, with a passage of 108 days, she established her three-voyage record average of 105 days. Only seven vessels at that point, out of hundreds, had been able to make a selected best passage as fast as her average for three.

The evocative name *Flying Cloud* brings us close to the apex of the clipper ship era. Those who are comforted by ultimates often have nominated her as the perfect sailing ship. When compared with her extreme contemporary the *Challenge*, Donald McKay's first miracle reveals a balanced refinement of lines excellently calculated for the California trade. This meant that she should perform superbly in all weathers, helpful or hostile—scant breezes, furious hurricanes—the best and worst offered by every ocean.

The *Challenge* can be likened to a *Sea Witch* with measurement tonnage more than doubled and with the important Griffiths departures from conventional design pressed to a dubious extreme. The *Flying Cloud* came closer to being simply an enlarged *Sea Witch*, with a little less than twice her measurement tonnage and similar lines. In this strenuous marine activity of mid-century America the early theoretical primacy of Griffiths is evident. The influence of practical shipmasters as campaigners

Clipper ship cards, distributed to mercantile houses, advertised available shipping space.

Telegraph Hill, inside the Golden Gate, is seen in the painting below covered with tents of forty-niners awaiting nails, glass, and other building materials. William H. Webb's extreme clipper *Challenge* *(Smithsonian model at the left)* was the knife-like response to a need to move such freight rapidly, even at a severe sacrifice of carrying capacity. (See pp. 205–11, 213.)

for principles of design appears strongly in Palmer. Webb was the progressive, knowledgeable, steady producer throughout the era. His own notes on surviving plans prove that some extreme features of design were insisted upon by the owners or their captains, against his judgment. His original sail plan for the *Challenge* survives. It is daring enough for most tastes, but seems commonplace by comparison with the wild one substituted by Captain Waterman as an expression of his own phenomenal self-confidence in all weathers.

Although Palmer had not been able to persuade his owners to incorporate his concept of the flat floor in a forthright way in the three moderate ships most associated with his name—the *Samuel Russell,* the *N. B. Palmer,* and the *Oriental*—the idea won general recognition soon after mid-century among builders of large, fast ocean carriers. Such extreme departures from it as the *Challenge* and the *Gazelle* of 1851—another Webb ship, probably the sharpest of the large clippers along the keel—expressed a sort of commercial cultural lag. Shipowners of the sort who had jeered at the lines of the *Rainbow* when she was being built had taken five or six prudent years to convince themselves that Griffiths's principles were producing remarkable results. Some of them began to insist upon extremely sharp bottoms when most of the clippers being built had doubled in size and no longer needed this sacrifice of cargo space for the sake of weatherliness. When Griffiths himself was commissioned in 1851 to design a clipper for owners in Hamburg he gave her a very capacious midsection and an almost flat floor, with lines fore and aft about as sharp as those of the *Sea Witch.* But in the meanwhile the heroic performances of that relatively small clipper, setting records even in the Cape Horn trade for which she was never intended, had persuaded some hardheaded businessmen to insist that her principles be applied to excess in much larger ships.

THE YACHT *AMERICA*

The schooner *America* was designed as a decently capacious, practical vessel, competent to cross the Atlantic at a brisk pace, under her own sails unaided, to the area of a contest. As such she performed a variety of useful chores for later owners. She was a fine expression of the mature New York pilot boat experience, with a sail plan much elongated from that of the Chesapeake Bay prototypes of half a century earlier. And she was considerably larger than any vessel of her day primarily intended for pilotage. By contrast with recent defenders of the cup she brought home from Cowes, she was built for a long life. The closely calculated racing machines that have succeeded her have for almost a century now been rich men's toys, good for no other purpose. The rich men who financed the *America* gave her ample living quarters below for a crew, something not to be found in recent cup defenders.

Commodore John C. Stevens, of the newly established New York Yacht Club, formed a syndicate to share the building cost: $20,000. He selected as her designer George Steers, who had produced a number of particularly successful pilot boats. At this point Steers was moving toward an essential simplicity of design. The rig of the *America* was free of gadget sails that complicated management and contributed little to a vessel's force. By comparison with the tall, spiky sails of a modern schooner yacht, made feasible by the use of wire for shrouds and stays, her canvas stretched fore and aft to a bizarre degree. Well-known pictures, notably the Currier & Ives profile, show her with the single headsail that survived the famous ghosting match around the Isle of Wight, but at the outset she wore a huge jib in addition, stretching 25 feet beyond the cap of the bowsprit on a jib boom that snapped during the race, just to prove that it was not all ghosting. The long boom of her mainsail extended an equivalent distance beyond the stern. The soaring sail plans of recent cup defenders have been no longer than the length of the deck itself.

Steers, elongating his canvas horizontally, made his plain, practical compromise with the best materials of his period. Still the rig of the jib boom proved to be basically ill-calculated. The spar carried away on later occasions: a risk of the experimental simplicity of the *America*'s rig throughout. Her light main topmast was hardly more than a flagstaff. When the elaborate canvas of cutters and other favorite British yacht rigs is considered, it seems the more curious that the English yachtsman who bought her after the race lowered her already stubby masts by five feet: a fact to remember when she is criticized for dubious performances in the races of 1852. In her famous contest she was skippered by Dick Brown, a seasoned New York pilot, who had familiarized himself for years with the characteristics of similar, if smaller, vessels. Mere survival as a New York pilot was quite a trick in itself. One reason for continuous experimentation in design was the high replacement rate of the pilot schooners smashed in equinoctial hurricanes or winter gales, sometimes with all hands lost. But the competition for business was such that the pilots held to their cruising in all weathers.

An amiable dispute between recent partisans of New York and Boston vessels extends to pilot schooners. Off-shore shoals diminish north of Cape Cod toward the deep waters of coastal Maine. This circumstance invited the use of larger, deeper vessels for Boston pilotage. Some built in the 1890's reached the dimensions of the *America*. A Boston schooner of 1896 that was given her name to perpetuate had almost her precise measurements, although different principles of design make the overall comparison deceptive. The 1851 schooner had a clipper bow and a sternpost that raked slightly forward. The stem of the 1896 schooner was almost vertical above water, but her sternpost had an excessive rake aft up to a longer overhang. Both were sharp under water. The earlier *America*'s entrance lines were hollow and her keel comparatively flat. The Boston *America*'s keel rockered upward much more sharply forward, following the practice that her designer, Thomas F. McManus, developed for his fishing schooners. McManus was a yachtsman. This may have been a reason for his interest in producing a hull that was decently comfortable to live in and also very fast: qualities of obvious interest to pilots as well as to banks fishermen. Each had to spend a lot of time bouncing around and waiting for ships to appear or dories to return with their catches, but speed was as necessary to race for the ships as to bring fish to market in good condition.

Commodore Stevens, who had attained an undervalued place in history almost 50 years earlier at the helm of the twin-screw steamer *Little Juliana*, sponsored in the *America* of 1851 a much less revolutionary craft. Whether she was in fact an example of the very best in up-to-date schooner design is an argument not likely to be resolved to the general satisfaction. What can be unquestionably documented is the shock wave that her victory at Cowes sent rudely splashing into progressive shipyards of Great Britain and the Continent. Perhaps better

The print at the right, celebrating American manufactures exhibited in London at "The Great World's Fair" of 1851, reveals the prominence with which the yacht *America* had assumed the central position in her country's attentions. Her lines *(below)* were made available to John Willis Griffiths in time for inclusion in his treatise on naval architecture that bears the date 1850. (See pp. 144, 213–15, 218.)

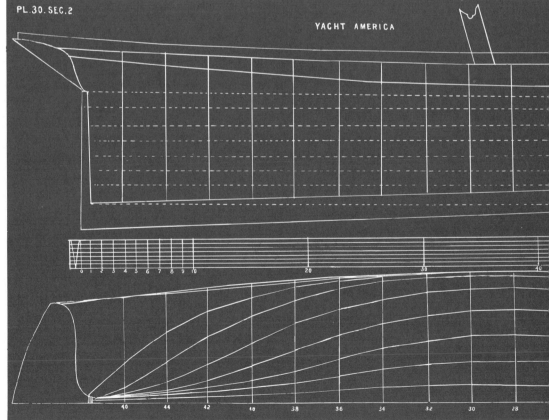

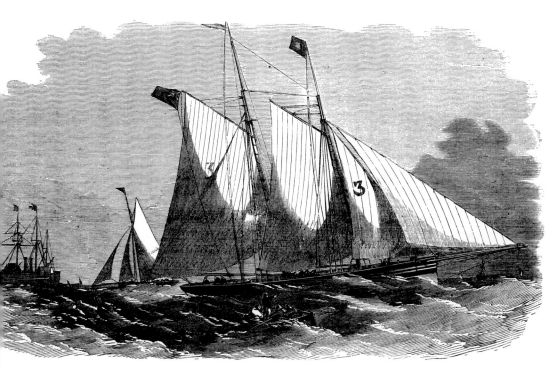

Liverpool pilot craft were cutter rigged, conservatively, until June 9, 1852, when six new ones were launched with rigs almost identical to the *America*'s. Despite the compliment to Yankee enterprise, the Liverpudlians continued to wait their turn in the channels. No racing. (See pp. 216, 218.)

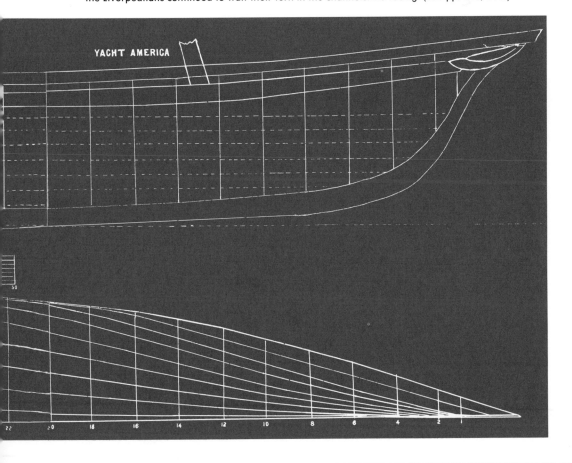

YACHT AMERICA

and certainly earlier examples of a new American tradition
in naval architecture had been given curt notice in the British
press. The yacht *America* dramatized that newness and forced
the reconsideration of basic problems of design. She had the
prompt effect of altering profoundly the lines of a new fleet of
pilot vessels for the busy port of Liverpool.

Sail or Steam?
Wood or Metal?

MATERIALS AND PROPELLANTS

Growing parliamentary support in Britain for free trade had been somewhat offset during the 1840's by a program of subsidies for British steamships in the transatlantic service. The Cunard Line was ostensibly being paid to carry the mails, but the Admiralty added a stipulation that the vessels should be suitable for naval use in wartime; consequently they must be made of wood. One outcome was a contest between wooden American sailing packets and wooden British steamships for the passenger trade. Before the decade's end it was evident that the British, using a more steadily helpful and reliable propellant than the wind, were winning. American wooden steamers were consequently projected, to be similarly subsidized as potential warships. The strategists of both armed services were convinced at the time, from experimental evidence on the firing range, that heavy, somewhat elastic wooden walls of large ships afforded a substantially better protection against cannon shot than the plates of iron thus far used in shipbuilding.

This concurrence of military belief on both sides of the ocean caused a postponement of the genuine contest that was shaping up between American timber and British iron as the basic material for shipbuilding. Many national factors added up to the circumstance that British shipyards could build iron vessels more cheaply than wooden ones, while American yards for about half a century would continue to rely upon wood as cheaper and more readily available. A separate contest of steam against sail was complicated at the same time by the use of sails on all deep-water steamers, and by intermittent experiments with auxiliary steam engines in sailing vessels.

The common idea that there was a last great victory of sail over steam in the clipper ship period does not stand up well against these complexities. If anyone was mounting a glorious ten-year stand against the upstart stinkpot, it would have been the remarkable group of self-taught theorists and inspired mechanics who produced the great American sailing ships of mid-century. But John W. Griffiths, William H. Webb, Donald McKay, Samuel Hartt Pook, like several others of marked ability, all were interested in both sail and steam as propellants. Webb even tried to challenge the subsidized Cunarders with a wooden steamer laid down in the same year as the *Sea Witch* and of twice her tonnage. Aided by his government, Cunard slashed his freight rates 50 per cent and put the Webb ship out of business because Congress was offering no equivalent help.

The chief novelty of the period was the emergence of independent naval architects who did find it possible to stand somewhat apart from the tyranny of habit in particular shipyards. Webb and McKay were designer-builders, but Griffiths and Pook were able to blend mathematical planning with tank experimentation to produce designs that were not mere attempts at refinement of the last job completed in the same yard. The contest between sail and steam was shaped, not by any preference that such naval architects might have had for one or the other, but by the current state of the art in each of these methods of propulsion. Wooden sailing ship construction had, in the Liverpool packets, been brought close to an ultimate technical excellence. The art of translating the pressure of steam into propulsion in deep water was still so unsure of itself that in some cases, when different engines were installed or when propellers were substituted for paddle wheels, coal consumption dropped by two-thirds.

Because of these wide differences in the point of development reached at mid-century by sail and by steam as propellants, it was natural that both shipowners and ship designers should rely primarily upon the more assured device for propulsion —sail—when an intense need arose for many new vessels. But it was not an exclusive reliance. The most difficult long route, to California, was recognized as strategically important by an act of Congress of March 3, 1847, authorizing a $200,000 annual subsidy for a line of steamers to carry mails by way of an over-land link at the Isthmus of Panama. The Pacific Mail Steam-ship Company was formally organized in the following year by William H. Aspinwall, who was sufficiently interested in sail to be principal owner of the *Sea Witch*. The steamers *California* and *Panama* were built for this new enterprise by William H. Webb in 1848, two or three years before he built his most notable clipper ships. The steamer *Oregon* was built for Aspinwall's line in the same year by Smith & Dimon, who had produced the *Rainbow* and the *Sea Witch*. The first three New York steamers built for the Pacific averaged 1,081 tons in meas-urement. They would undoubtedly have been larger if news of the discovery of California gold had been confirmed a few weeks sooner than it was. Later vessels for the Atlantic side reflect a response to that prospect of increased business. Smith & Dimon built in 1849 the *Georgia*, of 2,745 tons, and in 1851 the *Illinois*, of 2,123 tons.

Except on the run from New York to Panama, which includes a broad belt of chronic calms, the best sailing-ship passages were considerably faster than the fastest made by these steamers over each significant part of the route and over the total dis-tance around South America, even though the steamers could take the shorter and relatively calm route through the Strait of Magellan. But after steamers had established themselves in the Pacific, operating between the Isthmus and San Francisco, the steam route including the adventurous few miles across the Isthmus became the quicker and more reliable.

All the California steamers carried a considerable amount of sail. Most were bark-rigged, but one was a stumpy brig. The two largest were four-masters of mixed rig. All were built of wood, and Webb continued to build large wooden steamers for use in the Pacific. Three of these, the *Constitution*, the *Golden City*, and the *China*, were larger than all but one of the clippers. The largest, the *China*, of 3,836 tons, was laid down about a year after the conclusion of the Civil War. But long before that, with the increasing size of both passenger vessels and freighters, the problem of suitable material for shipbuilding had become acute, in a manner that profoundly affected the destiny of both the United States and the British Empire.

Unlike pilot boats and whalers, deep-water packets were limited in ideal size only by the passenger lists and the freight that could be built up between scheduled sailings. These factors were controlled by the number of competing vessels in the service, but the general trend well into the clipper ship era was for packets to become larger every year. Sailing packets, run on schedule, were a Yankee monopoly. Challenged by British steamers in the forties, the Americans soon lost the luxury passenger traffic but made up for it by taking on the vast human flood of the immigrant trade, which justified a further enlargement of individual ships.

As the clipper ship era crested, newly built packets had attained three or four times the size, in measurement tonnage, of those that had inaugurated the regular competitive sailings about three decades earlier. In 1853 and 1854 a few were built that measured almost 1,800 tons. Many clippers were substantially larger than that. An important mechanical question was arising: how large a structure, fit to ride out a hurricane, could be fastened together out of multitudinous sticks of wood? Large pieces made stronger structures than smaller ones, both in resistance to torsion and in a reduction of the amount of wood wounded by fastenings. But America was sensing England's ancient problem—dwindling sources of the right kind of timber. Tall trees near coastal rivers were being used up far more rapidly than new ones could grow. The difficulty, becoming acute in 1850, had been felt in some measure for half a century.

On November 23, 1798, Enos Briggs of Salem had published an advertisement addressed to "all true lovers of the Liberty of your Country . . . in possession of a White Oak Tree," urging the delivery of the timber to Salem for use in building the frigate *Essex*. "Your largest and longest trees are wanted, and the arms of them for knees and rising timber. Four trees are wanted for the keel, which all together will measure 146 feet in length, and hew 16 inches square."

Twenty years later, when the packet era began, there was hardly a white oak of such size left in any neighbor's back yard.

The shipyards of Manhattan, which acquired in the packet ship period a reputation as the world's best, had to import all their material, a factor that became so onerous after the Civil War that the center of wooden shipbuilding moved northeast-ward to Maine and Nova Scotia, where timber could still be felled and floated directly to the yards. This was the last tran-sition. The problem had been evident much earlier. John Wilkinson had been the forerunner of its solution when in 1787 he built in England an all-iron vessel of 50 tons. In 1825 the *Codorus,* of 14 tons, a curious 80-foot steamboat that drew 6½ inches, went to work on the Susquehanna River. She was strictly a homemade job—plates rolled from iron mined nearby, engine fashioned in Philadelphia. In 1828 she got her first official listing at Baltimore and was sent south for several years of useful employment on shallow rivers. But the *Codorus* was a lonely forerunner. The first thoroughly successful Amer-ican iron vessel was built for the Navy about a decade later, and not many of either iron or steel were launched until the end of the nineteenth century.

THE FORBES-ERICSSON AUXILIARIES

In a pamphlet entitled *Notes on Navigation,* Robert Bennet Forbes at the age of 80 mentioned his efforts before 1838 to sell shares in a projected twin-screw iron tugboat. "The general answer was that a tug boat was not wanted; that the propeller could not tow so well as the paddle, and finally, that an iron boat would rust out in a few years." In 1844, having made an extended commercial visit to China, followed by experimen-tation in the production of vessels specifically for the China trade, Forbes revived his earlier project for a compact but highly powered, quickly maneuverable tug to operate in deep water. Forbes at this time was the most imaginative merchant adven-turer in Boston, a friend of the great factor Houqua of Canton, of the Parsees of Hong Kong, and of the self-styled Brahmins of his own home place. In the cozy atmosphere of mutual support among groups of relatives that marked the financial assumptions of the Bostonians, Forbes had taken his time in amassing a middling fortune by age 33, when he lost nearly all of it again in the Panic of 1837. He recouped his losses in China and returned to play a significant role in the experimental 1840's —a role that paralleled, with a difference, the concurrent experimentation of Griffiths and others in New York. Forbes was interested not so much in the idea of a developing contest between sail and steam as in their supplementary applications.

The second time he tried to sell shares in a twin-screw iron steam tug he succeeded:

Mr. Otis Tufts was engaged to build the boat, and on her completion she was named "R. B. Forbes" as a punishment for my temerity in recommending such an expensive craft.

Cutler writes, "Busily engaged in laying down her lines and working out her specifications was a boy of twenty named Samuel Harte Pook. He will be heard from again." He will indeed, from writers who as a rule seem to have found it difficult to credit the true spelling of his name. In this matter Cutler, with "Harte" for "Hartt," is the least offender. Captain Hartson H. Bodfish, who will appear in a more dubious connection later on, called him "S. H. Peck" in a laudatory magazine article when Pook was still alive, and the Navy's official historians, when Samuel Hartt Pook was an officer of high rank, repeatedly confused him with his father, whose middle name was Moore. Cutler commits a more serious error in overstating Pook's age. If Forbes did add to his many other temerities the selection of a boy who actually was 17 at the time to do exacting work on a revolutionary vessel, he fails to say so at the points in his writings where he mentions the tug *R. B. Forbes*. It is possible. Pook supplied information for a biographical notice which asserts that after his apprenticeship had been completed, "under the kind guidance of his friend, Robert B. Forbes, he opened an office as a naval architect."

Forbes, a practical shipmaster of long experience as well as a far-ranging businessman, had enlisted for the production of two earlier steamers with wooden hulls the Swedish immigrant John Ericsson, another of the many famous men who chose on purpose to be Americans. One of these vessels had twin screws, but both were essentially sailing craft with engines of modest power. The combination of Forbes, Ericsson, Tufts, and perhaps Pook produced in the *R. B. Forbes* the first thoroughly successful American iron steamship, capable not only of independent operation on the ocean in all weathers under steam alone, but able also under such conditions to contribute the better part of her strength to a larger vessel in tow. Her specifications, dated July 13, 1844, provided for several water-tight bulkheads. Despite the early uneasiness of some of her owners, she was for 15 years a boon to ships entering and leaving Boston; she performed many successful salvage operations on the adjacent stern and rock-bound coast. Forbes's insistence upon two screws instead of two paddle wheels was the great difference that accounted for her variety of successes. In ocean waves, paddle wheels tended to lift clear of the water as the vessel rolled, losing power and putting a strain on the machinery.

Captain Arthur H. Clark has an affectionate description of her in *The Clipper Ship Era*:

Her hull was painted a brilliant red up to the bulwarks, which were black, while the deck fittings, houses, and the inside of the bulwarks were a bright green. Altogether, with a rainbow of bunting over her mastheads, the brass band in full blast, and champagne corks flying about her deck, she contributed liberally to the gayety of many festive occasions. She was also usually the first to introduce a new-born ship to the end of a manila hawser, and for several years she towed most of the eastern-built clippers to their loading berths at Boston or New York.

But these were only the odd jobs at which she put in her time when not engaged in her more serious work of salvage operations, for she was the best equipped and most powerful wrecking steamer on the Atlantic coast, and saved much valuable property abandoned to the underwriters.

Henry Hall, who has credited only Ericsson with the design of this vessel, implies that the *R. B. Forbes* was the first screw tug of any sort in America, but notes that at the beginning of the year in which she was projected 42 American vessels had been equipped with screw propellers, many times the number then in use in British waters. Whether he counted the *Little Juliana* does not appear. Forbes was not the first to risk an investment in screw propulsion, despite his claim that he tried to assemble investors in a twin-screw iron tug almost a decade before he succeeded in doing so. He does appear to have produced, even at the end of that long delay, the first sizable prototype of the metal, twin-screw steamer that in the long run was to supplant wooden hulls, paddlewheels, and sails.

Forbes was a blithe and handsome man who emerged from

The transitions from sail to steam and from wood to metal did not reflect a sharp division between partisans. Captain Robert Bennet Forbes *(lower right),* an eminent plank-and-canvas seaman, argued in the middle 1830's for a twin-stack, twin-screw iron tug. When launched at last in 1844, she was named by other owners the *R. B. Forbes (below).* William H. Webb, who later built famous sailing ships, produced in 1848 the Pacific Mail Steamship *California,* a side-wheeler, whose owners also held shares in the clipper *Sea Witch.* Forbes chose the Navy's sailing ship *Jamestown (right)* for his dash in 1847 with donations of food to relieve the Irish famine. (See pp. 221, 224–25, 228–32, 253–55.)

a sickly childhood into great vigor. He seems to have taken generosity for granted in the ordering of his life. In a brief review of his activities, midway in his autobiography, he writes:

Beginning in 1817, with a capital consisting of a Testament, a "Bowditch," a quadrant, a chest of sea clothes, and my mother's blessing, I left the paternal mansion full of hope and good resolutions, and the promise of support from my uncles. At the age of sixteen, I filled a man's place as third mate; at the age of twenty, I was promoted to a command; at the age of twenty-six, I commanded my own ship; at twenty-eight, I abandoned the sea as a profession; at thirty-six, I was head of the largest American house in China. . . . from 1817 to 1832 . . . my first thought was to form for myself a character for my future capital. . . . When, however, I had fully established my mother in her new house (1833), had seen John fairly embarked in business with good prospects, I began to dream of an establishment for myself. . . .

In 1826, when Forbes was a young shipmaster of 22, he chanced to encounter in a Peruvian port "several American whalers; among them a ship,—the 'Commodore Perry,' I think,—whose bottom was covered with leather, and she was very foul." It seems that the briefly tested expedient was no substitute for copper. The *Commodore Perry* was in the Pacific at the time, but she is not identified in Starbuck as leathered. Forbes in his old age perhaps was recalling the *Kingston*, commanded by a Captain Perry, which was leather-bottomed and was also somewhere west of South America at the time.

It is not clear in Forbes's "List of Vessels Built under my Order or Supervision, or in which I have had an Interest" which ones actually profited from his supervisory skills. Of the 20 launched prior to 1843, the *Ariel,* a schooner of 100 tons, seems to be the only one in which he made a substantial alteration. The terse note in his "List" reads merely, "Model by Joe Lee, for himself and me; went to China." It seems unlikely that she would have got to China at all under her original spar plan, which Forbes described as "altogether forbidding to my eye." Lee said, "Try her and if you can capsize her I will give you my head for a football." On her second trial run out of Boston harbor Forbes did capsize her without much trying. Lee kept his head but agreed to cut six feet off the masts and step them two feet farther aft. She then made an extremely fast passage out to China and became one of the two notorious opium runners of her name.

In the list appended to his autobiography and also in his *Notes on Navigation* Forbes dates the earliest of his steamers as having been built in 1841. This vessel, the *Midas*, of 180 tons, has a historical interest both for her rig and for her auxiliary power. It is consequently important to correct a slip of the author's memory—particularly because the date is followed without question by later writers. In the 1884 pamphlet there is internal evidence that it was a slip: Forbes says, "Failing to drown Captain Poor in the 'Ariel,' I built in 1841, a schooner the 'Midas,' fitted her with twin screws and machinery designed by Ericsson, and dispatched her for China under Captain Poor." But Poor had already taken the *Ariel* of 1842 out to China and had come home again in another vessel before his assignment as the first master of the *Midas*.

Late in the 1830's Ericsson had begun to experiment with screws strengthened by a hoop of metal around the tips of the inner blades, usually with a larger number of blades sprouting outward from these rims. The propellers that he designed for the *Midas* had four inner blades and five outer ones, I suppose on the theory that there was more water to deal with outside the periphery. In his autobiography Forbes says that the *Midas* sailed from New York for China on November 4, 1844, on what was clearly her first commercial voyage, "with her wheels shipped." This meant that both propellers were on their shafts, ready for use. It was, Forbes comments, "a fatal error." They could be "ungeared" so that their shafts would merely spin free when the engines were not in use. Under such conditions the vessel once sailed 230 nautical miles in a day. But the boilers were seldom fired on the passage out to China, and corrosion was at work all the way. Her machinery when she arrived was in a sad state, a fact that appears to have been kept in confidence, because the *Chinese Repository*, in its issue of May, 1845, gave her a cheery welcome:

The American steamer Midas, *captain Poor, arrived in Hongkong on the 21st instant. She is moved by propellers, and seems admirably adapted for the Canton river. Fitted up with proper accommodations, and running daily between Canton and Hongkong,*

she will greatly facilitate the intercommunication, and would,
we should think, liberally remunerate her owners.

The services of the *Midas* in China have been deprecated,
even by Forbes himself, but she evidently was tinkered into
adequate running order. Contemporary port records for the
China coast indicate that she made something less than the
forecast daily runs on the Canton River between Hong Kong
at its mouth and Whampoa, the island settlement for foreigners
on the edge of Canton. For almost a year she made two such
runs a week with time between for some salvage operations.
On April 5, 1846, she cleared from Hong Kong for Manila and
is entered as having returned on June 1. On July 28 she cleared
from Canton for Shanghai, and again on August 18 cleared from
Hong Kong for the same port. On November 1, 1846, she sailed
from Canton for Rio de Janeiro with her propellers unshipped—
stowed in the hold. When she reached New York her machinery
was removed and she began a useful second career as a sailing
vessel under different owners. She deserves something better
of history than the mere usual notice that she was the first
American steamer to quit the Atlantic for an Asian port.

The Ericsson Papers indicate that the inventor was involved
with eight steamers during the years 1844 and 1845, one of
them referred to as the "188 ton twin screw propeller" *Midas.*
There is nothing in any of the accounts to suggest that she
spent three years on the stocks in Hall's shipyard. Thus the
limiting date of her departure from New York indicates that
the first American steamer in the orient seas was begun and
finished not in 1841, but in 1844.

In his reminiscences Forbes declares that he "purchased some
experience in steam" by investing in this first attempt and
consequently improved the second auxiliary steamer he promoted, the *Edith.* Like the *Midas,* she was produced in Samuel
Hall's East Boston yard, with propulsive mechanisms below
decks designed by Ericsson and those aloft specified by Forbes
himself. The "experience" to which he referred could hardly
have been transmitted by sea letter in time actually to influence
the design of the other vessel, since she was launched within
a few weeks of the *Midas's* departure from New York, but the
shakedown cruise from Boston to that port may have suggested

last-minute alterations in the *Edith*—a vessel named after Forbes's daughter and variously recorded as of 400, 407, and 450 tons. She thus had two or three times the capacity of the *Midas,* which was listed as of 148, 180, 186, and 188 tons.

Instead of twin screws, free to spin and ruin their bearings when sails alone powered the vessel, Ericsson provided the *Edith* with a single large screw. The shaft ran slightly off center, to port of the sternpost. Its end was keyed to receive a propeller carried on a separate arm affixed to another shaft parallel to the powered one and several feet above it. By a geared mechanism inside the hull the upper shaft could be turned 180 degrees so as to swing the propeller up against the ship's stern, well above the water line, or drop it to a position exactly aft of the drive shaft. When the screw was thus positioned under water, the upper shaft could be hauled a few inches forward, pulling the hub of the propeller to a locking position on the keyed end of the powered shaft. The propeller ran aft of the rudder, which was slotted to keep it from encountering the shaft when the helm was put over to starboard.

On her first trial run the *Edith* made a top speed of 9.8 statute miles an hour. Ericsson had guaranteed 7 and was well pleased. He wrote that his "patent invention for unshipping the propeller" worked in a "most gratifying" way. The *Edith* sailed for British India to compete in the opium trade only ten weeks after the departure of the *Midas* for China. Thus the changes that Forbes recollected as having been "purchased" by his costly experience with the smaller vessel probably reflected Ericsson's own constant experimentation. Between one ship and the next, he always had something new to try.

The third of the Forbes-Ericsson auxiliaries, and the largest, is foreshadowed in a note sent by Ericsson to his lawyer soon after the *Edith* sailed for Bombay:

In confidence, *our Boston friends have about made up their minds to build at once a large packet with my auxiliary propeller for the Atlantic. I am almost crazy with joy in consequence.*

This was to be the *Massachusetts,* of 750 tons, powered in the same fashion as the *Edith;* but in the case of the *Massachusetts,* Ericsson abandoned the hoop that had distinguished his former propellers and provided something closer to the kind pioneered

by Stevens between 1802 and 1806, which has since become
conventional in sizable vessels.

Like many other marine innovations, the screw propeller had
to wait a long time for circumstances that would reveal its
merits. Ericsson solved the problem of inadequate power not
with the curious forms his propellers sometimes took but by
the development of faster engines. When he is credited, as he
is by Hall, with the design of an entire vessel, it should be borne
in mind that he took a highly prudent measure to make certain
that the effects of the two kinds of power on the same hull could
be fairly demonstrated. His biographer, William Conant Church,
makes the point. Ericsson "built his ships precisely on the
model of sailing vessels of the first class." The performance
of a ship equipped with a screw that could be hoisted up out of
the way was thus made purely competitive with what the same
vessel could do under sail. Such precautions were necessary.
An absurd prejudice had developed against screw propulsion,
especially in the Navy, which needed it most.

It is ironic that the armed services eventually chartered, then
purchased, not only the R. B. Forbes but also the Edith and the
Massachusetts, propeller-driven vessels financed through the
imaginative persistence of a private citizen and engineered by
Ericsson at the very time when the Navy was haughtily turning
down his persistent offers to build for the government directly.
There was of course a reason.

An eminent American naval officer, perceiving forceful
originality in the work being done in England by Ericsson,
persuaded him to come to the United States to design machinery
for and oversee construction of a recently authorized large
fighting ship. The result was the U.S.S. Princeton, the world's
first deep-water naval steamer that was not cumbered with a
pair of suicidally attractive targets, outboard paddle wheels;
the first also, being screw driven, that could have its vulnerable
boilers and machinery entirely below the water line.

Claims made for the British Rattler do not withstand inspection. She was begun sooner, but as a side-wheeler. While she
was being built she was converted to screw propulsion and
launched after the Princeton. Thus the American vessel, designed by a Swede, was the first fighting ship planned for screw
propulsion and the first of the sort to be launched.

Ericsson, independently, had been experimenting with heavy naval guns. The *Princeton* mounted two unprecedented giants of 12-inch bore, supplemented by a conventional battery. One of the two 12-inch guns had been manufactured for Ericsson in England. The other was an American imitation, heavier around its powder chamber but of inferior metal. It burst during a first ceremonial cruise, killing the Secretary of State and the Secretary of the Navy. A responsibility-fixing hassle followed, of the sort that only hierarchical organizations can produce. Irrationally, since the gun was not even of his design, it deprived the Navy of the foremost marine engineer in America. Ericsson then turned to private shipowners, who handsomely sustained him. Forbes was the most adventurous of these; he was the organizer of several risk-sharing groups to finance not only auxiliary steamers for long voyages but the *Iron Witch* as well, a 614-ton Hudson River steamer designed to travel at more than 20 miles an hour.

The *Massachusetts,* launched to the illumination of sheet lightning in the midwatch of the nautical day that began at noon on July 22, 1845, was intended by Forbes and his fellow investors as an answer to the most vexatious problem of the Atlantic packet lines—the frequent experience of a fast passage from soundings to soundings, marred by several days of beating about or waiting for a wind to get clear of the land in the first place and into port at last. The design of her hull is credited in U.S. Navy records to Forbes and E. H. Delano.

The *Massachusetts* was not meant to compete as a steady steamer. A letter from Forbes, published shortly after her launch, declared that her owners did not look for "steamboat speed *except under canvas,* her steam power . . . is intended, *as a general rule,* to be used only in calms, or against moderate head winds; *occasionally* when near land." Her stack seems to have been an innovation. Ericsson had fitted the *Princeton* with a telescoping stack, but he gave the *Massachusetts* a simpler device, one that hinged at the base (like James Beetle's mast for a whaleboat) and so could be folded down parallel with the deck, out of the way of the rigging and sails.

Two months were spent in fitting her out at New York, where her machinery had been built under Ericsson's supervision. Although Forbes later wrote that he had planned to use her "for

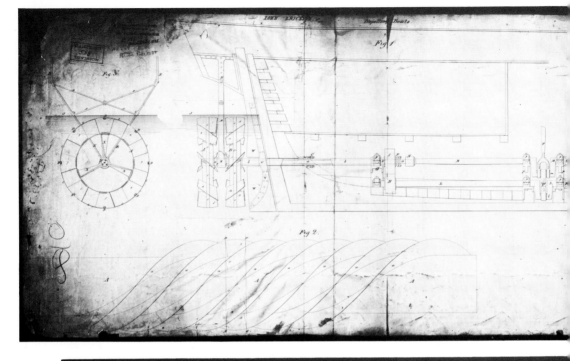

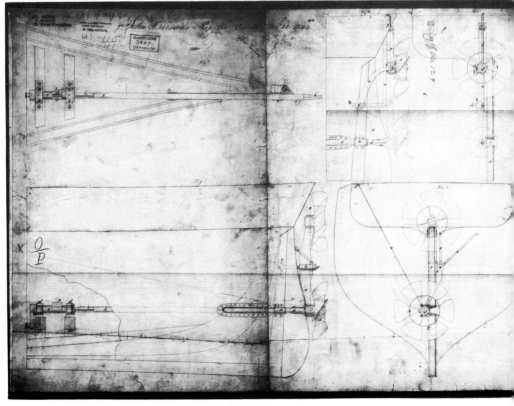

John Ericsson painfully rediscovered the merits of simplicity for screw propulsion. His 1838 patent *(left, above)* had two screws in tandem, turned in opposite directions, the solid shaft of one turning the hollow shaft of the other. His hoistable propeller *(lower left)*, patented in 1844, was used in R. B. Forbes's *Massachusetts (lower right)*. Forbes's *Midas (above)* had two Ericsson hooped screws. The Smithsonian model of the *Massachusetts (below, with detail)* shows one, although Ericsson's chief biographer says that the hooped screw was first discarded in her. (See pp. 228–29, 230–31.)

a pioneer to a line of auxiliary steam packets to run from Boston to Liverpool," she began her first commercial voyage by steaming out of New York harbor on September 16, 1845, toward the same British destination. Her elapsed time, 17½ days, was better than the best ever achieved by all but a few sailing packets on their lucky passages.

A reporter for the *Illustrated London News* called her "the most extraordinary vessel, as a specimen of consummate engineering skill, that ever crossed the Atlantic. . . . Her screw is of a novel construction; it can be drawn completely out of the water at pleasure, by a most simple process, and placed in a perpendicular position against the stern; and, in such circumstances the *Massachusetts* is, to all intents and purposes, a sail vessel." The reporter's eye was equally taken by novelties of her rig.

Perhaps it should be noted that the *Massachusetts* got to sea just in time to miss the first homecoming of Griffiths's *Rainbow*—a vessel within two tons of the same measurement and strongly expressive of the parallel experimentation toward ultimate development of sail alone. As it turned out, the *Rainbow* was a notable advancement in a process for which great splendors and more than half a century of usefulness lay ahead; while the Forbes-Griffiths auxiliaries were experiments of the sort that give a nudge to the future in more closely defining what is feasible by demonstrating their own shortcomings. John Endicott Gardner, a publicist much concerned with shipping, contributed a piece in 1849 to Hunt's *Merchants' Magazine* in which he remarked:

Errickson's plan of one propeller abaft the rudder, and having an arm to it to hoist it up to the stern when disconnected, as in the Massachusetts and Edith, can only work decently in smooth water; . . . in rough water, it would not work at all.

Forbes in his mellow years, after the issue had been long decided, admitted that, "the rough Atlantic requiring full power," there had never been any real prospect of success for the idea of auxiliary steam upon which he had hazarded with Ericsson so much of his money and effort. When he wrote, however, that idea was already being revised for a different purpose in Arctic whalers.

The *Isaac Newton (above)* was named after her New York builder, not after the mathematician. Billed upon her launch in 1848 as "the largest in the new or old world," she had 39-foot paddle wheels. Since she was intended for the deep Hudson, she had little to fear from the terrible "sawyers" and other snags that ripped out the bottoms of many steamers on shallow midland rivers. Snag boats such as the *A. H. Sevier* were developed in the later 1820's, largely by Henry Shreve, to remove such menaces. The *A. H. Sevier* was sunk by a sawyer during her first year of use. James B. Eads, who later built the Pook turtles, contributed to the improvement of snag boats. (See pp. 239, 335–36.)

Huge paddle wheels, as in the *Empire City* and *Bay State (above)*, made docking difficult. John Ericsson unsuccessfully tried small, high-speed paddle wheels in his *Iron Witch*, then side propellers. Renamed the *Erie (below)*, she ended up with conventional big wheels. (See pp. 239–40.)

The wide-ranging list of Forbes-Ericsson ventures included, in 1846, the *Iron Witch* and the little propeller-driven *Firefly*, of 20 tons, sent out to China as freight in a sailing ship and later carried in the same fashion to booming San Francisco. The *Iron Witch* was Ericsson's attempt to provide adequate power in a river steamer without a further increase in the already gigantic dimensions of its machinery. He sought compactness with small paddle wheels driven by fast engines, hoping by this combination to go a step beyond the big conventional side-wheelers, such as the new *Isaac Newton*, of 1,332 tons, which had wheels 39 feet in diameter. She made 20 miles an hour with them, but they were so wide that they created serious docking problems. With competition producing larger vessels every year in all categories, Ericsson decided that wheels five or six storeys high were not the only possible answer. When his small, high-speed paddles produced only 17 miles per hour, he removed them and substituted a pair of side propellers amidships, but these did not improve the speed.

Experimenting with many such novel concepts, he had important successes that could have been arrived at only by this method of trial and error. The three Forbes-Ericsson steam auxiliaries also turned out to be errors in the specific competitive services for which they were intended—compromises of the sort that sacrifice more of some virtues than they gain in others— but two of them later served the Navy well in a fashion possible with none of its existing ships. Off Vera Cruz the economic balance sheet was not the test. General Winfield Scott added his bit to a traditional strain between the services by ignoring regular naval vessels and choosing the chartered *Massachusetts* as his flagship.

The *Iron Witch* was the only metal-hulled vessel in use on the New York and Albany run until 1880. Her career with small paddle wheels and side propellers was brief. Renamed the *Erie*, she was given conventional machinery and diverted to the task of carrying passengers between New York City and a pier near Nyack, the eastern terminus of the newly opened Erie Railroad. An 1851 woodcut in *Gleason's Pictorial and Drawing Room Companion* shows her with the usual lofty paddle boxes of the period. Ericsson's impulse to reduce the size of these excrescences can be appreciated from a glance at such contemporary portrayals

as one of the same year in the *Illustrated London News* introduc-
ing its startled subscribers to the American coastal steamers
Bay State and *Empire City,* with an admission that the 40-foot
paddle wheels of the former were not as large as those used on
the Hudson. In this dubious contest the *Isaac Newton,* advertised
in 1846 as the biggest steamer "in the new or old world," had
been outclassed within a year.

When Robert Bennet Forbes was compensating for his government's crass boycott of the talented Swedish immigrant, the
source of Ericsson's great fame, his prototype monitor, lay about
15 years in the future. Naval authorizations for Ericsson's work
on the *Princeton* and on the *Monitor* were issued 20 years apart,
almost to the day—and even at the end of this period (1841–61),
the problems of technical adaptation of steam power to hull
structure were not yet well understood. The record of one remarkable group of naval steamers, built hastily in 1861, will be
examined a little later. It indicates that orthodox wooden hulls
could be driven by steam in a fashion highly reliable and predictable, while the experimental *Monitor,* laid down at the same
time, was a transient device delivered only by luck and heroism
to the waters where it was desperately needed. Along the way
it had been in constant peril of flooding and had almost cooked
its engineers. Monitors were prophetic sections of larger ships
not yet conceived of. As soon as "Timby turrets" were placed
on hulls of adequate dimensions, monitors were obsolete. It was
a wild bit of historical luck that Ericsson's *Monitor,* a truly
original concept, was less faulty in construction than the hastily
reconceived *Virginia,* her first opponent, which was converted
from the captured orthodox steam frigate *Merrimack.* The point
is that events seldom give a sufficient warning to the inventive
mind, which produces what it can with what it has. In this
comparison of two parallel trends in nautical development
during the 1840's and 1850's, the developers of engines, of propellers, and of iron hulls were much less sure of their relatively
new applied technology than the sailing ship men were of their
ancient craft and art.

It is curious that R. B. Forbes, while he was generously en-
couraging the engine builder through seasons when he most
needed such faith, equipped three of their joint productions
with innovations aloft for the use of wind power that proved

A vast change in the structures and stuff of fighting ships pivoted upon the Civil War. It is dramatized in the conversion of the captured U.S.S. *Merrimack*, a wooden sailing steamer, into the ironclad C.S.S *Virginia (lower picture)*, which fought a famous stand-off battle with the all-iron U.S.S. *Monitor*: the first fight for each. (See p. 240.)

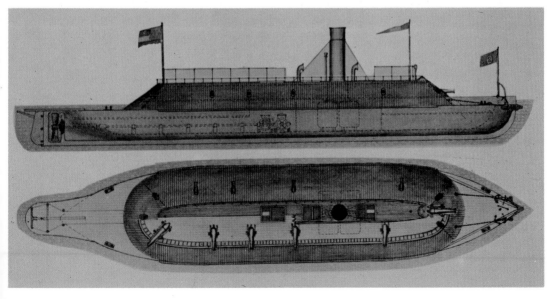

throughout three-quarters of a century to be much more important to ocean carriers than Ericsson's novel mechanisms in the same three hulls. The competitive edge, throughout the long twilight of commercial sail, quite literally was provided by the relatively simple idea of double topsails—a device first made practical, and first widely championed, by Forbes.

DOUBLE TOPSAILS

A persistent increase in the size of sailing ships during the packet era, with no basic alteration in the concept of their rig, produced the corollary of larger and larger individual sails. How did it happen that the small topsails of Columbus's day, and the modest ones set by Drake, continued to grow disproportionately until they were larger, in many early-nineteenth-century ships, than the "main" sails above which they were located? Topsails were fighting sails, in armed merchantmen as well as in naval vessels. That probably was the significant reason. It was best to get the lower sails all out of the way while "clearing the decks." Otherwise, shot that missed the men mangled the canvas. To maneuver briskly, any ship that might have to fight was given topsails of a size to drive her by themselves. They continued to be standard for three or four decades of the generally peaceful period that followed the settlement of the Napoleonic wars.

It was the increasingly deep topsails of the Western Ocean packets, more than anything else, that got them in the late thirties their reputation as brutal mankillers. Each of the three topsails of a modest packet at that time contained more than 3,000 square feet of heavy canvas. Imagine the task of handling a frozen wet rug, measuring about 50 by 60 feet, high aloft in a hammering winter gale, with only an icy footrope to stand on. Yet when the increase of the tempest made this area of sail too great, the only way to reduce it was to haul the buffeted stuff up to the yard and secure a part of it there with a multitude of also frozen reef points. Usually there was the choice of single, double, or triple reefing. Occasionally, as in the *Harald's* main topsail, there were four reef bands. Almost the worst of it was the call to shake a reef out again if the wind lessened a little a few minutes after the agonizing task was completed. The highly competitive packets were driven night and day close to the edge of disaster to their spars and rigging.

The size of the usual sails had been controlled somewhat by superimposing new ones on taller masts. To the mainsails and topsails of the early explorer's ship, topgallants, royals, and skysails had been progressively added—with an occasional even loftier skyscraper or moonraker—but still the topsails grew. The seemingly simple answer, to divide them in half laterally and have the option of setting only one of the two resulting sails, must have occurred to many sailors. The weight aloft of an additional yard and the complexity of all the duplicated gear to manage it were valid objections, but the chief resistance to change was the ancient, obdurate indifference of shipowners and shipmasters to the suffering of foremasthands. Seamen were obviously better off in the 1830's than a hundred years earlier, when ships for long voyages were manned on the calculation that half the crew would die of scurvy and other occupational hazards. Still, it was more probably the prospect of making do with fewer seamen to pay, rather than any humanitarian concern, that finally persuaded the owners and officers of ships that double topsails would sweeten the balance sheet with a little harmless compassion into the bargain.

Whether Robert Bennet Forbes "invented" double topsails is a matter of definition. Forbes's rig included mechanical innovations, the most important being an arrangement for controlling the upper topsail and its yard from deck level, quickly, instead of sending several men aloft to shorten sail. Forbes rigged his upper topsail yard so that ropes belayed on the customary pinrails could be slacked to drop it to a position close to and parallel with the lower topsail yard, thus causing the entire upper topsail to droop, in the lee of the lower topsail. The effective size of an old topsail occupying the same space was thus reduced by 50 per cent. The equivalent of the slow, difficult task of close reefing was achieved in seconds with a great economy of manpower. The "reef" could be "shaken out" and the full power of both sails restored merely by hoisting the upper topsail yard to its former position.

Claims for the several "inventors" of double topsails have been argued through many issues of the British historical quarterly *The Mariner's Mirror,* beginning in its very first appearance in January of 1911. A scanning of queries and confident answers affords a wholesome exposure to the traps into which one can stumble when marine pictures have been misdated by forgery

Deep topsails could be endearing to the artist's eye, as in Robert Salmon's 1829 oil, "The Wh
of Boston" *(upper right)*, but as late as 1866, when the woodcut at the right was published, they
still in many ships a cruel horror to foremasthands. One reason for their bizarre overgrowth ap
in the lithograph *(below)* of Perry's 1813 victory on Lake Erie. They were fighting sails, made
enough for brisk maneuvers when the "main" sails were brailed up in an action. The *Harald* of
(above) had four main topsail reef bands to "shorten" sail. Half a century later, double topsa
in the *Warner* of 1851 *(lower right)*, made the task quick and easy. (See pp. 242–43, 400.)

or honest zeal. Different vessels carried the same name on their sterns. At least ten well-remembered ships have borne the name of Forbes's fourth steamer, the *Massachusetts*. New York's favorite China packet, the *Sea Witch*, had been in the water less than two years when the Blackwall opium runner *Sea Witch* was launched and promptly diverted to the tea races. Smaller and less sharp, she nevertheless made several brisk passages out of ports on the South China Sea — an invitation to confusion with Griffiths's famous tea ship.

The case has many parallels, some arising when accurate pictures were painted of ships after they had been rerigged. Where no painting date appears, it has been the innocent practice of museums to assign the known date of the ship's launching. During the 1850's many old ships were rerigged with double topsails. Late pictures of them consequently have been cited to "prove" that the rig was in use at the time of their construction. That is the reason why the launching date of the Forbes-Ericsson *Midas* has historical consequence insofar as such technicalities matter at all. Forbes repeatedly identified the *Midas* as the first vessel to carry his rig. In a pamphlet issued in 1849 he wrote:

The rig, which I call mine, is entirely original, so far as I know, with me. It is true I have seen a ship in Boston harbor with two yards and sails on an ordinary foretopmast, and that was something like mine; and there are several ships in the East India seas fitted with similar sails and yards, but not arranged like mine, and having no symmetry, as I am told, for I have not seen them.

Griffiths, discussing in 1855 "improvements of the past twelve years," said that the rig "first introduced by Mr. Forbes in 1844 . . . Stands foremost on the list." The first issue of Forbes's own pamphlet, *A New Rig for Ships and Other Vessels, Combining Economy, Safety and Convenience*, carries the printed date 1844, the year in which Ericsson certainly installed the *Midas's* machinery.

In his late *Notes* Forbes said that the *Midas* "was rigged as a top-sail schooner, with her topmasts fidded abaft, and double topsails, the first of that rig built by me." A model that he probably made himself may be seen at the Peabody Museum in Salem. A footnote in his *Personal Reminiscences* refers to it as being, in 1876, "at the rooms of the Massachusetts Historical Society," from which there is a record of his having borrowed it at least once in connection with a public lecture.

The *Midas*, as a schooner, had square sails only on her foremast. Forbes progressively tried his rig out afterward on vessels with two and three masts for square sail. The second use of it, again above steam machinery by Ericsson, was in the auxiliary bark *Edith*. Two paintings, now at the United States Naval Academy, show the *Edith* carefully posed in different kinds of weather so as to display her two unusual features: hoistable propeller and double topsails. In one painting she is headed toward the left on the starboard tack, under all plain sail, close hauled. The main in consequence eclipses the stack completely, but the propeller in its swung-up position on the starboard side exhibits one blade under the counter in this profile view from off the port side.

The other painting shows her in brisker weather, steaming in the opposite direction with the help of courses and lower topsails only. It meticulously exposes the "doublings" of the topmasts "fidded abaft"—that is to say, the long overlap of the two spars. Ordinarily the topmast was fastened forward of the mainmast, overlapping a quarter of the lower spar's length above deck. For the Forbes rig the lower masts were taller to begin with, and the minimum overlap was about a third. The fittings of the topmasts were so fashioned as to permit them to drop still further and be hoisted again with little effort. The second *Edith* painting shows that when the skipper chose his option of "housing" his topmasts—as Forbes put it—hardly a fifth of their length extended above the caps of the tall lower masts. This was a much less arduous procedure than to send down the topmasts completely, as the whalers did upon approaching the weather off the Horn. It had the enormous advantage of allowing them to be hoisted into the usual position in minutes instead of the hours required to reinstall and rerig ordinary topmasts.

Forbes made much of this feature in another of his pamphlets, *The Forbes Rig*, printed in the second year of the Civil War. Noting that only one small naval vessel, the *John Hancock*, had been fitted with his rig, he elaborated its advantages particularly for a blockader:

*. . . if she sends down topmasts and lower yards, she is in no
condition to guard the port. With the new rig she can hold on
longer, and, when obliged to get under way, will be comparatively safe. While the new rig is a necessity in our short-manned
merchant-ships, it is hardly less so in a man-of-war.*

His main argument concerned the ability of a blockade-runner,
in an enterprise where unusual risks were normal, to crowd
on full sail and slide past the guardian vessel in much less than
the time it took even a large naval crew to get the upper spars
in place and the sails drawing. When the weather was bad, the
ideal blockader had to have all his sails bent all the time, ready
to be sheeted home for a chase. The blockade-runner, on the
other hand, needed to crowd on canvas in dangerous weather
only as he hove in sight, approaching the forbidden port. The
blockader thus had the disadvantage of trying to maintain his
canvas in a perilous state of readiness. Forbes had developed a
cogent answer to a chronic difficulty, but the Navy was unwilling to be instructed, for its own good, by a civilian.

The 1862 pamphlet concludes with the admission, "It certainly looks odd to see masts fidded abaft; but this want of
symmetry is a mere trifle compared to the manifold advantages
of the new rig." The pamphlet was probably an attempt to revive
interest in his version of the double topsail arrangement, which
had been challenged in the meanwhile by at least two strong
competing systems, both of which achieved their major purposes without offending the eye of nautical orthodoxy and without sacrificing lower masts of the usual dimensions to taller
ones. The one persisting advantage of the Forbes rig, after about
a decade during which the others had become standard, was its
provision for keeping the topmasts "housed" during bad storms
but quickly available. This was a point of not much interest
to merchant mariners, considering the extra trouble and cost
of the conversion, but it should have interested the Navy.

The long controversy in *The Mariner's Mirror* was overlooked
by the British historian Harold A. Underhill, whose works on
the details of rigging are even so the best we have. He fixes the
introduction of double topsails in 1853, although Forbes's use
of them nine years earlier was noticed in prominent British
journals. The *Illustrated London News*, when it welcomed the
Massachusetts to Liverpool with great praise for her appur-

tenances as a steamer, expressed fascination as well with her novel arrangements aloft:

She is . . . ship rigged, with a few exceptions, the most striking being, that her top masts are fidded abaft the mast. The lower masts are also unusually tall. . . . The sails and rigging abound in the most curious contrivances to ease the labour of reefing, shortening sail, &c., perhaps the first instance in which modern machinery has been carried aloft.

The actual first vessel with modern machinery aloft, the *Midas*, at this point had been at sea for about a year.

Early in 1851 the same popular weekly carried a description of the new British steamship *Iberia*, which had been fitted with "Cunningham's patent topsail":

The sail can be close-reefed in heavy weather by one man and a boy, in two seconds and a half—an operation which otherwise would occupy at least half an hour, and require many men.

This independently developed British rig may have been the occasion for a letter addressed by Forbes to the *Nautical Magazine and Naval Chronicle,* explaining the advantages of his own rig. He admitted the "unsightliness of the doublings," but pointed to merits that outweighed "small objections." In this magazine, distributed worldwide from London, he claimed that his rig had been used on three steamers and several sailing vessels, naming examples. It had been tried on all three auxiliary steamers more than a year before he first tried it on a pure sailing ship, the *Samoset,* of 734 tons, built by Samuel Hall at East Boston in 1847.

The *Samoset* had the odd task of carrying on deck to California in 1849 the *Mint,* an iron paddle-wheel steamer belonging partly to Forbes. Space was made to accommodate the *Mint* only by breaking a hole in her bottom through which to step the *Samoset*'s foremast. The steamer's machinery was designed by Ericsson.

The second vessel Forbes mentioned in the *Nautical Magazine* was Donald McKay's first Cape Horner, the *Reindeer,* of 806 tons, launched in 1849. The third was the relatively full-modeled *Lantao,* 593 tons, a China packet launched by Hall in the same year; the fourth was the phenomenal *Race Horse.*

It is clear, then, that the Forbes rig had been tested in a variety of vessels and had been adequately described in the press of both

The bark-rigged auxiliary steamer *Edith*, built for Captain Robert Bennet Forbes in 1844, was the first vessel to carry his double-topsail rig on more than one mast. The overlong "doublings," which allowed the topmasts to be dropped aft of the lower masts promptly in bad weather, may be seen in the carefully posed picture of her above, as well as in that of Forbes's much larger *Meteor (below)*, built 21 years later. The latter picture and that of the *Edith* at the top right show Forbes's double topsails at work. Many captains objected to "topmasts fidded aft," so Forbes supplied a more conventional rig—still with long doublings—for the *Lantao (lower right)*, built in 1849. (See pp. 242–49.)

America and England—over a period of six or seven years—when
Captain William Frederick Howes of Brewster, Massachusetts,
evolved his simplified arrangement to fulfill the same purpose.
Several fine skippers named Howes or Howe were active in this
period—an invitation to error that has been frequently seized
upon. One ship of unusual historical interest, the *Three Brothers,*
was jointly owned by George, Henry, and Jabez Howes, at least
two of whom have been wrongly credited with the invention of
her Howes rig.

The right Howes redesigned the double topsail rig in such a
way that it could be adapted to the customary masts. An extra
yard with special forgings was about all that was needed, with
some rope, blocks, and belaying pins. But Howes's rig and Cunningham's both lacked what Forbes with his taller lower masts
had provided for—the means of temporarily housing topmasts
in heavy weather.

Underhill seems to have had in mind the clipper ship *Climax,*
of 1,051 tons, laid down at Medford under supervision of her
publicist skipper, W. F. Howes. She was completed early in 1853,
carrying double topsails of his own design. In an era when the
America's contest off Cowes was a minor side show beside the
great races of clippers to California, Howes with his *Climax*
challenged another brand-new Medford clipper, the *Competitor,*
skippered, to compound the confusion, by Moses Howes, Jr. The
Competitor was the smaller by 180 tons, but she carried twice
as many foremasthands. When the two vessels sailed a dead heat
in 115 days, Captain William Frederick Howes lost no chances
to emphasize that he had sailed with only 14 men and 2 boys.
He promptly swallowed the anchor and devoted his energies
thereafter to the installation of Howes's patent rig on other
men's ships.

Forbes had faced the issue of monopoly four years earlier:

*It will be asked by some, why I am so desirous of recommending
this peculiar rig to merchants and seamen,—having no patent,
and no desire for one, I can expect no pecuniary advantage;
true, but I wish to introduce it for the reason that I believe it
will go far to reduce the risk and labor and anxiety of sailors,
and the losses of underwriters. . . . I shall be happy to furnish
plans of spars and sails, in my rough style, to any who may wish
to adopt the rig, without any charge therefor. I shall feel well*

*compensated for the labor in the reflection that I have done
something to lessen the hardships of sailors.*

While the *Climax* was running her shrewdly calculated
race, "the largest and strongest ship ever built," McKay's *Great
Republic,* was taking shape in East Boston, an experimental
vessel in more ways than hugeness alone. She is of special
interest here because, just before Howes completed his demonstration of the merits possessed by his particular rig, she was
equipped with Forbes's double topsails on conventionally
fidded topmasts; but when rebuilt a year later, after a fire that
destroyed most of her structure above water, she was given
fore- and mainmasts 17 feet shorter than before, with the suddenly popular topsail rig of Howes.

It may be that the well-tested merits of Forbes's rig were
what made it seem possible for McKay even to contemplate a
vessel that was not only the largest and strongest to date, as
Gleason's Pictorial pointed out when she was launched, but
larger by a heroic margin than any preceding clipper—a jump
in measurement of more than 2,000 tons. McKay's own *Sovereign of the Seas,* whose building he had had to finance entirely by himself the preceding year (she was regarded as much
too large to be practical), had less than two-thirds the tonnage
of the *Great Republic;* yet her sail plan required a crew of
more than 100 men. Even with double topsails, the *Great
Republic* was going to need 120, and they were to be given the
assistance of a 15-horsepower engine nicknamed the Steam
Tar to power winches for hauling rigging and ground tackle
as well as for hoisting cargo. The Steam Tar could also be
transferred into a longboat and used to tow the ship in a calm.

The iron tug *R. B. Forbes* had confounded gloomy predictions
by failing to rust her bottom out in a hurry. Nine years old,
she was assigned to haul a ship of 15 times her tonnage from
East Boston to New York to take in cargo. The *Great Republic,*
riding far too high in the water to set much canvas, did try
out her topsails during the journey and tugged the tug part
way. She never had a real chance, under Forbes's rig, to exhibit
her sailing qualities.

Griffiths noted that more ships had been fitted with Forbes's
rig in 1854 than ever before. Admitting that Howes's rig was

well liked and cheaper, he wrote that Forbes's was worth the extra first cost. But Howes, in the years of panic that followed, quickly prevailed. The competitive edge, in the long twilight of merchant sail, quite literally was provided by his simplification of Forbes's device for eliminating the necessity of sending large numbers of skilled men so frequently aloft.

There is a kind of grace note to the story of Forbes and his rig. In 1847, the year of its first trial on a vessel with no auxiliary power, the Irish famine that was to have a profound eventual effect upon the political life of Massachusetts produced a particularly spirited response of sympathy and aid in that state. Although the divisive Mexican War was still unsettled, Forbes and some of his friends by a special act of Congress got the use of the U.S. ship sloop *Jamestown*, of 985 tons, to rush a cargo of relief supplies to Cork. Despite the uneasiness of his wife, who believed that he had retired from the hazards of command, Forbes donated his services as skipper, thus completing the 100 per cent charitable aspect of the enterprise. His old friend Captain Joseph C. Delano warned him on Saint Patrick's Day—in case he had forgotten in the coziness of retirement—that the tail end of March was the very worst time in the year to sail for the British Isles. Delano's 20 years under the Swallowtail house flags gave his opinion great authority. In 1830 he had made the 16-day westward passage in the *Columbia*, which was not bettered on the uphill run until 1846. But the Irish were dying. Forbes made his way out of the harbor so impetuously that he even refused to heave to when the moment came for dropping the pilot. A delegation of well-wishers was pacing him in the controversial steam tug that bore his name. Forbes ordered the *R. B. Forbes* under the *Jamestown's* counter and advised the pilot to grab a rope's end and jump.

Captain Delano had estimated that the voyage would, to judge by his own experience, require 30 days. On the second day, in a cabin awash with ice water, Forbes made these entries in his journal:

March 29. . . . Set all studding sails. . . . The number of effective men to go aloft, including one mate, 31; sick, lame and blind 4. . . . much of the time we had single reefs in the topsails, with topgallant sails over them, all of which would have been unnecessary had the ship been rigged after my plan.

His ingenuity cropped up in other ways during the voyage. On April 2 he wrote:

Necessity being the mother of invention, I devised a method of partially warming my cabin, by suspending a grapnel and keeping on it four 32 lbs. shot heated in the galley.

One day he logged 265 miles in a crossing that required less than 15 days, with no serious calamities until his arrival off the Cove of Cork, where the pilot stove his port quarter gallery in running alongside and promptly demanded indemnity for his own damages.

Having completed his errand of mercy in half the time forecast by his experienced friend, and in a vessel normally operated by a large crew of disciplined enlisted men, Forbes made a last grumpy comment: "If she had the double topsail rig, I think we should have saved at least two days."

THE PUZZLE OF DONALD McKAY

If all competitors are eliminated, Donald McKay can be justly credited with having produced a somewhat delayed American clipper ship era all by himself. A larger number of individually famous clippers were launched from his East Boston yard than from any other. There are a dozen reasonably well verified instances when sailing ships have attained a speed of 18 knots or over; nine of these were recorded aboard ships built by McKay, including the two fastest—of 22 and 21 knots.

Out of 14 occasions when similarly verifiable day's runs of 400 miles and over have been logged under sail, 10 are credited to McKay clippers. These include the greatest of all, 465 miles. When the 26 records are scanned together, five McKay ships appear in both categories—fastest rate and highest day's run. The *Great Republic* scores once in each, the *Sovereign of the Seas* and *Champion of the Seas* both appear twice in the first list and once in the second. The *James Baines* is entered once in the first list and three times in the second; and the *Lightning* is the most impressive—she turns up twice in the first and three times in the second category.

Only two other ships were able to set such records more than once. A bizarre Canadian vessel, the *Marco Polo,* makes a single appearance on each list. Pook's *Red Jacket* is registered twice on the second one.

The Southworth and Hawes daguerreotype of Donald McKay *(above)* suggests a new medium's artistic power to define character: a sense of competence and of dogged assurance that could produce the *Great Republic (upper right)*, by far the largest merchantman of her time. The particular view of her, painted by James E. Buttersworth for a Currier lithograph, probably was meant to emphasize Robert Bennet Forbes's revised double topsail rig, with long doublings of the forward-fidded topmasts. McKay's *Chariot of Fame (right)* was a sturdy medium clipper of 1853 that made fast passages on the run from Liverpool to Melbourne under conventional topsails. (See pp. 253, 255, 260–61.)

Despite this phenomenal pre-eminence of his products, McKay has been sharply criticized by some professionals, particularly by the naval architect William Armstrong Fairburn who—in praising William H. Webb as a designer-builder of varied and continuing accomplishments over a long period —wrote by contrast:

Donald McKay, with a sort of fanatical frenzy and a blind belief in his infallibility, drove straight ahead to his doom —with extravagance, poor judgment, and a defiance of the dictates of common sense and the laws of cause and effect and of compensation.

Such conflicting elements appear, nevertheless, in the quality of greatness that in many other eminent men has produced vast accomplishments and ultimate downfall, chiefly because the use of their best talents was urgently needed in a period of transient and peculiar stress. McKay's abilities answered at its apex the phenomenal needs of such a period: the clipper ship era. When it was suddenly over, he found it difficult to conform again, as he had begun by doing, to the orthodoxies of supply and demand.

McKay, a year younger than Griffiths, was one of the many eminent citizens of the United States who chose their nationality on purpose. The son of a poor Nova Scotia farmer, he was indentured in 1827 to Isaac Webb, New York's most eminent shipbuilder. At 21 he was employed by Brown & Bell when they had the famous Black Baller *North America* on the stocks. Thereafter he took a curiously methodical route toward his eventual fame. At a time when excellence and innovation in shipbuilding had gained worldwide primacy for New York City, he left it in 1840 for Newburyport to work as master builder for another man. In 1844 he was able to move to East Boston when it seemed likely that the scanty and sporadic packet service between Boston, Liverpool, and London would be reorganized on the pattern of the New York lines. The Forbes project of auxiliary steam packets had a contemporary counterpart in Enoch Train's White Diamond Line, which after a shaky start became moderately prosperous, aided by nine ships built for it between 1844 and 1853 by Donald McKay. Train evidently encouraged McKay to re-establish himself

close to the heart of New England's maritime activity, and
the reliable performance of McKay's packets helped Train to
compete with the Cunard steamers as well as with the sailing
packets out of New York. Oliver Wendell Holmes, in a burst
of regressive mockery, was soon to allude to Boston's state
house as the Hub of the Solar System, but America's primary
early port had long been overshadowed by the booming focus
of most transatlantic traffic at the mouth of the Hudson. Ter-
rain was a factor: there was no such great Massachusetts river
for the easy dispersal inland of large cargoes. Railroads were
already moderating this disadvantage in the 1840's, but the
suddenness of achievement in several Massachusetts shipyards at mid-century suggests that complacency, and the cozy
familic structure of commercial endeavor, had for some decades
previous been blunting a competitive edge kept keener at New
York.

In a biography of his grandfather, Richard McKay says that
the shipbuilder tried hard to convince the Bostonians that
they should let him follow principles being developed at New
York but was balked by their preference for sensible capacity
at the expense of speed. A comparison between the last packet
Donald McKay built before dissolving his Newburyport partnership and the first he launched at East Boston—both in
1844—bears this statement out. The *John R. Skiddy*, ordered
for the New York Swallowtail Line, was 50 per cent larger
than the *Joshua Bates*, first of nine ships built for Train. This
merely reflected conditions of traffic at the two ports, but a
significant distinction appears in their length-to-breadth
ratios. That of the New York ship built earlier was 4.94 to 1,
the highest to date and probably not exceeded in any packet
built anywhere before 1850. McKay's next ship, for the Boston
owner, had a 4.6 to 1 ratio, a bit venturesome for the place
and date but already standard among New Yorkers.

In 1846 New York ordered the *New World*, of 1,404 tons,
which on September 9 gave McKay the first of his many launchings of "the largest merchant ship in the world."

A year later Enoch Train lunged dramatically beyond the
caution that so far had kept all Boston ships well below the
1,000-ton level, ordering from McKay the *Ocean Monarch*,
of 1,301 tons, which for three years was to be the only Boston

packet measuring more than 1,000 tons. By that date New
York had 18 of at least that size; but only four of these were
larger than Boston's lonely giant.

The strength and sailing qualities of the *John R. Skiddy* had
received at the outset a merciless test: on her maiden voyage she
was steered precisely through the eye of a hurricane. If her skipper had paid proper attention to a passage on the Law of Storms
recently inserted into his Bowditch he would have known how
to keep out of the swirl of greatest violence surrounding the quiet
eye. His naive description of two frightful buffetings, just before
and just after an inexplicable period of dead calm, reveals that
he had no idea of a hurricane's structure or of the new sailing
directions for using a circular storm's own power to steer away
from its vortex.

No-one has seriously questioned McKay's steady achievement
as a superb master builder. Fairburn says, "The McKay clippers
did not win any honors for longevity nor for sturdiness of build,"
but the figures he quotes to demonstrate this are puzzling.
Noting that it was not the builder's fault if some of his vessels
were burned or wrecked, he claims that their average service was
"less than twelve years." Yet, of the 16 that enter into his calculation, all but 2 were burned, lost, or wrecked—the eventual
fate of most clippers—and only the 5 in the "lost" category
might have got into difficulties because of structural weakness.
All of these had been at sea at least 9 years, and their average
service was more than 15 years; any fault ascribable to the
builder should have shown up long before the final calamity
occurred to each.

Of the two McKay clippers that were condemned as unseaworthy, the *Donald McKay* was converted into a coal hulk after
26 years of service, much of it in the grueling Australian trade;
and the *Star of Empire* provides the only instance of a brief life
possibly ascribable to insufficient strength. She was built as a
transatlantic packet for Train about two years before his White
Diamond Line ceased its operations. Although she had the lowest
length-to-breadth ratio of any McKay ship classed as a clipper,
she made what appears to have been the fastest recorded passage
from Boston to Liverpool. Transferred to the Australian trade,
she put in at Algoa Bay, South Africa, in the middle of 1856 and

was condemned, at age three years and two months; but it should be noted that her sister ship, the *Chariot of Fame,* of exactly the same tonnage and other measurements, built at the same time, lasted for 20 years before being sold to England. Her fate thereafter is uncertain. The *Staffordshire,* the shortest-lived of all, struck a rock on Christmas Day of 1853, when she was two years old; but she was far off course in a violent storm. Fairburn's generalizations about McKay thus seem to be unsupported by his own choice of evidence.

McKay's clippers and clipper packets demonstrated at least an average sturdiness in the extraordinary conditions to which all packets and clippers were subjected as a matter of course at a very unusual time. The *Cornelius Grinnell,* a packet of 1,118 tons produced for New York owners in 1850, had an experience that justified *Gleason's Pictorial's* description of her as "by all odds the strongest ship of her size ever built." That was written in 1852, when she was two years old. A year later the same journal reported that she had been wrecked on Squam beach and would "probably be an entire loss." When the storm abated she was got off, patched up, and put back into service of the London Red Swallowtail Line, for which she had been built in 1850. She was still sailing regularly under its flag in 1881 when the line went out of business.

It seems clear enough from their performances that McKay's packets were sound examples of a standard product that had been perfected at New York. His special distinction comes from his clippers, but the clipper also had been developed—as a class with important variations—in New York. A few notable opium clippers produced at Boston in the early forties by Samuel Hall and other builders were outgrowths of the Baltimore experimentation with schooners and were quite unrelated to the square-rigged clippers of Palmer and Griffiths. When word of Sutter's discovery in California reached Boston in 1848, to unhinge the prudent policies of Long Wharf and Back Bay, there was no local tradition upon which an ambitious shipbuilder could base his recommendation. A few merchants did share the risk of letting McKay build for them his first Cape Horner, the Forbes-rigged *Reindeer,* variously reported as measuring from 770 to 806 tons.

The curious result casts some doubt upon his biographer's

claim that McKay at this point was "familiar with John W. Griffith's clipper productions." If he was, he evidently wanted to produce something distinctive of his own rather than an approximation of the already famous *Sea Witch*. No model or draft of the *Reindeer* seems to have survived, but her major dimensions for registration present questions. She was 13 feet 9 inches shorter than Griffiths's masterpiece, a difference not quite accounted for by the smaller tonnage. In breadth, the *Reindeer* was only 6 inches narrower than the *Sea Witch*, for a ratio of 4.7 to 1—fairly high for a packet of her date but already too low for a clipper. The startling difference is that the smaller vessel was the deeper by at least 30 inches. Registry figures for her depth vary; the smallest, 21 feet 6 inches, is the same depth that McKay was to use three years later for a vessel of more than twice the tonnage, his famous *Flying Cloud*. So great a depth for a vessel of the *Reindeer*'s length and breadth can hardly be accounted for except upon the assumption that she had an extremely sharp bottom.

A principal stockholder in the ship was John M. Forbes, which may explain the fact that she tried out his brother's double-topsail rig. Her performances were generally undistinguished. She was launched on June 9, 1849, but did not get away until November 22 for a voyage of 122 sailing days to San Francisco, with time deducted for a pause at Valparaiso. Her skipper claimed a record run of 36 days from that port northward. The *Alta California* on April 3, 1850, called it "the shortest passage known." The departure and arrival records indicate that it was 38 days, still very smart sailing. The *Sea Witch*, according to her log in the National Archives, arrived from Valparaiso about ten weeks later in 36 days 8 hours, but the final record was made at year's end by the somewhat larger *White Squall*: 31 days, Valparaiso to San Francisco. The *Reindeer*'s average for her five California voyages was 140 days. No-one rates her as a clipper. It is unclear whether McKay was hampered or encouraged by her shareholders in an effort to make her into one.

No such doubts can reasonably be entertained about McKay's first outright clipper, the *Stag Hound*. In her case we have a pair of the most detailed descriptions surviving from skillful contemporary observation: an account of about 4,000 words in the Boston *Atlas* for December 21, 1850, two weeks after her launch, when she was still untried; and another almost as long in *The Monthly Nautical Magazine* for August, 1855. John W. Griffiths, while at work on the latter, evidently had the former before him, since he picked up an occasional phrase from it verbatim. The first account, probably written by the nautical specialist Duncan MacLean, presents a multitude of precise figures and is unequivocal on the circumstances that determined the *Stag Hound*'s model. The second comments upon these circumstances and judges her comparatively from her performance during three San Francisco and three China voyages. From the Boston *Atlas:*

> . . . her model may be said to be the original of a new idea in naval architecture. She is longer and sharper than any other vessel of the merchant service in the world. . . . Every element in her has been made subservient to speed; she is therefore her builder's beau ideal of swiftness; for in designing her, he was not interfered with by her owners. He alone, therefore, is responsible for her sailing qualities.

Griffiths in his later account elaborates upon the passage above:

> Her model was not undertaken without a thorough exploration of all discovered mysteries in modeling for speed, and the most celebrated models were sought out and examined with care. The result was . . . a vessel designed with special reference to her builder's beau ideal. . . . His intelligent owners gave him the entire responsibility of design, model, construction, rig, and finish, while they stood by, having no other duties to perform than the financial task of footing the bills. To the wise and generous course of the owners, Mr. McKay was indebted for his success.

It is probable that Griffiths had been approached in the process of seeking out "celebrated models." Earlier in the article he finds occasion for referring to his own "famous *Sea-Witch*," justifying himself with this statement:

> It will be entirely proper to add, that the model of the Sea-Witch had more influence upon the subsequent configuration of fast vessels, than any other ship ever built in the United States.

Griffiths stresses also the lag of several years before "Boston awoke to distinguish herself with *clipper* building." In his comments there is a hint of regret that New York had allowed its clipper ship pre-eminence to be overshadowed by McKay's suc-

cession of very large ships; but Griffiths's sense of the interrelationship of sail and steam, the marked shift of his own interest
within the clipper ship era itself, appears in this passage:

*In 1848 and 1849, New-York entered upon the era of steamship
building, and by her late experience in modeling sailing vessels
for high speed . . . set afloat steamer after steamer, which found
no match under any foreign flag upon the ocean.*

Both accounts leave no question but that McKay did, in the
Stag Hound, produce a model of his own rather than an enlargement upon the lines of any famous New York clipper. The chief
difference was an extremely sharp entrance that did not have
the hollows under water of the Griffiths bows. Despite her 1,535
tons register (Griffiths says 1,600), she was conventionally rigged.
Some objected to her look of a steamship forward: her stem was
more nearly vertical than had been the fashion at New York.
Griffiths, by the time he wrote his article, had so far abandoned
the concept of a sharp bottom that he criticized her excessive
"dead rise" of floor. As with Webb's even larger *Challenge,*
launched at New York five or six months later, this feature was
a reversion, sacrificing costly stowage space on a theory that had
some merit for vessels of modest size but none for large ones.
It can be demonstrated in a comparison of logbooks that some
ships have made passages of many weeks in listless weather
while others at about the same time, on somewhat different
courses between the same ports, were driven almost all the way
by strong winds. The *Stag Hound's* good passages were over-
whelmed by the great ones of other vessels that soon followed
from the yard of the same builder. All the larger McKay clippers,
commencing with the *Flying Cloud,* have been so thoroughly
treated in many other works that there is no reason to examine
them singly here. It should at least be noted that with the swing
of major clipper ship production from New York to the yards of
Massachusetts, New Hampshire, and Maine, the developed New
York model was generally settled for—with small variations—
by the principal builders of New England. Both the *Reindeer* and
the *Stag Hound* appear to have been unsatisfactory models in
McKay's own judgment; with the *Flying Cloud* he produced a
vessel differing not very much from an enlarged *Sea Witch.*
When discussing McKay's last four great clippers, the *Light-*

ning, Champion of the Seas, James Baines, and *Donald McKay,* Fairburn implies that the builder was rescued from domestic ruin by the chance interest of the Liverpool firm for which they were built. It seems more to the point that his domestic fame at the height of his career was capped by a phenomenon without parallel at the time: of a British shipowner repeatedly patronizing an American yard. Some new American ships, and many Canadian ones, were "bought British" after a speculative first voyage across the Atlantic, but it long had been the invariable assumption that British owners must place their orders for new ships with British yards.

Fairburn objects that the models of these four clippers were so different that McKay must have been uncertain of the requirements of the Australia run for which they all were intended. It did indeed have an unprecedented aspect—the routine necessity, for a speedy outward passage, of a long great-circle course through the roaring forties that cut across one-quarter of the earth's meridians, with an equally long homeward run in even higher southern latitudes, much of it in the furious fifties, on another arc of a great circle from Melbourne to Cape Horn. The Cape Horners of the California trade were built to buck their way head on against a few hundred miles of this weather. The Australian clippers had, as their chief requirement, to be fit to take the huge waves and steady gales from astern for thousands of miles. It is the impulse of any experienced seaman in really bad weather to head up into the wind and ride a storm out, taking the force of it on the strong, wave-splitting bows. Since waves almost invariably travel faster than a sailing ship, one that runs before the wind is in constant danger of a big sea breaking over the stern, where the mechanical controls and the brains are concentrated. Mere size helps, in these circumstances. Except for Pook's *Red Jacket* and McKay's own phenomenal *Great Republic,* three of the four clippers built for James Baines & Company of Liverpool were the largest merchant sailing ships afloat.

All four of McKay's Australia clippers did so well that an argument over differences in their mould becomes a pointless quibble. As noted at the outset in this chapter, all of them made both kinds of ultimate record: highest rate of speed and longest day's run. There is no best ship for all purposes and occasions. These answered excellently to the only universal test: quality of performance in the specific trade for which they were designed, at the particular time when they were needed. All four were launched within 13 months. When the first and smallest, the *Lightning,* of 2,083 tons, returned to Liverpool on October 23, 1854, from her first round voyage to Australia, the last and largest, the *Donald McKay,* of 2,594 tons, was already building. The particular performance of the *Lightning* in high southern latitudes could not in consequence have been considered in the design of the others.

It is at least evident that in the last of his famous clippers McKay produced a conscious response to rapidly altering conditions that were about to bring the clipper ship era to a close. She is listed by Richard C. McKay simply as a "clipper," the designation he uses for all four vessels built for Baines, and for the *Great Republic* as well. This is in comparison with the term "extreme clipper," by which he distinguishes 13 other ships built by McKay prior to 1855; but there was so great a difference in model between the *Donald McKay* and each of its three predecessors that the ratings do not make sense. The *Lightning* was more "extreme" than most so designated by the biographer, and the *Donald McKay* was a medium clipper, capable of stowing a much larger cargo per registered ton than any of the others. The special adaptation of all four to conditions in high southern latitudes was dwelt upon in a Boston *Atlas* description of the first of them:

Her after motions, therefore, will be easy in heavy seas, and when she is going at her highest speed, the after vacuum in the water will be filled by the run, so as to enable her to sail upon the same lines forward and aft. It is well known that ships with hollow counters, when in a heavy sea, bring up aft with a tremendous splash . . . and that when going swiftly through the water, they settle down almost to the taffrails. The Lightning's after body was designed with special reference to obviate these defects.

Despite such accurate foresight in design, McKay was visited, as all other American shipbuilders were in the latter 1850's, by the consequences of overproduction. Prior to James Baines's four orders, the Boston shipbuilder's increasingly ambitious designs had gone begging for investors. The *Sovereign of the Seas, Empress of the Seas,* and *Great Republic* all had been financed by McKay himself as owner, the factor providing Fairburn with his most cogent reason for criticism. When the vast boom fused by California gold discoveries collapsed into commercial depression, the hundreds of fine ships that had been built quickly were more than enough for even the normal needs of a commerce that slumped to a level far below normal. Many in which carrying capacity had been sacrificed to speed could not, with freight rates sagging, be operated at all. Throughout 1857 McKay's yard was closed. In the two years following he launched a modest ship and three small fishing schooners. In August of 1859, having decided again to seek orders abroad, he addressed a letter to Griffiths that is a curious mixture of the peremptory and the unsure. It points up the extent to which, even among eminent contemporaries, repute rests upon evidence that can be verified in print. Griffiths was a diligent writer of books published in England as well as in America. McKay advertised a forthcoming book that he never produced. His great ships were the emissaries of his fame, but only one of them wore his own name in gold letters—an act of grace on the part of Baines, her well-satisfied owner—and a ship's name has hardly ever bespoken her builder.

Dear Sir.

As you are extensively known abroad . . . particularly in Naval Architecture, and as I intend visiting Europe and all the Navy Departments therein, soon, therefore I would ask of you an introductory letter, (stating I am an American Shipbuilder, also my standing at home). . . . Mr. Maury has given me a certificate that the ships of my build have attained a speed, higher than that of any other builder in the world. I have built in all 88 ships, mostly large size 3 Deckers, and not one up to this date has ever sprung a leak at sea,—or abandoned at sea,—or in a foreign port under repairs,—or made a port short of her destination. . . .

Will you give your earliest attention to the above & Oblige
Yours respectfully,   *Donald McKay*

Lieutenant Matthew Fontaine Maury's name would have been even better known abroad than that of Griffiths. With tremendous energy he had established an international scheme of reporting upon weather conditions all over the world. The fastest passages in the fifties were tributes as much to Maury's sailing directions as to the qualities of skipper and ship. On May 14, 1853, *The Economist* of London had enthusiastically urged governmental support for Maury's cooperative scheme, concluding, "It is, perhaps, curious to notice that the suggestion springs from a Lieutenant of the United States; it is enforced by an English Peer; and it is to be carried into effect for behoof of all the mariners of the world. . . . Governments must go with society . . . more and more on cosmopolitan rather than on national principles."

In his request to Griffiths, McKay admitted one exception to the fine record of his ships—the damage done when the *Great Republic* shipped a huge sea off Cape Horn. He was being excessively scrupulous: the damaged parts of her structure had been installed by Captain Palmer when he rebuilt her as a three-decker after the disastrous fire that had consumed her fourth deck on the day after Christmas, 1853, as she lay at her New York pier. Even then, reduced by 1,200 tons in measurement and much diminished in rig, McKay's *Great Republic* continued for 17 years to be the largest merchant sailing vessel afloat, and one of the fastest.

THE MARCO POLO, "A VERY ORDINARY WOODEN SHIP"

If the convenient test of covering more than 400 nautical miles in a day rightly divides the very greatest clippers from the merely excellent ones, then the only two others that ranked with Donald McKay's seven should concern us. One, the *Marco Polo,* is a true puzzler. Frederick William Wallace, a Canadian historian moved by at least customary patriotism in assessing his country's marine achievements, calls the *Marco Polo* "the most celebrated of all Canadian-built sailing ships"; but later he remarks, "There was absolutely nothing of the clipper model about her."

She was built on Courtenay Bay, St. John, New Brunswick, at the yard of James Smith, who specialized in the production at his own risk of capacious vessels for sale in England. John Frederickson, the foreman in charge when she was laid down in 1850, referred to her as "a very ordinary wooden ship." Things went wrong. Her frames, ready for planking, were blown apart in a great gale. When launched, she ran up on the opposite bank of the bay and strained her keel out of shape: in sailor's jargon, she was "hogged." It is a part of the persistent mythology of the sea that vessels suffering this accident, an upward curve of the keel amidships, often sail much faster than they did before. Maybe so. At least, the fact that this one was hogged at the outset

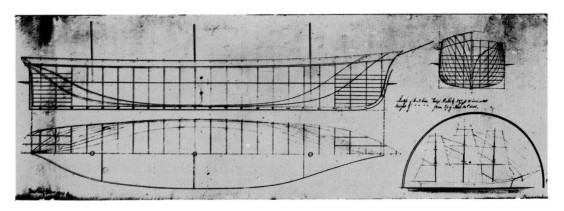

Two ships that made phenomenal records on voyages between England and Australia in the 1850's. The logs of Donald McKay's *Lightning* recorded extreme rates of speed and very high day's runs more often than those of any other great clippers. Her builder's original plans are reproduced above. From the surface of the water on up the *Marco Polo (below)* looked and was at least 50 years out of date when she was launched in 1850 from a New Brunswick yard. In spite of that, the unusually fine lines of her submerged hull made her one of the dozen or so vessels of the clipper ship era capable of the highest rates of speed as well as of consistently fast voyages. (See pp. 255–68, 270–75.)

has been given as one structural clue to the *Marco Polo's* phenomenal performances.

The *Stag Hound*, the first McKay vessel generally recognized
as a clipper, had taken to the water four months earlier than the
Marco Polo. A comparison of size is relevant because the latter
at the time of her launch was the largest Canadian vessel ever
built. She measured 1,626 tons by the British formula, which
produced figures varying by about 5 per cent from equivalent
American measurements; the real change was to come with the
Moorsom system a little later. The *Stag Hound*, at her official
American measurement of 1,534 tons, seems to have been somewhat the smaller vessel. McKay's *Flying Cloud*, launched in the
same month as the *Marco Polo*, measured 1,782 tons and was thus
somewhat larger. The point of interest is that the *Flying Cloud*
was the smallest of the seven McKay ships that sailed more than
400 miles in a day, but the freakish *Marco Polo* was the very
smallest ever to do so. Wallace claims, moreover, that "she was
such an ugly ship that everybody connected with her building
disowned her." She had the snub-nosed look of a frigate of the late
eighteenth century, complete with a painted stripe of false gunports, an obsolescent form of camouflage against pirates and
privateers that the Yankees had given up early in the clipper era.

Although Smith surely was influenced by the gold rush demand for larger vessels, he seems to have expected nothing
remarkable of his *Marco Polo*. He threw in some iron scrap for
ballast, stuffed her with the lumber that was the staple product
of the Maritime Provinces, and pointed her for Liverpool. Unable
to find a purchaser in that port, his British agents sent her out
to Mobile for a load of cotton. Her 35-day return passage from
that Gulf port interested James Baines, who was soon to become
the principal customer of Donald McKay.

Baines, aged 30, had recently founded the Australian Black
Ball Line with one stodgy New Brunswick ship bought at a
bargain and sent at a lucky moment when the new gold rush
was getting past the rumor stage. He may merely have been
following the same tactic when he bought the *Marco Polo*,
which was described by Basil Lubbock, on the basis of memories
of Liverpudlians, as being "square as a brick fore and aft, with
a bow like a savage bulldog." The latter feature can be seen in
a contemporary woodcut done by one of the scrupulous en-

gravers of the *Illustrated London News,* in which it appeared on February 19, 1853, soon after the ship's return from her first phenomenal Australian voyage. A lusterware crockery platter was later prepared, following the details of the engraving with the omission of one flag and a different tilt to the spanker gaff, perhaps to take the curse off a too slavish plagiarism. Such mementos were sold to members of a ship's company and former passengers. A decent accuracy in the portrayal can usually be assumed at this date because wrong details would have been objected to by the best customers.

It is the beakhead of the *Marco Polo* that suggests a bulldog's underslung jaw: an outthrust structure beneath the bowsprit, the diminished remnant of the traditional ram used in men-of-war prior to the joyful invention of explosives. For some centuries it had persisted as the "head"—the crew's decidedly wet water closet. Its last vestige had vanished from the clipper bow advocated by Griffiths ten years before the launch of the *Marco Polo.*

Yet the anachronistic visible profile and the unqualified negative of historian Wallace's statement—"absolutely nothing of the clipper model about her"—are, respectively, misleading and misled. A description accompanying the *Illustrated London News* woodcut reveals, in the second of the excerpts following, what was hidden to viewers of her profile above water:

When the tide of emigration . . . first set in toward the Gold Regions of Australia . . . 100 to 120 days were actually consumed on the voyage out. An improved class of vessels . . . it was confidently predicted, would reduce the voyage to eighty days.

In the meantime, however, a noble British ship—the Marco Polo—*had already sailed from the Mersey . . . and made the voyage out in the unprecedentedly short space of sixty-eight days; and the passage home in seventy-four days!*

Her elapsed time "from her leaving and regaining the shores of Great Britain" had been a week less than six months. The article further reports that the vessel on her return voyage by way of Cape Horn crossed her own outward track in the South Atlantic (whether in 32 degrees south latitude or 32 degrees west longitude is unclear) 69 elapsed days later. Since she had spent 28 days in an Australian port, she at this point had circumnavigated the globe in 41 sailing days. The description continues:

The distinguishing feature of the Marco Polo *is the peculiarity
of her hull. Her lines fore and aft are beautifully fine . . . while
she makes amidships a displacement that will prevent unnecessary "careening," she has an entrance as sharp as a steamboat's, and a run as clean as can be conceived. Below the draught-
line her bows are hollow . . . with a bottom like a yacht, she has
aloft all the appearance of a frigate.*

The hull thus was very similar to the hollow-bowed, sharp-
ended, flat-floored clipper model that Griffiths was advocating
in the year of the *Marco Polo*'s launch. McKay did not fully
express all these features in combination until a couple of years
later. The *Stag Hound,* his first clipper, did without the underwater hollows and was fairly sharp along the bottom. The ships
that followed were hollow-bowed, but he did not try a really flat
floor until he modeled the first of his ships for James Baines,
the *Lightning.*

It is likely, therefore, that the first clipper thoroughly well
designed for the specific conditions of the Australian circumnavigation was given the right features by accident, in Nova
Scotia, more than a year before the need for such a model was
made evident. What the conditions of this particular navigation
meant to the foremasthand can be hinted at in a few excerpts
from Cutler:

*. . . for long-drawn-out misery, running the easting down the
12,000 miles that lay between the Cape of Good Hope and Cape
Horn stands unmatched. . . . Decks full of water for weeks on
end; men soaked to the skin . . . completely exposed to the fury
of icy, sleet-laden gales . . . on to full hurricane force that
pierced stiff oilskins like flimsy cotton. . . . They moved in a
nightmare of suffering, in which the lesser tortures of earache,
toothache and throbbing boils—the usual accompaniment of
the conditions they endured—passed almost unnoticed in the
greater agony that gripped them from head to foot. . . .*

*One cannot describe that sort of thing. Perhaps only those
who have sought the infinitely grateful shelter of a freezing
fo'csle with its sea chests bumping around in six inches of
sloshing ice water; who have found in a sodden dripping bunk
an all-too-brief glimpse of heaven on earth, can appreciate it.*

*. . . It was on this run that the clippers learned the trick of
converting a heavy gale into a stiff breeze by merely continuing
to run before it at 18 knots or so.*

The reason why a buoyant, flat-floored midsection and wave-dividing bows were both important, at least from the crew's standpoint, should be evident from that description by one who had sailed the route.

Any single test for great performance in a ship is subject to the criticism that out of thousands of voyages, the weather might by luck, in this one instance, have been favorable all the way. As with the *Sea Witch*, one should also ask whether the commander's skill was as important as the shape of his ship. When the *Marco Polo* broke several records on her first Australian voyage, she was driven by Captain James Nicol Forbes, whose given and middle names hardly ever appear in print because he was "Bully" Forbes to the world of water—another of the magnificently self-assured captains who at last took one voyage too many.

Forbes did less well with the *Marco Polo* on his second voyage, although the elapsed time of exactly six months was almost as impressive. He then left her to take charge of Baines's new McKay ship, the *Lightning*. Again as with the *Sea Witch*, the mate trained by the original master became the *Marco Polo*'s second skipper; Charles McDonald took her out in 69 days, land to land, and home in 78. Her third Australian voyage bettered Forbes's time for the second by 6 days on the outward run and by 17 homeward bound. Her fine performances were not dependent upon a single fabulous commander. It was on the outward run of this third voyage that she joined the 400 club. On January 7, 1854, the following item appeared in the ship's newspaper:

The extraordinary run made by the Marco Polo *in the last twenty-four hours has taken us altogether by surprise. We could not have believed the fact had we not seen our position on the chart, and been well assured that the statement subjoined is the result of actual observation and agrees almost to a tittle with the dead-reckoning. We ran 366 miles from noon on Thursday to noon on Friday, and from that time until noon today we have made 438 miles. Thus we have eclipsed every former exploit of either our own ship or any other sailing vessel ever known.*

The reader should ask, "How reliable is this kind of evidence?" In the first place, it is comparatively reliable within its own category. All the claims for remarkable speed and distance at sea rest upon navigational entries made at the time on the log slate and transferred within hours to the ship's official journal.

As with other examples of the raw stuff of derived history, special interest, fraud, or mere mistake may have warped the contemporary evidence. Tampering would be easier in a logbook to be delivered at the end of the voyage than in one available to the editor of a newspaper promptly distributed on board. Many of the long-voyage clippers published weekly periodicals. They helped to keep up the morale of several hundred passengers crammed into close quarters. These passengers were sure to include experienced voyagers who would want to see the evidence. The editor was a passenger, the printer a member of the crew. The captain might have wanted to make a dishonest reputation for his ship and so for himself; but this would have required the collusion of other navigating officers and the acquiescence of at least some knowledgeable readers, all in the compressed, gossip-filled world of a ship. For such reasons the evidence seems about as trustworthy as most that passes into the historical record when observers have not been appointed under controlled conditions in advance.

The first great day's work of the *Marco Polo* broke by a handsome margin of 27 miles the only previous noon-to-noon record of more than 400 miles—that of McKay's *Sovereign of the Seas.* One of her logs, preserved at Washington in the National Archives, records on March 18, 1853—about ten months earlier—a day's run of 411 miles. The only good evidence for a higher mileage in one day than the *Marco Polo*'s best appears in the newspaper published aboard another McKay clipper, the *Champion of the Seas Gazette.* On December 12, 1854, nearing Australia in about 50 degrees south, she covered 465 miles.

The average rate of speed on the *Marco Polo*'s best noon-to-noon run works out at 18½ knots. No top speed was entered in the newspaper account, but since the wind is never steady even in a gale it can be assumed that the ship was at times moving at least a knot faster than this 24-hour average rate. The seven much larger McKay ships for which great day's runs are claimed touched 20 and 21 knots, with the top claim of 22 for the *Sovereign of the Seas.* An idea of the fineness of that ship's lines can be got from the drop of almost 1,000 tons in her registry figure under the Moorsom system. She fell from 2,420 to 1,461.

The most extravagant claims for high speed at sea all cluster to a period of seven years in the early to middle 1850's. Some have regarded this fact as a reason for suspicion, but it should be noted that almost all these achievements took place in the roaring forties and in even higher southern latitudes, where nothing but the jut of South America's southern archipelagos breaks the world-circling rush of winds and waves. The worst weather gave the best chances to the Australia clippers because they stayed for weeks at a time in waters avoided on purpose by everyone else. Ships that never knew what it was like to have a full gale astern for a month did not have the same probability of encountering favorably excessive conditions throughout some one heroic day. It should likewise be noted that all the records were made by over-sparred eastbound ships driven by westerly winds "against the sun." Thus the noon-to-noon total represented something nearer to 23 than 24 hours by the clock. This factor is commonly ignored because it is offset by the helpful effect of the current. The dead-reckoning account of a ship's speed, computed by casting the log, measured speed through water that itself was in motion at an average rate of 1 or 2 knots.

For her fourth Australian voyage the *Marco Polo* again swapped skippers; she made an old-fashioned fast run to Melbourne that was logy by her own standards—95 days; but she would have had to lower her precedent-shattering first performance by yet another day to equal that of a new champion—the Maine-built *Red Jacket* had departed from Liverpool ten weeks ahead of her and had reached Melbourne in 67 days.

SAMUEL HARTT POOK, NAVAL ARCHITECT

Samuel Hartt Pook's *Red Jacket* was the third vessel to chalk up on the slate a reasonably authenticated day's run of 400 miles or more. This was accomplished in a snowy North Atlantic gale that expedited her 12-day maiden voyage from her pier at New York to the bell buoy off the mouth of the Mersey, where her pilot required that she loiter to await a lessening of the fog. Her final time, alongside the quay at Liverpool, was 13 days, 1 hour, 25 minutes. By the longer of these calculations, her voyage is still the shortest ever completed under sail from any United States port to any in England or on the Continent. It was made before the ship was coppered.

Pook's clipper, larger than the *Marco Polo,* should by that test alone have been the faster. Under British registry the Ameri-

The fast bark *Race Horse (left)* of 1850 probably was the first vessel put skillfully into final form by the young genius Samuel Hartt Pook. His first outright clipper was the *Surprise* of the same year *(below)*. His *Red Jacket (above)* won the highest praise from his somewhat older contemporary John Willis Griffiths. In the view of some experts her combination of extreme speed and unusually high carrying capacity makes her the greatest, most versatile achievement of the clipper ship era. (See pp. 282ff., 290, 296–99.)

can *Red Jacket* measured 251.2 feet long, 44 broad, and 31 deep. When her lines and spar plan were published by Griffiths in the June, 1856, issue of his *U.S. Nautical Magazine and Naval Journal* he gave her dimensions as 250 by 44 by 24. The Hall *Report* gives the molded figures as 251¾ by 42½ by 26, and there are other variations. Such divergences in measurement records typify one problem of comparing ships' performances when size is an inevitable factor. None of the sets of measurements given for the *Red Jacket* produces, by the American formula, the often reported tonnage figure: 2,400. At least we have her exact shape: "Her design," Griffiths wrote, "is the result of a *carte blanche* given to Mr. S. H. Pook, of Boston, by whose politeness we furnish the lines of this fine vessel."

Since we have the Lloyd's measurements for both vessels, a meaningful comparison can be made. The *Marco Polo* was entered in the St. John Shipping Register as measuring 184.1 by 36.3 by 29.4. Lloyd's, which trusted only its own yardstick, put down 185 by 38 by 30. Thus the *Marco Polo* was the shorter by about 65 feet, with a length-to-breadth ratio befitting an extreme packet. Her performances remain a puzzle.

While the *Red Jacket* was making her wild first transatlantic passage to Liverpool her designer celebrated his twenty-seventh birthday. Samuel Hartt Pook was born in Brooklyn, New York, on January 17, 1827. He was the grandson of Charles Lee Pook, a Boston cooper, and the son of Samuel Moore Pook, an eminent constructor of vessels for the Navy. Like Griffiths therefore, but unlike the farmer's son McKay, the younger Pook took to naval architecture by inheritance. At the age of 14 he graduated from Portsmouth Academy, near the Portsmouth, New Hampshire, Navy Yard, where his father in the same year— 1842—was promoted to top rank in the Bureau of Construction: United States Naval Constructor. In the following year Samuel Hartt Pook became his father's apprentice at the Boston Navy Yard.

The elder Pook had earlier helped in the design of a number of notable fighting ships. Together with Naval Constructor Samuel Hartt, a relative, he had championed flat floors for the Navy at about the time when they were gaining favor for packets. Hartt provided the younger Pook with a commonly misspelled middle name and reinforced his nautical heritage.

Samuel Humphreys, competent son of the great Joshua, was another of the elder Pook's associates. Together they designed the heavy corvette *Saratoga,* launched at the Portsmouth yard July 26, 1842: a durable ship that did useful chores for Uncle Sam until 1907. For his next assignment Samuel Moore Pook had entire charge of both design and construction of the *Plymouth,* a corvette that according to Chapelle "was much admired abroad and was considered by many officers to have been the finest vessel of her class in any navy." Her admirers included Japanese artists who drew curious and fearsome pictures of her as a member of the American squadron that put to a close Japan's long determination not to let herself be corrupted by the barbaric West. The *Plymouth* was chosen as a vessel likely to stand the buffeting when Commander John A. Dahlgren, in 1857, was authorized to test for six months his theory that a few heavy 9-inch and 11-inch bore guns would be a more effective armament than the traditional broadside batteries of many smaller ones. She helped him make his point, surviving unshaken.

It was thus a well-designed and superbly constructed vessel that provided Samuel Hartt Pook, at the outset of his apprenticeship, with an opportunity to develop his heritage. From 1843 to 1847 he worked at the Charlestown yard, a mile or so north of the state house dome. Half a mile due east, on the other shore of the Mystic River, Otis Tufts began late in 1844 the unprecedented task of constructing a "twin-screw, double-engined, iron steamer"—the *R. B. Forbes,* registered at Boston on February 24, 1846. She had been launched the preceding August, after a period spent in newly creating all the equipment needed for the novel procedures of shipbuilding with iron. The task of "laying down her lines" therefore must have been accomplished long before Pook's eighteenth birthday. It is not unlikely that the protean Robert Bennet Forbes had got wind of the unusual talents of a particular apprentice at the navy yard. A youth of 17 might well have been assigned to help in "laying down" the lines of any vessel in a nearby yard, as a part of his training. But other writers have picked up Cutler's statement quoted above, including the error in Pook's age, and have elaborated upon it. Fairburn, whose selective disparagement of McKay is counterweighted by enthusiasm over Pook's achievements, claims that the deep-sea tug was "designed by young Sam Pook of Boston (when a twenty-year-old boy)."

Since it is a factor of critical importance to an understanding of Pook's unusual career, the distinction between "designing" a vessel and "laying down her lines" calls here for some emphasis. The designer created the original shape of a vessel —usually, in Pook's day, in the form of a lift model. As a rule the designer transferred this three-dimensional object to three two-dimensional plans on paper. A study of the paper plans and their comparison with others on file often resulted in further whittling of the three-dimensional model, still the designer's task. When the model and its paper surrogates had been approved by the owner, the intricate job of translating the shape of each frame of the small drawings into full-size chalk lines on the mould-loft floor could begin. This was the process of "laying down," which could be accomplished under skilled supervision by anyone who knew his multiplication table and had a respect for precision. To match the full-size lines on the floor of the loft, moulds of thin wood were made as patterns for the shipwrights to use in shaping the heavy timber or iron frames.

Cutler's statement can be read to mean nothing more than that the younger Pook had some part in laying down the lines of Boston's first iron tug as an exercise of his apprenticeship. It is certain at least that his career had its origins in work under his father's supervision on one of the last and finest wooden sailing ships built for the United States Navy, and within view across the river of a remarkably sophisticated prototype for the twin-screw metal vessels of a future that was still remote in the real world of American shipbuilding. Samuel Hartt Pook learned his trade at the outset of the triumphant climax of wooden sailing ships, but he was interested also in the new technology of steam and iron. Fairburn was elaborating unduly when he said that Pook "made all the drawings and calculations and laid out the lines of the . . . R. B. Forbes, which became famous in Boston as a big seagoing ocean towboat."

Pook himself made no such claim on the several occasions when he was being questioned for printed accounts of the full scope of his career.

Having come of age, he found his first free employment at the Portsmouth Navy Yard under Naval Constructor Benjamin F. Delano, in helping to build the United States Steamer *Saranac* —a wooden side-wheeler that survived the Civil War by cruising uneventfully with the Pacific Squadron. The ways were made ready for her in May of 1847; she was launched in November of 1848.

Within the following year Pook firmed up his decision to establish an unprecedented enterprise amid the traditional shipbuilders. A biographical notice published shortly after his retirement states that "under the kind guidance of his friend, Robert B. Forbes, he opened an office as a naval architect"—but the date is not given. A letter written by Pook to Forbes in the panic year 1857 confirms the fact. It accompanied a model for a propeller steamer, presented in "gratitude for your kind Patronage at the time of my commencement in business"—but here too the time is not revealed. The writer may have hoped that the gift would prod its recipient into breaking the hush that had fallen over the shipyards with an order for such a vessel.

A business card printed in the Boston *Atlas* on February 15, 1850, shows that the new enterprise was under way at least by that date. Substantially the same wording turns up in the Boston *Post* for May 31, after intermittent appearances in the *Atlas.* Both papers carry it sporadically for several months thereafter:

TO SHIP OWNERS AND BUILDERS.
Plans, Models and Moulds of Sailing
Ships and Steamers,
Furnished by
SAMUEL H. POOK,
Naval Architect
Cunningham's Wharf—East Boston.
☞ Please address orders to Cunningham's wharf, or to
Charlestown Post Office 1s6m mh28

Cunningham's Wharf was located where East Boston juts its southwest elbow into the confluence of the Mystic and Charles rivers, a central place for any maritime enterprise. McKay's yard was less than a mile to northward, up the estuary. Samuel Hall, who had pioneered in the region, built his ships

halfway between. Three blocks east of Cunningham's lay the
Otis Tufts wharf, thrusting outward from sheds and foundries
where the frames and plates for the *R. B. Forbes* had been
prepared, and her engines built. Two mast yards, a graving
basin, and a marine railway somehow found room for themselves close to Cunningham's.

Pook's plans evidently had not matured soon enough for
him to arrange a listing in commercial directories dated 1850,
but he turns up in their issues for 1851. You have to hunt to
find him. Among standard categories no provision had been
made for the unheard-of profession "naval architect." The
editors put him under "Architects," amid the designers of
houses and shops, but with the adjective "naval" uniquely
following his name. Donald McKay was not provided for any
more imaginatively; throughout the brilliant part of his career
he lingered under "Shipwrights and Caulkers," and so did
Samuel Hall. It was not until 1856, with business calamitously
dwindling, that "Shipbuilders" were recognized separately
in the *Boston Almanac.* In that year Pook's listing suddenly
became "S. H. Pook & Co.," but it reverted thereafter to simply
his name.

A letter written by John M. Forbes on April 9, 1850, may
provide the clue to the "kind Patronage" that R. B. Forbes
provided at the outset of Pook's career as an independent professional. It mentions negotiations with Samuel Hall for a
bark to cost $31,000 "complete with one suit of sails—not
coppered but he to put the copper on." The resulting vessel
was the little China Packet *Race Horse,* intended for the interlocking Forbes enterprises in Boston and at Canton. The elder
Forbes had left for China on June 20, 1849, and did not get
home again until July 3, 1851. He may, before his departure,
have arranged financial backing for Pook. "Patronage" implies,
however, the placing of one or more actual orders. The earliest documented connection I know of, between Pook and a
Forbes ship, is his work on the second *Antelope* of 1855; but
since the independent designer was certainly working with
Hall by the early summer of 1850, the likeliest meaning of
"Patronage at the time of my commencement in business"
would be that he had something to do with the last Forbes-
Hall vessel built prior to 1855, the *Race Horse.*

Fairburn heads a list of clippers "admittedly designed by

Pook" with the *Race Horse,* but fails to say who admits it.
The little bark in any case has an importance of her own, at
the outset of Boston's belated participation in the clipper ship
era, that has not had adequate notice. The new and sudden
standard of excellence she set on her maiden voyage perhaps
resulted somewhat from a scientific designer's corrective touch.

THE FAST BARK *RACE HORSE*

Before the China packet *Race Horse* was ready for her midyear
launch, California fever had swept up the coast to infect even
stolid Boston. Vessels crafted for different weather and waters
were lumbering off toward Cape Horn and the Golden Gate.
The *Race Horse* was designed for the generally pleasant eastward
route toward Canton, passing the Cape of Good Hope both outward and homeward bound; but at about the time of her launch
the lure of booming California brought a decision to try her
as a Cape Horner, headed for China by way of San Francisco.
On July 30, 1850, she was registered at $514^{49}\!/_{95}$ tons, 125 feet
long, 30 feet 3 inches broad, 16 feet in depth. David S. Babcock
is listed on the certificate as master, and John M. Forbes as
sole owner at that date. Shortly thereafter, I. Goddard and
Company seem to have acquired the controlling shares.

In the frantic preceding year, all the tea clippers were already
far at sea, eastbound, when the forty-niners began their first
desperate scramble to charter ships. Two modest Baltimore
clippers, the *Greyhound* and *Gray Eagle,* were among the first
three sharp vessels to be diverted to the new California trade.
These cleared the Virginia capes on January 12 and 22, 1849.
The third of a speedy trio, the Baltimore clipper *Architect,*
sailed from New Orleans in the interim, on January 18. The
average tonnage of these three ships of special design was
almost exactly that of the *Race Horse.* If handicap adjustments
are made to compensate for the clearance of one from a Gulf
port and for the pause of another at Valparaiso, their uniformity
of performance seems remarkable. On a route that formerly
had offered no great incentive to the nimble—normal voyages
having used up six or seven months—each of the three Baltimore clippers went out in the equivalent of 120 days sailing
time from Boston or New York. Their actual passages were 117
days from Philadelphia, 119 from Baltimore, and 127 from

New Orleans. The corrected average of about 120 days, as it turned out, was the measure for the best passages made by other forty-niners.

The first true clipper that got back from China in time to make her next voyage into a westward circumnavigation by way of San Francisco was the *Memnon,* built by Smith & Dimon to beat their own incomparable *Sea Witch.* Measuring twice the tonnage of her predecessors on the route, the three little Baltimore ships, the *Memnon* was in her prime at two years of age. She sailed from New York on April 11 and arrived at San Francisco in 122 days.

Toward the year's end, on November 22, 1849, McKay's *Reindeer* took her departure from Boston. Although not classifiable as a clipper, she was one of the first vessels designed for the unrelenting, head-on weather of the Cape Stiff route. She too made a passage in 122 days. All the other gold rush vessels took much longer. Cutler computes the average for the year at 200 days. The Forbes-rigged *Samoset* of 1847—the last vessel built by Hall for the Forbes brothers prior to the *Race Horse*—did better than most with her passage of 173 days.

Lieutenant Maury was the inadvertent originator of a practice, much elaborated by later writers, of dealing with Cape Horn voyages to California somewhat in the spirit of the planned races between big yachts. Maury was virtuously concerned with an examination of the courses of four clippers that had sailed for California within a period of 33 days; he sought to deduce from their logs evidence that would improve the accuracy of his own sailing directions from New York to San Francisco. Captain Arthur H. Clark, in *The Clipper Ship Era* (1910), confirmed the fashion with high authority. "The first contest of clippers around Cape Horn," he wrote, "took place in 1850, between the *Houqua, Sea Witch, Samuel Russell,* and *Memnon,* old rivals on China voyages, and the new clippers *Celestial, Mandarin,* and *Race Horse.*"

Clark, who learned the duties of an officer in the Pook-designed *Northern Light,* later became an eminent yachtsman. As such he was reading into this first "contest" around the Horn aspects that apply more sensibly to the larger numbers and specific challenges by shipowners in the "races" that followed. Since three of the seven ships he named had completed their 1850 voyages before the last two even sailed, it was hardly a contest in the usual sense; rather it was the first occasion, on the world's most steadily exacting route, when something like the trials of speed and stamina in competition that had long been going on between North Atlantic packets began to sort out the remarkable Cape Horners from the ordinary ones.

Later scholars do not follow Clark in rating the little *Race Horse* as a clipper. If she is to be fairly included in the sporadic contest of 1850, other vessels with a reputation for speed that sailed at about the same time should also be compared: Waterman's old *Natchez*, under a skipper whose name does not appear in the usual accounts of heroic voyaging; the *Wisconsin*, of 925 tons, a fast New York packet and general trader with a commander of the opposite sort; the *Thomas Wattson*, of 349 tons, another remarkable Baltimore clipper; and the *Cohota*, of 691 tons, a seven-year-old Canton packet built by Webb.

First to sail, on January 4, 1850, was the *Natchez*—an over-size liner when built in 1831 but the third from smallest in this mid-century group. The *Samuel Russell* sailed 11 days later. Her arrival at San Francisco on May 6 caused the *Alta California* to remark:

The ship Samuel Russell—the favorite and fastest ship out of the Atlantic ports . . . reached this port yesterday in the unprecedented short run of 109 days from New York. . . . Old canvassback is not dead yet.

When the *Natchez* made port on June 3 the same paper reported her elapsed time from New York, 150 days, "via Valparaiso 50," but without any deduction for the time spent in that port. Something evidently had gone wrong, since she sailed under Captain Duryee and arrived under Captain Braman. Fifty days up from Valparaiso was a good deal better than the average, but it does not suggest that her corrected time would have been comparable with her earlier performances under Waterman. She continued on around the world, headed next for the more leisurely afterlife of so many grand old packets, sailing out of New Bedford in chase of leviathan.

The *Wisconsin*, third to sail and third to arrive, chalked up the fast time of 121 days. Oliver R. Mumford, her commander, added in his log, "ahead of all the ships that sailed 30 days

before us." The figure "30" saved him from comparison with
the faster passage of the *Samuel Russell*, which had sailed
37 days before him. It was in this sense that a conscious contest was under way: each skipper was sailing against the as
yet unknown time of all the ships that would have entered
port ahead of him. Unless he picked up news from an outward-
bounder, he could evaluate his own success, as Mumford in
this case did, only upon arrival when he submitted his log
for inspection by port officials and reporters. It was the latter,
compilers of "Marine Intelligence" for shrill young California
newspapers, who stressed the competitive aspect and kept the
score in view.

The two smallest competitors, the *Thomas Wattson* and the
Houqua, were fourth and fifth to sail. They arrived in the
same sequence, but the Baltimore clipper bettered the big
Wisconsin's time by eight days with a score of 113 days from
the Delaware Capes, which a few weeks earlier might have
been declared the record. The *Houqua*'s time was 130 days.
When she made port the fastest run from any North Atlantic
port had continued through seven weeks to be the 109-day
passage of the first vessel "built to beat the *Sea Witch*"—the
Samuel Russell. A few hours behind the *Houqua*, Captain
George W. Frazer brought the head of the *Sea Witch* to the
wind at nightfall on July 23, 100 days out of New York, including a four-day pause at Valparaiso. The *Alta California*'s
marine reporter was ready to greet him next morning off the
foot of Sacramento Street. His story appeared on July 25:

*THE QUICKEST TRIP YET.—The Eastern press boasts of the
performance of their steamships, and with good reason, for
they can beat the world. With the self same pride in American
naval architecture, we can boast of our sailing craft. "Britan-
nia rules the waves!"—rules a fiddle-sticks-end, why she can
scarcely rule anything. The ship Sea Witch, Capt. Fraser,
arrived yesterday, in ninety-seven days from New York, "all
around the Horn." What do you think of that! And only thirty-
eight days from Valparaiso. She was kept under easy sail all
the while, and never tried once. This is the very quickest trip
on record, beating the Samuel Russell, which was but 109 days,
half a month. There is no knowing what the Sea Witch could
do if she was put to it, and just spread herself once. Her trip
excels in speed that made by the steamship Carolina, which*

made the quickest trip then recorded. Why would it not be a good idea for the Pacific Mail Steamship Company to run her in connection with their steamers?

The *Cohota* had sailed six days ahead of the *Sea Witch* but came in three weeks later. The *Memnon*, next to appear, was the first clipper to complete a second California voyage. To demonstrate her reliability, she did it in exactly the same time as her first: 122 days. The *Memnon* was the largest of the 11 vessels we have been considering. Since she too had been designed to do better than the *Sea Witch*, she must have disappointed her skipper, Joseph R. Gordon, who had been slowed up off the Horn on his prior passage by his crew's refusal to obey orders. Perhaps that was what drove him on to the fine achievement following. In a special supplement crowded with shipping advertisements the *Alta California* carried this announcement:

For Canton—The splendid ship MEMNON, Capt. J. R. Gordon will have immediate dispatch for the above port. Freight and treasure taken at the usual rates.

She cleared for Hong Kong on November 8 with 20 passengers —it was hard to get a berth to California but even harder to get home again. Captain Gordon did his best for them, rounding up at the Whampoa anchorage in 36 days, the fastest passage that has ever been made under sail from San Francisco to Canton; but on the next leg of her circumnavigation, loaded with teas for London, the *Memnon* perished on a reef and was stripped by Malay pirates in Gaspar Strait.

Webb's *Celestial*, of 860 tons, often referred to as the first outright clipper specifically designed for conditions of the California trade, was one of the last group of three ships that ran between them in the second half of 1850 something more like a race than the spread-out performance of their eight predecessors. The *Celestial, Mandarin,* and *Race Horse* sailed within a period of 19 days, on July 16 and 25 and August 4. They all arrived in the month of November. In designing the *Mandarin*—one of the smallest of outright clippers, measuring only 776 tons—Smith & Dimon had taken Griffiths's revised advice. She had exceptionally flat floors.

Boston's little *Race Horse*, being last of the 11 to leave port, was in competition with the entire group; the two larger vessels against which she was pitted in the same season had both been designed, as she had not, to cope with particular difficulties of the Cape Horn passage.

According to her remarkable commander, David S. Babcock, the *Race Horse* raced from land to land in 94 days 14 hours —a day or two faster than the 96 sailing days of the *Sea Witch* to her landfall off the Golden Gate. Special pleading is no more justified in this case than in innumerable others when splendid runs in deep water were lengthened exasperatingly, just off port, by days of fog or calm. The reported time of the *Race Horse*, anchorage to anchorage, was 109 days. She had cleared at Boston on August 3, a date when the *Daily Advertiser* noted that "nothing sailed." She got to sea on August 4 "in tow of steamer Hornet . . . with thick weather and some showers."

On November 22, 1850, the *Alta California* carried this item:

Nov. 21: About twelve vessels are reported to be off the Heads, among them the barque Race Horse and the French ship Arabella.

The elapsed time between these notices is 110 days, although the hour of day could justify one day less. Nothing entered San Francisco on November 22 because it was still, as the paper noted, "thick outside." Nineteen of the backed-up group made their way in on the twenty-third. On the twenty-fourth, midway in another large batch, the first vessel to which Pook may have contributed a touch of his magic found her turn:

Barque Racehorse, Babcock, 109 ds fm Boston, 1 passenger, to master.

The last two words indicated that Babcock himself was the consignee of his cargo, empowered to sell it in the booming city where the owners as yet had made no arrangement for a local commercial representative.

Next day an exultant piece announced a break in the weather:

One of the finest mornings. . . . The ships . . . with wet sails drying in the sun, looked like some immense flock of huge birds. . . .

What these entries, in the absence of the log, do not tell us is the span of time that the *Race Horse* may have endured in the fog off the Heads before her presence there was first ascertained, probably by a fisherman who knew how to work his way in and out by the color of the bottom.

A fair evaluation of this unusually well designed bark, which on a later Mediterranean voyage made a still unequaled record, should include some stress upon the excellence of her commander, who had no need to fabricate the report of 94 days 14 hours. The vessel and her master were well suited to each other and to the task that called for something remarkable in each. Captain Babcock was one of the men who made the clipper ship era by the consistency of their performances. He confirmed this early achievement through several extraordinary California voyages in the *Sword Fish* and *Young America*: 94 days, port-to-port, in the former, claimed sailing time 90 days 16 hours.

By the longest computation of her elapsed time, the first vessel with which Samuel Hartt Pook's name has been associated was beaten by only two ships in the year's final tally. Both were substantially larger: Webb's celebrated *Celestial*, perhaps the first extreme clipper, rated by Howes and Matthews as "the sharpest ship built up to that time . . . launched especially for the California trade"; and the incomparable *Sea Witch*. The little *Race Horse* also earned herself a numerical tie with the *Samuel Russell*, of almost twice her tonnage, in which the eminent Captain Charles Porter Low had had some troubles along the way but none in making port. It should not be overlooked that these four were not only the most impressive of the 11 unusual vessels listed above—they were also the four best out of hundreds that sailed in the first year of the California trade in which shipowners had a chance to prepare with some adequacy for its peculiar conditions.

POOK'S CLIPPERS: A CONSISTENT EXCELLENCE

Apportionment of credit for a ship's qualities between owner, naval architect, and builder is always difficult. It is particularly so in Pook's case, since records are scanty. Alongside published acknowledgments that he "assisted" with the design of some, there is the certain fact that one of the few most famous ships of the age—thought by several experts to be the best of all—expressed his own, completely unaltered, concept. I assume here that Pook deserves preponderant credit for the ships with which his name is credibly linked, because his participation seems consistently to have lifted the products of otherwise good but uneven builders to a level of excellence.

This process involved the unhappy task of exposing older men to the inference (stressed by Griffiths in his writings) that the foremost shipbuilders had little knowledge of the principles of scientific ship design. The independent naval architect's efforts, to say the best of the situation, were consequently pitted against a stubborn Yankee self-reliance. Beyond this there was an attitude often remarked by British visitors, a slyness in commercial dealings that even contemporary American writers tended to celebrate fondly: the Yankee was a smart bargainer who liked to go to court. Ericsson, who worked with both Pook and Forbes, was in almost constant litigation over claims of theoretical priority that were raised after his ships and their propulsive mechanisms had shown practical results.

The most credible of several biographical notices for which Pook himself would have had to supply most of the relevant information was printed in L. R. Hamersly's *Records of Living Officers of the U.S. Navy,* issued in successive editions late in the century. The fact that it is somewhat disorganized in time sequence suggests that it was prepared from Pook's own dictation or from his informal notes. It early presents the surprising statement, ". . . opened an office at Boston as Naval Architect, where he continued for fifteen years, during which time he designed nearly one thousand ships of various kinds, among them the celebrated clipper-ship 'Red Jacket;' he laid out all the work for the builders, as well as designed their ships for them, having about fifty customers. . . ." This implies more than one ship a week for the entire period. Elsewhere in the account, however, distinctions are carefully made between the process of design in some cases and of laying out (or laying down) in others. I assume that the word "designed" in the original summary statement was an editorial simplification and that the total represented the number of vessels with which Pook was in some way helpful.

The 16 very fast sailing ships usually credited to him were all designed within the first five years of his independent activity. They were built in ten different shipyards, a fact that has suggested to Fairburn and other writers that it was a shrewd Yankee practice to purchase one model from him and then reuse approximately the same lines for larger, later vessels, with no acknowledgment or remuneration for Pook. As primary designer, Pook worked with Hall for about half a year at the outset of Boston's postponed clipper ship era, beginning probably with the *Race Horse;* certainly he shaped the *Surprise,* referred to by most marine historians as Pook's first clipper—which is not to say his first vessel. Confusions between designer and builder begin with her.

In the first book-length account of the clippers, Clark says that Pook "designed" the *Surprise.* Referring to her on an earlier page, he writes, "Mr. Hall was a master ship-builder and had figured the weights, displacement, and stability of his ship with the same exactness with which an astronomer foretells the transit of a planet." Yet these calculations were the designer's primary task. Cutler writes, "To Hall belongs the honor of constructing the first large clipper ship built outside of New York. This was the *Surprise,* of 1261 tons, designed by Pook." It should be noted, however, that the Lows of New York employed Pook to design her, and Hall to build her, when the yards around Manhattan had more gold rush orders than they could handle. This first outright clipper launched at East Boston carried, as if to stress the point, a carved representation of the great seal of New York on her stern.

It is understandable that Gothamites, ordering a ship to be built where whittler's eye and rule of thumb had shaped most models, would have sought out a Bostonian acquainted with the recent New York revolution in marine architecture; but the drain of the California crisis had produced also a shortage of shipmasters. In a letter published five years earlier in the Boston *Post,* Robert Bennet Forbes had remarked, "The brig *Antelope* and her commander are too well known to require any comment." This original Forbes-owned *Antelope,* built by Hall, was one of several vessels into which Forbes had put his favorite skipper, Philip Dumaresq. Writing in the last days of sail, Clark called them still the only combination of square-rigger and captain that had ever been able to beat through the Formosa Channel against the unrelenting northeast monsoon. It was a jolt to Boston when the Lows of New York hired the most distinguished Boston shipmaster to take command of the only clipper laid down so far in Massachusetts. It seems also to have irked Hall, who rightly regarded himself as an exemplary mechanic, to have Dumaresq put in charge of construction of the ship he was soon to command. A master builder was responsible for the work on each ship, answerable only to the operator of the shipyard. Her intended commander, meddling in this role, could be a wonderful nuisance.

The looming up at Hall's yard of a big clipper for New Yorkers encouraged the Bostonians to look at last to their own share of the cream of the California trade. Richard McKay states that a contract for "the pioneer of the 'extreme' clipper fleet"—Donald McKay's *Stag Hound*—stipulated delivery within 60 days. If so, her builder was allowed more time. The diligent marine reporter of the Boston *Atlas* announced on August 26, 1850, that he had seen her half-model and that McKay had made a point of it to stress his familiarity with the models of all previous notable clippers. Work on the *Stag Hound* began before the end of August. She was launched on December 7, 1850.

Two months earlier, in its issue of October 5, the Boston *Daily Advertiser* carried this announcement:

The splendid ship SURPRISE, *of New York, of about 1200 tons, will be launched this (Saturday) forenoon, about 11 o'clock, by Mr Saml Hall, at East Boston.*

In calling the *Stag Hound* the pioneer extreme clipper, Richard McKay was stretching a point unless he meant to confine his candidates to Boston. The *Celestial* and *White Squall*, built earlier at New York, earned the adjective "extreme." It should be stressed, however, that Pook's *Surprise*, the only Boston clipper launched before the *Stag Hound*, was described by contemporaries as a beautifully balanced sharp ship rather than as an extreme model. This is significant because she proved herself on the San Francisco run to be the better performer.

Something of the difference between these first two clippers built at Boston may be gathered from their measurements.

The *Surprise* was registered at 183 feet 6 inches by 38 feet 8 inches by 22 feet. The *Stag Hound*'s equivalent dimensions made her about 32 feet longer, a foot wider, but a foot less deep. Chapelle, after comparing the original plans, made the *Stag Hound* 27 feet longer and 2 feet 9 inches less deep. By either comparison, Pook's relatively as well as absolutely deeper vessel was much more capacious per registered ton. If McKay consulted Griffiths, as contemporary sources indicate, the decision in favor of a very sharp bottom defied the latter's revised doctrine: that flat floors in a large ship would better her speed as well as her capacity. Where Pook had gone a little way beyond the example of the *Sea Witch*, giving the *Surprise* 30 inches of "dead rise" at half floor, the *Stag Hound* had close to the extreme for any clipper: 40 inches.

The usual drop in tonnage between original and Moorsom measurement shows the extent of this particular sacrifice. By the misleading original registry figures the *Surprise* was the smaller by 273 tons; when the two clippers were remeasured by rules revealing actual capacity the difference between them was only 94 tons. Pook's was consequently the more economical vessel to operate. She continued to be a moneymaker throughout the difficult years when most clippers went begging for cargoes. McKay's first clipper had no chance to demonstrate her ability to adjust to the worst of times. She died by fire at sea in 1861. Pook's first clipper lived 14 years longer than that before being wrecked by an alcoholic scamp who posed as a pilot.

The impatient owners of the *Surprise* had her fully rigged before launching. They hurried a partial cargo into her in Boston and hired the iron tug *R. B. Forbes* to tow her down to New York lest Dumaresq have any problem with her, lightly laden, in the boisterous late fall weather. Six days after the Boston launch of her larger competitor, Pook's *Surprise* cast off her Manhattan hawsers and headed for the Golden Gate. On this first voyage her elapsed time from Sandy Hook was 96 days 15 hours to the Clark's Point anchorage in the bay at San Francisco. It was the fastest passage on record, a few hours better than that of the *Sea Witch* completed eight months earlier. The *Stag Hound*, sharper and larger, spent 114 days on her first passage to California and an average of 122 on her first three, against 111 days average for the three voyages made by the *Surprise* in this trade.

On Christmas Day of 1850 the Boston *Daily Advertiser* recorded the launch, four days earlier, of "the TORNADO, owned by Daniel C. Bacon, Esq. and others. . . . This is the ship which it was at first intended should be called the Game Cock." When registered on January 22, 1851, she was again the *Game Cock,* her intermediary name thus having become available to another notable clipper not to be launched until a year later.

The last clipper on which Pook probably worked with Hall was this disputed *Game Cock,* of 1,392 old-measurement tons. The author of *The Clipper Ship Era,* who made a San Francisco voyage as second mate in Pook's *Northern Light* and who writes of him as of an acquaintance, ascribes the *Game Cock* without qualification to Pook, but there are reasons for thinking her the somewhat disappointing upshot of pressures from builder and owner as well. Pook's name does not appear in contemporary announcements, perhaps because of a dispute later aired in the press when Hall claimed—as Chapelle summarizes it—that Pook had designed their preceding vessel, the *Surprise,* under the "detailed supervision" of her builder, who "had determined what characteristics the ship should have."

The *Game Cock* seems to be one more example of a merchant's belated notion that his failure to recognize an improvement some years before could be compensated for by applying it even more emphatically now. There on the stocks when she was laid down stood the *Surprise,* with 30 inches of dead rise; nearby stood the *Stag Hound,* with 40 inches. Bacon, a successful skipper who had swallowed the anchor to become an even more successful merchant, could have regarded the sharper bottom of the larger ship as indicating the direction of progress—since the *Stag Hound* was by a few weeks the later of the two to be designed.

In his extensive study of the *Stag Hound,* published in 1855, Griffiths wrote, "Perhaps the greatest mistake in her model consisted in the great amount of deadrise, detracting from her stability and capacity. . . ." Despite one or two bizarre excesses, New York in 1850 was working its way out of the early Griffiths influence and accepting his own revised recommendation for flat floors in any large fast ship. The Bostonian

Samuel Hall specialized at East Boston in building fast vessels for Boston's ventures in the Far East, including the illicit opium trade, for which speed and weatherliness were essential. In 1843 he launched the opium brig *Antelope*, painted in Boston harbor 20 years later by Fitzhugh Lane. Below her is the much larger *Game Cock*, built by Hall in 1850, perhaps from Samuel Hartt Pook's model. Forbes's rig is evident. (See pp. 290–93, 295.)

owners seem still to have been relying upon the known records of earlier and smaller sharp-bottomed New York ships, and that probably was what prevailed in the case of the *Game Cock*. As might have been predicted from this feature of her design, she gained a reputation for working to windward, an advantage offset by her crank behavior in heavy seas and generally with the wind abeam. She established fine records on two lucky passages when the weather was right. Hall's craftsmanship is attested to in her life span of 30 years. But whoever had the final task of harmonizing the conflicting principles of her design is to be credited with the fact that she still found employment when many other fast ships did not, having had only one period of idleness: when Confederate raiders were busy.

For more than five years after her launch, Hall and Pook went their separate ways to produce other notable clippers. The suggestion that the owner, not the builder, was responsible for the *Game Cock's* excessive dead rise is made plausible by Hall's reversion to models more nearly resembling the *Surprise*. He produced eight that measured above 1,000 tons, all but one of which have usually been listed as "medium clippers." The exception, his own favorite, was the *Wizard*, of 1,601 tons, launched in 1853. His eighty-fourth vessel, she obligingly celebrated the fact by establishing the record of 84 days from Manila to New York, which stands unequaled, but her showing was otherwise uneven. When the performances of Hall's clippers as a group are compared with those of clippers similar in size designed by Pook in the same years, for other builders, the inference emerges that any changes which Hall did make in Pook's primary design for the *Surprise* could not have hurt her very much. Their association in producing three of the first four fast Boston ships, in 1850, looks like a case of a highly competent and self-reliant mature man resenting the intrusion of a young outright genius.

At a time when patents were being issued for multitudinous contraptions, ships' lines were not patentable. Rule-of-thumb builders were in the habit of making small changes from one vessel to the next. Thus it may be unjust to think of Hall's production of more ships resembling the *Surprise* as plagiarism. Several builders in three states purchased a Pook design and

then launched other vessels, without credit, that seem to have
been closely based upon it. Fairburn assumes that disgust
with such practices caused Pook in his latter thirties to follow
his father into government service, but there are more explicit
reasons for that decision, which was not made final until a
decade after the clipper ship era had ended.

Pook's fame rests upon the unexampled steadiness of excellence in the ships he designed during the five most adventurous
years of that era, centering upon one in particular, his largest.
Among clippers separated out for the highest praise, the three
most often mentioned are Griffiths's *Sea Witch*, McKay's *Flying
Cloud*, and Pook's *Red Jacket*. When their dates are considered
and their models compared, the third appears as the climax
of technical response to an extraordinary kind of commercial
need. Tonnage had been steadily rising. The jumps among
these three, from 908 to 1,782 to 2,435, as first registered, are
representative; but a fairer view of the increase can be got
by looking at the Lloyd's measurements for the two latter.
When the *Flying Cloud* was sold to the British in the Civil
War her registry tonnage dropped to 1,139. The *Red Jacket*,
as an Australian clipper, was remeasured at 2,305 tons. Thus
the McKay clipper was reduced by 36 per cent, and the Pook
by only 5 per cent, a reflection of the serious misstatements
of true capacity arrived at in the United States under the Old
Custom House Measurement system, which persisted in use
for some years after the last Yankee clippers were launched.

It is one warrant of Pook's magic that of all famous large
clippers, his *Red Jacket* succeeded best in outwitting this antique irrationality of the tonnage laws. First devised as a handy
means of calculating the taxable stowage space in a merchant
vessel of average proportions, the old formula for measurement
had invited malformation—blunt ends, excessive depth, cum-
brous deckhouses—to keep taxes as low as possible. It became
an advertised lure that a vessel could lade half again as many
cubic tons as she was taxed for. Nothing at that point was
said of her chances of working to windward in the tides off
Hatteras, or of the extra stores and wages used up in long,
slow voyages.

It is therefore one of the remarkable features of the entire
clipper ship era that four or five hundred vessels were pro-

duced over a ten-year period in defiance of the previous economic edict that a ship must have at least as many measurement tons of stowage space in fact as the theoretical number arrived at by the tax formula. Another reminder perhaps is in order here that cubic tons are not tons by weight. Some clippers could carry almost twice their measurement tonnage in avoirdupois tons of spikes and nails.

Excepting the *Fearless* and the *Ocean Telegraph*, with drops of about 23 per cent, no Pook clipper dispensed with as much as a fifth of her first tonnage rating when remeasured under Moorsom rules. This proof of high original stowage capacity gives his ships a particularly creditable standing when compared with the products of Webb and McKay. Four of Webb's celebrated clippers—the *Flyaway, Invincible, Sword Fish,* and *Young America*—dropped between 25 per cent and 30 per cent when remeasured. Four comparably notable McKay clippers —the *Champion of the Seas, Chariot of Fame, Empress of the Seas,* and *Stag Hound*—were reduced by 20 per cent to 28 per cent. McKay has been criticized for sacrificing too much carrying capacity to attain mere speed, while Webb has had a reputation for resistance to structural extremes. Yet by this test he was the evident extremist—except for the extraordinary case of McKay's *Flying Cloud*, an unemployable marvel when freights were low.

Toward the end of the clipper ship era there was a return to a more prudent balance of qualities in the medium clippers, a few of which were large enough to attain high speeds and to make notably quick passages in high southern latitudes. In this progression, too, the priority of the *Red Jacket* is significant. The two McKay ships most suitable for a fair comparison were the *Champion of the Seas* and the *Donald McKay*, launched, respectively, about six and fourteen months after she was. By American measurement the former seemed to be 12 tons more capacious than Pook's masterpiece, but under Moorsom's formula she measured 358 tons less. The relatively full-bodied *Donald McKay* announced her builder's abrupt move toward prudence. Her lines expressed something of the magic Pook had earlier developed for accommodating a weatherly hull of least resistance within the irrational stipulations of the measurement formula. The *Donald McKay* dropped 6 per cent in tonnage rating when remeasured at Liverpool, which was not significantly different from the *Red Jacket's* drop of 5 per cent. But Pook managed to produce what was universally judged to be an extreme clipper with approximately the same true capacity per measurement ton as McKay's medium one. This latter description was deliberately celebrated in the well-known verses in her praise written by old Captain Frank Waters, with the subtitle "Pioneer Medium Clipper Ship." She was not that either, but rather the large culmination of a trend that throughout the clipper era paralleled the development of outright clipper ships. By McKay's own designation his earlier *Blanche Moore, Santa Claus, Commodore Perry,* and *Japan* were all "medium clippers"—while his next vessel in this sequence, the *Donald McKay,* was the last that he himself described simply as a "clipper," neither medium nor extreme.

Size, but not size alone, continued to be a requisite factor in the extraordinary speed records of the middle fifties. Under British rules McKay's fifth and largest medium clipper measured 144 tons more than Pook's extreme one. Both made, in wild North Atlantic weather, the kind of day's run that a few other great ships found it possible to make only in high southern latitudes: 421 miles for the *Donald McKay,* 417 for the *Red Jacket.* These occasions came 13 months apart, on maiden voyages, the *Red Jacket's* being the earlier. It was in between, on December 12, 1854, that the *Champion of the Seas* made the highest day's run of contemporary record for any sailing ship: 465 miles in the roaring forties. In such an exceptional case it is tempting to assume that steadily extreme luck of the weather, throughout afternoon, night, and morning, was the most significant factor. But she was sharp as well as large—another of several McKay ships publicized on launching day as the largest merchant sailing vessel in the world. By the more meaningful British test of capacity, however, she was on that day 358 tons smaller than her predecessor the *Red Jacket.*

These numerical intricacies frame the particular climax of design represented in Pook's masterwork. By cubic calculation she continued, during the rebuilding of the *Great Republic,* to be the largest merchant sailing ship afloat until the launch of the *Donald McKay*—claims for the *James Baines* and

Champion of the Seas notwithstanding. In Pook's extraordinary balancing of contours for both maximum speed and maximum lading, the "extreme" *Red Jacket* pointed to the feasibility of "medium" clippers to come, but close attention to her secret awaited Griffiths's publication of her lines in June of 1856, when she had been startling the world with her performances for more than two years.

A famous quartet of McKay clippers followed the *Red Jacket* into the Australian service. The first three sacrificed far more cargo space than she did to attain comparably high speeds. Only the *Donald McKay*, after more than a year, gave evidence that the practical designer had profited at last from the example of two notable theoreticians who were his contemporaries; and all of his work that followed was a dwindling anticlimax, in years of commercial retrenchment.

Griffiths's phrase *"carte blanche,"* used in praise of Isaac Taylor for his willingness as owner to let Pook design a ship of the largest size exactly as he thought best, was written in evident celebration of a rarity. Since size aids speed, the reminder is also in order that most of the Pook clippers were smaller than the contemporaries with which they so successfully competed year after year. This is particularly evident in comparison with McKay's. Pook designed what others asked for. McKay, increasingly, designed larger and larger ships on a gamble, financing them himself when he could get no backers. His four clippers built for James Baines and launched between January, 1854, and January, 1855, were all much larger than any of the five fast ships designed by Pook that followed the *Red Jacket.* Of these, only the *Blue Jacket* turned in a claim—not adequately authenticated—to the highest order of speed.

Sharpness helped. McKay's *Lightning*, which appears five times on the lists of ultimate performances, was very sharp indeed. But the evidence favors a combination of both size and sharpness as requisite for the greatest performances. Pook was steadily more successful than McKay in designing ships that could attain high speeds and make fast passages without an undue sacrifice of carrying capacity.

There were mysterious factors too, and the aesthetic was seldom overlooked in the days of great sailing ships. Thomas F. Hall, who spent four and a half years of his teens in Pook's *Belle*

of the West, recalled her in his old age in words that would have
delighted Griffiths:

She was, in my opinion, the finest specimen of naval architec-
ture ever seen. Every line in her hull was grace and beauty.

It was my good fortune . . . in a foreign port, to see that beauti-
ful ship, full rigged, hauled out of the water, to be recoppered.

I still suffer the regret I then felt, on observing for a week or
two that beautiful picture, silhouetted against a fleecy Indian
sky, in a grand panoramic view, that it could not at that time
have been wrought in marble, to vie in artistic beauty through
the ages with the choicest Phidian statues, and to immortalize
the name of her designer, the youthful Samuel Hartt Pooke of
Boston, the Praxiletes of his time. . . . She at last became my
sweetheart, my idol . . . before which, for years, I daily bowed
and worshipped. . . .

It is doubtful if there is any other inanimate thing in existence,
except the home, that has such a grasp upon ones affection as a
merchant sailing ship.

Fairburn's free and easy researches, for the most part undocu-
mented, led him to assign to Pook many more clippers than he
is usually credited with. Since no previous book brings together
the basic information on even a substantial proportion of his
fast ships, Appendix B at the end of this volume presents a list of
them arranged chronologically by launching dates. It includes
all I am aware of that were ascribed to him on good contemporary authority.

Other clippers that have been credited to Pook by recent writers
include the *Flying Childers, John Gilpin,* and *Polynesia,* all built
by Hall within the 12 months following his assured association
with Pook at the outset of Boston's clipper ship production; the
Sea Serpent, Wild Pigeon, and *Witch of the Wave,* built by
George Raynes at Portsmouth; Samuel Hanscomb, Jr.'s *Nightin-*
gale, and Fernald & Pettigrew's *Typhoon,* both likewise of Portsmouth. For these claims I have found no contemporary verification.

THE YEAR 1853

The year that brought the clipper ship era to its zenith was
marked by other excitements. On February 11, 1853, a number of
eminent merchants, scientists, and editors were taken for a pleasant ride in New York harbor aboard the *Ericsson,* a new vessel of

2,200 tons propelled by an engine that had been built under conditions of secrecy at the Hogg and Delamater Works. The witnesses to its performance later signed a statement declaring that "the new motor presented to the world by Captain Ericsson . . . is likely to prove superior to steam" for seagoing vessels. One of the guests, James J. Mapes, had been an editor of the *Journal of the Franklin Institute* and vice president of the American Institute of the City of New York, which a decade earlier had provided a forum for Griffiths's lectures on the shaping of ships. Professor Mapes thought this event of 1853 a genuinely pivotal one, referring to "but two epochs of science—the one marked by Newton, the other by Ericsson." Horace Greeley's newspaper proclaimed that "the age of steam is closed, the age of caloric opens."

Ericsson was trying, in his new engine, to use hot air rather than hot steam as the expansive force in his cylinders, with an arrangement providing for the reuse of the heat wasted in the exhaust of a steam engine. Although he was as well aware of the law of the conservation of energy as any man living, he was attacked in the popular press for trying to achieve perpetual motion. His caloric engine did run with a remarkable economy of fuel, but in an age that worshipped velocity it was incapable of competitive speeds. Operating at a temperature recorded at 444 degrees Fahrenheit, it destroyed its lubricants in a manner that contemporary technology could not correct. The owners of the vessel converted her into an ordinary steamship. When she was 20 years old all her machinery was removed and she became a notably successful square-rigger—a fact reinforcing the claim of Ericsson's chief biographer that his mid-century steamers had the lines of the best contemporary sailing ships.

The inventor himself wrote, in 1875, "I regard the hot-air ship as by far my best work, it was simply a mechanical marvel," but the financiers of shipping did not agree.

The sadly foreshortened age of caloric coincided with a much more stubborn challenge to the age of steam: in 1853 the American clipper ship era brought the ancient technology of sail to its magnificent crest. Carl C. Cutler, whose researches are still definitive 40 years after publication of his findings, listed in *Greyhounds of the Sea* 426 ships built between 1850 and 1856 that deserve, on the basis of their lines and rig, to be classified as clippers. Of these, 24 were launched in 1850, 54 in 1851, and 75

For two decades prior to the *Monitor* contract that forced a deep revision in naval tactics, the talents of John Ericsson were crudely ignored by his adopted country's government, but at his death in 1889 he was apotheosized amid oak and laurel boughs. Late in life he expressed the view that the engine of the "caloric ship" *Ericsson* of 1853, which used hot air instead of steam, was his most important invention; but the caloric engine was not fast enough for the speed-worshiping clipper ship era. A steam engine soon was substituted. Later, shorn of her four stacks, the *Ericsson* was converted into a particularly fast sailing ship. (See pp. 223–49, 300–301, 469.)

in 1852. Then came the peak year, 1853, with 120 clipper launchings. Production fell off thereafter at a rate somewhat steeper
than that of its rise. Launchings numbered 71 in 1854, 42 in 1855,
and 40 in 1856. Total production in the three-year period following the peak year was, curiously, the same as in the three years
preceding it: a fortuitous, old-fashioned, seven-year business
cycle. Then depression struck. No more than ten vessels describable as clippers were built in 1857 and nine in 1858. The
size of the ships was dwindling as well. The three launched in
1859 were all of less than 1,000 tons measurement, and they had
no successors. The California gold rush, with the added stimulus
of Britain's relaxation of her navigation code, had caused the
swift rise in the building of fast ships in America. A demand
for such ships for the emigrant traffic to Australia, following
the verification of large gold deposits there, eased what would
have been an even more rapid falling off of production in the
over-expanded American shipyards.

The year 1853 was marked also by an extravagant conceptual
overreaching on both sides of the Atlantic. The climax of skill
and ingenuity in fashioning large structures out of sticks of wood
was expressed in Donald McKay's *Great Republic;* but at about
the same time something known only as the great iron ship was
taking shape in the mind of the English engineer Isambard King-
dom Brunel. Eventually Brunel's prophetic monster was to be
given the name *Great Eastern*—a reference to the service for
which she was at first intended. This symbolic overlapping in
1853 of the wooden nautical past and the metal nautical future
had little reference, on either side of the water, to the real needs
of commerce. Both vessels were to have opportunistic afterlives
in consequence. A comparison is difficult because McKay's
largest clipper was never measured in her original form under
the Moorsom rules; but her Old Custom House tonnage, 4,555,
represents so minor a fraction of Brunel's ambitious design that
exactitude loses significance. When finally launched in 1858,
the *Great Eastern* measured 18,915 tons, something like four
times the capacity of the *Great Republic.* She was about ten times
the size of the largest American passenger carrier of the classic
wooden sailing fleet, J. A. Westervelt's *Amazon,* of 1,771 tons.

The *Great Eastern* was not meant to be a competitor in the
transatlantic traffic, but she became one; originally she was

The *Great Eastern*, Britain's "great iron ship," announced in the 1850's the seriousness of a coming contest over shipbuilding materials. (See pp. 303, 305.)

supposed to stitch the far places of the British Empire together. Her huge jump in tonnage was in fact a bad miscalculation. The vessel was a mechanical triumph for her period but a financial disaster. Nothing so large was tried again until the turn into the twentieth century. She served many practical functions during her 40 years at sea, including the laying of the first successful Atlantic cable, but she was ruinous to her investors. Nevertheless, the rumors that began to spread in 1853 of Brunel's intentions, confirmed in the spring of the ensuing year when work on his colossus was actually begun, dramatized for the public what the engineers assumed: that British metal ships could be made practically limitless in their dimensions, while vessels of American wood were already nearing the limits of their feasible size.

Amid all the excitement, Griffiths was not impressed. In an editorial published as the hull was taking definite shape he called "The Great London Steamship . . . overburdened mechanically with herself," and added the prediction, "so will she be financially too expensive to be profitable, both in first cost and in management." He was right, but even as he wrote, the business of supplying ever larger wooden ships for the passenger lines of the United States had reached a climax well short of the structural limitations imposed by the nature of America's logical shipbuilding material.

The *Amazon*, likewise conceived in the closing weeks of 1853, was in two respects the ultimate Yankee sailing liner. Although dwarfed by the vast iron shadow to come, she was not only the largest Western Ocean sailing packet that would ever be built, but also the sharpest—the only one to creep into the clipper ship bracket for length-to-breadth ratio, which in her case was 5.1 to 1.

The year 1853 may also be said to mark the acceptance of the screw propeller as a device at least as important as the paddle wheel for propulsion in deep water. Brunel's drafts for the *Great Eastern* made provision for the use of both—a good thing too, on the occasion in 1861 when her paddle boxes were torn off in a storm, one after the other, while her propeller survived to take her back to port.

Before mid-century it had become evident that the Yankee lines of sailing packets were not going to recover the luxury passenger traffic that was being taken over by Samuel Cunard's steamships. In 1847 Edward K. Collins, who had organized the Dramatic Line about a decade earlier, got from Congress a contract to carry the mails that would make competition with the subsidized Cunarders possible. The first of his large paddle-wheel steamers, the *Atlantic,* left for her maiden voyage to Liverpool on April 27, 1850. A little later, with a crossing of 10 days 16 hours from New York, she bested by 12 hours the previous fastest time of any Cunard ship. The new Cunard *Asia* promptly moved the British into the lead again, according to some calculators, with a first homeward run from Boston of 9 days 14 hours. The *Atlantic* was the larger vessel, measuring 2,845 tons against the *Asia*'s 2,227. The Cunarder had a graceful clipper bow, with bowsprit and jib boom to carry conventional headsails. The straight, sparless bow of the Collins steamer caused much comment at Liverpool; it was a portent of the typical shape forward of deep-water steamers as their reliance upon sail lessened.

Three more Collins liners of about the same model and dimensions went into service a few months after the first one. In their case too, 1853 was to be the year of maximum triumph. Collins insisted upon the old promptness in departures of his earlier sailing packets, with steam engines adding a regularity in arrivals that sailing packets could not match. Collins offered a better wine card than the prudent Cunard's, as well as a hard-driving policy of operation that was a dubious reflection in steam navigation of the spar-smashing tradition of his square-riggers in the Dramatic Line. By 1853 the British were seriously on the defensive, and many on both sides of the ocean were ready to concede that sail itself was done for—but disaster struck in the year following. The Collins liner *Arctic,* operating in foggy weather in a reckless fashion that drew strictures from R. B. Forbes and many others concerned for safety at sea, was sunk in a collision, drowning Collins's own wife and children among the 500 passengers who perished. Fifteen months later the Collins liner *Pacific* simply vanished; she is supposed to have struck an iceberg. A public that had taken great pride in all four vessels promptly reversed itself and became critical of a policy involving too much risk. Although Collins tried to regain his position with the largest of wooden Atlantic steamers, the *Adriatic,* of 4,144 tons, the depression that made a bankrupt of McKay ruined the steamship operator too. The *Adriatic* had made only two voyages when she was put up at auction for the line's debts in March of 1858.

During the Civil War it was a convenience to the United States to have the transatlantic carrying trade revert entirely to protected neutral flags. The Cunarders regained their lead and held it, with their usual calculated prudence. Up until the submarine attacks of World War II the British line could boast that it had never lost a passenger.

The panic that ruined Collins and McKay added to its many other casualties the nautical magazine published by Griffiths. Its last issues reveal an evident striving to justify its continuation because an industry loath to support it was most deeply in need of a public forum for discussion of its problems in the difficult times when no-one seemed to know what to do next. The editor appears to have been pondering the recent experience of railroads when he recommended a separation of functions to put an end to a muddled sort of competition that had marked the recession from the great year 1853, when there had seemed to be an abundance of employments for all ships of all kinds:

A division of service and special adaptation is needed now for sailing ships and steamers. The former should be designed wholly for freighting, and suited to the special trades. The latter, where intended for freighting, should carry emigrants or second-class passengers only; and the highest type for speed should take no freight, but only first-class passengers, mails, express packages, and precious property. Steam vessels as at present constructed are only superior to sailing vessels in the regularity of their trips. Sometimes sailers have proved the faster. . . . Steam machinery must be vastly improved before sailing ships, if well designed, can be displaced by steamers in distant trades.

Heroic elements in the design, construction, and use of sailing ships had been somewhat stimulated by the economic challenge of steam, but the time when the clipper ship records would be bettered by steamers was still far ahead. Henry Hall, in his report of 1882, noted that no steamer had at that date equaled the best day's runs of three McKay clippers. Although the *Alaska,* in steaming 419 miles in 24 hours, had come close to the lowest of them, she was still 18 miles below what was then thought to be the fastest sailing ship record, 437 miles, logged by the *Sovereign of the Seas.*

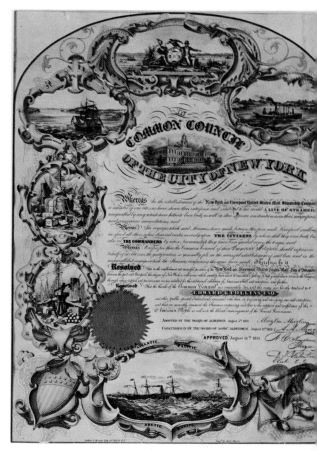

This certificate of 1851 authorized Edward K. Collins to operate his four new transatlantic mail steamers out of New York. The *Atlantic (right, middle)* was their prototype. The prudent Cunard Line countered with its new, more traditionally shaped *Asia (upper right)*, but Collins, after his early success, was undone by disasters that came from too much risk taking. In 1853 the *Arctic (lower right)* was wrecked. A year or two later the *Pacific* simply vanished. The *Adriatic (below)* of 1856 joined the line too late to avert bankruptcy in the depression that followed. (See pp. 306-7.)

The odd career of the *Ericsson* underlines Griffiths's sense of a need to choose particular forms and propellants properly suited to specific uses. For a few months in 1853 the caloric ship was a conceptual marvel that was never adequately tested. After her uneasy investors equipped her with orthodox engines, she helped for a year to keep the Collins Line going. Later services such as a hitch on the transatlantic run to Bremen and her use by the government to haul supplies in the Civil War brought her finally to the point of conversion to square rig for two last decades in what Griffiths called the distant trades, and as a west-coast collier.

The distant trades were what had stimulated the sudden development of fast models of large capacity to a high point of production in 1853: first the westward dash around the Horn to California, then the eastward plunge under the Cape of Good Hope to Australia. Sometimes the first of these continued into the ultimate distance of a circumnavigation; the second characteristically did so. When the two mid-century gold rushes had given way to commercial stimulants of a more normal sort the distant trades ramified: guano to Europe from islands off the west coast of South America, wheat from California. The *Ericsson* as a square-rigger eventually distinguished herself in the wheat races out of San Francisco. In the 1874 race she equaled the fast time of Webb's extreme clipper *Young America*, another product of the year 1853. Both took 103 days. In the same race Donald McKay's last large ship, the *Glory of the Seas*, measuring 2,103 tons, took 118 days; that, in her fourth year at sea, was one day above the commendable average she made altogether during ten such passages from San Francisco to British ports.

In an inspection of the long tussle between sail and steam the circumstance should not be overlooked that the merits of two individual ships with different propulsion, side by side on a particular ocean course, could be judged only in a larger context. A ship under canvas that sensibly followed Maury's sailing directions for one of the distant trades would have the source of its power, the wind, almost constantly available in some modest measure throughout a voyage of perhaps 10,000 miles. A steamer of 1853, on the same course, would have been lucky to limp the same distance if she had given all her cargo space to nothing but fuel—and refueling ports, along such routes, did not yet exist.

The failure of ocean steamers, for several decades, to match speeds achieved by the clippers in 1853 did not reflect a technical inability to do so. The best river steamers of the early 1840's could make 20 miles an hour on demand, not as a miraculous brief exception; and before the Civil War a speed of 25 miles an hour had been reached. But these vessels were voracious gobblers of fuel. Some of them, to save a maximum of space for passengers and freight, refueled several times a day. They were of shallow draft and top-heavy, unsuited to oceanic waves. An ocean-going equivalent could undoubtedly have been built in 1853 to outpace in reasonable weather the very best of the clippers; but such a vessel could not have carried fuel enough to reach the roaring forties and fifties, where the clippers' great records were made, and her life in such waters would probably have been brief indeed. Such efforts at comparison soon show themselves to be irrelevant.

Why relatively slow, sturdy sailing ships could persist in competition with steam long after engines had attained a considerable sophistication is therefore clear enough. Commercial stringencies of the late 1850's dampened innovation of all sorts. Ericsson's experience in 1853, after the lavish backing he had received from Forbes and other private investors, was an advance warning. His own durable faith in his caloric engine may mark an instance of better judgment in the world of commerce than in that of technology—which wealth supports at its own discretion —but as things turned out there was to be no recovery in kind after the long recession from the confident upsurge of mid-century. Before that phenomenal crest the principal changes in nautical technology were made by men who envisioned an attainable perfection—Griffiths called it beauty—a perfection that would bring to a prosperous economy even greater rewards. After 1853 the changes in the shaping and management of ships were mostly of a sort that retreated from any such ideal in the hope of sustaining an ailing enterprise by imaginative prudence. Only the heavy requirements of government in wartime were to bring the stimulus of creative innovation back into American shipyards.

9 The Distorted Shapes of War

THE TURN TOWARD IRON AND STEAM

Sentiments such as those that Seaman Hall carried into old age from his exhilarating love affair with Pook's *Belle of the West* did not hamper her designer or his eminent shipyard contemporaries when the condition of commerce or the ill-foreseen needs of the naval establishment called for a quick shift from wood and sail to steam and iron. McKay, in following his large extreme models with a baker's dozen of smaller wooden medium clippers, was exceptional. Webb, an early producer of noteworthy clippers, was also the first to stop building them on principle: he foresaw the results of overproduction when the real need for speed-above-all began, toward the end of 1853, to decline. After that pivotal year he launched none except the medium clippers *Black Hawk* (2) and *Intrepid*, both begun in 1856, the former a full-bodied ship that perhaps has been listed as a clipper without sufficient reason. Webb had no difficulty in accommodating himself to the transition to steam. Prior to the launch of his last clipper he had laid down 20 steamers, beginning with the large transatlantic side-wheeler *United States* in 1847.

Even in his two huge ironclads, however, Webb persisted in relying upon wood to frame as well as to plank a basic hull. Pook was flexible. He moved smoothly from his remarkable climax in the efficient use of sail and wood alone, through a few intermediate experimental vessels of mixed construction, to concentrate upon the design of iron ships driven wholly by steam. In the fashion of the time, these had sail for emergency use, but all were intended to operate efficiently without it. The first of Pook's six compromise structures was noticed in Griffiths's magazine as the "Japan and China Packet Antelope . . . well furnished with sail and steaming power. . . . Through the kindness of Captain Forbes and Mr. Pook we have been furnished with the mould-loft tables of the ANTELOPE. . . . In regard to her lines, Mr. Pook writes as follows:—'The model was altered somewhat from the original design, being made *one* foot deeper, and ten feet longer, and having a drag line of two feet put on the bottom, which made her somewhat different from Mr. Hall's original design; but, in my opinion, the lines are still too full aft to get the best result from her propeller, and her midship section entirely too square for speed.'"

This time Pook had had a rare chance to reverse the builders' alleged practice of tampering with his models. Hall was absent from Boston at a critical juncture; R. B. Forbes turned to Pook to complete the design and "superintend her building." The little steam packet, rigged as a barkentine with Forbes's revised plan for double topsails on her foremast, was rather a comedown from the *Ocean Telegraph* and *Blue Jacket* of the preceding year, but the general situation of Pook's employment was probably normal.

Forbes registered the *Antelope* at Boston on July 14, 1855: 155 feet 6 inches long, 26 feet 11 inches broad, 10 feet 6 inches deep. She arrived out at Hong Kong on November 17.

At about the time the *Antelope* was being laid down, Pook took as apprentice a 17-year-old youth from Wolfeboro, New Hampshire, who had developed a distaste for his job of counting money in a Boston bank. His name was William Henry Varney. His addition to the enterprise may explain the directory listing, S. H. Pook & Company, for the year 1856 only. Varney was destined to carry forward—if in a less spectacular fashion—the function of independent naval architect, beginning at an age even younger than Pook's when he created it.

William H. Sumner, in his history of East Boston published in 1858, devoted a long notice to "the iron steam-ship 'Le Voyageur de la Mer'" and claimed that the "honor" of applying iron "for the first time to the construction of a first-class vessel, belongs to East Boston," where she had recently been launched on February 25, 1857. She measured 1,300 tons.

The models and details of the ship were furnished by Samuel H. Pook, our distinguished naval constructor, who has done full justice to his high reputation . . . frames are of iron, in the shape of a right angle, with a base of three inches, to which the outside

The lower of these pictures is a lithograph by Fitzhugh Lane of the steamship *Antelope*, which was produced for Robert Bennet Forbes and associates by Samuel Hartt Pook, who had to begin with a model already supplied by Samuel Hall. Pook altered it considerably. He was in control from the beginning of design of the *Merrimack (upper picture)*, a much larger passenger steamer intended for service to the Southern ports. The Civil War interrupted this plan and she became a government transport. (See pp. 313–14, 318.)

plates are riveted, and a perpendicular of six inches. Between the perpendiculars she is filled with hacmatack frames. . . .

The account further notes the use of red-hot rivets to produce a smooth outer surface. These contemporary details of construction are explicit enough to offset the misleading opinion of Fairburn (himself a designer of large steel ships around 1900) that the *Voyageur de la Mer* had "a wood framing, ceiling, and decking" with "some intermittent iron framing." Rather than wood braced with metal strapping, in the manner of early composite construction, her basic structural frames were of iron braced by additional wooden ones. Although a transitional experiment in construction, she does appear to put to Pook's credit, in the difficult year 1856, the design of the first large iron steamship constructed in the United States. (The supplier of his middle name, Naval Constructor Samuel Hartt, had designed in 1841 the modest iron paddle-wheel steamer *Michigan*, of 582 tons, which was to stay in commission for 80 years continuously, thanks to fresh water.) The fact that the *Voyageur de la Mer* could be financed at all in a year of calamity can be ascribed to the Yankee enterprise of a wandering Bostonian who convinced the pasha of Egypt that he needed such a vessel. Business at the East Boston shipyards otherwise was at low ebb. McKay, after much overreaching, had become insolvent in September, and his principal backer, Enoch Train, soon followed him into bankruptcy.

The knowledgeable did not mislead themselves. Griffiths, in October of the panic year 1857, asked, "What will be done with the clipper ships to render them profitable?" He lamented the diversion of some of them to "a trade which of all others is the most revolting to humanity, although not yet proscribed by law, and though as yet only known by the term Coolie, is but another type of the *slave trade.*" He had a strong personal reason for detesting the cruel swindle of the traffic in indentured coolies. His own beloved *Sea Witch*, the marvel of the age, had been diverted to that employment for want of a better and had met her death on a reef near Cuba in April of the preceding year.

With the best of ships perverted to such purposes, there were very few orders for new ones. It is not surprising to come upon Pook's inquiry to Forbes, dated December 9, 1857, asking whether a job of which Forbes had spoken was the same that Hall had just called to his attention: the superintending of a dry dock at Shanghai. The letter likewise reveals that Pook had already applied for a post as Naval Constructor and had been told that there was no vacancy.

Efforts will be made this winter to establish a Dry Dock at San Francisco. I have been asked if I would go to San Francisco, if I should receive an appointment. Now in view of this, will, you please give me your advice. The probable effects of the climate upon a person of my Temperament at Shanghai The Duties required, and the Compensation.

I find myself wondering whether Hall hoped to get for the naval architect a job that would locate him about as far from East Boston as it was feasible to go. Pook hung on through the slump. In the meanwhile another young man of vision, Harrison Loring, changed his entry in the Boston directories. For several years his name had been followed by the phrase "builder of engines." In 1857, with prospects dismal and costs accordingly low, Loring took his cue from the founders of the old Black Ball Line, expanded his South Boston plant, and advertised himself as "builder of engines and of iron vessels." He first launched two small steamers for clients in the Far East, and in 1859, with business recovering, he asked Pook to design two sizable sister ships, the *Massachusetts* and the *South Carolina,* intended for a new line between Boston, Charleston, and New Orleans. They measured about 1,160 tons apiece and were originally described as of composite construction, which at this time had begun to mean wood planking on iron frames; but they were both listed as "Screw steamer; iron" when bought by the Navy on May 3, 1861, for use as transports. The purchase price second-hand was $172,500 apiece. They were fast for their day, rated at 11 or 12 knots, and as blockaders they took many prizes.

It was in the winter of 1858–59 that Pook's apprentice Varney, aged 20, set up his own mould loft at East Boston, where McKay's effort to reorganize his shipyard with European business had brought no results. In 1860, however, a New York builder called upon Pook to design three fighting ships wanted by the Spanish government. The old system of naval rates was dissolving; these, all referred to as frigates, were to carry 60, 50, and 40 guns.

Dahlgren's experiments with larger and fewer pieces of ordnance evidently had not been taken seriously in that corner of Europe. Work on the Spanish frigates was held up when the long-sputtering fuse of civil war, toward year's end, neared the point of explosion. Ships of other sorts, rather than antique broadside platforms, seemed a better gamble: ocean-going steamers particularly. Loring again turned to Pook for plans for the *Merrimack*, of 1,991 tons, and the *Mississippi*, of 2,008, the former screw driven, the latter a paddler. These, intended like their smaller predecessors for the Boston line to southern ports, are also listed as composites.

On March 26, R. B. Forbes, worried by the southerners' seizures thus far of forts pierced for 1,099 cannon, went to Washington to urge the Secretary of the Navy to build "at once a number of gunboats." He was informed that it was a matter for Congress, but the attack of April 12 on Fort Sumter was one portent too many to be evaded. Swift moves followed to put into action plans already on file, a few even in the dry-rotting bureaus of the Navy Department, which was awakening to its particular disaster that turned out to be a salvation: many of its senior officers bestowed their moribund talents upon the Confederacy, and no-one tried to stop the defection. Others whose respect for their oath of allegiance was regarded as dubious—Matthew Fontaine Maury was one—were cashiered. In the peculiar chivalry of the time, such able men as Maury, who could help the South greatly, and did, were simply allowed to go. But such ornaments of the peaceful Navy as Commodore Josiah Tattnall turned out to be lumbering tacticians in the cause of Dixie.

Beyond his advocacy of gunboats, Forbes had a plan in mind for a rather ambitious armed vessel that he proposed as civilian contractor to build for the government. A few hours after the arrival at Boston of news that Fort Sumter had been surrendered, Pook wrote Forbes a revealing letter concerning the proposed vessel. In it he was careful to sketch the substance of a clause to be included in the agreement with the shipbuilder:

That the Naval Architect under your direction, furnish model, moulds & Drawings complete for all parts of the fabric in detail (with the exception of Engines & Engine Room and parts attached thereto) all which plans to be subject to your revision, and issued only with your approval with signature attached, to *the Master Builder for his guidance, which cannot be altered or varied but by your permission or such person as you may direct for this duty—for which service the Naval Architect should be allowed say $1500 more or less dollars. . . . I would make this suggestion hoping it may . . . prevent any misconception on the part of the Builder—or others as in a case of this kind it might occur.*

Pook trusted Forbes to make sensible changes under consultation, but evidently had had his fill of the behavior of master builders. He also requested that if he were expected to design gun carriages, the design should be subject to the approval of his father. The family relationship appears to have been happy and close.

THE 90-DAY GUNBOATS

After the depression years Samuel Hartt Pook's talents were again in high demand, not only in the commercial shipbuilding industry, which was bracing itself for a gust of government contracts, but in direct employment by the Navy itself. John Lenthall, chief of the Bureau of Naval Construction, wired him to drop everything and come to Washington at once. But Pook had already made wartime agreements with Forbes and others. In a letter dated May 16, 1861, he told Forbes of Lenthall's telegram, which he had just received. With strong underlining for emphasis that almost never appears elsewhere in his correspondence, he wrote, "*I can't come,* as I much prefer to stay at home."

"Home" meant Charlestown, where he had married Ellen Maria Frothingham 11 years earlier and had settled down to a career of stubborn independence, which he was not yet ready to forgo. Some of the brief recent accounts of him imply that at this point, in disgust over sharp practices in the shipyards, he began his long stint as an employee of the Navy—but this is less than a half-truth. Although his preference for home soon did give way in the national crisis, there was still the complication of his local commitments. He consequently recommended that Forbes employ Albert G. H. Pook, a draftsman at the Brooklyn Navy Yard, to substitute for him: "Start him with your work at my loft—at anyrate until my return," with the added promise that "Father & myself" would help the newcomer and that "there need be no delay with your work if he will come."

Forbes, as it turned out, accompanied Pook to Washington, along with three other representatives of the shipbuilding industry. All five urged upon Gideon Welles the imperative strategic need for ironclads. Lincoln's new Secretary of the Navy was disposed to listen. Welles knew nothing whatever about shipbuilding and very little about the Navy, but his layman's objectivity was put to the test immediately with a decision he reported succinctly at year's end: "No sailing vessels have been ordered to be built, for steam as well as heavy ordnance, has become an indispensable element of the most efficient naval power." Luckily the traitors, Ingraham, Tattnall, and the rest, did not have to be coped with at such a time.

The only quick way to retake coastal forts that had been seized by the Confederates to protect their centers of shipping was by bombardment from the sea, a task for which the sailing vessels of the Navy were almost useless and the steamers far too few. It was fortunate that Forbes in his earlier visit had helped prepare the way when Lenthall urged upon Secretary Welles the immediate production of some modest, screw-propelled wooden gunboats that could maneuver briskly in the tides and shoals of intricate estuaries. They could serve also as attack vessels in support of the few large steam sloops-of-war that were available—or as blockaders. This time Welles assumed that the impending special session of Congress would support him; he approved the gunboat program in advance of the act that authorized it. Forbes wrote in his reminiscences that "instead of twenty-five, fifty should have been begun before July." Twenty-three were decided upon in fact, a number probably representing the count of available slips in private yards where keels could be laid immediately. All the navy yard space was taken or committed for fourteen much larger sloops of war, seven approved in February and seven more for which authorization was to be sought at the special session; but it was not likely that these could be ready within a year. The gunboat program stressed alacrity.

The importance of these orthodox little ships has been largely shadowed by the overhanging glamour of major and more innovative ones. Lenthall had wired for Pook to aid him in shaping up one prototype so nearly foolproof that the building of exact copies could be insisted upon as the very first order of business in the most prominent shipyards from Maine to Delaware.

It has become the standard precaution in such cases to subject a prototype to rigorous tests before risking its multiplication. At this high moment of crisis, Pook and Lenthall were on the verge of producing the first numerous class of identical naval vessels. There was no room for delay. They had to be right the first time—and they were. The result was a remarkable emergency fleet; it promptly established for the Union a tactical superiority in coastal waters and on the Mississippi that continued throughout the war and was probably the chief controlling factor in its outcome. On a number of occasions when the Confederate armies were moving into position to capture centers of heavy industry—the agricultural South's great lack—they were stopped as much by logistic shortages as by the Union armies; and the shortages were the result of naval blockade.

The nature of Pook's task as an independent naval architect is illuminated in this particular connection. The Hamersly biographical notice quotes him as saying that "at the opening of our Civil War, he offered his services to the Government and was called to Washington, where he laid out the plans, under the Chief of the Bureau Lenthal, for the ninety-day gunboats; he superintended the construction of six of these steamers, with others. . . ."

His emphatic "I much prefer to stay at home," written when the call came, makes the claim of a prior offer of his services puzzling. It may be another disturbance in the time sequence of the article, intended to refer to Pook's earlier attempt during the depression to get a government job. Editors necessarily truncate, in such works, creating unforeseen anomalies. The first extensive posthumous notice says, "His services were accepted by the government, and he was called to Washington, where, under chief constructor Linthal, he completed the plans of the first ninety-day gunboats."

The first three contracts were signed on June 29, the last one on July 10. Forbes visited New York five days later for a conference on his own new task as inspector of the nine gunboats to be built in Massachusetts and Maine. He later listed the nine as having been "built under the inspection of myself, S. H. Pook, and Mr. Ellis"—the last a joiner. I assume that the six gunboats which Pook said he superintended—a word implying a larger, continuous responsibility—were additional. At some time in the summer he left the Boston field to his 23-year-old former apprentice Varney and transferred his activities to Connecticut. Thus he probably was concerned directly with the two gunboats built at East Haddam and at Mystic.

Pook, in his often frustrating career at Boston, had been pioneering almost alone to create the full function of the naval architect as it came to be understood two or three decades later. He was prepared to do all the conceptual, mathematical, and supervisory tasks for a particular vessel, or any part of any of them. The intricacy of the undertaking, when he had elevated it above the ancient practice of judging a whittled model by weather eye and rule of thumb, is helpfully explored for the diligent armchair navigator in Chapelle's *The Search for Speed Under Sail* (1967), which gave a little more attention to Pook than he had previously been allotted.

It was during the war years that Pook, for the first time, appears to have had the opportunity to control all the work, from concept through construction, on a series of vessels. As is the case with designers of shoreside dwellings, he of course had to accommodate his concepts to the wishes of their purchasers. But the practices of master builders to which he had objected, the making of alterations without necessary compensations elsewhere in the fabric, did not have to be endured during most of this period. Griffiths, when he wrote that Hayden & Cudworth had been "assisted in maturing the plans and calculations" for the *Herald of the Morning* "by Mr. S. H. Pook," was stressing a happy exception to the "very general rule" of distortions caused by merely common sense.

Pook's great contribution appears to have been his attention to the ultimate refining of balance. When he was able to create a ship from beginning to end of the process, most notably the *Red Jacket,* the result was magnificent. By "maturing the plans and calculations" he brought other men's models to something like the excellence of those that were entirely his own. Lenthall must have had a gunboat design in an advanced state of readiness when he sent off his imperative wire to the man likeliest to make it foolproof in detail. At any rate, that is what Lenthall

When shooting began in the Civil War, John Lenthall *(above, left)*, chief of the Navy's Bureau of Ships, and Samuel Hartt Pook *(above, right)*, civilian naval architect, combined their talents to produce the first numerous class of identical fighting ships, the "90-day gunboats." Their *Cayuga (below)* was heroically successful, and all 23 served with distinction. (See pp. 319–22, 324–35.)

and Pook accomplished, with a brilliance that has never had sufficient notice.

Casual references in standard naval histories leave an impression of these small warships that stands in curious contrast to Secretary Welles's statement of December 1, 1862: "No vessels were ever constructed on better terms for the government, or have better subserved the purposes for which they were designed, than the twenty-three gunboats for which the department contracted . . . without waiting for the action of Congress." Although speed in construction was assured by building no two in the same shipyard, engine builders were too few to follow that scheme with them. Three New York factories powered twelve gunboats. Nine firms in seven other cities equipped the remaining eleven. The hulls cost between $52,000 and $56,500, the more expensive ones with the earliest guaranteed delivery dates. Mechanical equipment cost from $43,000 to $46,000, except for the first four, which had smaller boilers than the others. Like the hulls, the engines were identical in specifications: two for each vessel, horizontal back-action, surface condenser, 30-inch cylinders with 18-inch stroke. The propeller could be operated by both engines working together or by either one with the other disengaged, thus permitting repairs while under way or even during an action. Each boiler could serve either engine. Working steam pressure was a moderate 30 pounds.

The hulls were strengthened throughout by a diagonal bracing of strap iron, $\frac{1}{2}$ inch thick and $3\frac{1}{2}$ inches wide. They displaced 691 tons and measured 507: length 158 feet 4 inches, breadth 28 feet, depth 12 feet. Despite identical specifications, top speed varied. The *Seneca*, first to be launched, was fastest with $11\frac{1}{2}$ knots; the average was a little better than 10. The much larger, unarmored screw sloops—in use and building—were as a group no faster. Most ironclads made only 6 or 7 knots. In a new navy of small experimental types and ponderous transitional ones, the Lenthall-Pook gunboats could thus assume the old function of frigates—scouting around the slow line of battle, nipping in quickly to the point of need, blockading wherever the blockade-runners were nimblest. But in the pinch of new conditions they also were soon to get assignments in the line. They were schooner-rigged with gaff topsails, one square yard on the foremast, and a vestigial light bowsprit of metal. The foresail's clew comfortably cleared a stack a little abaft of amidships. There was working room between mainmast and stack.

The *Ottawa, Pembina, Seneca,* and *Unadilla,* products of efficient New York yards, were the first in service. Only these four actually deserve to be called 90-day gunboats. Contracts for three of them were let on June 29, stipulating delivery on September 27. A fourth, the *Seneca,* was contracted for on July 1, to be delivered on September 28. The other contracts required delivery in from 105 to 148 days. First to be commissioned was the *Unadilla,* on the ninety-third day after her contract was signed. She must therefore have been delivered to the New York Navy Yard well ahead of time. The commissioning of a new vessel involved the mounting of guns, stowage of munitions and stores, quartering of the crew, and a test of all machinery before the hoisting of her national flag and the commander's pendant announced that she was "in commission": ready for sea.

How much of the lapse between launch and commissioning was spent by the contractor in fitting the engines, and how much thereafter in the navy yard to convert a vessel into a fighting machine, is in some cases uncertain. *Harper's Weekly* reported on September 28 that the four named above were all in the water and that the *Winona* had been launched on the fourteenth "fully sparred and rigged, with the propeller and main shafting fitted up in her," after only 46 working days. The *Seneca* had been launched on her fifty-eighth contractual day; her pendant was hoisted 48 days later. The average time between the last swing of a maul at a dog shore and the recital of captain's orders was five weeks. Most of the engines took longer to make than the hulls. New York's Novelty Iron Works, which had powered the largest transatlantic liners, had already developed an engine for foreign gunboats. The model was adaptable to the sudden needs of their own country. It went at a particularly favorable price into the four gunboats first rushed to completion.

The Novelty Works then made three more sets with larger boilers for the *Aroostook* and *Kennebec,* built in Maine, and the *Owasco,* which I assume that Pook himself was supervising at Mystic, Connecticut. The *Aroostook's* builder clearly was at fault for her late commissioning. Her contract called for delivery on October 19, but she did not reach the Boston Navy Yard until January 24 and was not ready for sea until February 20, 1862,

On August 31, 1861, *Harper's Weekly* celebrated with a full page of woodcuts the six 90-day gunboats nearing completion at New York shipyards. One, the *Seneca*, appears above. Another, the *Winona* *(below)*, had a full page to herself in *Harper's* two weeks after she slid into the water, fully sparred, on September 14. (See p. 325.)

one of the last three to go into service. The *Kennebec's* launch on October 5 left 22 days for engine installation, but she did not reach the Boston yard until December 15. Her commissioning was delayed until February 8. The *Owasco* was likewise launched on October 5, but her contract provided 31 additional days before her delivery at the New York Navy Yard. For whatever reason, she took twice as long and was not commissioned until January 23.

Harrison Loring, skillful and well established, seems to have taken on more orders than he could manage. His engines for the gunboats *Chocura* and *Huron*, both built within a few miles of his factory, probably were not delivered on time. The *Huron* went down the ways on September 21 and the *Chocura* on October 5, each with 26 days to go before the stipulated date of delivery just across the river at the Charlestown Navy Yard. But the *Chocura* did not get there until January 29; she was commissioned 17 days later. The *Huron* was commissioned on January 8, 110 days after her launch. Engine-delivery trouble seems the likeliest cause of both delays.

Loring had previously been a joint contractor for engines for the first-class screw sloop *Hartford*, of 1,900 tons measurement, launched at the Boston Navy Yard three years earlier and destined to be the flagship of fleets in which many of the 90-day gunboats would support her. (The wooden *Hartford*, probably the busiest and most steadily effective Union vessel in the Civil War, sank without fuss at her Norfolk Navy Yard slip, to celebrate her ninety-eighth birthday two days ahead of time.) Loring supplied engines for the *Maratanza*, a large side-wheeler launched at the Boston Navy Yard on November 26, 1861. Later in the war he built both hull and engines for a monitor and an iron double-ender.

Delays, foreseen and unforeseen, in the 90-day gunboat program should not shadow the fact that the fleet was produced with unexampled promptness, despite shortages of manpower and material, during a vast expansion of manufacturing in general. Twelve were commissioned before the end of the year, four more in January, six in February, and the last of all on March 8, 1862. Equipment and guns were the most evident variables, yet the speed with which the navy yards could work is revealed in a letter of September 30, 1861, from Dahlgren to Welles, reporting that the recently purchased iron tug *R. B. Forbes* had been refitted within a few hours and had steam up "ready to join the flotilla and go into action by 9 p.m." He had added "the rifled 80-pounder" to her rated armament of two 32's. On October 12 Welles ordered the *R. B. Forbes* to report for duty to the South Atlantic Blockading Squadron, which included the first four gunboats. The fleet sailed south from Hampton Roads on October 29 into a punitive, Caribbean-born hurricane. The *Isaac Smith*, another converted steamer, not designed to carry guns above her normal center of gravity, had to jettison them to stay alive. Two transports sank. Boston's old iron tug for a while had the *Unadilla* in tow. Otherwise the new gunboats plowed through the violent storm without incident.

The fleet had been sent to take Port Royal, South Carolina, for conversion into a naval base. Its marine defender, the traitor Tattnall, offered only a gesture of opposition with his river steamers, which were inadequate to engage the Union fleet. Captain Samuel F. Du Pont had been uncertain of the strength needed to reduce heavy shore fortifications. He ranged three of the Lenthall-Pook gunboats in his line of battle, directly behind his four heaviest ships. The *Unadilla* had second place in the flanking line. Each gunboat was armed at this point with one 11-inch Dahlgren smoothbore, one 20-pounder Parrott rifle, and two 24-pounder howitzers.

The ease with which Port Royal was taken confirmed the tactical superiority of Dahlgren's theory of armament—fewer, heavier, more versatile guns—over the classical assumption that land batteries could best be reduced from the sea by the relentless flinging in of broadsides. High-lofted shells from gunboat howitzers were particularly effective in driving the enemy from their emplacements. As Admiral David D. Porter put it:

This affair showed conclusively that the time-honored theory that one gun on shore was equal to five on shipboard no longer held good, when applied to the heavy artillery carried by modern ships and served with skill and precision. . . . Its moral effect counted prodigiously. It opened the way for the more important operations with wooden ships against the enemy's forts at a later period of the war.

All four gunboats came through the Port Royal exchanges of fire without any crippling damage. A grimmer test of the ability of unarmored wooden vessels to endure the fire of guns as good as their own was impending when Captain David Farragut approached the Mississippi delta on February 20, 1862, with his flag in the screw sloop *Hartford*. He had three other new screw sloops of about the same size, three more modest ones, and the 21-year-old side-wheeler *Mississippi*, which had served "Old Bruin" Perry as his flagship both in the Mexican War and at the outset of the expedition for the opening of Japan. The fleet also included 9 of the Lenthall-Pook gunboats and 20 sailing schooners, each mounting one 13-inch mortar. The mortar schooners were to be towed into position by six additional steamers. One of these was the *Owasco*, a tenth 90-day gunboat. The Mystic-built *Owasco's* task was to shift the schooners under fire and supply them with shot and shell. Since their mortars were useless at short range, it was also her job to defend them from surface forays.

The versatility of the gunboats was promptly emphasized when a couple of vital weeks were spent, with their help, in getting the bigger ships over the bar. The heaviest of all, the new *Colorado*, is not enumerated above because she never did make it into the river. The 90-day gunboats *Kennebec* and *Wissahickon* were the first Union vessels to reconnoiter the Mississippi. They brought back news that chains—supported by eight hulks—and other evident obstructions had been placed to close the river below Forts Jackson and St. Philip. Both structures were then heavily bombarded by mortar schooners, and two more gunboats, the *Itaska* and *Pinola*, were sent at night to break the chain across one of the main channels. They succeeded under fire in doing so.

From such assignments and many others it is clear that the hastily built little vessels were regarded as expendable. In the main attack that forced a passage between the forts, Farragut's officers squelched his determination to lead the way in the *Hartford*. He then bestowed the suicidal honor of first place in the line upon the gunboat *Cayuga*, with four major vessels following. Another group of 90-day gunboats came next, with the nasty assignment of discovering subsurface obstructions by becoming enmeshed in them, thus giving a better chance of survival to the large ships of the second division. Three gunboats were trapped as a result and badly pounded, but all managed to extricate themselves.

Thirteen Confederate gunboats and two improvised rams were

The condition of the United States Navy shortly before the Civil War is hinted at in the logbook sketch *(below)* of the landing in Japan from "Old Bruin" Perry's squadron on March 8, 1854. For this momentous errand the President sent three obsolescent side-wheelers and five obsolete sailing vessels. The flagship *Mississippi (above)* was drawn by a reasonably objective Japanese artist; the oddity at the right by another of the several surprised Japanese viewers. (See p. 329.)

waiting above the forts. The *Cayuga,* outrunning most of the seven other vessels in the first division, which she led, engaged the fleet alone until her sister ship the *Oneida* came up with the 1,300-ton U.S.S. *Varuna* and helped her to disperse the opposition. The *Varuna,* a speedy wooden merchant propeller recently purchased in Connecticut and given heavy armament, was sunk by the two rams, which she managed to take down with her. The nimble *Cayuga* continued to fight until Farragut's second division arrived and (in the words of the contemporary chronicler B. S. Osbon) "ranged in one after another, leaving their broadsides in spiteful revenge for the ill treatment of the little *Cayuga.*" After accepting surrender of three of her Rebel antagonists, the *Cayuga* banked her fires for a count of her wounds. She had been hit by something sizable in 42 places. Farragut's General Orders, issued before the battle, had prudently included this paragraph:

Have light Jacob-ladders made to throw over the side for the use of the carpenters in stopping shot holes, who are to be supplied with pieces of inch board lined with felt and ordinary nails, and see that the ports are marked . . . to show the locality of the shot hole.

Lieutenant Pierce Crosby's report to Farragut of the gunboat *Pinola's* participation in the same action is too detailed to reproduce here but is worth looking up. (Pages 319–21 *Executive Documents,* House of Representatives, 37th Congress, 3rd Session, Volume 3.) It details exactly what each of 12 shot that entered the hull did on its journey. An extensive report of the *Owasco's* perilous task, nursing her mortar schooners, appears on pages 351–54 in the same volume.

This is not a history of naval actions, beyond the minimum needed to indicate the capabilities of a particular and hasty design produced to prop up a neglected navy until heavier and technologically more novel vessels could be built. The first two tests, at Port Royal and in the breaching of the Mississippi's defenses, were passed in a praiseworthy fashion. The 90-day gunboats took on perilous assignments for which larger ships could not prudently be risked. They emerged, battered but still serviceable. Of the ten that helped open the lower Mississippi, the *Sciota* perhaps had the most adventurous career. She led the third division past the forts below New Orleans, which by this time in the battle had perfected the range of their fire. Two months later, with four others of her class, she attacked and passed the forts at Vicksburg when eight of the heavier Union vessels for which they were opening the way dropped back down the river. On July 15, when the armored ram *Arkansas* slipped out of a side stream and ran through an anchored Union fleet, the *Sciota* swapped broadsides with her, quickly got up steam, and joined in the pursuit of her under the Vicksburg batteries. In the Donaldsonville action in the fall the *Sciota's* executive officer was killed. She continued on active patrol until July of 1863, when the U.S.S. *Arizona* sank her in an accidental collision. She was raised, repaired, and put back to work. On the day of President Lincoln's assassination, April 14, 1865, she ran into a submerged torpedo in Mobile Bay and settled to the bottom with her decks awash. The war at sea was over, her emergency function long since fulfilled; yet, lying there, she was still a ship in being. As such the *Sciota* was formally decommissioned on July 27. She was judged to be in sufficiently good shape to be bought at auction in the fall, where she lay, for $16,000. Warships twice her size and still afloat brought less.

When the shooting stopped, every one of the 90-day gunboats was in commission, and the *Sciota* was the only one not in fighting trim. The Navy could have raised her and put her back to work a second time if there had been a need for her. Other warships, new and not so new, were sunk alongside the Lenthall-Pook vessels in the same actions. Monitors swamped and sank of their own accord, or, in the manner of the *Tecumseh* at Mobile Bay, went down like sudden stones when torpedoed. Shallow-draft ironclads with high-pressure boilers slaughtered their crews in live steam. The remarkable innovations of the war did change the nature of naval warfare, but not by producing good ships while it was still in progress. The 90-day gunboats, built with the idea of getting something into the water to hold the edges of a continent together until more powerful fighting machines could be produced, outlasted a series of innovations expressing up-to-date technology. The 23 little vessels represented the confident best experience of ages of wooden shipbuilding, and of the engineers who recently had developed reasonably safe, low-pressure steam engines. The importance of the latter was demonstrated when the *Itaska,* at the battle of New Orleans, was pierced by a 42-pound shot that drove through a bunker full of coal and smashed a boiler. Two men were scalded but none was killed, by contrast with the frightful mortality on such occasions from ruptured high-pressure boilers in river craft.

More than half of the unarmored 90-day gunboats fought repeatedly in regions of intense fire in critical naval actions of the war. After the last meaningful shot and shell were fired, one patrolling gunboat encountered a moored submarine torpedo, an accident hardly describable as a battle casualty. Sturdy, simple design made the battered gunboats easy to repair. An official list of 327 vessels destroyed in the Mississippi by both sides included many armored and unarmored naval steamers, but not one 90-day gunboat was fatally hurt. There were too many of them to credit this astonishing record to luck. Their individual histories attest that they were more skillfully designed for a foreseen purpose than any other class of Civil War vessels and that the final credit for their excellence rests with the disciplined skill of Samuel Hartt Pook.

Their success as blockaders was also notable. Only the *Kineo* failed to participate in the taking of prizes afloat, but she did something more surprising: she captured 1,500 head of cattle to weaken the defenses of Donaldsonville. When the big Union sloop *Monongahela* was driven ashore by Confederate fire, the *Kineo*—less than half her tonnage—passed a hawser under severe bombardment and pulled her off to safety. The most important single contraband cargo of the conflict, including engines and rifled heavy ordnance for two big Confederate ironclads, was taken unaided by the *Unadilla.*

In 1868, when some seized ships were still being adjudicated in the clogged courts, the 90-day gunboats had been credited with 146 valid captures. The *Sagamore* had the highest numerical count: 15 schooners and 4 sloops. The *Kennebec* participated in the taking of six steamers that sold for $1,343,773; she also took five schooners, to raise the total to a million and a half. This was the activity that bled away the South's capacity to fight on.

The Lenthall-Pook gunboats that contributed so significantly to the Union's taking and patrolling of the lower Mississippi

River should not be confused with "Pook's turtles," which a few weeks before Farragut's assault began to open the river from the north. It is curious that the younger of two distinguished naval architects named Pook was producing up-to-date orthodox vessels while the father who had taught him was hastily working out a hazardous experimental design. The Pook turtles emerged from an Army-Navy game of protocol and mutual obstruction that probably would have produced nothing if James B. Eads—in method a forerunner of Henry Ford—had not been willing to undertake an inland program similar in urgency to that which was producing the seagoing gunboats on the continent's edge. He found himself working as a contractor to the Army, under supervision of a deep-water naval officer who knew nothing of inland navigation. Eads fortunately did. He thought Samuel Moore Pook's basic design somewhat dubious but was grateful for the Naval Constructor's help with problems of armament, armor, and consequent calculations of displacement and fighting trim.

When Secretary Welles, in response to congressional poking, issued a stout report on armored vessels in 1864, he included Rear Admiral David D. Porter's opinion that "monitors would have done much better on this river than the old Pook gunboats did, which were built for temporary purposes only, or until Monitors could take their place." The admiral, amid a turbulence of technological change, had his dates blurred. Bids for the "old Pook gunboats," the shallow rivercraft, had been invited soon after the first contracts for the Lenthall-Pook gunboats were let, delivery required by October 10. The Eads contract is dated August 7. Both new classes were in production some weeks before anyone in the Navy knew what a monitor was, and eight months before the first of them demonstrated her qualities at Hampton Roads.

The elder Pook is not to be posthumously harassed for shortcomings of the turtles that have dragged his name into the footnotes of river warfare. They were knocked together from materials at hand: length 75 feet, breadth 50 feet, with a single 22-foot paddle wheel that turned in a 60-by-18-foot slot in their afterbodies, extending not quite to the stern. Thus they were clumsy, shallow-water approximations of Fulton's suave *Demologos* of half a century earlier. Forward they were armored with

James B. Eads *(right)*, a dynamic industrial manager, somehow composed stuffy rivalries of the armed services and hastily produced for the Army, under the Navy's supervision, several effective river gunboats. They were called Pook turtles, from the design *(below)* of Naval Constructor Samuel Moore Pook, father of the clipper architect. The side-wheeler *Michigan (far right)* was earlier built inland, in 1841, by the elder Pook's relative Samuel Hartt. She was the Navy's first iron ship. (See pp. 329, 335.)

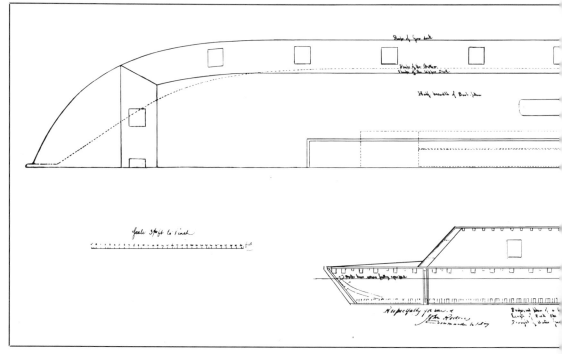

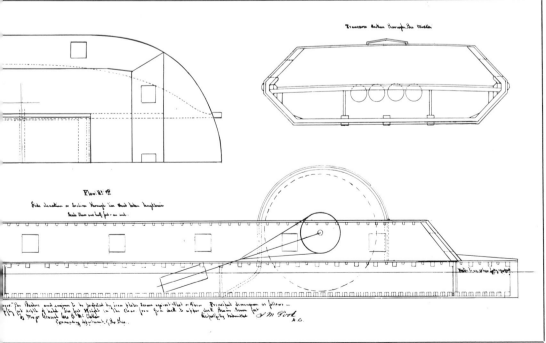

2½ inches of iron over 20 inches of oak. The sides had the same thickness of iron only where it might give some protection to boilers and engines, which could not be placed below the surface of the water since rivercraft had to be of minimum draft. Most of the deck spaces and all of the stern were unarmored. These seven improvisations of the elder Pook and Eads mounted about twice as many guns apiece as the more versatile vessels designed by Lenthall and the younger Pook.

The 4-knot, desperately ugly turtles had a rougher time of it. Their frugal armor was located for head-on fighting, a not always controllable posture in the swirling river. The *Mound City* scalded 82 of her crew to death and drowned 43 others when a shot reached her ill-protected high-pressure boiler. The *Cincinnati* was sunk by the Vicksburg batteries. The *Cairo* and *St. Louis* were lost to torpedoes. But a stress that has properly been put by historians upon an indecisive skirmish in Hampton Roads between an ironclad and an oddity all of iron has diverted notice from the fact that vessels of the Pook-Eads *Cairo* class a month or two earlier had been the first American ironclads to engage a shooting enemy.

The shrewdness of the decision to give first priority to a wooden gunboat program for the Union navy is underscored by the South's immediate concentration upon ironclads. If Farragut had had to wait for ironclads of his own, of a seagoing model capable of adventuring the voyage to the Mississippi delta, the defenders would probably have had ready two major invulnerable river vessels that with the support of the forts should have been able to stop anything built to endure wild weather. The big C.S.S. *Louisiana*, 264 feet long, 62 feet beam, was propelled by an untested innovation: internal paddle wheels in tandem. The second wheel, churning in the turbulence raised by the first, proved ineffective. She would have been better off with the second wheel alone, placed near the stern as in the Pook turtles. The *Mississippi*, almost as large, was also an innovation: she was to have three screws. The third shaft had not been made when Farragut passed the forts and she was burned in her slip to forestall capture. The *Louisiana* was towed out to fight, but the quick-steering gunboats kept off her quarters, where her guns could not be brought to bear. As the battle ended she too was burned by her officers. Both ironclads could probably have been

Most new Union ships of the Civil War had to be fit for long sea voyages to reach their Southern objectives. The Confederacy concentrated upon defensive, heavily armed and armored, shallow rivercraft. The *Louisiana*, a ram built to defend the lower Mississippi, had the unsuccessful innovation of two tandem paddle wheels in a well, here symbolized as if horizontal. (See pp. 338, 340ff.)

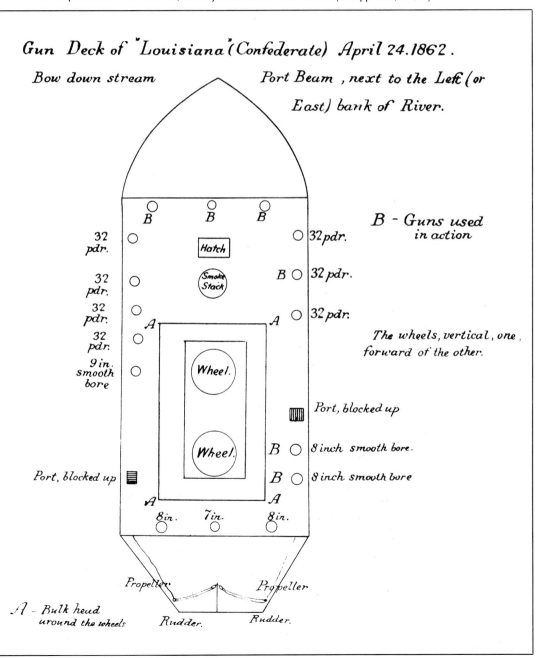

Gun Deck of "Louisiana" (Confederate) April 24.1862.

Bow down stream

Port Beam, next to the Left (or East) bank of River.

B
B
B

32 pdr.   ○ 32 pdr.

B - Guns used in action

Hatch

Smoke Stack

32 pdr.   B ○ 32 pdr.

32 pdr.   A   A ○ 32 pdr.

32 pdr.

The wheels, vertical, one, forward of the other.

9 in. smooth bore

Wheel.

Port, blocked up

Wheel.   B ○ 8 inch smooth bore.

B ○ 8 inch smooth bore

Port, blocked up

8 in.   7 in.   8 in.

Propeller.   Propeller

A - Bulk head around the wheels   Rudder.   Rudder.

In the War Between the States neither combatant had time to develop vessels with much of the aspect of design that John Willis Griffiths thought essential in his "complicated art": beauty. Many were hideous improvisations. The Confederacy concentrated upon big ironclad rams, such as the *Atlanta (above)*, that were too cumbersome to defend themselves. The Union knocked mortar boats together *(left)* with tiny refuge decks aft. The *Cairo (below)* was the prototype of the Pook turtles, some of which are shown *(lower left)* along with mortar boats in the attack on Island No. 10. (See pp. 335–39, 342.)

made effective within a few more weeks, but—thanks largely to Lenthall and Pook—Farragut's entirely wooden fleet arrived in time.

THE COASTAL IRONCLADS

At the war's end Secretary Welles wrote, "Three hundred and twenty-two officers traitorously abandoned the service. The embarrassment . . . was temporary. Better men from the merchant marine, educated and vastly more efficient, promptly volunteered." Nearly all of Farragut's 20 mortar schooners were commanded by their former skippers, who joined up in their purchased vessels. Farragut expressed to Welles the highest admiration for their coolness and skill under fire.

The Bureau of Construction was at the outset more luckily staffed. Most of its experienced officers had been born and trained in the North. Chapelle has called to notice the "coincidence that all of the naval constructors had experimented with steamship design long before such craft were desired by the Navy. The rather peculiar circumstance that had allowed the constructors to engage in outside work was undoubtedly the reason for their progressiveness, as compared with the naval officers as a class." Furthermore, the Navy had the flexible options of building ships in its own yards, buying them ready-made, or contracting for them with private shipbuilders. Confronted by a sudden expansion of need, Lenthall as chief of the bureau was in a better position to make contracts with private suppliers than to expand the government's own overtaxed shipbuilding facilities. He himself had had a thorough schooling in his task, as Samuel Humphreys's apprentice in the twenties and later as a close associate of Hartt's. Lenthall designed the large ship-sloop *Germantown*, launched in 1843 and called particularly sharp, fast, and handsome. While at the Philadelphia yard, where she was built, he also designed ships for the city's merchants and did his best to divert some naval funds to the building of steamers, a project opposed with horror by traditional deep-water commodores.

The new Secretary of the Navy was consequently lucky in having Lenthall as bureau chief. When a torrent of concepts for novel men-of-war began to wash across his desk, Secretary Welles asked Congress for authority to build ironclads, as had been advocated by Forbes, Pook, McKay, and others. The concept was not new. John Saris, an English wanderer in the East in the days when Shakspere was writing *The Tempest,* reported having encountered in Japan "a great town where there lay in a dock a junk of eight hundred or a thousand tons of burden, sheathed all with iron, with a guard appointed to keep her from firing and treachery." But the act of August 3, 1861, was the first official American recognition of the possible merits of iron sheathing. It appropriated $1,500,000 for the experimental program, directing the secretary to appoint a board of officers competent to review the proposals. His scope of choice was fortunately constricted by the desertion of many oak-and-canvas diehards. The two commodores and a commander whom the secretary fixed upon made a cautious statement of guiding principles, which they managed nevertheless to ignore at the perfect moment for doing so.

On September 16 the board of three officers submitted a report on 17 proposals, all but one of which included bids to build ironclads. Donald McKay, who earlier in the year had emerged as a public advocate of large armored ships of the sort he had inspected under construction when he was unsuccessfully seeking orders in France, wanted a million dollars for his entry. It would displace 3,100 tons and have a top speed of 7 knots. The hull and armor were approved, but the board thought her cost too high and her speed too low. Another helpful patriot offered a "*rubber-clad* vessel, which we cannot recommend."

The officers were intrigued however by a "plan of a floating battery" supposed to be "shot and shell proof. We are somewhat apprehensive that her properties for sea are not such as a sea-going vessel should possess." The officers were proved to be quite right in their doubts over the sea-keeping qualities of the suggested craft, but they decided to risk experimentation with "one battery of this description . . . with a guarantee and forfeiture in case of failure." In so doing they at last gave John Ericsson, who at this point had been a naturalized citizen for 13 years, his chance to change the nature of naval warfare forever. As the board had foreseen, the first *Monitor* was an abominable sea boat. She almost sank on the way to her first fight and did founder near Cape Hatteras while being towed to a new battle station on the last day of 1862. Fourteen of her crew perished.

Patriotic fervor and private profit, in the customary combat mix, produced a complex situation in the financing and construction of the first ships approved by the ironclads board. A reflection of the broad options that Lenthall enjoyed confronted his employee Pook as well. The naval architect could obviously at this point have entered the service that four years earlier had turned him down for lack of a routine opening. He could have gone on working for Lenthall as a civilian employee. He chose instead a job in private industry producing ships under government contract.

The board divided its $1,500,000 among what may have seemed the three best bets; but together they suggest a compromise between orthodoxy and startling experiment. More than half of the appropriation went for a moderately conceived major ship for which there was encouraging precedent. The plans resembled those of the French *Gloire,* the first large ironclad to be laid down and the second to be launched. The British *Warrior,* begun later, had been completed more briskly. Since the *Gloire* was the pilot model for a large fleet of ironclads approved for the French navy, Welles's board of advisers was not being notably adventurous in recommending the proposal of Merrick & Sons of Philadelphia, whose ship would displace 1,500 tons less than her French prototype. McKay, in urgent letters to the press, had been advocating deep-water fighting ships like the *Gloire,* not merely adapted to a ponderous envelope of iron but designed from the keel up to carry armor and armament. Merrick, with the same prototype in mind, underbid the still overreaching McKay by offering at $780,000 an ironclad of 3,296 tons displacement with a speed of 9½ knots. Modifications, provided for in the contract, raised the cost of Merrick's *New Ironsides* to $865,414.66. On the Navy list she was rated at 8 knots, somewhat better than the 6 or 7 that the board had thought slow in their comments on McKay's higher bid for a smaller ship.

The French had taken several years to build their pioneering *Gloire.* Merrick promised nine months and completed the task a few weeks ahead of time. It was foreseen however that almost a year altogether would have to be spent before she could have her guns in place. The board consequently divided the remainder of its appropriation between Ericsson's "novel" proposal, which was to be ready in 100 days, and that of C. S. Bushnell & Com-

Ironclads of the Civil War were derived partly from France's *La Gloire (above)* and Britain's *Warrior (right)*, steam frigates of the latter 1850's, but the Union was largely dependent throughout the war upon wooden screw sloops such as the *Hartford (below)*, of 1,900 tons, launched in 1858, Farragut's flagship in the actions that opened the Mississippi. (See pp. 327, 344.)

uilt in Boston 1858, Length 225 ft. Beam 44 ft. Draught 18 ...
...lacement tons 2900

pany of New Haven, Connecticut, for a small ironclad "on the rail and plate principle, and to obtain high speed": delivery in four months. It is clear from the contracts and their grim forfeiture guarantees that both proposals were regarded as risky prototypes.

Experience demonstrated that the board had chosen well. The *New Ironsides* honored the inferences behind her updated name. When speed was not a vital consideration she turned out to be the most powerfully effective member of the Civil War fleets. In 1863, within seven weeks, she fired 4,439 11-inch projectiles in action. She became the particular prey of Confederate "Davids," small suicidal craft with spar torpedoes. On October 5, 1863, a David at last put the *New Ironsides* out of action and sent her home for months of repairs. The small surface steamer and most of her men miraculously survived.

Ericsson's *Monitor* was the naval innovation of the century: an unsuccessful particular vessel, able nevertheless to convince the world that all the other warships afloat were in principle obsolete. It was the rare triumph of a Platonic idea of form over an inadequate physical expression of the form itself. The suddenness of this change is highlighted by the persistence, even in the *Monitor* contract, of a provision standard in all previous ones for fighting steamers that she be equipped with masts and sails. Ericsson merely ignored the clause and no-one called him to account. The *New Ironsides* went into commission bark-rigged, as stipulated, but her masts were promptly taken out by her commander at the new naval station at captured Port Royal "and replaced with light clothes-poles, with which rig her appearance was remarkably like that of a modern war vessel."

"Modern" meant 1896, when the opinion was published by Frank M. Bennett in his useful book *The Steam Navy of the United States.* Bennett describes the *New Ironsides* as "large and decidedly shipshape in appearance, with a projecting ram bow, the sides for the main battery being sheathed with four inches of iron plate armor." Still, she was obsolescent when launched and obsolete as soon as the war was over. When she caught fire and was burned to wreckage on December 15, 1866, the *Army and Navy Journal* called the loss "unimportant" because she was "unwieldy and slow . . . too thinly clad to resist the impact of modern missiles." Iron armor on a wooden hull was by nature a transitional compromise, combining the merits and short-comings of both materials into a needlessly ponderous product. The ancient seesaw between offensive and defensive capability in naval actions was tipped only for a short while in favor of defense by the use of slow ironclads. The continuous, brisk development of heavy ordnance by Dahlgren and others soon swung it the other way again, and the third vessel approved by Welles's three-man board was something of a victim to the process.

The *New Ironsides* and the *Monitor* were the board's tactical extremes, one needing plenty of room in deep water for her maneuvers, the other unsafe in offshore weather but brisk and versatile in rivers and roadsteads. The third accepted proposal came from Cornelius S. Bushnell, president of the New Haven, New London, and Stonington Railroad Company—who was also the most effective of four equal partners backing the *Monitor* at the same time. Bushnell had made his money originally as a wholesale grocer in New Haven. Later he was the principal investor in the Union Pacific venture. His transient interest in an iron navy reflected the circumstance that he, with the other backers of Ericsson, had investments in heavy industry: foundries and processing plants. They would all profit by it, but they also controlled the means and skills to rush their vessels to completion with a speed that startled the ministries of England and France.

Bushnell behaved like something of an ironclad himself when hauled up before a congressional committee to explain some peculiar transactions in which he had concurrently served his country's and his private interests. The legislators were annoyed by a company that he had organized to purchase steamers and lease them to the government at a whopping profit. It would obviously have served the public interest better if the Navy had got there first to buy and own them. After the Bureau of Ships began to insist upon outright purchase, Bushnell had charged his own company fat commissions for selling its vessels under compulsion. Questioned about this, he coolly said that all the money went back into his enterprises that were producing war materials. Who could object to that kind of patriotism? The *Varuna*, rammed and sunk below New Orleans, had been bought from Bushnell's firm.

First and last innovations of the Civil War. The rotatable turret of John Ericsson's *Monitor* *(below)*, modestly dimpled by close-range fire, announced a new era in naval construction. The torpedo boat *Spuyten Duyvil (right)*, redesigned and built by Samuel Hartt Pook, was ordered too late in the war to see action. Here, visible only as a thin line on the surface, she is seen on April 2, 1865, blowing up obstructions in the James River to make way for President Lincoln's visit to Richmond two days later. (See pp. 239–40, 343, 347, 349–54, 371–74.)

Of the three proposals approved by the ironclads board, Bushnell's got the first contract, on September 27, 1861.
middling concept and the least costly: under 30 per cent of the
price asked for the *New Ironsides*. The resulting *Galena,* 738
old-measurement tons, was to draw about five feet less water
than her big contemporary, and only a foot or two more than the
Monitor. If the latter proved as foolish a failure as Ericsson's
critics predicted, then Bushnell's compromise should be a second-
best for the *Monitor's* intended inshore functions. The board
probably was reassured by Bushnell's employment of Samuel
Hartt Pook to draw the basic plans. His work on the 90-day
gunboats, of which half a dozen were already afloat, confirmed
his reliability.

On August 17 Bushnell had given Pook's ironclad drawings to
Ericsson with instructions to adapt the midships section for
steam machinery of adequate power. With his usual assurance,
the engineer had produced a revised drawing before nightfall,
altering the entire structure. The gun deck was raised an extra
foot above water "in order to obtain sufficient space below for
the boilers," a change that would seriously disturb the ship's
stability. A compensating change extended the armor four and
a half feet below the water line. "Less would not answer," he
wrote, "during the slightest rolling of the vessel."

One reason given by Ericsson for lifting the gun deck poses a
puzzle: "I need not remind you that owing to the extraordinary
rise of floor, the height under deck at a very short distance from
the midship section diminishes very rapidly." At a time when
it had become the almost universal custom to give steamers flat
floors amidships—not only because it provided a more economical use of space in accommodating the machinery, but also
because the revised Griffiths theory had for some years been
upheld by experience—Pook had drawn a V-shaped bottom for
an ironclad. I can only speculate upon the reason. It was to be
a relatively small ship, less than half the measurement of the
steamers Pook had recently designed for Loring and about one-
eighth the tonnage of the seminal ironclad *Gloire*. Rise of floor
in the Pook clippers had varied with their size, the smaller
having the sharper bottoms. When inviting bids for ironclads,
the Navy had stipulated that they must be able to maneuver
under sail alone. A sharp bottom would help a sailing steamer

of modest size, overburdened with armor, to get to windward if disabled off a lee shore. Pook, under Bushnell's direction, was designing a vessel primarily intended for versatile offshore use, but one that would be 200 tons smaller than his smallest clipper. For such aspects of design, the frantic weeks in which a new navy was being conceived on many drawing boards do not encourage fair comparative judgments. The government had advertised for bids. It is uncertain whether the builders got wind of one another's intentions. One, E. S. Renwick, was given an almost favorable nod for a huge 18-knot ironclad thoughtfully conceived to pick up the entire million and a half. It was more a competition in speculative concepts than in capability at lowest cost to fulfill a known need.

The *Monitor* herself became a belated competitor almost by accident. Bushnell testified that he had got his first glimpse of her model—which had loitered in a dusty box for seven years— when he visited Ericsson on August 17 to deliver Pook's plans for the *Galena* and ask the eminent engineer to design her machinery. Napoleon III, to whom the *Monitor* model had at first been offered, is said on uncertain authority to have turned it down with a flattering letter and a medal. Ericsson assumed that enemies in the United States Navy were preventing his employment in any capacity. Bushnell therefore took the model directly to his friend Secretary Welles, who thought it expressed "extraordinary and valuable features . . . involving a revolution in naval warfare." Bushnell then lined up two other politically muscular industrialists to share equally with him and Ericsson in the investment and armtwisted his way to an appointment with President Lincoln, whose favorable opinion at a later conference clinched the matter. If the *Monitor* seemed a weird freak to the traditional officer corps, she proved a sound investment to men used to financial risk-taking for high return. The contract stipulated a ruinous loss if she should not be approved when tested, but she gave her backers a net profit of $80,000 to be divided between them—67 per cent of her cost. Career officers continued to dispute the merits of the *Monitor*'s first stalemate in action, but Welles was well satisfied with his audacious gamble. In his official report written less than nine months after the conflict at Hampton Roads he showed that he was convinced of what naval historians finally conceded: "The most remarkable naval combat of modern times, perhaps of any age," he called it, adding, "a new era was opened in the history of maritime warfare."

Bushnell's *Galena*—the first of three naval vessels so named—had an escape clause like the *Monitor's* in her contract. Because of the advisory board's "fear that she will not float her armor and load sufficiently high, and have stability enough for a seagoing vessel," she could be rejected outright for any of these failures. Bushnell subcontracted the building of her wooden hull to Maxson, Fish & Company, who were just completing the 90-day gunboat *Owasco* at their yard near the present site of Mystic Seaport in Connecticut. The Delamater Iron Works of New York was to produce the *Galena's* machinery.

Pook, in the information he supplied much later to Hamersly, made in this instance one of his careful distinctions: he "laid down for Mr. Bushnell, and superintended the construction of the iron-clad 'Galena' for the Government"—no claim to having designed her, although he did make the original drafts. Ericsson had meddled with the *Galena's* lines, and this pioneering ironclad—the first seagoing example to be contracted for and commissioned in the United States Navy—acquired an evil reputation which in later years Pook would have found it difficult to forget. Explaining the changes he made in her model, Ericsson wrote Bushnell, "Your plan evinces, on the part of the constructor, a perfect acquaintance with the laws of hydrostatics. The great difficulty of protecting the upper part of a floating body by heavy materials, is the unavoidable top weight and tendency to tip over. This difficulty can only be met by such a form of vessel as you propose."

These courteous acknowledgments of Pook's prior work, however, did not stop Ericsson from making a change that was the chief cause of the *Galena's* worst few hours in combat and of her consequent unpopularity. He lowered the extreme breadth of her hull to a point well under the surface "in order to present a considerable slope of the side immediately above water." His intention was to confront the enemy gunner with a sloping bank of iron that his shot would hit at an angle of about 45 degrees and from which it would be deflected upward with its force largely spent. The theory did not take into account the effect of plunging shot that might hit an ironclad's sloping topsides at an angle of about 90 degrees.

The *Galena's* first significant action, during an attempt to

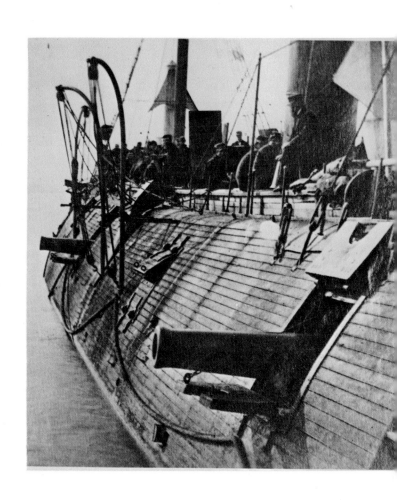

Samuel Hartt Pook designed the *Galena*, the Navy's first ironclad, but John Ericsson altered her topsides *(external view upper left, interior of gun deck right, center)* to deflect close-range fire. The change proved calamitous. Her thin armor plate, rolled by Brooklyn's Continental Works *(lower left)* and laid over iron rails, was vulnerable to plunging shot. Her armor was stripped off late in the war, and she survived an evil reputation to become flagship of the North Atlantic squadron *(top, right)*. Designers responded quickly to the war's harsh lessons. The monitor *Dictator* *(adjacent picture)* of 1863 had a more seaworthy, faired hull than the first "cheese box on a raft." (See pp. 346, 349–51, 354–58.)

reach Richmond, Virginia, brought her under a battery perched high above the James River on Drewry's Bluff. Her armor was pierced several times by plunging shot. Twelve men were killed and 15 wounded. The *Galena* was the United States Navy's first ironclad wooden ship to go into action, a calculated experiment. More than half of the Army's also experimental Eads-Pook turtles were sunk, despite their armor; but the Pook-Ericsson vessel, like every one of the Lenthall-Pook gunboats, despite a severe drubbing outlived the war. Her armor, on the "rail-plate principle," was Bushnell's idea, a compromise to speed production. Rails were available in quantity, and it was natural for a railroad magnate to perceive in them the answer to an urgent need. A third subcontractor, the Continental Iron Works of Greenpoint, Long Island, applied the rails and added an overlay of iron plates to bring the thickness to four inches. Rails alone buckled and spread when hit, but the extra inch of plate iron turned out to be less than enough either to balk shot of middling weight or to prevent the spreading of the rails beneath it.

Prior to the launch of the *Galena's* wooden hull at Mystic on February 14, 1862, Thomas F. Rowland of the Continental works had been able to produce five-inch plates for the side armor of the *Monitor* while the Novelty Works was constructing her eight-inch-thick turret. Four inches, even of solid iron, would not stop the heavier projectiles already in use by the time the *Galena* went into action. Robert MacBride, in his book *Civil War Ironclads* (1962), says of the *Galena,* "Throughout her career she had a poor reputation, although it is hard to see why." A review of her record fixes the difficulty in one ship-to-shore duel from which she withdrew in good order only when all her ammunition was expended and her onshore opponent was still banging away from his deadly trajectory node far above her. The casualties on this occasion were no worse than those suffered by many vessels in later fights, but she had the prototype's burden of carrying into her first serious engagement high expectations of invulnerability. It was the reverse of the recent *Monitor* fight, when hopes were so low that a stand-off encounter seemed a great victory; but the *Monitor's* armor was solid, and twice as thick, where it mattered most.

In the *Armored Vessels* report of 1864, Rear Admiral L. M. Goldsborough wrote that he was "putting the Galena aside as a sad mistake, unworthy of naval criticism . . ." and went on to give a prudent, old-guard view of the merits of ironclads generally. He regarded the *New Ironsides* as much more efficient than the monitors and reminded Welles that two of them had gone down when not even under fire. Dahlgren, by this time a younger rear admiral, defended the monitors more briskly in the same report. He noted that while they were under his command the *Montauk* had taken 412 hits and the *Weehawken* 187, by 10-inch shot. "What vessels have ever been subjected to such a test?" he inquired.

As Goldsborough, on February 26, 1864, was scribbling his contemptuous assessment of the *Galena*, she was steaming up Chesapeake Bay. Her inadequate iron clothing had been stripped off and she had been recommissioned 11 days earlier as a wooden gunboat, but the conversion appears to have been badly managed. Ice had opened her seams. After more adequate repairs to her hull at Baltimore she headed south to join Farragut's blockaders in the Gulf of Mexico, ready to play her important part in the Battle of Mobile Bay. In that assault Farragut used the tactic of lashing a minor vessel on the port side of each of his major ones as a help in maintaining speed and stability while passing Fort Morgan to starboard—also as insurance of some maneuverability if the large ship sloops should be disabled. The 90-day gunboats *Kennebec* and *Itaska* fulfilled this function for the fifth and sixth ships in the line; the *Galena* did so for the *Oneida*, of 1,032 tons, which came seventh, bringing up the rear.

The pairing was a prudent precaution. The *Galena* was struck seven times, without serious damage, but one hit among the *Oneida*'s several found her starboard boiler. The *Galena* not only carried her crippled companion on into the harbor; she took aboard some of the *Oneida*'s casualties, sent her assistant surgeon into the bigger ship, and assumed all navigational functions when the commander of the *Oneida* was severely wounded. His executive officer's report concludes, "The safety of the ship after the explosion depended upon the 'Galena.' That we are here, quietly at anchor, attests how nobly Lieutenant Commander Clark H. Wells stood by us."

The effectiveness of ironclads again came into question at Mobile Bay when the greatly relied upon armored ram C.S.S. *Tennessee*, according to Admiral Porter, "never once struck a

Sinkings in the Civil War. Monitors, the startling new shapes of 1862, proved wretched sea boats, much more vulnerable below the surface than above. The *Weehawken (upper left)* bounced back 187 ten-inch shot, but sank in a storm. The *Tecumseh (lower right)* was sunk by a torpedo. When disabled, the Confederate ram *Tennessee*, celebrated in a wallpaper panel *(upper right)*, was sunk by her own people. Both sides hoped to sink the enemy with submarines, like the imagined one below. The stone fleet of old whalers *(right)* was sunk in futile attempts to block Southern ports. (See pp. 333, 355, 358–61.)

vessel of Farragut's fleet, while she herself was rammed at least four times." The only Union vessel lost was the all-iron monitor *Tecumseh*, which "was seen . . . to careen violently over, and sink almost instantly" when she struck a torpedo. It was within a few moments of witnessing this dismaying occurrence that Farragut spoke the war's most famous order.

The *Tennessee*, with five-inch armor, did manage to bounce back almost everything that hit her until the surviving three monitors pounded her with 15-inch guns, jammed her gunport shutters, and cut her foolishly exposed steering chains. She had battered most of her swarming wooden opponents severely until these occurrences put her out of action; but once more, as at New Orleans, it was the speedier wooden sloops and gunboats of sophisticated design that had the best of it. The enormous and heavily gunned *Tennessee* sacrificed too much to the concept of being impenetrable. Her offensive fire was at times devastating, but she was too unwieldy to keep it concentrated long enough to sink any of her smaller opponents. Her failure as a ram was preordained. All the Union ships were faster by at least 3 knots and much more responsive to a hard movement of the helm. They simply sidled out of her way.

After the Battle of Mobile Bay the *Galena* served as a blockader with the Gulf and North Atlantic squadrons. She participated in captures, including the warships *Gaines*, *Selma*, and *Tennessee*, that brought a distribution of nearly $800,000 in prize money. Somebody in the Bureau of Ships had a better opinion of her than Goldsborough's: she was retained in the Navy at the war's end when all the 90-day gunboats and most of its other vessels were sold at auction. Clearly she was a "committee boat" at her origins, in a worse sense of the phrase than in the usage of discontented yachtsmen. It was not unusual that her conceptual lines were changed by another hand, but it does seem to have made a substantial difference whether the last hand to alter a vessel's lines was Pook's, putting someone else's draft to rights, or the hand of another draftsman, upsetting the result of his "perfect acquaintance with the laws of hydrostatics."

WAR UNDER WATER

In the autumn of 1861, when Pook's time was being put chiefly to the production at Mystic of the Navy's first experimental ironclad, a ghost that had troubled nearby Connecticut waters in an earlier war quickened rumors in the editorial offices of both Northern and Southern journals. *Harper's Weekly*, on November 2, offered a double-spread engraving of the Port Royal expedition, including pictures of three of the 90-day gunboats, and followed it a few pages further along with a cigar-shaped "infernal machine" containing a navigator and a propeller cranker who were heading it for the U.S.S. *Minnesota*. That vessel had supposedly been attacked some weeks earlier by a submersible, but there seems to be no satisfactory record of the event. The imagined submarine was equipped with a kind of snorkel.

The first well-documented Civil War submersible was the *Alligator*, built by Neafie and Levy of Philadelphia to designs by the French specialist Brutus de Villeroy. She was launched on April 30, 1862, and went into service on June 19. As the Navy's records put it with appropriate punctilio, she "left Philadelphia for Hampton Roads, under charge of Mr. Samuel Eakin," a civilian. She was 47 feet long, 4 feet 6 inches broad, and 6 feet in vertical measurement. At first she was equipped with special folding oars. When these proved unsatisfactory she was sent on July 3 to the navy yard at Washington and there fitted out with a screw turned by 16 men. The alterations took nearly a year. On April 1, 1863, she was towed out of Hampton Roads by the U.S.S. *Sumpter*, a small converted merchantman, bound for Port Royal. Next day, in a storm, she was cut adrift, and has not been seen since.

Except for the problem that postponed effectiveness in all undersea craft for another generation—a source of power not heavily dependent upon oxygen—the *Alligator* was a fairly sophisticated vessel. She had a watertight, double-doored compartment in the bow through which her men might exit or enter, and an apparatus for chemically regenerating her air supply. Her armament was a torpedo at the end of a long spar.

As the war intensified, a variety of anchored and drifting torpedoes were quickly developed, inexpensive devices attractive to the weaker naval power. The eminent physical geographer Maury, after he was cashiered, devised for the South a system of anchored torpedoes electrically exploded from the shore, thus providing in narrow channels for the passage of friendly ships and the destruction of those belonging to the Northern enemy.

Fortunately for the North, the electrical systems tended to become waterlogged. When Farragut defied the torpedoes ahead, after the sudden death in Mobile Bay of the monitor *Tecumseh,* watch officers were certain that their Union vessels bumped into many objects that did not explode. The particular torpedo that sank the *Tecumseh* (in the words of her chief engineer Harrie Webster, "the ship pitched out of sight, like an arrow twanged from her bow") had been newly placed just off the sea walls of Fort Morgan a few days before the battle.

Floating mines, sent usually in pairs connected by a line like those tried nearly a century earlier by David Bushnell, proved less effective, but spar torpedoes had important successes, as when one of them put the *New Ironsides* out of action. This was done by the prototype *David* herself, an almost submerged steamer measuring 50 feet by 6 feet by 5 feet, carrying a complement of four men. The extent of the damage she inflicted has been in dispute. Some sources say none, but the Navy Department, in its recent monumental *Dictionary of American Fighting Ships,* has decided that the "*New Ironsides,* though not sunk, was seriously damaged by the explosion." The attack occurred on October 5, 1863, and the ship remained in service; but she was out of commission for several weeks during the following summer, undergoing repairs at the Philadelphia Naval Yard.

One of the most peculiar underwater offensive operations of the war also got secretively under way when Pook was beginning construction of the ironclad *Galena.* Mr. Lincoln's Assistant Secretary of the Navy, Gustavus Vasa Fox, unlike his immediate superior Welles, was an experienced naval officer. He had been recalled from five years of civilian life to organize an expedition for the relief of Fort Sumter, but only a part of his fleet had reached the vicinity when the fort fell. As assistant secretary he conceived a plan to stop up the ship channels leading into Savannah harbor with a barrier of stone-laden hulks.

The superintendent of the coast survey supported Fox. Welles consequently ordered the purchase of "twenty-five old vessels of not less than 250 tons each . . . as secretly as possible before any knowledge is obtained that the government is in the market." Old vessels of that tonnage were likely to be whalers, with no prospect of other use until the Confederate commerce raiders were coped with. Eventually 45 whalers were acquired (most of them at about $3,000 or $4,000 apiece), loaded with stone, and sent southward.

Captain Du Pont, commander of the Union fleet of fighting ships based at Port Royal, sent Assistant Secretary Fox the surprising news that the traitor Tattnall was "doing the work for us"—sinking old steamers in the Savannah approaches to keep the Yankees out. Du Pont said he had sent a message to Tattnall offering him half a dozen of the aged whalers; but his kind proposal was ignored. As a consequence of Tattnall's cooperation at Savannah the stone fleet was diverted to Charleston, where the first fleet was sunk on December 20. The formerly caloric ship *Ericsson* was one of several steamers and tugs employed in towing the whalers into place in a "checkerboard or indented form." Sixteen ships were sunk in the main channel, and after the arrival of the second stone fleet a month later, 20 more were used to block another. That left two minor passages still open, but these could be more easily watched by the blockaders.

When a torrent of angry editorial opinion flowed out of England and other countries concerned for the cotton and tobacco trades, the Yankee press offered many historical examples of the same practices indulged in by the principal objectors; but from the North's own point of view these were called to notice a bit late. A study of earlier results would have made the project seem as dubious as it turned out to be. Estuaries tend to take care of their subsurface patterns in their own way. About 16 months after the whalers were sunk, the Coast Survey discovered that a fine, deep channel, providing 21 feet at low water, had cut its way to the sea "south of the southern-most wreck." About a year later the stone-stuffed whalers could not be located at all.

To assist its blockaders, the United States Navy had been willing to spend several hundred thousand dollars on a naval officer's insufficiently researched scheme, but it was unwilling to listen to the civilian Forbes, who offered it free of charge his thoroughly tested double-topsail rig, which would have enhanced the versatility and nimbleness of the Navy's blockading vessels. Narratives of the blockade-runners are full of instances of narrow escapes when an extra knot of speed for the intercepting vessel would have meant capture. Forbes's housed topmasts,

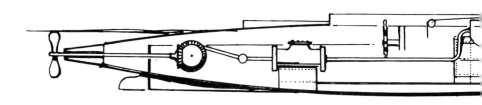

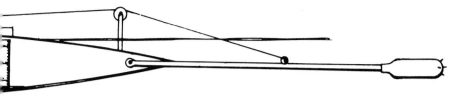

Confederate torpedo boats called Davids—after the first of their class—had some success against Union warships. The *New Ironsides*, most useful of the Northern ironclads, was seriously damaged in the attack of October 5, 1863, shown in the lithograph above. Note the clothes poles that replaced her original bark rig. A modern plan of the *David (top)* shows her spar torpedo. The photograph at the upper left is of a captured David moored at the Naval Academy after the war. Conrad Wise Chapman's oil of the original *David*, painted in 1863, appears at the lower left. (See pp. 344–46, 360.)

when the seas were turbulent, would have offered that extra knot in a hurry.

The only famous submersible built by either side during the War Between the States is usually listed as the C.S.S. *Hunley,* although in Confederate documents she is given her designer's initials as well. One dated January 20, 1864, orders First Lieutenant George E. Dixon to take "command and direction of the Submarine Torpedo Boat *H. L. Hunley,* and proceed at his discretion to the mouth of the harbor, or as far as the capacity of his vessel will allow, and will sink and destroy any vessel of the Enemy with which he can come in conflict."

The usual brief references to the *H. L. Hunley* give an impression that she was hastily riveted together out of a large marine boiler. Some such available structure probably formed her midships sector, but a contemporary drawing by Conrad Wise Chapman, and a reconstruction of her interior arrangements by one of the men who built her, both suggest that the long, straight tube of her shape was an intelligent container for a row of eight men of similar dimensions who occupied more than half of her length to provide her motive power. The wedge-shaped ends of an engineer's later plan of her seem in the Chapman drawing to be faired away somewhat more subtly into vertical vanes that would have added something to her stability. The one aft had an important function in support of the propeller guard and rudder. Her dimensions are variously given. Lieutenant William A. Alexander of the Confederate army's engineering corps, one of her builders, gave her length as 30 feet, breadth as 4 feet, depth as 5 feet.

The *H. L. Hunley* was the third submersible with which Horace L. Hunley was involved. The first, the *Pioneer,* was built at New Orleans as a privateer. To exemplify what he calls the comedy in submarine development, Simon Lake repeats in his history a vicious anecdote told by "an old southern gentleman" about the death of her original crew: two slaves. She probably was sunk to forestall capture by Farragut's forces.

Hunley and his associates then transferred their projects to the Parks and Lyons Ironworks in Mobile. Their second submarine went down like the *Alligator,* at the end of a cast-off tow line. A tow line, adapted from the theories of the revolutionary Bushnell and of Fulton, was the device by which Hunley's third submersible was to make her torpedo strike home. She was meant to dive beneath her victim while dragging after her at a distance of 60 or 70 yards a floating copper cylinder charged with powder and studded with triggers that would explode it as it touched the ship's bottom.

When originally tested in Mobile Bay by Dixon (he and Alexander were the pair of army engineers who had overseen her construction), the *H. L. Hunley* worked well enough to warrant her transfer in August of 1863, on two flatcars, to beleaguered Charleston. There she was put in the charge of a naval lieutenant who seems to have been less deft than the engineer Dixon in managing her tricky controls. He made some successful dives on August 29, but later in the day she flooded when a steamer to which she was moored moved unexpectedly. The lieutenant and two crew members got out; five drowned. She was fished up about three weeks later and turned over to Hunley for reconditioning. He brought her former crew from Mobile; but one day in mid-October when Dixon was absent, Hunley himself did some practice dives under an anchored vessel, from the last of which he failed to resurface. Hunley and his crew of seven died in nine fathoms.

Like Fulton's *Nautilus,* the *H. L. Hunley* was equipped for diving with both ballast tanks and vanes, but many years were to pass before either device was made reasonably foolproof. The tanks were a particularly unstable device in all submarines of the period: the longer the vessel, the worse their effect. When water was valved into the forward tank to bring her head down, it ran downhill within the tank and could cause an almost vertical nose dive, which the vanes could not correct. Each time she was salvaged, the *H. L. Hunley* was found with her nose fixed in the mud. In such a predicament an escape lung in the bow, like that of the *Alligator,* might not have been usable.

A much more ambitious contemporary, France's *Le Plongeur,* with a length of about 140 feet and compressed air engines rated at 80 horsepower, proved similarly difficult to keep in trim. On some of her trial runs, in water with a depth of about a quarter of her own length, she alternately bumped her nose against the bottom and broached it through the surface.

General Pierre Beauregard, who had resigned his post as superintendent of West Point to assist the rebellion, witnessed the "indescribably ghastly" removal of Hunley and his suffocated companions from the vessel when she was yet again raised. The indomitable Dixon wanted to recondition her and try again, but Beauregard, who was in command of all operations at the port, forbade any more diving. Dixon consequently fitted her with a torpedo spar to replace the tow-line weapon and continued the hunt awash for the *New Ironsides.* He made about 50 attempts over a three-month period in the difficult tides and currents of the estuary. Unlike the steam-propelled *David* that had damaged a big Union ship from the same base in the preceding October, the manpowered *H. L. Hunley* had to make her bargain with both predictable and unpredictable movements of water that sometimes had a higher speed than her own. Her best chance, like the 1776 turtle's, was to reach her target at turn of tide, getting help from it both in going and coming. All Union blockaders at anchor, after the almost successful attack by the original *David,* mounted the most attentive of watches and kept steam up, ready to make quick sternway from slipped anchor chains. All the Davids had stacks several feet tall. The converted submarine did have the advantage of a lower profile and of almost silent machinery, even though her officer was forbidden to dive.

Dixon's phenomenal persistence was rewarded on February 17, 1864, when he was able to approach the Federal screw sloop *Housatonic,* a vessel of 1,934 displacement tons completed at the Boston Navy Yard about two years earlier. She was not his particular chosen prey, but the Confederates had special reasons to resent her presence off Charleston. A year earlier, after the Lenthall-Pook gunboat *Unadilla* forced ashore a big British blockade-runner loaded with rifled cannon, marine engines, and other vital munitions, the little 90-day gunboat and the *Housatonic,* both unarmored, had between them fought off the Confederate ironclad rams *Chicora* and *Palmetto State* when they ran out to try to rescue the enormously important cargo.

In the winter darkness at 8:45 P.M. the acting master of the *Housatonic,* J. R. Crosby, saw something moving toward his vessel at a distance of about a hundred yards. He instantly ordered the chain slipped and the engine backed, but the *Housatonic* could hardly have moved two minutes later because the explosion that sank her occurred just forward of the mizzenmast. The experienced Dixon undoubtedly would have headed for the big sloop's stern, anticipating that she would run astern with the tide if her people saw him.

Reports of the fate of Dixon and his crew are confusing. Admiral Porter's detailed account of the occurrence includes the statement that "when the 'Housatonic' was inspected by divers, the torpedo-boat was found sticking in the hole she had made, having been drawn in by the rush of water, and all her crew was found dead in her." A recent summary by the United States Navy's own researchers says simply, "The exact cause of her loss is not known: she may have gone down beneath *Housatonic*; or in backing away, been swamped by waves caused by her sinking victim; or she may have been swept out to sea."

The incident is often cited as the first sinking of a surface ship by a submarine, but this is not quite true—even in a technical sense. Vessels adapted to new uses are customarily described by their latest functional form. The *R. B. Forbes*, when she was taken into the Navy and armed, was a gunboat, not a tug. The rebuilding of the *H. L. Hunley* with a torpedo spar, and her use under orders only as a surface vessel for about 50 missions, made her tactically a David, differing from the other Davids in that she lacked a steam engine.

The revolutionary Bushnell, about nine decades earlier, had set himself two governing conditions that would distinguish his submersible: she must be capable of making her attack completely submerged, and her crew must have an assured means afterward of navigating her—still submerged—to a safe distance from the point of explosion. The original *H. L. Hunley*, if she had been used as a submarine dragging a torpedo, might well under Dixon's skillful management have sunk her victim and slipped away. Since she was never so used in actual combat we can only guess. Her action with the *Housatonic* fulfilled neither of Bushnell's primary stipulations, which have continued, despite suicide submersibles of Japan, to be the basic tactical requirements of submarine warfare. His turtle fulfilled both of them, even though a particular operator failed to sink a ship. The first submarine to fulfill both in a successful attack was the German U-21 a few weeks after the beginning of the First World War, in 1914.

The need for a source of power stronger, more durable, more efficient, and less hungry for oxygen than human muscle was not satisfactorily solved in submarines until the close of the nineteenth century, when Simon Lake and John P. Holland experimented successfully with storage batteries and electric motors. Holland *(right)* tried steam on the surface, batteries when submerged, then settled for a combination of gasoline and electric motors in the *Holland (far right)*, shown at her launch in 1898. She was sold soon afterward to the government. (See p. 370.)

The Confederate submersible *H. L. Hunley (left)*, depicted by Conrad Wise Chapman, earned her nickname "the drowner." She was nevertheless the most successful submarine built during the Civil War. In two of her practice dives she pitched nose downward into the mud, drowning 12 men in all, including her designer Hunley. Condemned to operate thereafter as a surface craft, just awash, she ended her career by again killing her own crew as she took the U.S.S. *Housatonic* with her to the bottom. The plans below are reconstructions made after the war had come to an end. (See pp. 364–67, 370–72.)

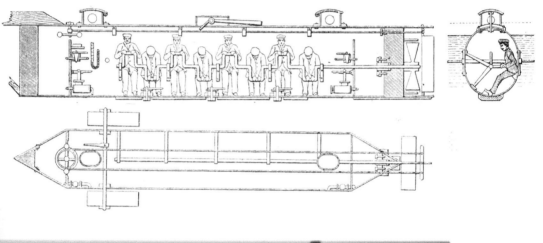

Lake, who wrote his history of submersibles while that war was in progress and after they had become calamitously reliable on Bushnell's own terms, noted that most of their nineteenth-century forerunners had been unable to cope even with the problem, common in estuaries, of abruptly different densities of fresh and salt water. The reaction produced by ballast tanks was almost always too little or too great:

The movement of the crew fore and aft, or the effect of the sea, which imparts a vertical motion to the water beneath the surface, all tend to destroy both trim and equilibrium to such an extent that many failures have resulted.

From such considerations it can be argued that throughout more than a century of experimentation with vessels capable of diving and resurfacing with some reliability, Bushnell's primary design was the best of all. Fulton substantially extended the cruising range and added one knot of speed by tripling the manpower, but Hunley's eight-man cranking crew got no more speed than Fulton's three. On the other hand, smallness in the last minutes of approach was a virtue. No diving mechanisms of the Civil War period were as sensitive and reliable as those designed by Bushnell, whose inspired choice of a round clam for prototype eliminated at the outset the vexatious problems of balance in a submerged cigar.

SAMUEL HARTT POOK, NAVAL CONSTRUCTOR

The career of Samuel Hartt Pook pivots upon the Civil War, and offers a convenient running measure of the conflict's effects upon maritime activity. When the old, deep tensions between North and South erupted inescapably in the spring of 1861, shipyards that had made only a modest recovery from the panic of 1857 had much more business than they could cope with. At the war's end, their greatly expanded capacity was useless. The consequences of the gold-rush boom were repeated. The market for new ships was destroyed by a surplus of government vessels auctioned for small fractions of their recent cost. What happened after that is reflected in Pook's own experience: an unhappy story, but one that should be told. During the war he began as a brilliant practitioner of sound orthodoxy and ended by producing one of the two or three most notably original fighting ships of the period.

About six months after the sinking of the *Housatonic* by a Confederate David, the New York *Herald* announced on September 9, 1864, under a headline of considerable typographical prominence for the period:

SUBMARINE WARFARE

A NEW ERA IN NAVAL WARFARE INAUGURATED— LAUNCH OF TORPEDO BOAT NO. 1. . . .

The first torpedo boat worthy of any notice which has been planned since the rebellion was launched yesterday afternoon at half-past three o'clock, at Fairhaven, Conn. Her hull was built and modelled by Mr. S. H. Pook, son of the naval constructor of that name.

The Navy's *Official Records,* with its customary devotion to one particular error of ascription, says that the hull was "built by contract with Mr. S. M. Pook." It notes that machinery was furnished by the Mystic Iron Works.

The concept for this vessel originated with William W. W. Wood, Chief Engineer, United States Navy, although a torpedo expert who worked with him, First Assistant Engineer John L. Lay, should probably be credited with the ingenious apparatus for placing and exploding her charges. Pook's contract called for a vessel 75 feet long, 19½ feet broad, and 9 feet "more or less" deep. The *Herald's* reporter, who made a point of the secrecy shrouding his visit, gave her dimensions as 75 by 20 by 7. Bennett, however, is precise in saying, "As actually built the boat was 84 feet 2 inches long; 20 feet 8 inches extra beam; 7 feet 5 inches draft, and of 207 tons displacement."

Northern torpedo specialists learned more from Southerners than vice versa because the South was driven by a sense of desperation, amid chivalrous expressions of the shame of it, to employ torpedoes in circumstances that simply did not arise in the North. No major Confederate vessels were blockading Union seaports or intruding into Northern rivers. The Pook-Wood-Lay torpedo boat, at first named the *Stromboli,* was in her general form and concept a David, substantially larger than any built in the South and conceived of as an attack vessel that should be able to survive in combat conditions of considerable give and take. Tanks, similar in principle to those used by the Revolution's Bushnell and by Hunley, would lower her to a fighting trim with her curved deck barely submerged and only her squat conning tower, ventilator, and smokestack showing. Lay had evolved her torpedo strategy from the contributions of several predecessors.

The first two workable fighting submarines had been designed to approach unseen and affix a magazine of powder to a ship's bottom with a screw, but Bushnell's time clock was replaced by Fulton with a lanyard—to be fed out by his submarine as it backed away—with which the gunlock in his torpedo could be tripped from a safe distance. Hunley's torpedo, barely lighter than water like the others, was dragged at a safe distance behind the attacker as she dived beneath a victim, one of its multiple triggers exploding it upon contact with the ship's bottom. The Davids, including the converted *H. L. Hunley*, counted upon a straightaway surface lunge—either to affix a torpedo at the end of a spar by driving it into the enemy to be exploded by a lanyard after the attacker had backed away, or simply to explode on contact.

The problems in each case are evident. Lay tried to resolve them in the *Stromboli* by using a spar considerably longer than those of the Confederate Davids, one that could be retracted for its full length within the vessel and that when protruding could be dropped at a fairly sharp angle. The head of this spar could be entirely withdrawn into a water lock in the bow that could be swiftly emptied or filled by a steam pump. When it was fully retracted, with the lock pumped dry, a torpedo attached to a coiled trigger lanyard could be inserted in the spar's socket. The inner gate of the lock was then closed upon the shaft of the spar, water was pumped in, and the outer gate opened. As the *Stromboli* came up with its target, the spar was angled down so as to thrust its head beneath and beyond the ship's keel. The released torpedo then would float toward the surface on the opposite side of the victim, to be exploded by a jerk of the lanyard as the *Stromboli* backed away, with the protection of her victim's hull between her and the explosion.

This procedure made the *Stromboli* effective for repeated attacks. Her spar should not be damaged by her own torpedo and

could be promptly retracted to receive the next one. The Davids
were extremely vulnerable, even to small arms fire. They had to
count on an unobserved approach in darkness to a position so
close that a ship's guns could not be depressed enough to aim
at them. Although the *Stromboli*'s armor had not yet been installed when the *Herald*'s reporter made his security-conscious
visit, her whale-shaped deck soon thereafter was given three
inches of iron plate, her sides and pilothouse five inches. If contemporary pictures are to be believed, navigator and steersman
of a David sat with their torsos in full view. The *Stromboli* was
large enough to house her entire crew below, well protected by
her armor from the normal fighting hazards. She had a powerful
engine—18-inch cylinder with 18-inch stroke. Her speed was
rated by the Navy at a maximum of 8 knots, although one account credits her with 12 knots when pushed. Bennett notes,
in substantiation of her revolutionary aspect as a versatile fighting ship, that "the weight of the torpedo handling machinery
was ten tons while that of the motive engine was only two and
one-half tons." Early in her career she was renamed the *Spuyten
Duyvil,* and so she appears in most references.

Pook evidently told Hamersly that he "designed and built for
Mr. Lay the 'Spuyten Duyvil' torpedo-boat," a phrase which
implies that the engineers had given him in the contract approximate dimensions for accommodating their mechanisms,
but that he had altered them in accordance with his hydrody-
namic computations. By the time she was completed the only
notable enemy vessels left that might have merited her lethal
attentions were far up the James River, past Drewry's Bluff and
beyond a wild subaqueous jumble of obstructions planted to
protect the approaches to Richmond. Land operations against
the city early in the spring of 1865 were of a sort that made a
concurrent naval assault seem unnecessary. Bennett says that
"the *Spuyten Duyvil* was in service in the James River during
the last months of the war and had the honor of taking President
Lincoln to Richmond when he visited that city after its abandon-
ment by the enemy." The report, like that concerning another
head of state who is alleged to have made a journey in Drebbel's
submarine of the 1620's, eludes verification. Lincoln did go up
to City Point, General Grant's headquarters, in the steamer *City
Queen.* After several days of what would be regarded as lunatic's

behavior by the security standards of our times, and a review of
the naval flotilla that doubtless included the *Spuyten Duyvil*,
the President proceeded on April 4 in the *River Queen*, transferred into Admiral Porter's flagship the *Malvern*, and made
the last part of his journey to the smoking wharves of Richmond
in the admiral's 12-oared gig. The city had fallen the day before,
and again Lincoln exposed himself in a manner that Porter found
dismaying.

When they had returned to the *Malvern*, three odd characters
made separate attempts to get aboard to see the President, and
one succeeded, giving him a ferocious scolding. Porter expressed
the opinion, in his *Naval History*, that one of the other two
probably was John Wilkes Booth, who did get close enough to
fulfill his intentions ten days later. As for the *Sputyen Duyvil's*
activities at this climactic time, it is most likely that she helped
to clear the way for the visit by blowing up channel obstructions—a task at which she functioned with success on many
occasions when the fighting was over. Having attended to that,
she was transferred to the New York Navy Yard and used frequently for experimentation with torpedoes. The Navy's chief
specialist in the theory of submarine warfare, writing in 1868,
called her "the most formidable engine of destruction . . . now
afloat of which the public have any knowledge." In 1880 she
was dropped from the register.

During the war Pook continued his intermittent exchange of
letters with Forbes, whom he urged on August 6, 1862, to visit
Washington to "look after the Ram—and close a Contract with
Mr. Fox & Com Smith in my name.—Mr. Bushnell advises it.
. . ." This was something of a reversal of their earlier roles.
Forbes replied testily that he was unwell and would have no in-
clination toward a "wild goose chase"; he asked for better assurances that the government was serious, which it seems not
to have been. They also discussed a proposal being advanced by
several zealots, although the earlier Bushnell, David, had
demonstrated its error nearly a century earlier: a submarine
gun to be fixed under water in the bows of Union vessels. Forbes
tried it out in April, 1862, in a dock at East Boston, with "a
twelve-pound rifle, carrying a Shenkle-elongated shot weighing
seventeen pounds; charge, three pounds. . . . Passing through
twelve feet of water, the shot went into the target of hard wood

about two feet; the recoil of the gun, nine feet." Pook had warned him that the gun would cause more damage to the vessel in which it was mounted than to an enemy, and this the violent recoil seemed to demonstrate. Forbes nevertheless got a government contract, then changed his mind: "I begged off, thus saving myself from considerable loss."

On January 31, 1863, Pook reported to Forbes that he had delivered two steamers to the government and had a number of others under way:

I have a large steamboat in frame for the New Haven & New London RR for the crossing at Connecticut River—which will be a novelty as she has a Propeller at each end. . . .

At least 65 steamers of more than 100 tons measurement were built in Connecticut during the war years—seven at Fairhaven, where Bushnell established Pook as manager of his own yard. All the Fairhaven ships and some of the six built at New Haven probably were included in the sixteen that Pook said he "designed, built and launched for Mr. Bushnell." The *Admiral,* of 1,248 tons, and the *Commodore,* of 940, upon their completion in 1863 were sold to the Navy by Bushnell's associate George Griswold. These were renamed U.S.S. *Fort Morgan* and U.S.S. *Iuka.* In 1864 the builder himself sold to the government the *Hibiscus* and *Spirea,* both of 406 tons, to join an already extensive roster of horticulturally identified supply ships and transports. The government's published records in each case identify the seller as S. M. Pook. The younger Pook also designed, constructed, and launched "while ship-builder for Mr. Bushnell . . . the famous yacht 'Idler,'" a contestant in 1870 in the first race for the America's Cup.

The stagnation in merchant shipping that preceded the Civil War had brought other naval architects and shipbuilders— along with Pook—into connections of an exigent sort with their government. Griffiths in 1858 got a temporary appointment as Naval Constructor to design and supervise building, at the Philadelphia Navy Yard, of the twin-screw wooden sloop of war *Pawnee,* of 1,289 tons, which participated with the Lenthall-Pook gunboats in the capture of Port Royal. The *Pawnee* was probably the first vessel in which all elements of design were reconsidered for the purpose of carrying the heavy naval ord-

The jaunty steam schooner *Tillie (above, left)* was built in 1862 at Fairhaven, Connecticut, in the shipyard financed by Cornelius S. Bushnell for Samuel Hartt Pook. Bushnell promoted the workable submarine *Intelligent Whale (above, right)*, launched too late for combat, as was the huge ram *Dunderberg (below)*. Her builder, William H. Webb, sold her to France. (See pp. 375, 381.)

nance that Dahlgren had been developing. The tactical problem that persuaded the conservative Navy administrators to employ a civilian came of a desire to mount four 11-inch Dahlgren guns in a vessel drawing no more than ten feet. Bennett comments:

Besides having to carry the unusually large battery, the engines to drive the two screws were considerably heavier than in other vessels of the class, and this necessitated further calculation on the part of the constructor, who so modified the form of the hull that when the vessel was completed her bottom was actually concave.

Although most of the naval constructors, as Chapelle has demonstrated, were flexible far beyond the rigidities established by old-line commodores, such heresy could have hardly been looked for in any of them. Yet it permitted the *Pawnee* to carry her devastating guns into shallow waters, again and again, where no other Union ship of equal speed and power was able to operate. She first went into action with two 12-pounders and eight 9-inch Dahlgrens instead of the four 11-inch guns for which Griffiths had designed her scantlings. In 1864 she was carrying twelve 9-inch Dahlgrens, and when the war ended a 24-pound howitzer in addition—probably the maximum for firepower in any vessel of her tonnage. In the *Official Records* her terse entry concludes, "sometimes spoken of as the Griffith Ship." Like the smaller wooden gunboats with which another civilian designer was involved, the *Pawnee* outlived her buffets. She was not sold until 1884.

Donald McKay's efforts to adjust himself to the mysteries of naval bidding resulted in nothing of comparable interest. After his bankruptcy he built only two modest traders, launched in 1859 and 1862, and four little fishermen. He laid down no vessels in 1862 or 1863, but in the following year he began to build for the government the *Ashuelot*, of 1,030 tons, a paddle-wheel iron double-ender—stem and stern of essentially the same lines with a rudder at each end, permitting her to operate as a gunboat in shallow, narrow rivers and channels without ever having to turn around. She was one of seven built to the same design, another being contracted for by Harrison Loring. Thirty-nine somewhat smaller double-enders had previously been built, all but one of wood. McKay did not get his into the water until July 22, 1865, when the shooting was supposed to be over. Five of the other six had been launched or delivered before the end of the preceding year.

McKay was building at the same time the light-draft monitor *Nausett* and two additions to the Navy's horticultural fleet, the wooden propellers *Trefoil* and *Yucca.* The *Nausett* was delivered on July 18, 1865, commissioned on August 10, and decommissioned two weeks later. She never saw service, and was broken up in 1875 at a cost of $3,666. The *Trefoil* spent six months in commission. McKay's brother-in-law bought her two years later for a trivial fraction of her cost after an auction had failed to bring the stipulated minimum price. The *Yucca* was also sold soon afterward for a trifle.

These melancholy details concerning the steep drop in value of relatively new ships that had seen no rough service call to notice the conditions that confronted all shipbuilders as the war ended. Again there was an oversupply, as there had been about nine years earlier, of many kinds of well-built, up-to-date vessels: naval supply ships for general traders, troop ships for passengers. There was an abundance of transatlantic steamers under foreign flags and enough of the old sailing liners left to handle what they could get of the immigrant traffic. McKay's four naval vessels, launched too late for participation in the war, at least were completed. Many others under government contract were simply broken up on the stocks. A good deal of shipyard space was employed for a while in reconverting naval vessels to civilian employments, but facilities expanded to meet the needs of war got few orders for new ships.

These conditions again confronted Pook with a need to reassess his future. With the collapse of the Connecticut boom he returned to East Boston. There, in the latter part of 1865, he took up where he had left off by designing what proved to be his last two ships for civilian clients: the large and handsome *Ontario* and the *Erie.* These were transatlantic liners built at Newburyport, Massachusetts, by George W. Jackman, Jr., with engines supplied by Harrison Loring. They were of the same measurement as the huge Collins side-wheelers of the early 1850's— about 3,000 tons—but were screw driven. The new Boston–Liverpool service for which they were intended had trouble in raising capital. The *Ontario* did not make her maiden voyage until August, 1867. A picture of her at the Peabody Museum in

The long stagnation following the Civil War differently affected both principal founders of American naval architecture. The owners for whom Samuel Hartt Pook designed his graceful liner *Ontario* (*above*) of 1867 never could raise adequate operating capital. John Willis Griffiths spent four years waiting for appropriations to finish the stodgy training ship *Enterprise* (*below*), launched in 1877, which he built to the bureau's antique specifications. (See pp. 378, 380–82.)

In the 1870's America's most subtle naval architect, Samuel Hartt Pook, was reduced as an officer in the Navy's Bureau of Ships to the building of vessels conceived by others, ranging from the curious torpedo boat *Alarm (left)*, designed by Admiral David Porter and propelled by a Fowler wheel *(bottom)*, to the big *Trenton* "of bureau design." The picture of her, just below, is entitled "Reefing Topsails"—a full generation after Pook's own double-topsail clippers had helped make that dangerous and infuriating operation obsolete. (See pp. 382–83.)

Salem shows an unusually graceful hull, with a clipper bow. She had two stacks in tandem between the fore and main masts of her bark rig. But her backers did not have enough money to operate her properly in the stiff competition that Europeans had developed on the Atlantic while the Americans, North and South, were making the oceans uninhabitable for each other. The Boston line failed before the *Erie* was finished.

Iron ships cost a third more to build in the United States than they did in Britain. Wooden hulls, like those of the *Ontario* and the *Erie,* were still competitive in first cost with foreign hulls of metal, but the latter were cheaper to operate and maintain. Although the government had been able to subsidize a considerable expansion of the iron shipbuilding industry in wartime, nearly all the important battles had been won by wooden vessels. Private shipowners were content to see the forging and rolling mills swing promptly to the supplying of railroads. Such shipping financiers as Vanderbilt and Bushnell turned their wealth inland.

Foreign business had never been relinquished by some American shipbuilders, even while the war was on. The *Army and Navy Journal* reprinted without comment an article praising Webb for finding time to build two warships for Italy while keeping up his contractual deliveries to his own government. It reacted quite differently toward McKay's efforts to interest the Admiralty in a weapons system he was prepared to produce, judging as a "disgraceful piece of business . . . the unpatriotic course of Mr. McKay." The distinction reflects the fact that Britain had supplied the Rebels with commerce raiders and munitions.

Griffiths discussed knowledgeably the hard choices confronting his country's merchants upon deep water. No-one at the time, however, perceived that the exuberant world conquest of the Yankee whalers, packets, and clippers, owned and operated by private persons, was finished—that Americans would be strong again in international waters only when their government had compelling reasons to foot a very heavy part of the bill. Coastal trade recovered after the war because the government excluded competition. Riverboats proliferated throughout the protected inland waterways; but international seaborne trade continued its long decline. Scores of angry books and pamphlets, throughout the rest of the century and later, scolded the government for its colossal folly, but only another great war would change the policy that was no policy at all.

Pook saw the portents. If such fine ships as his *Ontario* could not be financed it was time to make the decision that would have bettered his present status if he had made it when the war began. In the diminished peace establishment Lenthall had only the rank of Assistant Naval Constructor to offer the country's most distinguished theoretical naval architect. Pook accepted it and got his commission on May 17, 1866. He could not have foreseen, however, conditions that would force the Navy's return to the sort of stagnation that had made it so perilously unready in 1861. His own recounting to Hamersly of work done in his years as a naval officer is sometimes pathetic. He designed vessels that he was not asked to design; he reports the praise that his concepts elicited and goes on to explain that something smaller was wanted: that sort of thing. At first he was stationed at Washington, but soon, "at the solicitation of some of the people of Boston," was ordered back to the Charlestown yard. On April 15, 1871, he was advanced to the highest rank, Naval Constructor, and in the following year he made the journey west about which he had consulted long before with Forbes, to take charge of construction at the Mare Island Navy Yard, north of San Francisco.

A belated act of Congress, in 1873, authorized eight modest vessels. Griffiths, again under a curious temporary arrangement, built one of them by private contract, using the facilities of the navy yard at Kittery. McKay also built one at Kittery, another at Boston. They were classed at first as gunboats, later as corvettes. All were of wood, with a displacement tonnage of 1,375. Reversing the emphasis of the 1840's, they were described as steamers with auxiliary sail. Pook had the satisfaction of producing the only one of substantial size, the *Trenton,* a steam frigate that displaced 3,900 tons. In the Hamersly account he is careful to say that he "finished and launched" her, but he uses the bracketed phrase "Bureau's design." It was at about this time that he built, to the general design of Admiral Porter, a fantastically shovel-nosed torpedo boat, the *Alarm,* displacing 800 tons, made of iron throughout, and 173 feet long. She was equipped with an experimental Fowler Wheel, a paddle wheel that turned in a horizontal plane in the location usually given to a propeller. The blades were made to feather when moving forward and flatten for thrusts against the water when moving aft. The device proved less efficient than either a propeller or orthodox paddle wheels having the same paddle area. The care Pook took to avoid being given credit for the design of either of these vessels is understandable. Although an element of imagination appears in the *Alarm,* the *Trenton* when launched was 30 years out of date in almost all aspects except size. To give a large naval crew something to do, no doubt, she carried old-fashioned man-killer topsails long after Howes's rig had replaced them on most merchant ships.

In 1877, while Pook was still at the Brooklyn yard, his former apprentice Varney published *The Ship-builder's manual; or, Mould loft guide.* Varney too had found the career of an independent civilian naval architect frustrating and had followed Pook into the Bureau of Ships as Assistant Naval Constructor in 1869. He was given the top rank in 1875, with the relative rank of commander.

The practice now called moonlighting evidently continued among naval constructors. On October 14, 1870, Pook asked Forbes whether an ironclad design of his could be offered to "the Prussian or Russian consulate." Ten years later he was working on a yacht model for Forbes when "an anonymous person" made inquiries as to whether it was being done on government time. Evidently the climate was changing in such matters. Pook wrote that he was "ready to be investigated by the department" but that "the sorehead, whoever it is, will have to be content without further explanation." When Forbes sent him a copy of *The Tour of General Grant,* Pook acknowledged it with the confession, "I am a worshiper of that gentleman and nothing could have given me greater pleasure than to watch or read of his progress around the world."

The only published writing by Pook himself that I have come upon appears in the massive *Naval Encyclopedia* issued by Hamersly in 1881, which thanks him in its acknowledgments for "definitions of the terms pertaining to shipbuilding." The work also contains Pook's signed article, of about 1,000 words, entitled "Ship, Launching of."

The latter years of America's most versatile and skillful naval architect of the nineteenth century provide a commentary upon the condition of marine enterprise in the United States. After a phenomenal rise to world leadership in the forties and fifties, this eminence was allowed to dwindle away. A swift increase in population was accompanied by a steady falling off in tonnage of merchant shipping. The figure for vessels in foreign trade in the year before the Civil War was nearly 2,400,000 tons. Fifty years later, with three times the population to be served by it, tonnage in the foreign trades had fallen below 800,000. The proportion of exports and imports carried in United States ships had dropped from about nine-tenths in the year of Pook's birth to about one-tenth in the year of his death. During the period of his service as a full-time employee of the government, a Congress obsessed with internal exploitation of a rich continent had to be elbow-twisted into making appropriations to maintain a small, moribund naval force in commission. Very few new ships were authorized. Most of these were obsolescent monitors and obsolete wooden cruisers differing hardly at all from the steam sloops of the late fifties.

The fateful *Maine,* of 6,648 tons displacement—precursor of a new Navy—was authorized on August 3, 1886, and the first plate of her keel was laid on October 11, 1888, at the Brooklyn Navy Yard, where Pook was the ranking naval constructor, but the design of her hull is credited to Commodore Theodore D. Wilson. Pook could have had little to do with her since he retired with the rank of captain on his next birthday, January 17, 1889, at the age of 62. The *Maine,* bark-rigged for 7,135 running feet of canvas, was not launched until November 18, 1890, after sticking stubbornly on the ways in a fashion that might not have occurred if the author of "Ship, Launching of," had been in charge.

A modest headline in the Washington *Post* for March 31, 1901, referred to an event of the preceding evening:

DESIGNED FAMOUS CLIPPER SHIP
CAPT. SAMUEL H. POOKE, USN RETIRED
DIES SUDDENLY OF APOPLEXY

The Last Challenges of Wood and Sail

WHALING: THE SHIFT TO SAN FRANCISCO

The decline in American deep-water ventures was severe in the case of whaling. Registered tonnage of whalers early in 1861 was 158,746. Five years later it stood at 43 per cent of that prewar capacity. The count of bottoms had declined a little less, because many small vessels had been quickly converted into whalers after the lapse in hostilities. The fleet of 1860 had included 23 schooners. In the short postwar season of 1865, departures of schooner-whalers numbered 39. In the full year following, 70 put to sea. All but one fished the Atlantic—where, as in previous times when men had turned their energies to hunting men upon the oceans, gentler mammals had increased their numbers.

The fratricidal quarrel to which ancient hulks of the stone fleets were sacrificed eliminated scores of working whalers in the usual ways. Starbuck's terminal notes record the fiery end of many that had sailed in the three or four years before the fall of Fort Sumter and were homeward bound unwarned when intercepted by Confederate commerce raiders. Some that got word of their danger via the Isthmus mails to Honolulu and San Francisco were ordered to stay in the Pacific. Others that reached neutral ports were sold to foreigners. "*Alabama* Claims," a pivotal phrase in international law, recalls the dignified admission by Great Britain that she had done wrong in permitting a commerce raider to be outfitted from a British port: an admission followed by a payment of $15,500,000 to injured shipowners. The *Alabama*'s famous captures were the clippers *Golden Eagle, Talisman, Winged Racer,* and *Contest,* but her 64 others included 13 whalers. Other raiders, such as the ocean tug *Calhoun,* which sank the whalers *Mermaid, John Adams,* and *Panama,* operated out of Southern ports despite blockaders.

Between the gold rush and the Civil War, San Francisco's native whaling had been intermittent. Starbuck complained that "data in regard to San Francisco . . . are extremely hard to get at," a problem made no easier by succeeding earthquakes and fires. New Bedford's *Nile,* of 322 tons, was sold in 1844 "to parties in San Francisco for whaling thence." She was followed five or six years later by many whalers chartered to carry gold seekers. Of these, the *Mayflower,* of 350 tons, and *Russell,* of 301 tons, later made at least two whaling voyages apiece out of San Francisco. The *Nile's* departure in April, 1853, is followed by a laconic "no report." In 1853 the Nantucket-built *Charles Carroll* was "sold in California," from which she made at least two voyages.

Most New England whalers in the Pacific had rounded the Horn homeward bound with a catch intentionally short of capacity, pausing to fill up off Patagonia or Africa. When these grounds were fished out, the long periods spent merely in transit came to seem too costly. Hawaii, central to several areas where whales still clustered around the huge perimeter of the Pacific, consequently became the point for transshipment of oil and bone. The islands' economy under the Kamehamehas was managed by shrewdly commercial descendants of New England missionaries, factors who appear to have recognized the threat of San Francisco as a rival. On October 21, 1855, despite the fact that at least six firms were already refining oil and making candles, the *Alta California's* annalist wrote:

. . . at present the rates of repairing and fitting out in this harbor are so much higher than in the Sandwich Islands, whalers go there in preference.

At year's end, however, he pointed to San Francisco's "spacious dry dock" and its other "greater facilities than at any other port in the Pacific," some of which were not available at all in any "other port adjacent to the whaling grounds."

These advantages were capped by the completion in 1862 of a telegraphic ligature with the east coast, allowing New Bedford owners to execute decisions promptly through local managing agents—at least during considerable periods when the Indians left the wires uncut.

The oil rush of 1859 to western Pennsylvania was not taken

seriously at the time for its potential effect, but it turned out to be one of several concurrent factors that discouraged replacement of vessels sunk, burned, and sold away during the civil strife. The war's worst blow was struck belatedly by the raider *Shenandoah*. She had begun life in Scotland as the wood-planked, iron-framed steamer *Sea King*, of 1,160 tons, fitted with a hoistable propeller. She left the Thames October 8, 1864, ostensibly for Bombay, but was converted off Madeira with guns and equipment carried from Liverpool in another ship. Her particular orders were to destroy New England whalers that had found a haven at San Francisco.

Uncertain of the Union's naval force based there, Captain James I. Waddell brought the *Shenandoah* up the opposite side of the Pacific into the Sea of Okhotsk, northeast of Japan, where a whale chart given him by its compiler, Lieutenant Maury, led him to hope that Yankee whalers might be operating. On May 27, 1865, he found the ship *Abigail*, of 310 tons, which had been sailing out of New Bedford for 44 years. She had picked up a crew largely of foreigners, most of whom, lured by prize money, were willing to transfer their talents to the cause of the South. It was Waddell's good fortune to recruit also an American citizen from the disputed ground, the *Abigail's* second mate, Thomas Manning of Maryland.

Manning, transformed into a corporal of Confederate marines, offered to pilot the *Shenandoah* some 1,700 miles across the Gulf of Anadir to the principal fishing grounds of the American whaling fleet, which was clustered in an inescapable crescent of ice. A detailed account of this only circumnavigation of a Confederate ship, written by her executive officer, discreetly avoids any mention of Manning, but the impromptu pilot was regarded as distinctly unlovable by Cornelius E. Hunt, acting master's mate, who put to press the longest and best-written narrative of the cruise shortly after its conclusion. "It is always unpleasant," he wrote, "though sometimes necessary, to accept the services of the most disreputable of men."

Cape Thaddeus, a fang in the lower jaw of the Gulf of Anadir, was a point of particular reference for whalers because it lies very close to the International Date Line, in 179 degrees 42 minutes east longitude, a handy spot for the checking of chronometers. It was off Cape Thaddeus on June 20, 1865, that Corporal Manning conducted the *Shenandoah* within view of two stragglers from a fleet of about 30 whalers that had recently proceeded northeastward to scatter at prudent working distances in Bering Strait. Romanticized retellings of the episode represent Captain Waddell as making a cautious approach to the nearer vessel because she was too large for a whaler and crossed double topsail yards, still a rarity in whaleships; but there is nothing in Hunt's account to suggest that she was suspected of being a Union gunboat. In fact she was loitering to get the last blubber from a whale alongside, and Hunt states that she was identified as a whaler at a great distance by clouds of oily smoke from her tryworks. She proved to be the *William Thompson,* still wearing the name she had been given as one of the four new ships built for the Black Ball Line in 1821. After being sold to New Bedford in 1830, she was for a decade probably the largest whaler afloat: 495 tons. There were only nine larger ex-packets operating as whalers at mid-century; thus the yarn that Waddell thought she might be a disguised Union cruiser had something to grow out of. Waddell sent a prize master aboard, went after the other whaler, burned her, and returned to complete the destruction of the *William Thompson.*

A complex international economy had been building itself up south of Cape Krusenstern, where the earliest American whalers of whom we have respectable evidence were practicing their dangerous art 4,000 years earlier. New Englanders had made increasing use of the strait for about three decades, but its migrant Eskimos had been trading furs with Russians for a much longer period and more recently with Englishmen. Whalers dabbled in pelts as a sideline. They were somewhat dependent upon Eskimos for meat and fish. The mixed market lured modest provision vessels from San Francisco with something for everybody, and with stowage space upon returning for furs and bone.

In these circumstances it is not unduly surprising that a couple of whaling skippers, on the barren farthest edge of the Siberian Arctic, were well informed about the surrender at Appomattox Court House only ten weeks earlier, and that they protested the decision of Captain Waddell to burn their ships in peacetime. He explained his own reasoning in a letter written later in the year at Liverpool:

. . . from each I received San Francisco papers. These papers professed to have correspondence between Generals Grant and Lee concerning the surrender of Lee's army. They also stated . . . that Mr. Davis had issued a proclamation informing the Southern people that the war would be carried on with renewed vigor. . . . I continued my work until it was completed in the Arctic Ocean, on the 28th of June 1865, when I succeeded in destroying or dispersing the New England whaling fleet.

Waddell's most recent previous news of the fortunes of his war had been picked up while coaling at Melbourne, from which he had sailed on February 18. It could not have been much newer than the British newspapers dated in the first week of October that he had carried with him to Australia.

Between June 22 and 28 the *Shenandoah* added 1 brig, 15 barks, and 6 ships, taken in the mouth of Bering Strait, to the brig and two ships that had begun her subarctic depredations. These, with the five destroyed in the southern Pacific, gave her a total of 29 or 30 whalers for the cruise, all of which she burned, except four that were bonded as cartels to carry home the crews of the others; 29 or 30 because there is some confusion over the smallest, identified in a list appended to Hunt's account as the whaling brig *Susan and Abigail* of New Bedford, but referred to in his text as a trader from San Francisco. Starbuck has no listing for her as belonging to either port. Her function in history was to deliver to Captain Waddell some later issues of San Francisco papers. They carried news of the assassination of President Lincoln, but nothing sufficiently circumstantial on the collapse of the Confederacy to deter the commander of the *Shenandoah* from seizing the last 12 whalers counted above. Of these he burned nine and bonded the others.

Captain Waddell had been serving in a United States Navy ship in the Far East when the war broke out. After changing uniforms, he got his first chance to shoot at his former comrades-in-arms when he helped to send the plunging missiles from Drewry's Bluff into the Pook-Ericsson *Galena*. More specifically to be noted is Hunt's observation of umiaks and their Eskimo crews:

Their boats are ingeniously constructed affairs. The frame is something like that of a whale boat, over which is stretched walrus hide, which renders them completely impervious to water. They are very light and much better calculated to traverse these icy seas than wood or even metallic boats. . . . They first blow a walrus hide . . . full of air and to this they fasten one end of their harpoon line. . . . they dart the harpoon into the whale, and thus attach to him a great buoy. . . . Another and another is attached to him in the same way, until the poor animal can no longer get below the surface and is in the end, fairly worried to death.

Egede in the early eighteenth century had seen inflated seal-skins in use as drogues to tire the whale, and Bernard du Haut-cilly had referred to bladders, but the principle in all three cases was the same.

The relative capabilities of sail and steam early in the 1860's are hinted at in Captain Waddell's statement that his vessel, designed primarily as a steamer, could make 10 knots under steam, 16 under sail. Hunt noted that she had "Cunningham's patent reefing topsails, and under sail with a fair breeze, with a sufficient crew to work her, we had little to apprehend from a chase." On the other hand her value as a raider depended greatly upon her ability to steam into the wind's eye when her prey under sail alone would have to claw their way zigzag. Her efficient rounding up of most of the American whaling fleet, in the fogs and floes of Bering Strait, demonstrated the merits of auxiliary steam for future whalers. The Forbes-Ericsson principle, hoistable screw and all, was revived after a period of disinterest; but its potential good sense became evident only after a rapacious, worldwide attack upon the whale population had made nearly all the fishing grounds unprofitable except along the edges of perpetual ice.

The four cartels that carried the *Shenandoah's* prisoners to San Francisco turned loose in that port about a hundred of the most accomplished whaling masters and mates with their disciplined whaleboat crews. Many of these sought commands and berths on the San Francisco waterfront. Most went into ships locally managed for New England owners at the far end of the telegraph wire.

In the early postwar years, the pressure of charter parties seeking bottoms for grain carriers at the San Francisco wharves sent much of the entrepôt activity back to mid-Pacific. San Francisco owners for a while left the large risks of full-size whaleship operations to New Bedford. They instead sent out brigs or schooners—such as the *Manuella,* a brig of 128 tons, equipped for a variety of tasks. The captain of the disputatious *Susan and Abigail* sailed in the *Manuella* as his next command, "whaling and trading." The event is not mentioned by Starbuck, who records only a voyage resulting in her loss in 1871.

In the fall of that year the most famous Arctic whaling tragedy occurred on Alaska's northwest coast when 43 vessels lingered too long against advice of the Eskimos and were trapped. On September 12, after three ships were crushed, all the masters signed a document expressing their common judgment that none could be saved. The superb rescue operation that followed is unparalled as a demonstration of seamanship. Whaleboats were built up with additional strakes above their gunwales and given protective belts of copper. These, mostly under sail, carried 1,219 of the ships' people, including women and children, through 80 miles of shifting ice to the seven whalers that were operating in open water. The last few miles were accomplished under "the full force of a tremendous gale and a sea that would have made the stoutest ship tremble." Freezing brine almost swamped the constantly bailed open boats and ruined all their stores. The wind was so severe that the ship *Arctic,* just as the last refugee came up over her side, lunged with such violence that her chain cable broke and her starboard anchor was gone forever. Yet in these wild circumstances the delicate cedar whaleboats delivered every one of their passengers swiftly and safely aboard the rescue fleet. Descriptions by the participants, although they seem to take the performance of the whaleboats as something only to be expected, are probably the best testimonials ever written to the functional excellence under extreme stress of any particular small craft.

News of a similar tragedy of 1876 arrived just in time for Starbuck to make a footnote of it. Fewer ships were destroyed—12—but some of the crews had decided to stay the winter out in their trapped vessels, and of these 50 died. This aspect of the disaster confirmed in human terms what had been sadly evident on the ledgers: that efforts to stay north of Bering Strait long enough to make a profitable voyage were rendered unreasonably perilous by the short Arctic summer's capricious ending. The first winter gale that piles floe ice into grinding level avalanches could not be predicted within a month. A ship might be caught in any year, as the bark *Roscoe* was on August 19, 1872, but smashing of whole fleets, on the second dramatic occasion with heavy loss of life, called the whole enterprise into question. For some years whaling out of San Francisco almost ceased, and the main activity out of New Bedford was carried on in schooners.

Devastations of the American whaling fleet—during the Revolution and the War of 1812—had seemed to spur an inventive new experimentation. The decline in numbers of whaling vessels caused by the Civil War was less drastic than in the earlier conflicts. Yet a modest recovery this time was marked by no prompt technical advancement. In 1846 the American whaling industry employed 775 vessels, of which 678 were ships or barks; 292 of them were fishing the North Pacific. With the onset of the Civil War, even in these safest waters the count fell below 100 and never topped that figure again. After the third Arctic tragedy, in 1876, the total still fishing in the North Pacific was eight. By this time the chief reason was the swift rise of petroleum technology. A minor part of the surviving fleet of barks, without any additions except the taking up of schooners for the Atlantic, had been able to produce all the whale products the market would absorb. The sudden turn toward steam whalers, and the new importance of San Francisco as the best port from which they might be operated, were still a few years ahead.

Before the work of the *Shenandoah* recedes beyond too many pages of type, one particular humane note out of a period of fratricidal bitterness deserves attention. The later whaling captains, in most objective works, tend to appear as hardhearted money grubbers, adept at swindling their own crews. Acting Master's Mate Hunt of the Rebel raider had this to report of those he encountered:

I must say that American whalers are officered by some of the noblest, most high-minded and generous men belonging to the great brotherhood of seamen. A kindness they seldom forget,— to a friend their hand is ever open, and an enemy they can look upon as one who might have been a friend, but for some political accident. . . .

THE DOWN EASTERS

If the builders of wooden sailing vessels ever did consciously project a concerted challenge for the survival of their ancient industry, it was not in the clipper ship era, which ended abruptly without having resolved a contest that continued for half a century in a series of less spectacular intermittent endeavors. A few square-rigged whalers built in the latter sixties probably were expressions more of habit and erroneous confidence than of need. The industry, like the stock market, had a surrounding fringe of hopeful investors in the share system of its separate voyages, causing a profitable year to be followed by too many departures, with consequent overproduction and falling prices. As the whole enterprise dwindled, only the managing owners who were experts survived. These, in the 1870's, did order a few fine new whalers; but after the Civil War, orders for wooden ships of any kind were so hard to secure that most of the New York shipyards vanished. Some around Boston led a diminished existence, while the center of the industry moved to the jagged, still largely wooded coast of Maine. Here, 20 years after the launch of the last true clipper, builders of wooden sailing ships organized their impressive final challenge to iron and steam. With plenty of bulk freight to be moved, and with small ports newly dredged for the wharfside lading of sizable carriers, the challenge took two concurrent forms. One, evolved for what Griffiths had defined as the distant trades, became known as the down easter —a large, prudent expression of knowledge gained in the latter part of the clipper era, a capacious and sturdy vessel to be stuffed by preference with bulk cargo on one side of the planet and sent by a route that kept favorable winds in her square sails for most of the journey to the planet's opposite side. The other form was an extraordinary overgrowth of the schooner concept, likewise designed for bulk cargo but intended to lug it for modest distances up and down the coast, out of and into comparatively shallow estuaries.

The ultimate down easters were shipentines, rigged like the *Great Republic,* with square sail on three masts, fore-and-aft sail on a jigger aft. Of these the *Shenandoah,* of 3,406 tons, launched in 1890, and the *Roanoke,* of 3,539, completed two years later, were the largest, both slightly larger than the *Great*

Republic as rebuilt. Their lines were much less fine than those of their famous predecessor. As was common in the tightly interwoven economy of Maine, they were operated by their builders, Arthur Sewall & Company of Bath. Some students of nautical performances, unimpressed by mere speed at the sacrifice of carrying capacity, have praised these wooden down easters as better ships than the best clippers. It should be noted, however, that the construction of new down easters ended even more suddenly in 1893 than the building of new clippers had done in 1857. The reason was the same: a particular kind and size of vessel was lying idle in too many ports. Sound and well-rated examples could be bought for a lot less than the building cost of new ones.

Although somewhat ragged in its timing, the boom-and-bust cycle of uninhibited free enterprise appears in the production records of east-coast shipyards between the Civil War and World War I, half a century during which government left nearly all of them entirely to their own devices. After the auctioned 90-day gunboats were put to peaceful tasks, a modest boom crested in 1869, but production slipped to a low point again in the winter of 1871–72. Between this and the next low, in 1879–80, the down easter was firmly established as the dominant form of American sailing ship for use in deep water: a three-masted square-rigger with double topsails, measuring something like 1,500 tons. Fairburn, in his inventory of 320 of them built in the latter part of the nineteenth century, notes only a Neptune's handful of less than 1,000 or of more than 2,000 tons. Descriptions and resumes of the careers of most of the down easters can be found in *American Merchant Ships 1850–1900,* by Frederick C. Matthews (1930–31).

The fast *Clarissa B. Carver,* of 1,144 tons, launched at Searsport in 1876, set when she was six years old the record of 116 days from Philadelphia to Yokohama. She expressed a concept that came to full development in the *A. G. Ropes* and *Henry B. Hyde,* built toward the end of the next boom, in 1884, and measuring respectively 2,342 and 2,462 tons. Fairburn includes both of these in his list of eight down easters, of the decade concluding with the year of their construction at Bath, that made repeated Cape Horn passages to California in an average time as good as that of many notable clippers.

Another depression brought the construction of large vessels to a complete halt in the middle eighties. The average had been 28 a year between 1874 and 1877, but from the end of 1885 to the beginning of 1890 not one went into the water. A revival followed that was special and brief. When in 1893 the Phippsburg-built *Aryan*, of 1,939 tons, was delivered, none of the many Maine-coast builders knew that she would become wryly famous as the last wooden merchant square-rigger to be built in the United States. They had bided their time through other stagnant seasons, while the shipwrights of Maine planted their potatoes and cut wood and ice for shipment in vessels already in existence. The lime trade went on. People did not give up the practice of dying: headstones continued in demand in the coastal cities, and Maine supplied a lot of them. But the call for square sail on wooden merchantmen never came again. The problem centered more upon manpower than upon wind power.

For safe operation the last of the big square-riggers required skilled crews of about 35 men. Life in the sky, on slippery foot-ropes, had lost some of its romantic attraction with the very height of the masts in large vessels. Pay was wretched by comparison with that for easier work ashore. Adventure, for increasing numbers, centered in the inland west. To scrape up a crew for a square-rigger became a difficult task indeed.

In defiance of this particular disadvantage, the Sewalls made an abrupt decision similar to that taken by the organizers of the first packet lines. When everyone else was practicing retrenchment they decided to risk their ample capital on what for Americans was a novel venture. Arthur Sewall, guiding spirit in a firm that had launched scores of wooden vessels—including the "Sewall big wood four" of the early nineties, which were the largest square-riggers afloat—took off for England. There he inspected the technical factors of metal construction and came home with plans for a four-masted steel shipentine somewhat more modest than his largest wooden down easters. The resulting vessel, the *Dirigo*, of 2,855 tons, was the first American sailing ship built of steel. She was torpedoed on May 31, 1917.

Iron had been used for a few yachts. In 1883 and 1884 three sizable iron square-riggers had been constructed on the Delaware —the only vessels of that description registered in 1885. One of them was noted by Griffiths's partner Bates as having made five unusually brisk voyages in the California grain races to England, but the record of the others was too dismal to have encouraged the Sewalls or anyone else to shift to either iron or steel. Their *Dirigo,* designed in England and assembled in Maine from imported British steel sheets, has little interest for us as an American ship; but between 1898 and 1902 the Sewalls built seven more big steel shipentines slightly larger than their first one, all locally designed for more economical construction. In 1899 they launched the famous *Kaiulani,* of 1,430 tons, the only American steel bark. She had a notable second career as the *Star of Finland* of the Alaska Packers fleet. A sedentary spell as an antique museum ship followed, from which she was awakened by World War II, when she went to work again as a cargo hauler under schooner rig.

These nine turn-of-the-century vessels launched from the Bath yard of the Sewalls were the only steel square-riggers ever built in the United States. Except for the *Arthur Sewall,* which went missing in 1907, they were long lived, succumbing at last to the problem of all square-riggers: lack of competent American manpower. By the beginning of the twentieth century steamers were operating more economically than the best sailing vessels on all but the longest deep-water routes. The great Sewall steel fleet drifted into special trades. World War I disposed of three of them, two torpedoed, one wrecked. Five were bought by the Alaska Packers Association for tasks in which seamanship was secondary. In the depression of the 1930's, three of these were sold to Japan. The Sewall steel shipentines were fine examples of Europe's next-to-last concept of a long-voyage, economical, bulk cargo carrier under square rig. They mark the inevitable American transition to Britain's favorite building material, even in the still largely wooded state of Maine.

Commercial sail made its beleaguered final challenge in the Baltic, with some even larger steel square-riggers, including the only square-rigged five-master, the *Preussen* II, built for the nitrate run in 1902. The surviving steel barks were finally gathered under Finnish registry and continued to operate for a few years after the First World War; but it was a penurious affair, made possible only by the fact that ships with an original building cost in six figures could be bought for a few thousand. Their new owners manned them largely with unpaid apprentices and almost abolished insurance. It was an unrealistic endeavor in

With such large and moderately sharp square-riggers as the *Henry B. Hyde*, of 2,462 tons, built in 1884, the concept of the "down easter" came to its fullest development. Above, with her new copper gleaming, she is ready for her launch. The *Kaiulani (below)* of 1899 was the first and only American-built steel bark. Note the broad double topgallant sails, made feasible by steel yards and rigging. (See pp. 394–96.)

the sense that while it lasted no ship could possibly have been built for the purpose, and replacements could be had only at the door of the junkyard by paying a few cents more than the worth of the metal to the shipbreakers.

By such devices the combination of sail on metal was stretched to last a little longer than the combination of engines in wood, but the United States took no part in the last phase of the contest. Metal ships powered by steam really had won it before the nineteenth century ended.

THE MULTIMASTED WOODEN SCHOONERS

Maine's other contribution to the twilight of merchant sail—the multimasted schooner—was extravagantly American. A dogged myth that the primordial schooner slid under full canvas from the Jovian brow of a particular Gloucester builder in 1713 has to be punctured every few years all over again. The Dutch used fully developed schooners long before that. (For visual proof, see my book *American Sail*, pages 196–97.) But the Americans, beginning early in the eighteenth century, did make the schooner their own and pioneered thereafter in its development.

The traditional ship from the days of Columbus had had three masts. The traditional schooner has been a two-master. Working examples still afloat have this rig. There is some evidence of the trial of a third mast two hundred years ago. Three-stickers were certainly in use in the War of 1812, but with the ending of its intensive demands they appear to have been forgotten so vigorously that several Maine towns in the early 1830's—Ellsworth, Bristol, Eden among them—independently reinvented what Maine later liked to call the tern rig. The three-masted schooner *May*, a Boston-to-Baltimore packet, was built at Essex, Massachusetts in 1833.

Outside shallow waters the economics of shipping has encouraged a persistent enlargement of individual vessels of all sorts. So long as the wages and sustenance of seamen were modest factors on the balance sheets, bigger vessels were allotted moderately larger crews. Aspects of the industrial revolution, even before the rise of labor unions, put shipping at a disadvantage in the labor market. Sailing ships continued to use human back power for heavy tasks long after animals had been subdued into doing most of the lifting and hauling on shore. A few trials at

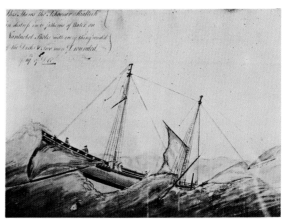

The *Baltick* of Salem, launched at Newbury, Massachusetts, in 1763, is probably the first American schooner specifically identified in contemporary pictures. Two that show events of 1765 and 1766 in her career are at the right. "Terns," three-masted schooners, were several times "reinvented." The tern *May* (below), built at Essex, Massachusetts, in 1833, was a Boston–Baltimore packet. (See pp. 143, 398.)

using animals in marine transportation failed, except on the towpaths of canals, and for rope ferries. Steam donkeys came late to the decks of sailing vessels. These are among the many factors that gave schooners an advantage over square-riggers of comparable tonnage as soon as skilled seamen became hard to find.

The square-rigger's foremasthand had to be a powerful, docile expert, able to cope with heavy freezing canvas in a strong wind. He had to know the locations of scores of lines in the darkness, and the function of each; but he also had to put his back to the task of breaking a two- or three-ton anchor out of the mud. The chief advantage of the schooner rig, as competent seamen drifted into other jobs, was the means for handling all canvas at deck level, or near it. There were no routine reasons for going aloft, except to free jammed gear.

To reef a square sail in heavy weather it was necessary to haul a probably wet and perhaps frozen part of it up against a lofty yard and tie it there with a large number of reef points. The comparable shortening of sail in a schooner was managed by dropping the canvas to be tied to the boom at its foot; but even this was not a wholly joyous alternative as the schooners grew bigger. A correspondent of *Scientific American*, arguing in 1905 for a system of roller reefing in the big schooners, wrote, "Reefing is practically out of the question on account of the size and weight of the sails themselves. These are from 80 to 90 feet in height and the canvas is of course of great thickness and corresponding weight, and as stiff as the proverbial board and quite as unmanageable."

Despite this handicap, the sails almost handled themselves whenever the schooner came about. A crew large enough to manage the canvas on one mast could do so on each of several in succession. Thus it was more economical to add an extra mast to a larger schooner than to increase the size of sails on the standard number of masts. As a substitute for reefing, one or more masts in heavy weather could be left bare of canvas. It was risky, because the strain on the working masts was very great. Still, it was often done to save wages afloat.

The shipbuilders of Maine did more than any others to keep commercial sail alive by their adaptive skill in the production of schooners, but the pilot schooners and the Baltimore clipper schooners were fully developed while Maine was still building a more practical model for the coastal trades. Maine's production of terns, despite proud disputes over the town that "invented" them, was not the almost exclusive venture of legend. In the 1850's, when shipbuilding at New York was already supplemented by many fine clippers launched in the New England states, the production of tern schooners still centered at Manhattan Island. Maine, Maryland, and Massachusetts produced 2 terns apiece in that decade, Delaware 4, and Connecticut 8, while the New York and New Jersey shipyards on New York harbor were launching 26. Griffiths referred to them, midway in the decade, when he was writing on the subject of brigantines: "Inasmuch as it has been proposed to denominate three-masted schooners, TERNS, . . . we suggest that this rig be called brig-an*tern*."

When the Bath schooner *Charles A. Briggs*, of 720 tons, was nearing completion in 1879, she was given a steam donkey to replace human back power at the capstan, winches, and pumps. This was not an innovation. The schooner *William D. Marvel*, built seven years earlier in Delaware, had been similarly equipped as an afterthought. It was the same device that had encouraged Donald McKay to regard his huge *Great Republic* as a feasible vessel in the early fifties. But its effect upon the evolution of schooners was important. A steam donkey could do almost any work it was told to do except go aloft. Occasions were frequent in a square-rigger when several men would have to go aloft at the same time. Persistent gentle weather might make it unnecessary for long periods, but the men had to be available. In a fore-and-after one man aloft could usually do what was necessary. Thus the steam donkey could eliminate a much larger proportion of a schooner's crew than of a square-rigger's. Before 1880 "schooner" had meant a vessel of modest size with a small crew. The steam donkey allowed it to become as capacious as a contemporary square-rigger, operated by about a third as many men.

Henry Hall (in his *Report* for the Tenth Census of 1880) mentioned the inland origin of the next advance beyond the tern schooners. "The four-masted rig," he wrote, "is common on one of the northern lakes," but, he noted, the *William L. White*, launched in 1880, was the first four-master built for service on the ocean.

*She is 205 feet long on deck, 40 feet beam, and 17 feet deep . . .
registers 996 tons . . . three masts would have required such large
lower sails that the strain upon the masts would have been destructive, and she was therefore furnished with four. This divided her 5017 yards of canvas into smaller sails and made her
a good schooner, sailing well, easily handled, requiring a crew
of only five men before the mast. . . .*

The *William L. White* was the first Atlantic four-master constructed as such. But Albert Winslow, who designed her, must
have known that a Civil War steamer, the *Weybosset,* had been
relieved of her engines at East Boston, a year earlier, and given
schooner rig on four masts. Winslow, regularly employed in the
manufacture of stoves at Taunton, was a perceptive genius of
the old model-whittling school who could be coaxed, but not
hurried, into shaping a schooner for a fee of about $100. He is
credited with the designs of the largest two-master and the largest
three-master ever built. Toward the close of his career he was
called upon for the lines of Maine's first five-master, the *Gov.
Ames,* launched at Waldoboro in 1888. As with the four-masters,
here too the inland lakers take precedence. The *David Dows,* of
1,419 tons, launched at Toledo in 1881, was the first of several
five-stickers built in the eighties to carry grain on the Great
Lakes. There is, however, a distinction: she was rigged as a kind
of barkentine, crossing four yards for square sail on her foremast
in addition to gaff and boom for fore-and-aft canvas.

The *Gov. Ames,* of 1,689 tons, was deliberately designed for
the deep-water trades, for which she also might better have had
the barkentine option of square sail forward. After the American
Revolution, two-masted schooners with square topsails had taken
to wandering all over the world, but as specialized varieties were
developed—for fishing, pilotage, slaving, opium running—a
standard model long persisted in the coastal trades. Its need of
square topsails diminished. Triangular gaff topsails were substituted, which made it less suitable for use in the long ocean
swells, but economical and more weatherly in the sudden intricacies of estuary navigation. After mid-century the suppression
of the evil trades and new refinements in square-riggers reduced
the occasions for employing schooners in deep water, although
chance cargoes when no other carrier was available continued
to send some on far journeys. While they were of modest size

there was no great problem; but the coastal schooners, following the usual economic urgency, had been growing much larger on the average, even though some were kept shallow by the use of centerboards. The tonnage of the *Gov. Ames* was almost twice that of the world-conquering *Sea Witch.*

Size under schooner rig did not make for either efficiency or safety in deep water. In a square-rigger the yards were held rigidly by lines affixed to both ends—and this was true of the yards crossed by the old topsail schooners as well; but the free-swinging lower spars of a big schooner could lift and slam with great force. When there was a stern wind they were kept more or less horizontal by nothing but their own weight. A single controlling line limited their outward swing; it could do nothing to prevent their swinging inboard again if the vessel was rolling. The least regrettable result was a rapid chafing of the gear. The real danger was that the controlling sheet would part, leaving a vast club of wood bashing at the shrouds before sail could be lowered.

Even in a light coastal swell a free-swinging boom could be nasty. The largest tern, the Winslow-designed *Bradford C. French,* of 920 tons, left Boston in 1915 with "a little swell running." As Captain O. R. Farrell described it, "She'd roll with it. When she did, that whoppin' big spanker would fetch up first one way and then the other, and the whole stern of that schooner would twist with it. Just like one of them Cuban rhumba dancers. I hollered to the mate, 'Haul that thing down before she tears the stern off'n her.'"

To diminish such effects the *Gov. Ames* was given relatively short booms, one for each 49 feet of her length. The smaller *Bradford C. French* had a boom for each 61 feet. By evil luck, a coastal howler that greeted the *Gov. Ames* on her maiden voyage raised such havoc that all five of her masts snapped. She was rescued and towed back to port. Rerigged, she persisted toward her intended destination, around the Horn, and somehow made it into the Pacific. The passage was so devastating, and so expensive in repairs, that her owners kept her in the more predictable weather of the Pacific for four years, after which she had almost as bad a time getting around Old Cape Stiff in the less onerous direction.

The *Gov. Ames* had one peculiarity that was not copied in any other five-sticker: an enormous centerboard. Countries that thought themselves sophisticated had been slow to adopt this descendant from the guara rafts of Peru, but toward the middle of the nineteenth century its advantages in whaleboats and other small craft were agreed upon. After the Civil War a separate centerboard schooner model was developed—flat, shallow, broad. It could get into small ports and up rivers. It was not stopped by the bars that closed some estuaries to conventional vessels of the same burden. But the board had its disadvantages. The trunk, or well, in which it could be hoisted, took up a significant amount of cargo space. No original ingenuity or faithful maintenance could keep it watertight. It was almost impossible to paint the interior, where dry rot developed more quickly than anywhere else.

The *Gov. Ames* was intended by Cornelius Davis, who employed Winslow to design her, to be a supremely versatile, economical vessel, fit for the longest journeys yet able to navigate in narrow waters and to handle cargo in small ports. Her initial dismasting was probably due to the relaxing of her new hemp shrouds, which it was the custom to "set up" after a few days at sea had taken the stretch out of them. The sudden storm gave her no time for that. The misadventures of the *Gov. Ames* had no relationship to the number of her masts. But her heavy repair bills seem nevertheless to have chilled the experimental impulse in schooner development for a decade during which shipping was beset by discouragements. The search for economy through increasing the size of vessels without enlarging their crews was pressed strongly in the nineties. Four-masters grew bigger, culminating in 1897 with the largest of all, the *Frank A. Palmer*, of 1,831 tons. Four booms for a deck length of 275 feet pushed the power concentration on each mast to the edge of hazard in a vessel managed by ten foremasthands. For the distant trades, smaller four-masters continued to be much more successful than their overgrown contemporaries. The *Samar*, of 710 gross tons, built at Alameda, California, in 1901, was employed in the coal trade from Newcastle, England, to San Francisco, which called for Cape Horn doublings in both directions. In 1909 she carried lumber to Cape Town and completed a circumnavigation on her voyage home. Maine continued to launch similarly modest four-masters, of which little is heard because they contrived to stay out of trouble. Attention centered upon the giants, and upon

Although the steamship *Great Britain* was launched in 1839 with schooner rig on five of her six masts, the *George W. Wells (above)*, launched in 1900, was the first pure six-masted schooner. Much smaller four-masters like the *Samar (below)* did better in the distant trades. (See pp. 404, 406–8.)

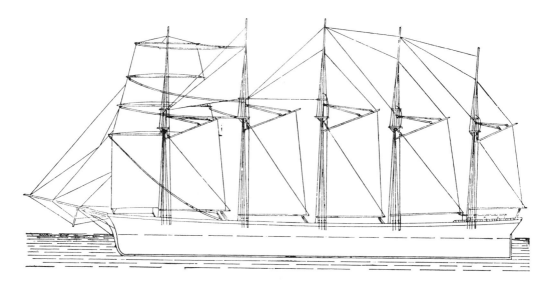

Multimasted schooners were supposed to provide for large increases in size without the enlargement of crews beyond the number needed to manage two or three masts of the same height. The *David Dows*, built in 1881 at Toledo, Ohio, was called a schooner although she was really a five-masted barkentine. The *Gov. Ames*, the first coastal five-master, had only fore-and-aft canvas; barkentine rig would have saved her some of the calamities she suffered in the deep-water trades for which she was designed. She measured 1,689 tons, 270 more than the *David Dows*. The *Frank A. Palmer (lower right)*, built in 1897, at 1,831 tons was the largest four-master. Her economy crews found her difficult to manage. Of these schooners, the *David Dows* was by far the most successful. (See pp. 402–4, 407.)

the increase in their number of masts. When J. S. Winslow & Company, builders of the *Frank A. Palmer,* produced in 1898 the *Nathaniel T. Palmer,* of 2,244 tons, she was the second schooner to sprout five masts.

The score or more of big schooners christened with various given names plus the surname "Palmer" need a good deal of sorting out. More than half of them were designed by William F. Palmer, mathematician and headmaster of a school in Taunton, the most important distribution center south of Boston for schooner-borne coal. He studied naval architecture on the side, in the city where many Maine-built schooners were designed, and emerged at the turn of the century as managing owner of a fleet based at Portland.

Palmer has been praised for doing more than anyone else to lengthen the period when sail could compete profitably. The 14 vessels built to his designs before 1909, in the final decade of big-schooner construction, were consistent moneymakers while they stayed afloat, but an appraisal of his accomplishment should not ignore the fact that the careers of 11 of these 14 ended in disaster. Six foundered, two with all hands lost. Two piled up on the coast. One was abandoned at sea. One burned, and another was torpedoed. Only one lived to the point of normal retirement. In almost all these sad endings the question of the vessel's responsiveness to the helm is a serious factor in the explanation of her fate. How much is Palmer to be admired for his designs of vessels that came so consistently to such bad ends? His profits largely reflected demurrage payments when his vessels loitered for their turn at the wharves. Particularly in the coal ports, labor troubles and shortages of railroad cars often kept a string of big schooners living comfortably on demurrage for weeks together. Palmer began to build schooners of average dimensions in 1894. His *Frank A. Palmer* of 1897, already referred to as the largest of four-masters, is not included in the count of 11 disasters to ships built in the last decade of big schooner production, but she too came to a violent end by collision.

Prospects of better times as the century ended encouraged the construction in 1900, for a Massachusetts owner, of the first six-masted schooner, the *George W. Wells,* measuring 2,743 tons. The eight additional wooden six-masters that followed created if nothing else a grand climax to the adze-and-auger shipwright's ancient art and mystery. Mystery, to the end, was always there: mystery and luck. Why did the first two six-masters, when they were the only ones afloat, collide with each other at night, far offshore, hundreds of miles from their different home ports, neither skipper having any knowledge of the other vessel's whereabouts? A writer of fiction would not dare to invent such a coincidence.

The last wooden six-master, the *Wyoming*, of 3,036 tons, was launched at Bath in 1909. She was 330 feet long, 50 broad, and 30 deep—larger in each of these measurements than any clipper except the *Great Republic* as originally built. After a lapse in schooner construction some sizable wooden five-stickers were built to ease the freighter shortage created by the U-boats of the First World War, but their tonnage averaged only a little more than half that of the *Wyoming*.

What had been happening to the old combination of human back power and canvas is revealed in a comparison of crews in the largest clipper and this largest wooden schooner. The *Great Republic*, despite a steam engine to help with her ground tackle and running rigging, was originally allotted a crew of 100 seamen and 30 boys; the *Wyoming*, also equipped with a steam deck engine, had a crew of precisely 11.

How many masts were too many? It is curious that one experimental answer had been worked out long ago, and forgotten. The steamship *Great Britain* had been launched in 1839 with six masts, carrying schooner rig on all but the second. She proved a smart but troublesome sailer and was soon reduced to a four-master. In the 1880's she ended her career as a sailing vessel with three masts.

John J. Rockwell of Rockland, one of Maine's notable designers and master builders, came to the point of saying, "Six masters were not practical. They were too long for wood construction." He had earned a right to his opinion by creating the first of them, but he pointed out that a part of the difficulty they all eventually experienced came from the practice of allowing such long wooden structures full of coal to lie on the mud at low tide, loading or discharging. The bottom on which they rested was never level, and this "grounding out," in his opinion, should never have been permitted in vessels of more than 1,000 tons measurement.

Diagonal strapping of iron—as in the 90-day gunboats—was used to strengthen the big schooners, and the keels were "rockered" when they were laid, curving upward toward bow and stern to compensate somewhat for the "hogging" that was sure to occur. One six-master, the *Edward J. Lawrence,* was found to have "risen" 42 inches amidships. The men who operated these vessels got used to their habit of "snaking": they would undulate visibly as they went through the waves. Cracks in the rails would open and shut to such an extent that sail would be shortened at this signal. Leakage was steady: steam pumps were always clanking to keep them clear.

There was a time late in the nineteenth century when dozens of big schooners competed profitably with the railroads in carrying coal from the middle Atlantic mining states to New England. Steam colliers then were the challengers of sail, at first with little success. Exclusion of foreign vessels from the coastwise trade was the basis for this last notable adventure in wooden shipbuilding; but, as the *Scientific American* sharply noted at the time, there were other factors. One was a shortage of skilled mechanics for the construction of iron and steel vessels after decades in which the Navy had been neglected and the transatlantic trade had been surrendered almost entirely to foreign enterprise. Maine still had her versatile thousands of potato-planting, ice-harvesting, lobster-potting shipwrights. Sudden rises and falls of the production chart make it evident that alternative skills of the coastal residents were essential not only to their own survival but to the survival of shipbuilding itself.

In 1897 the number of all kinds of sailing vessels produced and documented in the United States had reached the lowest mark for the century: 338, of which 160 were schooners. In 1898 the tonnage total, 34,416, although it did include the second of the five-masted schooners, was the lowest since the War of 1812. At that point conditions had been established for the genuine last challenge of sail to steam in the decade defined, roughly, by the first and last of the wooden six-masters, the *George W. Wells* and the *Wyoming.* In 1901, the second year of intensive production of very large schooners, eight five-masters were launched, and the annual tonnage figure reached a high of 126,165 for sailing vessels. With one exception this was the best year for new tonnage under sail since 1883. In the next year the count of sailing vessels built throughout the country, 581, was the highest—again with one exception—since 1884.

These were the peak years of the last challenge, which extended strongly through 1905, then dwindled. It was marked by one dominant quality that was relatively new in American shipping. The coastal trade was entered, rather suddenly, by exploitative big money: the sort of control through heavy investment that is not necessarily ruthless by intent, but that uses risk capital for quick high profits and cuts its losses without a qualm over the downfall of great institutions. The coastal schooner trade had kept a significant part of its management among participants in the production of the vessels themselves. Managing owners of the big Maine schooners frequently were their builders. The *Eleanor A. Percy,* of 3,401 tons, second of the six-masters, was built by Percy & Small of Bath for their own use. The partners, Captain Samuel R. Percy and Frank A. Small, at one time managed vessels totaling 25,000 tons measurement, a state of affairs in which two kinds of repute merged. They brought to both functions a profoundly experienced involvement in their art and craft, both as builders and as users of ships.

This was a tradition stretching its strong ground tackle back into the exuberant first half of the maritime nineteenth century in America, when decisions that shaped seaborne enterprise were typically worked out between retired shipmasters who had become managers of commercial houses and shipbuilders who had risen from apprenticeship. Robert Bennet Forbes is an articulate example of the former sort, which included the early Crowninshields of Salem and Cornelius Vanderbilt of New York. Samuel Hartt Pook best represents the latter. The distinction to be noted is that both kinds of men had an involvement in the past and a commitment to the future of shipping.

By contrast, some of the men who most significantly dominated the shaping of sail's last challenge were newcomers to the practical maritime scene: financial manipulators, politicians, and theorists whose cleverness was so partial in a complex problem that it produced dangerous distortions, which their moneyed backers lacked the practical knowledge to check. The group included the flamboyant Boston financier Thomas W. Lawson; the shoemaker William L. Douglas, later governor of Massachusetts; and a designer with a considerable talent for the development of special-purpose yachts, Bowdoin B. Crowninshield. Palmer, the mathematician-schoolmaster, designed big schooners for his own management on the basis of tardy theoretical training in the orthodoxies of marine architecture, but his vessels were not distinctive among their contemporaries, except for a higher than usual proneness to calamity.

The building of modest schooners continued, some with orthodox hulls, some shallow centerboarders. Their problems had been worked out long ago. They were decently responsive to the helm until they reached a size requiring the division of canvas among five masts. It was with five masts that the specific last challenge of sail and wood began, coming to an end with the six-master *Wyoming,* but producing along the way a bizarre variant, the world's only seven-master, a schooner with a steel hull, at the time of her launch the largest sailing vessel ever constructed. Some awed references to this colossus carry the inference that the *Thomas W. Lawson* provided a splendid, imaginative finale to the American experience with sail. She was, in fact, as much of a freak in origin as in her bizarre unsuitability for her intended employment. The financier whose name she carried and the yacht specialist who designed her were brought together in the course of a solemnly ludicrous sparring match among wealthy yachtsmen who aspired to defend the America's Cup against Sir Thomas Lipton's second challenger. Since this was the half-century anniversary of the influential race at Cowes, and also the season in which the future of American sail was casting about from business toward pleasure, we too should turn a last glance upon yachting and the cup races of 1901.

THE BRONZE SKIMMING DISH
INDEPENDENCE OF 1901

Perhaps the saddest of several acrimonious hassles over rules governing contests for the America's Cup crested in the spring and summer of 1901. The deed of gift, by which private owners of the original winning yacht had put their trophy under management of one particular club, was written out in 1857. About as simply as such a document could be worded, it made the ornate object "perpetually a challenge cup for friendly competition between foreign countries." Challengers should measure between 30 and 300 tons; six months notice was required; and the rules, unless amended by mutual consent, were to be those of the defending body.

As it turned out, the statement was too simple. Controversy arose over the first challenge. Whereas the *America* had sailed in 1851 as one yacht among several, each competing against the field, the New York Yacht Club construed its deed of gift as an authorization to sail a fleet against the single challenging vessel, with the odds heavily on the club's side that one of its yachts would accumulate more lucky moments in the always changing weather than the visitor on the average could expect. James Ashbery's challenger, the schooner *Cambria,* sailed in the 1870 race against 17 other starters, including the old *America* herself, repatriated after a turbulent interlude as British yacht and Rebel blockade-runner. The race was won by a light centerboard schooner, the *Magic,* with the *Idler*—designed by Pook for Bushnell—a close second, and the *America* fourth. The challenger placed tenth among 15 finishers. In his second challenge of the following year Ashbery sought to counter the New York Yacht Club's arbitrary rulemaking by stipulations of his own that he should represent a different British yacht club in each of 12 races, always against one or another single defender— centerboarders disapproved. If he won a majority of races, the cup would go to the club for which he was sailing the last race won. The cables and letters, which became unpleasant, produced a seven-race series, four to win, in which the defending club insisted upon making its own choice at the start of each race from among four defenders—two with ocean keels, two with centerboards. Having thereby the best bet ready for either light or heavy weather, the New York Yacht Club won the first and second races and lost the third with the centerboarder *Columbia,* then won the necessary fourth and fifth with the deep keel yacht *Sappho.*

Most of the nineteenth century's ten challenge matches for the America's Cup were marked by recriminations over the intent of a deed of gift that let a private club alter its own rules at every contest to its own advantage. One rule was that only members of the New York Yacht Club could enter vessels to race against the challengers. When it became evident that there would be no challengers if the club insisted upon having more than one contestant, the practice was evolved of setting up a series of preliminary races to choose the cup defender, a change that stimulated the design of racing machines for this one purpose. Challengers had been built for their task, shortly before each race, but most early defenders were pleasure craft that had been in use for several years. As competition stiffened, the design of successful defenders shifted suddenly to Boston, where the originator of the first family tradition in cup racers— Edward Burgess—produced three in a row for his fellow Bostonian General Charles J. Paine. These were the big sloops *Puritan* (1885), *Mayflower* (1886), and *Volunteer* (1887). They marked the shift to single-masters, which have since been the only yachts entered, and to the practice of seeking a more advanced design for every race. Since the general was a member of the New York Yacht Club, no problem was raised when the *Puritan,* owned by his syndicate, defeated Commodore James Gordon Bennett's new *Priscilla* in the trials. In view of later occurrences it should, however, be noted that the *Puritan* was enrolled at the Eastern Yacht Club of Marblehead under the name of her designer, Burgess, and that she flew his burgee number during the tryouts. The defeated *Priscilla* was one of the few iron-hulled yachts.

When Burgess died untimely of typhoid in 1891, Nathaniel G. Herreshoff of Rhode Island assumed in an even more spectacular fashion the task of creating a series of vessels that would reliably win the contests from which final cup defenders emerged. His first, the *Vigilant,* initiated the era of bronze hulls and of racing craft refined to the point of being almost useless for anything but the task of winning in moderate weather on a foreseen course. The change in shape can be gathered from a comparison of her principal dimensions with those of the widely versatile original schooner *America.* The *Vigilant* was 22 feet longer overall but 4 feet shorter on the water line, and 4 feet broader. Her hull when the centerboard was up drew 3 feet more than the *America's* 11, but with her board down the *Vigilant* drew 24 feet. Her sail area, 11,272 square feet, was more than double the *America's* 5,263 and was concentrated all upon a single mast.

Herreshoff's second defender, so named, carried this last aspect of competitive design past the edge of self interest—at least in the view of some contemporary experts. She had to be handled cautiously at moments when any of the earlier cup defenders would have been strapped down to get everything out of a puff that was in it. The *Defender* had bottom and keel plates of manganese bronze with aluminum plates elsewhere—the first marine use in America of that metal—saving 17 tons of dead weight where it counted most for stiffness. Her frames were of steel. By this combination Herreshoff achieved the technological pioneer's privilege of demonstrating in a costly fashion the error in a concept upon which he has spent too little time in mere research. When wooden ships first were coppered, galvanic action diminished the iron fastenings so promptly that some hulls fell to pieces. Forbes wrote morosely in his autobiography that in building the *Niphon* during the Civil War he had "proved satisfactorily" that even when iron fastenings were galvanized, "passing through oak planking, and carefully countersunk and plugged," the galvanic action set up between them and yellow metal sheathing soon destroyed them. The *Defender's* trimetallic hull structure suffered similarly. She had to be rebuilt after four almost idle years and was broken up after one more season.

While she lasted, however, the *Defender* was a disputatious marvel. She was handled with such bold skill in the trials, by her formidable professional skipper Hank Haff and his crew all of Deer Islanders, that her Herreshoff predecessor the *Vigilant* was withdrawn from further competition by an angry new owner with the complaint that if she had been held to her rights under the rules she would have had to sink the newer yacht.

Acrimony continued into the cup races, which in 1895 were marred by a foul in the second race and a refusal of Lord Dunraven to permit his *Valkyrie III* to finish the third one because of the crowding of spectator boats. The new challenger of 1899, Sir Thomas Lipton, restored international amity with his gay flair for publicity and a steady good sportsmanship that calls for no cozy commercial explanations. The first use of wireless telegraphy to report such an event increased the general excitement.

The *Defender's* mixture of external metals was avoided in Herreshoff's third marvel, the *Columbia,* which had a homogeneous plating of Tobin bronze. Her opponent the first *Shamrock* was one cycle behind in theory of materials, with a manganese bronze bottom and topsides of aluminum alloy. Neglect of naval architecture in the United States had allowed primacy in construction of specialized fast vessels to pass to England and the European continent. But with the concurrent building of the *Columbia* and the *Shamrock,* New England regained her old lead. When the *Columbia* took three straight races—even though the second was marred by the *Shamrock*'s loss of her topmast—nobody seriously questioned which was the better-designed or the better-built yacht.

Such was the state of affairs in the yachting world when Sir Thomas Lipton turned for the design of his second *Shamrock* to George L. Watson, the Scot who had crafted three *Valkyries* for Lord Dunraven as well as the earlier challenger *Thistle* of 1887. Several Bostonians who had grown discontented over the failure of their city to try again after the death of Burgess met on November 28, 1900, and selected Bowdoin B. Crowninshield as an imaginative designer. Crowninshield, a Harvard graduate of 1890, was a newcomer to naval architecture, having set up shop as a yacht broker only three years earlier; but the Harvard entomologist Burgess had had even less formal experience when his first contestant won the privilege of defending the America's Cup. Crowninshield had specialized in the refining of scows— small "skimming dishes," in the contemporary description— that were extremely fast on a broad reach or with a tail wind: forerunners of the planing hulls of more recent design.

Although the cost of metal racing sloops had soared, Boston's committee thought that $100,000 should be enough. Its members asked Thomas W. Lawson to head the list of subscribers with $10,000. He agreed, and promised to give $10,000 more if it should be needed. Lawson was a Renaissance man, dropped into turn-of-the-century Boston by some quirk of wrong timing. He was a writer of verse and fiction, with four books published and more to come. Born poor in 1857, he had acquired sufficient wealth in the stock market at age 21 to set up his own brokerage office. In 1900 he was reputed to be worth $50,000,000. He kept his financial associates and less friendly visitors a bit off balance by maintaining in the city of Cotton Mather an office crowded with works of art and masses of unusual flowers. After sparring with Lawson warily, Standard Oil and Anaconda Copper had made him in 1897 their manager for a financial "reorganization" that left the insiders richer than ever and ruined others who were not in the know. Some of those who did not unload their stock in time were, alas, members of the New York Yacht Club.

The Boston committee decided at the outset to avoid calculated publicity, but what it gained in punctilio it seemed to be losing in cash. In the upshot, Lawson was asked if he would "build, equip, and race the boat without the financial assistance of others." Writing soon afterward, he said:

I agreed to do so, provided, first, I could be satisfied that I, who was not at the time a member of the New York Yacht Club, could have the boat participate in the trial races and, if she proved the best American boat, sail for the cup's defence without being compelled to join the New York Yacht Club. . . .

Lewis Francis Herreshoff gave about ten years ago the somewhat different explanation that when Lawson

tried to join the New York Yacht Club, he was blackballed perhaps because some of the New Yorkers did not like his way of doing business. However, Lawson thought he could force his way into the club by building a cup boat that would beat any craft that the club owned and then he would be voted in, for one of the conditions of the final races was that the defender must be owned by a member of the defending club.

Lawson's own careful explanation of the episode hints that such a blackballing had previously occurred.

I explained fully to the committee all the conditions then existing which could in any way affect the eligibility of a boat owned by me for participation in the cup's defence: first, that I held pronounced views as to the right of any American to take part in the defence of the cup; second, that I was not a member of the New York Yacht Club and would under no circumstances become a member, at least until after the coming contest was over. . . .

In referring to the choice of a naval architect, which was made in advance of his own involvement, Lawson wrote:

The committee also decided that the boat to represent Massachusetts should be the product of home talent, and built from the designs of one of Boston's young naval architects, Bowdoin B. Crowninshield, whose small boats, of a pronounced type designated as the "scow," had met with success.

At a very early point in these maneuvers Lawson sent Boston's veteran marine reporter A. G. McVey to ask General Paine (who had managed the three Burgess defenders for the New York Yacht Club) whether the 1887 deed of gift would prevent entry in the trial races of a boat owned by a nonmember. Paine should have known, as he had helped to draft the revised deed. He replied, "No, the New York Yacht Club will not debar Mr. Lawson's yacht."

McVey added, "In view of such official authoritative opinion it will be impossible to find any member of the New York Yacht Club who will dare to whisper any objection."

McVey was wrong. The New York press suddenly was awash with planted articles quoting unidentified members to the contrary. One called it "a huge joke," adding, "Under no circumstances will anyone other than a member of our club be allowed to have a finger in the cup races."

Lawson, on December 9, 1900, responded with a press release, saying in part:

. . . I have this day perfected the arrangements.

My part will be to own the boat, furnish the necessary money and have a general supervision of the affair.

Mr. Bowdoin B. Crowninshield will design the boat.

Mr. George F. Lawley will construct it. . . . I shall meet conditions as they exist, even though they necessitate my giving the boat to any member of any eligible club that the committee decides is a good enough fellow to have her, while I personally withdraw from further participation.

There followed an exchange of correspondence between the club's commodore and the financier, marked upon its surface by a good will that proves, on closer study, to have been crafted at least into the New York part of it by subtle attorneys. When the jockeying was over, the issue still turned upon Lawson's original phrase "any member of any eligible club *that the committee decides* is a good enough fellow." Lawson was insisting throughout that the club must receive his vessel and assign it to a member, making itself responsible for its own offensive rule. The club was simply saying to the last that any member could enter his boat in the trials, it being no business of the club where or how he acquired it so long as it met the rules for the race.

It was Mr. Dooley who summed up the nonsensical sense of it, not quite accurately, but with the higher lunacy that the situation deserved:

. . . no more gallant sailor rides th' waves thin hearty Jack Larsen iv th' Amalgamated Copper Yacht Club. "What ho?" says he . . . "shiver me timbers if I don't look up th' law," he says. So he becomes a yachtsman. "But," says th' Noo York la-ads, thim that has the Cup on their mantel-piece, "Ye can race on'y on two conditions." "What ar-re?" says Larsen. "Th' first is that ye become a mimber iv our club." "With pleasure," says he. "Ye can't," says they. "An' havin' complied with this first condition, ye must give us ye'er boat," says they. "We don't want it," they says.

The touchy situation provoked a sudden and widespread uproar that swept the national press, running strongly even before Crowninshield had a design in final form. Viewed in retrospect, the durable involvement of Lipton as a contestant for the America's Cup, redoubled by Lawson's transient emergence as a contender, marks an emphatic turn away from sail's age-old commercial employments into an era of its use as a public reflection of the self-image of the very rich. Each successive *Shamrock* — there were five before Sir Thomas was done — seemed more than ever the expansive symbol of chivalry, courtliness, skill, and grandeur, such as few had the means to display and fewer still the temerity to risk. There was an overlap, of course. Commercial sail was briefly on the rise again, and Lawson was about to be involved in it. But new reasons for keeping sail in use were suddenly attaining, at turn of century, a flamboyant importance.

For some perspective upon the quality of this shift, dramatized with vast exuberance in the cup races, we should free ourselves of images of the comparative pygmies that have been challenging for the garish international trophy and defending it since the deed of gift was again changed by permission of the Supreme Court of the State of New York in 1956. These yachts have been hardly half as long, on the water line, as the original *America*. What is more significant, the modified cutter-sloop rig settled for by all contestants in the latter nineteenth and early twentieth centuries was gigantic in sail area. The climax came when the *Reliance*, cup defender in 1903, set 16,159 square feet of canvas on her single stick. The total spread of much lighter synthetic fabric on all five yachts that figured in the cup races of 1967 was only 9,070 square feet. If the canvas of the *Reliance* had been parceled out between them, there would have been almost enough left over for four more yachts of the same class. The big cutter-sloops had bowsprits and booms that carried their vast sail area a long distance outboard, both fore and aft. The *Intrepid*'s overall length of 64 feet covers everything. The total length of the *Reliance* of 54 years earlier was a bit over 201 feet. Her spinnaker boom was about 20 feet longer than the entire length overall of her puny descendant the *Intrepid.*

With the J sloops of the 1930's, sail area was reduced by about one-half from that at the turn of the century. Now, in the 12-meters, it is down to only one-quarter of what it was in the typical J. Such figures point to the grandiose circumstances of the challenge of 1901, when the New York Yacht Club employed extraordinary ingenuities to fend off even the chance of discovering whether a Boston-built defender would be more useful to it than one that a syndicate of its members was having built at Bristol, Rhode Island, by Herreshoff. The club had twice procured from the cup's surviving donor a revised deed of gift. By its own decision, it could overlook the new deed's stipulation that a challenger must "proceed under sail on her own bottom to the port where the contest is to take place." It had done so when Lipton requested that his first *Shamrock* be towed across the Atlantic. But the New York Yacht Club would rather risk losing its cup with a second-best defender than relax a vaguer provision of the deed to accommodate Lawson.

As is usual when confronted by tactical secrecy, reporters invented what they could not learn. That at least is a lenient explanation of stories concerning the theft of plans by Crowninshield, legal actions, confessions of chicanery, and the decision of the Boston committee to abandon its project. Some writers credited sources abroad with these scandalous inventions — although the reason why transatlantic correspondents could get information unsuccessfully sought by the local press was not explained. Lawson issued official denials. In March, as his challenger began to take shape at the Atlantic Works, editorial reaction to true and false news stories was running strongly in Lawson's favor — a factor perhaps in the tone of the New York

Around the year 1900, naval architecture probably was being advanced more usefully by the toys of rich men than by their investments in overgrown schooners. Contests for the America's Cup provoked experimentation with metal alloys for hulls and with the aerodynamics of enormous sails. The yachts on these pages carried about eight times as much sailcloth as can be set on today's contestants. The *Vigilant (far right)* announced in 1893 the era of extreme racing machines. The *Columbia's* accident of 1899 *(lower left)* resulted from too much strain upon a new kind of tubular metal mast. The *Reliance (right)* of 1903 carried more sail than any other single-master, before or since. All three were designed by Nat Herreshoff. Thomas W. Lawson's bronze skimming dish *Independence,* designed by the newcomer B. B. Crowninshield, had serious structural faults that eliminated her from competition, but she greatly influenced Herreshoff's *Reliance.* (See pp. 413–15, 418–19, 422–27.)

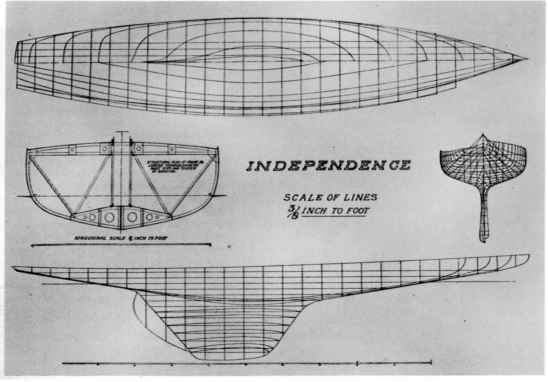

INDEPENDENCE

SCALE OF LINES
3/8 INCH TO FOOT

STRUCTURAL PLAN OF FRAME IN
LOOKING FORWARD SHOWING
MAST STEP AND SYSTEM
OF BRACING

STRUCTURAL SCALE 3/4 INCH TO FOOT

commodore's letters, which seemed affable until on May 18
he suddenly released the correspondence in support of his club's
decision to bar Crowninshield's *Independence* from the contests
by which the defender would be selected. Lawson claimed that
there had been an agreement to keep their interchanges confidential. He was annoyed, even though an open review of them
brought him a new outburst of friendly editorials, which insisted that America's best maritime skills, wherever they might
emerge, should have a fair chance to produce the final defender
in a contest that had come to involve the repute of the nation
itself.

The New York Yacht Club evidently had chosen May 18 for
release of the correspondence because the launch of the *Independence* was scheduled for that day, when wild rumors about her
contours would be settled. Writing in the late 1950's, Francis
Herreshoff told of his contemporary judgment:

> . . . when I saw the picture of the Independence I thought my
> father's cup boats would be beaten . . . but . . . she did not steer
> well, and her flat model had so much wetted surface that she
> was very dull in light weather. . . . As far as I can remember
> this was the only large racing yacht B. B. Crowninshield designed
> and he did well considering his lack of experience. Perhaps if
> he had made less of a freak he would have done much better.

Herreshoff's reference to his father's boats in the plural is a
reminder that the new *Constitution*, built with the greatest
secrecy at Bristol, would be in competition with the Herreshoff
Columbia, which had defeated *Shamrock* the first. A series of
trial races between the two would determine the defender against
Lipton's second challenger. It was from these trials that Lawson's
yacht had been barred.

Although Nat Herreshoff's new *Constitution* appeared superficially to be a somewhat enlarged *Columbia*, her hull was
lightened by the use of web frames, which from this beginning
were to be further developed for use in commercial craft, in air-
craft particularly. In all the aspiring cup challengers and defenders the problems of materials had become crucial. Masts of
various kinds and combinations were tried out. The first *Shamrock*'s hollow steel mast folded double when the king of England
was aboard, giving him an unpredictable chance to demonstrate
his aplomb. An experience of Herreshoff's when he was at the

helm of his own *Constitution* during the trial races was professionally more embarrassing. He held too much wind in his topsail until the topmast snapped—a common accident in the trials and even in the final races until jib-headed mainsails set on homogeneous masts appeared with the J boats of the 1930's.

The launch of the *Independence* revealed Crowninshield's gamble. He had in fact produced a much enlarged example of his successful skimming dishes, a broad and shallow hull with a thin, deep keel, the sort of vessel that if of modest size can climb up and seem to rush along on her own foam. The handicap of this form can be visualized if one compares the letter T with the letter V. It had too much wetted surface. In cross section the vertical line of the keel and the almost horizontal line of the hull add up to a considerably longer line than the hypotenuse of a V-shaped hull. In light airs every extra square inch of unnecessary wetted surface causes extra drag. In strong unfavorable breezes the skimming dish at best presented an inefficient entrance when heeling; at worst it could not be held to its course at all.

The preposterous impasse between Lawson and the New York Yacht Club got a preliminary solution when some eminent New York yachtsmen, unhappy over their own club's stand, joined with a group of Rhode Islanders to establish the Newport Yacht Racing Association and sponsor a separate series of races for which three very large yachts would be eligible that all just happened to be potential defenders: the New York Yacht Club's *Columbia* and *Constitution* and the Hull-Massachusetts Yacht Club's *Independence.* The *Columbia* had won three races in a row against the first *Shamrock,* which had been disabled in the second by a snapped topmast—the commonest indication that the big contestants were being designed with no adequate concession to the occasional buffets hidden in any strong breeze offshore.

An early mishap of the *Independence,* during her trials, suggests that she was probably more resilient aloft than her competitors. She began life with a balanced rudder, which produced an undue strain upon her steering linkage. During her second test under sail the linkage warped and jammed, causing a wild jibe too sudden to permit the weather running backstay to be set up. The spars stood the tremendous shock, but when the rudder was being replaced by a normal one, the tubular mast was reduced by 5 feet and the wooden topmast replaced by one 6 feet shorter.

Lawson described a more serious calamity at the end of June, when the *Independence* was on her way to the races at Newport:

She was sent around the cape in tow on a day when she should have lain at anchor . . . a short, vicious sea causing her to leak badly; while men stood by her tenders on deck ready to put them over and abandon her . . . on three occasions it was thought the moment had arrived. . . .

As a result . . . the yacht's floor forward was pounded up until there was a decrease of one and one half inches of headroom forward for a distance of eight frames.

Repairs were rushed, but the vessel had been framed too lightly. "The worst leak," Lawson noted, was "where the fin joined the hull."

Despite her condition the *Independence* sailed in six trial races, against the *Columbia* in all of them and against the new *Constitution* in four. In their first race both New York yachts were close together at the halfway mark with the *Independence* an hour behind. After the others finished, the wind fell and she had to be towed in. This melancholy performance seemed to conclude her career at the outset, but in the second race she finished about 18 minutes behind the new Herreshoff sloop. Some reporters guessed, correctly, that Lawson's yacht was carrying a lot of water ballast not called for in her plans. In the third race she lost to the *Columbia* by only seven minutes.

For the fourth race the *Independence* got the kind of weather for which she had been designed. She seemed to be handily outsailing her rivals, for all her disabilities, when a bit too much of just the wind she wanted knocked down her new topmast of Oregon pine. Hank Haff, her dogged professional skipper, took little more than ten minutes to cut loose the great dragging bag of her topsail and clear her jib topsail, which had been fouled in the wreckage. He continued under reduced canvas, sailing faster than his rivals until on the home stretch they were able to break out their spinnakers. Lacking a topmast, the *Independence* could not set hers. Even without it, she lost the race to the *Columbia* by less than 11 minutes, approximately the time spent in clearing the wreckage aloft.

After this race the *Independence* was dry-docked for repairs and alterations. All the cup defenders were in some degree new experiments in design that developed quirks discoverable only in their trials. Lawson's yacht undoubtedly had more than most because of her sudden departure from both the Burgess and the Herreshoff traditions—not that either designer was a traditionalist, but the first cup defender developed by each of them was somewhat less of a departure from previous tradition than Crowninshield's was from theirs. In addition to the vulnerability of her hull structure forward, far too much strain was developed by the original, supposedly balanced rudder of the *Independence,* and its orthodox replacement produced another symptom of drag under water: severe lee helm. In dry dock she was consequently given a fin near her forefoot, 17 inches deep and 11 feet long, to help keep her head from falling away.

The difficulty of foreseeing the behavior of these huge experimental yachts is revealed in a remark of the new *Constitution's* experienced manager after her second defeat by the older *Columbia* in two other series of races: "The *Constitution* was beaten because she was not fast enough. The boat would not go, and I do not know what is the matter with her." She in turn was sent back to the Herreshoff yard for alterations aloft, a taller lower mast and a shorter topmast among them. She was laid up while the last two races of the Newport association's series were run between the *Columbia* and the *Independence.* The latter still carried a hard lee helm; Haff could not hold his course as high into the wind as the sails were prepared to take him. He lost the first race by about five minutes, the second by only about one minute. When off the wind, during this race, the *Independence* sailed faster than the recorded maximum for any racing yacht so far, but when beating she lost more than she had gained. Clearly Crowninshield's big skimming dish was at best not a yacht for all weathers.

Perhaps another session in dry dock would have corrected her worst failing, but yacht races are won and lost for the record by vessels that have had a similar chance to discover their faults and tune up by the time they are due at the starting line. The assessment of the *Independence* that might be thought least prejudiced against her would be that of Lawson himself, who wrote, soon after these races:

Independence was the product of a new designer, without data gained by experience to guide him. . . . Her interior bracing was too light to properly support her overhangs, with the result that the vessel strained and leaked, and at the end of a season was good only for the scrap-heap.

The effect of her pounding forward while being towed around Cape Cod was described by her owner with the same candor:

The fore and aft diagonal steel rods running from the mast-step to within one station of the bow snapped like pipestems. The tubular upright struts buckled and snapped. . . .

Similar troubles developed aft while she was racing:

The braces abreast and forward of the rudder-post buckled . . . and were stiffened after being straightened with a maul, by anchor-stocks and capstan-bars lashed to them. . . . When the yacht lay down the braces to leeward buckled and those to windward straightened out; on the other tack those which had buckled straightened, and the others bent into crescents.

This description of the interior bracing of his yacht's hull, and its behavior under normal stress during the races, betray either Crowninshield's serious incapacity as a mechanical engineer or his choice of an excessive gamble in the severe contest to save weight. If he had lofted his huge skimming dish under the conditions that produced Herreshoff's first radical defender, the *Vigilant* of 1893, it is likely that her frames would have been strong enough. It was the odd fate of the *Independence*, as a contender in the preliminary contests, to impress Nat Herreshoff so much more profoundly than she did any other observers of her qualities that he patterned his next cup defender, the *Reliance,* rather more upon her than upon his own previous designs. A recent competent historian of the America's Cup races has called the *Reliance* "the most extreme of 'skimming dishes,'" and William P. Stephens, for many decades a devoted and objective recorder of the yachting scene, described her as "perhaps the most wonderful and useless racing machine known to yachting."

Crowninshield's *Independence,* consequently, may be regarded as the imaginative, daring prototype of the yacht that two years later brought the series of America's Cup contests to its most extravagant climax. The cost to Lawson, by his own account, had been $201,789.21. To this sum might be added $3,244.87, his bill from the ship breakers who, 90 days after her launch, knocked her to pieces again. Because of her prompt demolition, her owner was accused of a display of temper, but I believe he was following the disciplined impulse of a financial manipulator: to cut losses without a qualm and give full attention to the next project. His entire confrontation with the New York Yacht Club was part of the curious end-of-an-era generation gap. Lawson could probably have dealt in full understanding with the old bogus "commodore," Cornelius Vanderbilt, a self-made nabob of his own variety, but the inheritors of wealth were less direct in their dealings. For a last insight into this highly symbolic episode we may as well turn again to words put into Lawson's mouth by the thoughtful Mr. Dooley:

"Yachtin' is a gintlemans' spoort," he says, "an' in dalin' with gintlemen," he says, "ye can't be too careful," he says.

THE STEEL SCHOONERS

At century's end, when wealthy yachtsmen were fostering production of huge experimental sloops made of new alloys, the only sizable American steel schooners on the ocean were towing barges. While dilettantes pursued an extravagant contest to see who could hang the most canvas on one tall mast and keep it there in moderate weather, men of commerce followed an opposite impulse: to distribute between several stumpy masts just enough canvas to steady their barges while under tow and to save them from being blown ashore helpless if they should part their hawsers in a storm. Wilmington, Delaware, launched half a dozen steel sailing barges in 1900 and 1901 to operate out of Rockland, Maine. Others were converted from old steamers. Curious seagoing trains—several large barges under baldheaded rig hauled by a puny tug—were at first regarded with some derision, but they were one more symbol of the transition to nothing but steam in the ocean freight business.

Larger steel schooners and schooner barges had appeared earlier on the Great Lakes. In 1901 a total of 27 were registered —all built since 1895. The biggest was the sailing barge *John Smeaton*, of 4,725 tons, launched in 1899. She can be visualized in a fashion by comparison with the original *Great Republic*.

The laker was 123 feet longer than the clipper, 3 feet narrower, and had only two-thirds the depth; her length-to-breadth ratio was more than 9 to 1. The lake barges sometimes were towed well offshore and thereafter proceeded slowly under their own inadequate canvas until picked up near their destinations, but they were intended for towing.

The largest of the free-sailing lake schooners was the *John Fritz*, of 4,447 tons, launched in 1898 and unsurpassed in size for several years thereafter by any vessel intended to operate under sail without assistance. She was 22 feet shorter than the biggest sailing barge, but her breadth and depth were almost the same as the *John Smeaton's*. A popular size for steel schooners on the lakes, 3,000 tons, was dictated by dimensions of the Welland Canal and its locks.

Three large steel schooners built on the ocean coast in 1902 and 1903 were attempts to avoid both structural weaknesses of very large wooden hulls and high operating expenses of square-riggers. The last wooden square-rigger had been launched in 1893. By 1902 the Sewalls had abandoned their hope that square sail on steel bottoms would be the answer. What remained was the as yet untried combination: fore-and-aft canvas on a steel hull larger than any that it was prudent to construct from wood. The schooners that resulted were the seven-master *Thomas W. Lawson*, the six-master *William L. Douglas*, and the five-master *Kineo*. The first and second of these were built for a group of investors who entrusted their operation to Captain John G. Crowley of Boston, managing owner of 11 big coal schooners, including these two and the *George W. Wells*, the original wooden six-master. It was Crowley's task to operate the vessels for their many shareholders in a foredoomed, transitional enterprise. The mystery of Crowley's involvement with two vessels so notably unsuitable for the coal trade in which they were to be engaged does not yield to easy explanation, but this was the period when railroads were blithely ruined by managers who got control of them not for the purpose of operating them for a steady profit, but as a means of siphoning off their capital in the stock market.

Under the headline A TRUST IN SCHOONERS, *The New York Times* on January 24, 1903, announced the formation of the Coastwise Transportation Company, with a projected capital of $3,000,000, to operate "nine big schooners now in the coal trade, including the Thomas W. Lawson and another new schooner now on the stocks, measuring 6,000 tons." The un-completed vessel was the *William L. Douglas,* the reporter having confused a high estimate of her carrying capacity for heavy bulk cargo with her measurement tonnage. "Some of the best-known financiers of the country" were involved, among them representatives of the Cramp shipyards, and Lawson, who became president of the trust, with Crowley as treasurer and general manager. The "Coastwise Shipping Pool" was organized "to operate the boats owned by Capt. J. G. Crowley of Boston, owner of the seven-masted schooner Thomas W. Lawson," but Crowley himself probably owned no more than one-sixteenth of a typical vessel as a first move in promoting the sale of the remaining shares. Participation in this system of distributed risk rested upon the repute of the manager who had the task of keeping a vessel profitably at work by leasing her to charter parties, which might be shipping firms or the purchasers of bulk freight, usually coal. The schooner trust was to include "sailing vessels and barges towed by tugs." The president of the New York Maritime Exchange, asked to comment, said what was obvious: the shipping pool had been "gotten up" to prevent "cutting under." High freight rates could be maintained, if neces-sary, by the threat of an artificial shortage of shipping space. Thus the operating company issued its own separate stock, while the risk in ownership of each of its vessels was distributed among investors who might have bought shares in the holding company as well.

The six- and seven-masted steel schooners may have been con-ceived of as vast seagoing advertisements for the two self-made multimillionaires whose names they celebrated, but their fi-nancing at the time was reported as if it were orthodox. A promo-tional piece appeared in the *Scientific American* describing an unnamed seven-masted schooner long before there was any hint of Lawson's connection with her. The writer said that "as in so many other forms of construction . . . the bigger the unit, the less cost of operation, and the larger the profits." This was writ-ten in advance of the discovery—it is curious that the knowl-edgeable Crowley did not foresee it—that she could get into the coal ports when light but drew too much water to get out of them when loaded. There was no profit to be expected if the bigger unit had to be operated at two-thirds of capacity. This may explain why the second order placed through Crowley, a year later, by the same group of investors, was for a steel schooner 1,436 tons smaller than the first one. Even so, at 3,478 net tons the *William L. Douglas* of 1903 was larger than any wooden schooner. She too had a bad time in the coal ports.

Lieutenant W. J. L. Parker of the Coast Guard, who published in 1948 a modest monograph on the coal schooners, noted: "The Crowley fleet was the only schooner-collier fleet which succumbed to the modern big-business method of capitalization." Trusts and trust busting were much in the new-century headlines, with Lawson exuberantly active in both. He and Crowley were probably maneuvering toward a monopoly in the coal-carrying trade a year or more before their trust was incorporated, but it is hardly plausible that they projected on purpose two awkwardly oversized vessels simply to have large concentrations of cargo capacity to bargain with.

The *Kineo,* smaller and more versatile than the other two steel Atlantic schooners, had the advantage of Sewall's prior experience with steel shipentines. Wire standing rigging forestalled the slackness that 15 years earlier had proved costly to the pioneer wooden five-sticker. America's last steel square-rigger, the *Atlas,* was under construction in the Sewall yard when her builders, in a prospectus issued in 1901, offered a steel five-masted schooner "estimated to carry 3,000 tons of cargo, or over, on sea voyages, and about 3,500 tons in the coasting trade," with a crew of 11. Investors did not rush in: about two years were spent in financing and constructing the *Kineo.* Two more years of discouraging coastal voyages followed before she filled up with coal to lug to the Navy's Far Eastern squadron. Her captain, Frank W. Patten, was instructed to take her out on the sometimes benevolent route south of Africa, but her troubles began promptly in North Atlantic swells.

The *Kineo* had a desperately hard time of it throughout a voyage that turned into a circumnavigation. Captain Patten reported to his owners that the motion of his vessel "caused the sails to slat so badly that the jaws began to break. . . . Another thing against the schooner is the necessity of reducing sail in latitudes where gales are to be expected. . . . the sails have to be reefed in time or they cannot be handled with the heavy water washing across the decks." In such ways the characteristic economies of fore-and-aft rig were nullified. It was lucky that the Navy had no crisis on its docket requiring prompt delivery of its coal. On her way home the *Kineo* took the regular route for ships carrying her cargo, Hawaiian sugar: eastward around the Horn. But what was the better direction for a square-rigger proved the worse for a schooner. Much of her rigging was shredded under the relentless slam and jiggle of her spars.

To the discomfiture of those who had hoped that stronger materials would forestall the oceanic calamities met with by the wood-and-hemp *Gov. Ames*, this world-wrapping voyage of the *Kineo* seemed to demonstrate that long, deep-water swells and doldrum slatting had punished the earlier vessel's resilient structure rather less than they had that of the more rigidly built newer one. The basic fault was with the rig itself. When the big schooner rolled in capricious airs, tons of heavy metal zoomed back and forth across the deck to fetch up with a wallop before swinging back again. Schooners of modest size could go anywhere. Because they were more quickly responsive to the helm, their sails could more easily be kept full by a competent helmsman. As the whalers had determined early in the nineteenth century, in some cases there is an optimum size beyond which the bigger unit loses more than the money it was meant to save.

The *William L. Douglas* had two tanks amidships available for water ballast or liquid freight, a forecast of her eventual employment: all of the three steel ocean schooners became tankers. A few years earlier the *Quevilly*, a big French square-rigger, had been built as a tanker to fetch Philadelphia oil to the Continent under government subsidy, but case oil continued to be the favored method of shipment, employing several of the Sewall steel and wood square-riggers. It was more costly—for packages and for stevedore bills. Smashed five-gallon tins provided a thousand villages of the far Pacific with hideous roofing shingles. But to offset these demerits of the case oil trade, there was a suspicion that interior ripples of the cargo would do sad things to a sailing tanker's stability. Oil shippers proceeded with caution.

The *William L. Douglas*, as the *Times* pointed out, was named for "one of the principal shareholders in the syndicate that owns her." The fact was not unconnected with his candidacy for the governorship of Massachusetts; he won as an upset Democrat in the following election, which returned the Republicans to Washington with a landslide victory. Douglas was not much in need of extra publicity. His features, above the caption "The Boy who Pegged Shoes," had been appearing for years in advertisements all over the world. The vessel that publicized his name was calculated to carry a full cargo of 5,700 tons of coal. The running rigging of her six masts led to four deck engines. Photographs show her as a much less ponderous craft, forward, than her seven-masted predecessor.

Three big wooden six-masters had preceded the *William L. Douglas* into the coal trade. Six more followed her at a rate of about one a year—evidence that an excessive number of masts was not the only accusation laid against the steel schooners when 1903 brought a sudden end to their production on the coast of the Atlantic. A general revival of wooden schooner building continued. The year 1904 was the best one for launchings of large wooden schooners since 1890: there were 22 four-masters, 9 five-masters, and 1 six-master. After that the numbers tapered off into the lull that marks the panic of 1907. The fact that it came to be called the rich man's panic is a comment upon the way in which funds were misused in the era that prodded such an unlikely literary couple as Lawson and Lincoln Steffens into parallel activity as muckrakers, exposing from inside and out the ruthlessness of corporate wealth.

Crowley, like the Sewalls, appears to have forgotten the experience of the *Gov. Ames* or to have concluded that steel construction would overcome the difficulties of schooner rig in deep water. *The New York Times*'s announcement of his venture with Lawson in a schooner trust included the statements that its vessels "may go abroad" and that those in the coastal traffic might not be "confined to the coal trade either."

It is hard to sustain the argument sometimes heard that the steel schooners represented a grand climax in the heroic challenge of sail to steam. They were symptoms, rather, of a change in the procedures of investment after the final financial panic of the nineteenth century. To an unprecedented extent, risk capital came under the control of persons who had developed no particular competence in the technologies to which they applied it. The decision to inflate the dimensions of sailing vessels under a rig that demanded no increase in their crews was taken in the first instance by practical shipbuilders. It was pushed well past the danger point by theorists such as the mathematical Palmer, but Crowley and a few others who had an obligation to know better because of their own years in command soon were pressing the distortion still further, aided by restless, rich men with a willingness to hazard large losses, for themselves and others, in quest of larger gains.

In 1912 the unwieldy coal carrier *William L. Douglas* was converted into a sailing tanker for the Sun Oil Company and renamed the *Delaware Sun.* Her rig was cut down in 1917 to that of a baldheaded schooner barge. As such, on December 18 of that year, she struck a jetty at the entrance to the Sabine River, Texas, and became a total loss. The *Kineo,* at about the same time, was bought by the Texas Company and converted into the motorship *Maryland.* The effort to keep sail competitive by holding crews to a starvation minimum finds an appropriate footnote in the fact that the *Maryland,* during her prior life as a schooner, got along with a total of 11 officers and men, but as soon as all sail was removed she needed a crew of 25. Her long career was divided into three parts, similar in extent: almost 15 years under sail, than 15 more as an oil-powered freighter, and another 15 or so as a tanker. For the last function she was diminished drastically, losing 14 feet in length and more than 6 feet in depth, reducing her tonnage by about one-half; but the count of her people remained at 25. The first and largest of the multimasted steel schooners had origins and adventures deserving of more detailed inspection.

THE *THOMAS W. LAWSON*

The *Scientific American,* which took a wholesome view of the ever-expanding splendors of technological progress, published on October 19, 1901, a large conceptual drawing of "The First Seven Masted Steel Schooner" under full sail. The adjacent text is salted with exact statements about her construction, dimensions, and equipment. She "has been built from designs by B. B. Crowninshield, of Boston, the designer of many small and very successful racing craft, and of the 90-footer 'Independence.' Unlike her predecessors, the new schooner is to be constructed throughout of steel."

The article appeared less than seven weeks after the short career of Crowninshield's *Independence* ended with her delivery to the ship breakers. Between the first quoted words, "*has been* built," and the later "*is to be* constructed," we may suspect that this is promotional publicity, revised somewhat, but unevenly. The brand as well as the cylinder and stroke measurements of her six deck engines are given, with the cheerful assurance that they reduce her complement to 19 men, but the purpose of the article is best revealed in its last sentence:

We are informed by Mr. Frank N. Tandy of Boston, who was recently associated with Mr. Crowninshield, that so great is the confidence in the success of this vessel that preliminary steps are being taken by him and others toward the construction of a second seven-masted schooner.

A second seven-master, if it was ever in prospect except as a jog to investment in the first, never slid off the drawing board. Crowley, in his dealings with Crowninshield, seems, however, to have had either faith or an uncommon patience. Qualms must have arisen over the dimensions and rig of the *Thomas W. Lawson* even before her calamitous propensities were revealed, because the fabled "second seven-master" turned out to be the six-master *William L. Douglas,* less ambitious in all aspects. Crowley afterward turned to Crowninshield, in 1904, for two wooden five-masters—the *Margaret Haskell,* of 1,870 tons, and the *S. J. Goucher,* of 2,249. Both were reversions to the best Maine coast practices of design and construction. The former had a better than average career until she foundered on February 27, 1916, a couple of hundred miles east of St. Augustine.

These facts are entered in evidence of the extreme lunge revealed in each of Crowninshield's two most notable vessels: the first a vast metal enlargement of the skimming dish racing yacht, created at a time when the model was about to go out of favor among yachtsmen interested in something more than acrobatics; the second a schooner too big to take on the cargo it was designed to carry. The *Independence,* by testimony of her owner, was framed and braced in a manner seriously inadequate. Yet this daring prototype, displacing 146.75 tons, was Crowninshield's chief basis in experience for the prompt design of a vessel that according to first reports was to carry 75 times that tonnage of coal. How he managed to get the backing of a tough retired skipper like Crowley, and of the multimillionaire Lawson, remains a puzzle. Lawson's name does not appear in early references to the vessel that was to wear it. She was laid down within a few weeks of the appearance of her profile in the *Scientific American*. While she was building, Lawson found time to produce his extensive and handsomely illustrated *Lawson History of the America's Cup*. He wrote only a minor part of it, Winfield M. Thompson having researched and prepared with admirable clarity the main line of history through the second *Shamrock's* challenge; but the financier's own chapters in conclusion seem not only colorful and candid but fair. His few references to Crowninshield hint at no direct blame for structural failures of his expensive bronze toy, but they say nothing either in explanation of the financier's prospective willingness to invest heavily in an unprecedented all-steel seven-sticker that had been designed by an audacious neophyte.

News stories that announced the launch of the *Thomas W. Lawson* showed little disposition to regard her as a marvel. Everything was getting bigger and better—schooners too. She slid into the water early enough on the afternoon of July 10, 1902, for the Boston *Evening Transcript* of that date to include an account, describing it chiefly as a social occasion. The paper noted that she had been designed to compete with steam in certain trades. The *Scientific American* carried a photograph of the vessel beginning to move on the ways, with her seven steel lower masts already in place. She was 395 feet long overall, 368 feet on the load water line, which was placed at a draft of 25 feet 6 inches. Her beam was 50 feet and her depth of hold 35 feet 2 inches. The schooner's lower masts were 135 feet high from the steps on her keel, surmounted by 58-foot topmasts of Oregon pine. She was reported variously to have cost $250,000 and $300,000, the difference representing chiefly expenses in making her ready for her first voyage.

A hint of the functional relationship between Crowninshield's almost contemporaneous efforts to produce the fastest large metal yacht and the most economical huge metal schooner may be got from his specifications for their spars and canvas. The height of their masts above deck was roughly the same, but each of the schooner's masts carried about 6,000 square feet of canvas, while

the yacht—under mainsail, club topsail, foresail, and spinnaker—sustained on her single mast 18,000 square feet. Her
racing suit of sails in practice was somewhat less, but her specifications provided for that maximum.

Fairburn, who at the time was designing steamers, criticizes
Crowninshield for giving a sailing freighter the extremely high
length-to-breadth ratio of approximately 8 to 1. Hindsight, with
its usual confident clarity, does make it seem probable now that
she would have been safer and better able to get at the coal
wharves if she had been broader, sharper, and shallower, thus
attaining the same cargo-box capacity in a more stable form.
Crowninshield, during his earlier business ventures in the West,
may have studied the big steel lake schooners, which had attained a ratio of 9 to 1. The *John Fritz,* built four years earlier,
had the same breadth as the *Thomas W. Lawson.* The laker was
the longer by 41 feet but was 11 feet shallower. Her designer had
the depth of Lake Erie to limit him, which perhaps was lucky.
The *John Fritz* lasted more than ten times as long as the *Thomas
W. Lawson* and was still in good shape when sold to Canada for
a barge after World War II. The difference is not related to kind-
lier weather on the lakes, where in one storm on November 9,
1913, six steamers foundered with all hands lost for a total of
153 of the 346 American mariners killed that year on all seas
of the world in the loss of their vessels. It is perhaps significant
that no sailing vessel was lost on the lakes that fearful day.

It should, however, be stressed here that in the last fiscal year
before sinkings by German submarines began to complicate the
score, all but 13 of the 118 American sailing vessels lost throughout the world were schooners. Except for the loss of one man in
a yacht, all the 119 deaths resulting occurred in schooners, of
which 8 went down with all hands. These losses of vessels and
men, far out of proportion to the ratio of schooners to other sailing merchantmen (schooners constituted about 60 per cent of the
sailing merchant fleet), indicate the excessive hazard presented
by a class of vessels within which the *Thomas W. Lawson* went
to a new extreme in the effort to move more cargo without increasing the allotment for wages. The late schooners as a group
were killers. Their record as such invites a sad choice of general
explanations: on many of these fatal occasions either there were
too few men aboard to perform in time the saving acts of seaman-

ship, or the overgrown mechanisms in fact became uncontrollable. Perils of the sea are an ancient story, taken for granted by
shipowners and ship's people alike; but whereas the generation
of Robert Bennet Forbes strove consciously and well to amelio-
rate these hazards, the men who quite deliberately calculated the
cost of human beings against the cost of adequate controls for
huge spars, in the coal schooners, reversed the decencies awakened at mid-century.

The *Thomas W. Lawson* was the climactic, cold-hearted gamble in an effort to move the most cargo with the smallest pay-
roll. That conclusion is made no prettier by a reminder that the
coal which the vessel was intended to carry was mined with an
even more brutal disrespect for the lives and living conditions
of those who produced it. In this sense the enormous schooner
was a symbol of the commercial crudities of her era, but it is
still to be noted that the concept of a large steel schooner with
adequate deck engines, steam heat, and other provisions for
working and living conditions less arduous than usual, presented definite advantages. A somewhat more modest first example would have put these advantages to a fairer test, particularly
in a contest against competitors made mostly of wood. The spines
of the big wooden schooners had become huge scarfed masses of
lumber: keel, keelson, sister keelsons, far heavier than those in
square-riggers of similar tonnage. Steel promised even greater
strength from less than half the dead weight of material. Indeed,
the saving in this way was so large that Crowninshield thought
it necessary to provide his vessel with a double bottom that could
be pumped full of water ballast to stiffen her when she was
lightly laden. Here too, as in the *Independence,* his advance calculations fell short of the need. She was dangerously crank in
her trials. Having the greatest length-to-breadth ratio of any
ocean sailing vessel, she should have been exceptionally weatherly, but much of the advantage of her relative narrowness was
offset by bows as blunt as a silo. When deeply laden, she made
fairly good use of a leading wind; in ballast, however, the windward side of her huge hull above water had as much area as the
amount of sail she could set without lying down on her beam
ends. Thus leeway and sternway gathered from the wind's force
against her hull would practically cancel the headway of her
sails.

What was even more dangerous, her length and bluntness combined to make it extremely difficult to bring her about. Crowninshield in a late book admitted that to put her head through the wind was sometimes actually impossible: a potentially fatal circumstance on a lee shore. Awareness of it probably forced her skipper's decision to anchor in a perilously exposed position, instead of trying to beat around a headland to safety, shortly before she was destroyed by the sea.

In view of later references to this vessel as representing the grand climax of America's experience with commercial sail, as well as of persistent errors in the accounts of her loss, a look at more nearly contemporary evidence and opinion seems in order. The *Report of the Commissioner of Corporations on Transportation by Water in the United States,* dated July 12, 1909, singles out the only seven-master for special comment, beginning: "The climax of fore-and-aft vessel was reached in 1902. . . ." Acknowledging that multimasted schooners had for some time had almost a complete monopoly as carriers in the coastal coal trade, the commissioner stated that the *Thomas W. Lawson* was too large for the business for which she was built. It was Captain Crowley himself who confirmed the embarrassing circumstance. His troubles, during a trial voyage in command, were reported in *The New York Times* on the day after Christmas in 1902, under the headline "Ship Too Big for Coal Ports."

Capt. Crowley had to sail out of Philadelphia with about 1500 tons less than the ship's capacity . . . grounded twice in the Delaware River.

The unhappy skipper told a reporter that Newport News would be the only port where he could get 9,000 tons aboard—a severe limitation upon the bargaining power that a vessel of such large capacity was supposed to give him, and a poor advertisement for the "trust in schooners" to be announced a month later. Her actual load when she grounded was 7,347 tons. In such cases the cost of tugs probably offset the profit gained through the economy of her size. On her last voyage she grounded in the river, and it took a dozen tugs, according to *The New York Times,* to float her off.

After several years of such discouragements Crowley managed to foist off the *Thomas W. Lawson* on a five-year charter to the

Although the structurally unprecedented *Thomas W. Lawson* turned out to be the first and only seven-masted schooner ever built, her launch *(right)* was reported in Boston chiefly as a social occasion. The all-steel colossus sacrificed too much to the commercial ideals of large carrying capacity and a low bill for seamen's wages. At times, because of her bluntness and the excessive area presented to the wind by her topsides, she was unmanageable. Her largely frustrating career ended in sudden death for herself and all her people with the exception of her captain and her engineer. (See pp. 433–38, 440–45.)

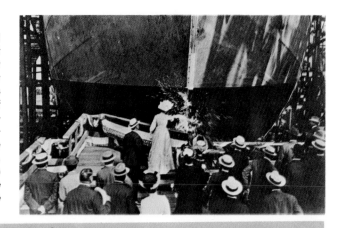

Sun Oil Company at $78,000 a year, a sum sufficient to cover her original cost as well as to provide for her conversion into a tanker. The commissioner of corporations concluded the above-quoted account of her with the statement: "In the summer of 1906 she was equipped with huge tanks for carrying oil in bulk, and transported oil until December, 1907, when she was wrecked." Fairburn disagrees. Having stated flatly that she was carrying case oil when lost, he concludes that she "was never built as a bulk carrier and was not constructed with subdivisions—transverse, horizontal, and logitudinal—for carrying any liquid cargo." More than three decades after her loss, however, the man who designed her referred with explicitness to the "fourteen tanks into which her hull had been divided." He did not say when it had been done, but they evidently were the tanks with which, according to the commissioner, she had been "equipped" when four years old. That she had such tanks before the fatal transatlantic voyage is proved by a reference in *The New York Times* to the drowning of two Negro seamen in one of her tanks when she was hove to, during her coastal service, to ride out a storm off Florida.

With the asperity that enlivens many of the historical skirmishes in the six tall volumes of his *Merchant Sail*, Fairburn reviews several crisscross reports of the biggest schooner's last voyage. He cites what he calls a "supposedly 'authoritative' article" (unidentified) and excerpts the comment:

The Lawson *should never have been sent to sea without extensive alterations which would have divided her up inside, confining the oil in tanks rather than allowing it to flow about, creating an inner swell which threw her off balance.*

Yet the evidence is abundant that this is precisely what had been done. Her designer, who testified to that, did his creation a disservice, however, in his statement of 1940 that she had sailed from Marcus Hook in November of 1907 and had taken six weeks to reach the western end of the English Channel. She met her end in the dark early hours of December 14, which would mean that a voyage of six weeks should have begun within the first two or three days of the preceding month. It is on record, however, that she sailed from the refinery port near Philadelphia on November 15, got aground as usual, was pulled off, and cleared the Delaware capes on the nineteenth. Thus she spent 25 days on the Atlantic—smart sailing for a blunt and deeply laden fore-and-after in a season when many other vessels reported an extremely bad voyage. Her loss has been wrongly attributed to the battering she took on her Atlantic crossing. But she did lose a lot of canvas, a fact that must have heavily affected her skipper's judgment of the options available to him on the tumultuous night that closed her career off the Scilly Islands.

I suspect that a good deal of the confusion over the last hours of the *Thomas W. Lawson* originated in a misreading of the prompt London *Times* report of December 16, 1907, which actually deals with the loss of two schooners. It is the second of these vessels, not identified in the article, that was seen by observers on shore to have "a heavy list to starboard, apparently due to her cargo having shifted." Because only one of the schooners is named, a quick reader might assume that the same one is being referred to throughout. The unidentified one did capsize, in view of spectators on shore, and vanish.

The *Times* of London covered the tragedy in four news stories, two on December 16 and two on December 17. The first, sent in haste from the islands, did say that the *Thomas W. Lawson* was "bound from Philadelphia to London with case oil," that she had anchored in a dangerous position to windward of one of the rocky islands, and that "at daylight it was found that she had capsized and become a total wreck." The St. Agnes lifeboat had got close to her, but the captain had felt that she could ride the storm out and had not asked for assistance. At this point he may have said that his cargo was oil, which the reporter who talked to the lifeboat crew assumed to mean case oil. News gathered under such circumstances would obviously need rechecking, and the opportunity came next day at the inquest.

There had been only three survivors. One, a seaman, died of his injuries after a few hours. Another, the captain, was too ill from shock and exposure to testify, but the third survivor chanced to be the man who should have had the most intimate knowledge of the ship's structure, Edward Rowe, the engineer responsible for her boilers, electric dynamos, steering and deck engines, and other contrivances. In a small crew he undoubtedly would have had responsibility as well for the problem of oil seepage and consequent explosive mixtures. Since he was found clinging to a rock in the icy seas, his information must have been given from memory, without reference to the ship's ledgers. A check on Rowe's accuracy as a witness, therefore, is provided in his testimony that the vessel measured 4,914 tons, the precise registered net figure rather than the larger gross tonnage usually given out for publication as being more impressive. He went on to say that she

had about 6000 tons of oil in 14 tanks. They sighted Scilly about 1 p.m. on Friday, but they were not certain at first what land it was owing to the fog. The captain hoped to clear the land but found it impossible, and two anchors were dropped. . . . They had only six good sails left owing to their having experienced two strong gales during their passage, by which they had also lost all their boats and their life raft.

The big schooners, when fully laden, had seas almost constantly breaking over their decks—enough to account, on a particularly stormy passage, for the loss of the life raft and all the boats. Crowninshield claimed that his seven-master, when deep in the water, "handled like a yacht," but she needed canvas to do so. With enough sails in the appropriate places she might have clawed around the headland to shelter, as her skipper had tried to make her do before anchoring off a rocky lee shore. No evidence was given at the inquest that she capsized as a result of the shifting of her oil. The storm increased during the last hours of her life to a furious level, which either caused her anchors to drag or her cables to part. She was driven broadside onto the rocks and broke in two: an accident that in the circumstances could have befallen a vessel of any design. It can be argued that she found herself in her final hopeless circumstance because her rig was basically unsuitable to the winter Atlantic crossing—but other kinds of vessels in stormy weather have had most of their sails go to leeward in small strips.

A pilot left aboard the *Thomas W. Lawson* by the lifeboat that reached her on the evening of December 13 was one of the men lost next morning before dawn. He may have been a reckless hero, but it is more likely that he shared the captain's confidence in the vessel's heavy ground tackle and considered her canvas sufficient to get her around the corner when the storm abated. Instead it increased to such a degree that when the men on shore saw her lights go out in the early dark of morning, they considered it impossible to reach her again.

Exactly what happened cannot be known. She may have capsized while still at anchor, or after a failure of fluke or chain.
The easiest moral to perceive is the dramatic helplessness of a
very large vessel in some circumstances when dependent upon
sail alone. Even under close reefs a small schooner can cast
quickly from one tack to the other to gain sea room off a lee
shore, but to put the seven-sticker about in good circumstances
was a major operation that might fail; it could not be risked with
an ironbound coast to leeward. Her heavy cargo, whether in
tanks or not, would have been more of a help than a peril when
riding to her anchors in such seas. It is light cargo that shifts to
throw a ship off balance, and a lightly laden vessel that bucks
and saws at her cables.

Sun Oil's decision to put a fore-and-aft-rigged tanker on a
deep-water run in winter still is hard to explain. I suppose it
was another outcome of corporate decision making, which dif-
fuses responsibility and often shunts aside the possessors of
particular knowledge. The Coastwise Transportation Company,
not the charterer, was responsible to stockholders in the *Thomas
W. Lawson*. As another oddity of such financing, the owners had
not insured their vessel, but the charterers had insured their
oil. Wide distribution of shares, both in Crowley's operating
company and in each separate vessel it managed, provided an
equivalent of insurance at less cost when losses were incurred
upon an average pattern—but the largest steel schooner was not
an average carrier.

An early British report of the disaster did contain the statement, repeated in some accounts, that the vessel was insured for
$200,000 against total loss and that there was separate insurance
upon the cargo, the latter reinsured in London to the extent of
£ 14,690, a significant sum because it approximates the annual
cost of the charter in dollars: $78,000. But the published figure
for insurance on the vessel, since the City of London was not
involved, probably was taken from the listing for a coastal voyage
at a prior date. Several American news stories asserted positively
that the vessel was not insured and that the personal loss to
Lawson would be $150,000: a reporter's guess, probably. Any
extravagant news of him found eager readers.

There is a choice of a sort between the wreck in 1907 of the
Thomas W. Lawson and the foundering in 1924 of the *Wyoming*
as a symbolic conclusion to the final American effort to keep sail

honestly at work upon the seas. The first and largest steel
schooner, the only seven-sticker, had a relatively short career full
of difficulties. The last and largest of the wooden six-masters
was a successful vessel usefully employed for 15 years. Drawing
about five feet less when full, she was able to take on a capacity
cargo of coal at ports that excluded her metal predecessor. Both
called attention to the cost of the commercial wager that produced them, in terms that were forbiddingly inhumane. The
Thomas W. Lawson killed all but two of her last crew; the
Wyoming was finally so shaken in a winter storm that she went
down with all hands near the Pollock Rip Lightship. It is curious
that both were reversions, after more than 400 years, to the
arrangement of canvas that Columbus, on his first voyage, had
found unsatisfactory in the open ocean: the fore-and-aft rig of
his *Niña,* to which at Las Palmas he added square sail. The first
and last reliance upon nothing but fore-and-aft sail on the
Atlantic coal schooners as they grew larger reflected a hardhearted gamble in human lives rather than an effort to select the
best rig for a particular task.

It is true that the *Thomas W. Lawson,* in her last hours, found
the worst kind of place for a test of her structural shortcomings.
Yet the measure of any vessel, as of any man, is to stand up to the
unexpected in a time of extreme stress.

WILLIAM LEWIS AND
THE SAN FRANCISCO STEAM WHALERS

In the last decades of the nineteenth century, as coastal freight
carriers increased in capacity and in the number of their masts,
a more modest kind of schooner went whaling as usual in both
our oceans. Bankers out of Gloucester continued to hoist their old
sparse rig on hulls of a design notably influenced by recent
experimentation with racing yachts as well as by pilot schooners.
An ambitious, technologically adept people does not take kindly
to the idea that an optimum of utility—even in the merest financial terms—may be reached at some point short of the maximum attainable dimensions. Yet any hundred-tonner of the New
England fishing fleet, built in the year 1902, was a better expression of mature nautical design than the overweening, crew-
starved *Thomas W. Lawson* of 50 times her measurement. The
bold experimentation paid for by rich amateurs, in the materials

and hydrodynamics of pleasure craft, did much more for naval
architecture than their blundering intrusion into the dinosaur
period of commercial schooners.

In the 1880's, as more and more barks with the few surviving
ship-rigged whalers were being put into the care of agents who
would thereafter operate them out of San Francisco, two-masted
schooners inherited all that was left of the Atlantic whale fishery.
A few brigs hunted in Hudson's Bay, and in 1889 a 121-ton brig
was the only vessel sent from New Bedford around the Horn.
The famous port's working tonnage had dropped to the level of
Provincetown's. The huge cruelty and uncontrolled greed of New
England's once most characteristically triumphant enterprise had
decimated throughout most of the watery world the animals
upon which it depended. It is probable that only a rapid rise in
the production of earth oil saved the whales from extinction well
before the nineteenth century ended. The height of irresponsible
ruthlessness was reached late in the 1890's when the steam
whaler *Beluga*, of 409 tons, brought 106,000 pounds of bone,
the largest catch ever, into San Francisco. A reporter noted that
"the captain took no blubber and boiled no oil. Had he done this
he would have had $63,000 worth more of freight and property.
But he had no time to spade out fat. . . ." It had become more and
more the practice in a swiftly maneuverable kind of vessel to
hack off the head and let the blubber-swathed carcass float away.
Captain Hartson H. Bodfish had destroyed 63 whales for the great
sieves of bone in their mouths, and had wasted enough blubber
to fill ten such ships with oil. The excuse given by his callous
welcomer, that "he had no time to spade out fat," was preposterous. He was returning from a longer than usual voyage for a
steam whaler—30 months embracing two winters in the Arctic.
The sea took care of its own. Carcasses cut adrift by Bodfish
nourished other creatures, but the whale herds had been almost
eliminated by such butchery when earth oil's underground
neighbor—iron—at last was satisfactorily processed into the
light, springy parasol ribs and corset stays that brought whalebone prices tumbling down.

Such steam whalers as Bodfish's *Beluga* were the one reasonably durable outcome of the Forbes-Ericsson auxiliary steamer
experimentation in the 1840's. The line of development had
crossed the Atlantic to Dundee, Scotland, where a few iron

auxiliaries were built for whaling about 1859. When the thick bows of the first and most ambitious one were promptly punctured by the ice, causing her to founder, and when four modest iron auxiliaries that went sealing were all badly mauled in the floes, Dundee and Peterhead reverted to resilient structures of wood. While the American fleet was being converted almost entirely to bark rig, the Scottish steam whalers continued to be full-rigged ships.

Britain's northern fishery fleet of steam auxiliaries was built up while Americans were savagely diminishing their active whaling industry in a civil war. When the fighting stopped, the New London whaling bark *Pioneer* was rebuilt as an auxiliary steamer. Starbuck lists her as having recently made out of her home port in 1864–65 "the best voyage on record," when she brought home a cargo worth $150,000 in an oil-starved wartime market. During the conversion her registered tonnage dropped from 235 to 202, reflecting subtraction of space under the new tonnage rules to account for what was occupied by machinery. On her first voyage as a steamer she was sunk in the ice of Hudson's Strait on July 6, 1867. This appears to have stilled for more than a decade any further urge to emulate the Scots.

In 1878 Captain William Lewis of New Bedford sent Captain Cyrus Manter of Martha's Vineyard to Newfoundland to have a close look at the Dundee steam whalers, whose crews often supplemented their main endeavors by clubbing seals off that island. Captain Lewis, a veteran in command but a relative newcomer to the management of whalers, appears to have been unencumbered with the sense of traditional ways that had partly accounted for the downfall of Nantucket. He first turns up as a "managing owner or agent" in 1872 with the little *Eunice H. Adams,* of 102 tons, built as a schooner at Bristol, Rhode Island, in 1845 and converted to a brig five years before Lewis began, with her, what was evidently a shoestring operation. By 1875 he had five barks and two brigs, all in the Atlantic fishery. In the year following he dispatched six vessels, two of them to the Indian Ocean and one to the North Pacific. In 1878, when he turned his attention toward steam, he was "managing owner or agent" for fifteen whalers scattered across the oceans: ten barks, three brigs, a ship, and a schooner.

Invigorated by Manter's favorable opinion, Lewis managed to

assemble the requisite group of investors and placed an order with the Goss, Sawyer and Packard shipyard at Bath, Maine, for the original and highly successful if short-lived *Mary and Helen,* of 420 gross tons. In his report published three years later, Hall called her "the pioneer of her class" and noted that she carried "coal bunkers and a small engine with a screw propeller capable of driving her at the rate of from 6 to 8 miles per hour. . . . With her steam power she could push her way through the ice floes." Lewis's impulse to build her must have been related to several events involving steamers or ice floes or both, and their effects upon sailing whalers. In 1863 his own command, the bark *Lafayette,* of 357 tons, had been caught and burned by the sailing steamer *Alabama.* After promptly departing again in the bark *Samuel and Thomas,* of 191 tons, Lewis diversified his wartime risk by shipping part of his catch home in another whaler, which was intercepted and burned by the sailing steamer *Florida.* The *Shenandoah's* devastating demonstration of maneuverability in the ice was only too well known in Lewis's home port, which had been the principal sufferer—as it had been also from the two calamities wrought by ice alone upon trapped sailers in 1871 and 1876. In all these cases, steam in reserve would have given the victims at least a chance to escape.

As the *Mary and Helen* was being readied for her first voyage, Lewis dispatched his bark the *Sappho,* of 263 tons, for a cruise in the Pacific, which she was to complete two years later at San Francisco. The practice seems to have been begun by the New Bedford firm of J. & W. R. Wing with their *Abraham Barker,* of 380 tons, which they sent to the Pacific in her thirtieth year, on October 26, 1875, to remain in that ocean for 19 additional years of whaling. Whether she sailed with orders to return to San Francisco, as she did do on November 4, 1880, with a very large catch, is doubtful. The orders probably caught up with her, but the logic of keeping Pacific whalers in the Pacific became, at about this time, too obvious to ignore at New Bedford. The Wings transferred three large barks and set up a West Coast office to manage them. They continued to fish the Atlantic with smaller vessels and with one bark, the *Charles W. Morgan,* now the lonely surviving square-rigged whaler. In 1881 they sent her westward around the Horn on a voyage in which it took her five years to bring back to New England a very modest catch of sperm, supplemented by less whale and no bone. That drove the point home. When next she sailed it was for a 20-year stay in the Pacific, where she concentrated upon whale oil and bone.

Lewis put his large sailing whalers and his steamers under the supervision of a San Francisco agent, keeping four or five schooners and a brig for fishing on the Atlantic side and in Hudson Bay. When his *Mary and Helen* sailed on September 9, 1879, she changed the character of two ports, being the first steam whaler to depart from New Bedford and the first to discharge at San Francisco. Conserving coal for the Arctic, she spent seven months sailing by way of the Strait of Magellan to Honolulu, where she arrived on April 7, 1880. Only six months and three days later, however, the *Alta California* reported that she had been spoken "going into Drake's Bay." On October 12 she docked at Beale Street to begin discharging her 2,615 barrels of oil and 45,000 pounds of bone. Her captain, Leander C. Owen, admitted to having bothered with only the head of most of the whales he had so swiftly taken, allowing a potential $2,000 worth of oil to drift away in each of the decapitated carcasses.

The competition of earth oil already had made bone the more desirable part of the catch. In the average whale, bone represented in that year about one-third of the potential value, but it could be made ready for stowage so much more quickly that there was a temptation to forget the trypots. The *Mary and Helen*'s oil sold for more than $45,000 but her bone proved to be worth $90,000. The most nearly comparable catch brought into any whaling port in the same year by a sailing vessel was that of the aged bark *Coral*, of 362 gross tons, newly transferred from New Bedford. She had needed two and a half years to fill up with a cargo worth somewhat less. Of sailing whalers returning to New Bedford in 1880, those with even moderate greasy luck had been out three years at least.

Soon after her first voyage, the *Mary and Helen* was purchased by the United States to go north again in search of the vanished *Jeannette* Arctic expedition. The unsuccessful rescuer was burned by accident a year later.

Restlessly ambitious San Francisco had vacillated since the Civil War over her evident destiny as the center most favored by geography and communications for a last upsurge in the adventure of American whaling. Her financiers, concerned with the swift expansion of agriculture and the consequent grain trade to Europe, had read the warning of earth oil. The tapering off of whaling everywhere was evident in public statistics. Three Arctic disasters in 11 years to the New Bedford fleet had opened the way for a nearer port to compete, yet fewer ships had brought more oil and bone than the market wanted. It was the promise of unprecedented operating economy, revealed by the *Mary and Helen*'s phenomenal single voyage, that reinvigorated an interest in whaling out of the Golden Gate. A steamer could do better in a single summer season than the luckiest of barks had been able to do in three.

William Lewis had not waited for news of the prompt success of his first steam whaler. Before she reached Honolulu he had a second, the *Belvedere*, of 339 tons, building in the same yard. When she sailed from New Bedford on August 17, 1880, she had on board a young seaman named Hartson H. Bodfish, who had been persuaded at the last minute to join her by his West Tisbury neighbor Captain Manter. Less than 15 months later she carried into San Francisco enough oil, ivory, and bone—consigned to agent J. N. Knowles—to credit Lewis for a second time with the most valuable catch of the year crammed into any vessel, and had given Bodfish the apprenticeship from which he presently emerged as the most eminent of the San Francisco whaling masters. After five weeks spent in outfitting, on December 14 she became the first steamer to originate a whaling voyage from a West Coast port. Under management of Lewis and his son she continued to sail out of San Francisco for three decades. As the longest-lived of the steam whalers designed for their particular function in the Alaskan Arctic, the *Belvedere* can represent the others. Her measurements were 140.6 by 31.3 by 17.2, and her registered gross tonnage was 442. Her net tonnage does not appear in the registers, but her usable space as a whaler was probably little more than the average for those under sail. She had a small engine, rated at 95 horsepower. The later steam whalers of her size were two or three times as powerful. As a group these vessels were heavily built. Bodfish described another of them as having 15 feet of almost solid oak in the bows with no stowage space. The four-inch oak planking was overlaid with a sheathing of ironwood, tapering from three inches forward to

half that thickness aft. Although iron hulls had been found unsuitable for use in the ice, the steam whalers were given protective metal shoes over their stems.

Robert Bennet Forbes and John Ericsson lived long enough to
take what satisfaction they could find in the demonstration that
their concept of steam auxiliaries had found at least one belated
area of fulfillment. Forbes spent some time in California in 1882.
The two pioneers died in the same year, 1889. Within the period
of less than three weeks preceding Forbes's death, eight auxiliary
steam barks similar in dimensions and in concept to his prototype, the *Edith* of 1844, came home from the Arctic to San
Francisco.

As soon as the chaos of the first gold rush had sorted itself into
a durable economy, which absorbed the usable bottoms abandoned during those wild years, shipbuilding became a competitive industry on San Francisco Bay. The first little steamers
shipped out by Forbes, with holes cut in their bottoms for the
masts of their sailing carriers, were supplanted by larger ones
built on the spot. John and James Dickie, Scottish brothers who
knew something about the steam whalers built at Dundee, emi-
grated to San Francisco in 1871 to set up a shipyard of their own.
They were followed by a third brother, George, a specialist in
marine engines who became associated with the Union Iron
Works. The Dickies were in readiness with all skills that were
needed when the local firm of Goodall, Perkins & Company
decided in 1881 that William Lewis's first steam whaler had
sufficiently demonstrated an economical direction for the future
of the fishery. Prices for all whale products had been slipping.
The partners, former Governor George Perkins and Captain
Charles Goodall, may have been subtle enough students of the
commodities markets to suspect that some persisting uses of oil
as well as bone would bring an upturn when the surplus had
been absorbed. Fine candles were still wanted, and nothing but
spermaceti had been so far produced to make them odorless.
"Petroleum, gas, and the shipping laws," as the *Alta California*
noted, had gravely affected "the whale fishing interest." What the
whalers contemptuously called earth oil was winning the competition for lamps, but the tanneries could not do without
whale. In the country's vast industrial expansion, in its railroads
particularly, "a thousand substitutes" had been tried for lubri-

The steam whaling bark *Belvedere*, of 339 tons, had a career embracing almost the entire history of Arctic steam whaling out of San Francisco. Launched in 1880 at Bath, Maine, she was the second such vessel built for William Lewis of New Bedford, who pioneered in the establishment of a new focus for whaling on the Pacific coast. By comparison with the longevity of hemp-and-canvas whalers, the average life of steam whalers in the San Francisco fleet was relatively short, partly because they took more risks and often wintered in the ice on the northern coast of Alaska or Canada. More than half of the American steam whalers had been crushed by the ice their metal-tipped bows and sheathed hulls were supposed to fend off, when the *Belvedere* herself, in her thirty-ninth year of service, succumbed in the pack ice off Siberia. (See pp. 449–50, 452–58, 472–73.)

Two strong factors contributing to the success of San Francisco in replacing New Bedford as the premier whaling port were the establishment of a shipyard by the Scottish immigrant Dickies and the building of the Arctic Oil Works *(below)*. The *Orca (above, Smithsonian model)* was the second steam whaler built by John W. Dickie, shown beside his son David. (See pp. 457, 464–68.)

cating journal boxes and other points of friction, "but nothing will do well except animal or fish oils, and after costly experiments the big transportation companies have fallen back on whale oil."

The year 1881 did turn out to be the low point, with sperm selling at 88 cents and whale at 48 cents a gallon, while bone brought $1.63 a pound. Oil prices rose in the next three years, then settled again into a long, slow decline, but bone zoomed with the assistance of *Godey's Lady's Book* and other persuaders to strait-laced fashions. Its value ten years later had more than tripled, and it did not fall below the 1881 figure until 1911, when changing waistlines and cheap metal "bones," for those who still relied upon the grimmer kinds of corsets, abruptly brought the average price of whalebone below a twenty-fifth of what it had fetched in the peak market of the early nineties. Bone kept the whalers afloat throughout the first three decades of the durable *Belvedere's* fishing. The price of bone gyrated weirdly after 1911, between a high of $1.59 and a low of 4 cents a pound: a product not to be wasted in hard times as oil had been, but one having an unpredictable value. Oil prices, as supply and demand both diminished, were relatively steady by comparison until the end of American deep-water whaling.

At about the time when the transcontinental system of chattering relays brought news of the departure from New Bedford of Lewis's second steam whaler, headed for the Pacific Arctic, Goodall and Perkins approved plans for her first San Francisco-built competitor, the *Bowhead*, of 533 gross tons, net measurement probably about 400. Trial and error, as with the sailing whalers, soon dictated an optimum practical size for those powered partly by steam. The British had tried a steam whaler in 1875—their second *Arctic*—of 828 gross and 522 net tons measurement. Lubbock reports "her great length was considered a drawback by old-timers, for it made her more difficult to manoeuvre and twist about in small water holes." As more American steam whalers were provided, their capacities diminished into the range of tonnages that had been found feasible for long voyages out of New England under sail alone. Appendix C, at the end of this volume, reveals year by year the size thought prudent for an Arctic steam whaler, whether she was built for her particular function at the outset or chosen as suitable for conversion.

The *Bowhead* was launched on April 21, 1882. The Dickies had so skillfully coordinated work on her hull, engine, and equipment, alow and aloft, that she made her departure for the Arctic only a week later. She was back again in less than seven months with a balanced catch—300 barrels of sperm, 1,750 barrels of whale, and 26,000 pounds of bone. Prices for these three products were up about 20 per cent, 10 per cent, and 5 per cent respectively over levels for the preceding season. The *Bowhead's* was the year's best catch for both sperm and whale and the fourth in rank for bone among all 30 whalers that discharged at San Francisco.

Most sailings to Bering Strait out of New Bedford had been timed to bring the whalers into summer weather off Cape Horn. The less boisterous Pacific invited winter sailings out of San Francisco, preferably in December but not later than March, in a calculated effort to be close to the chops of Bering Strait when summer's onset opened the first precarious navigable passages among the floes. The best hunting, off the northern coast of Alaska on both sides of Point Barrow, called for a perilous gamble that the whaling masters had lost so disastrously in 1871 and 1876 when the first wild gale of autumn arrived too soon. Ice, piled by northerly winds into the funnel of the strait, usually sealed it while the broad Arctic Ocean above it was still largely navigable. Sailers as well as steamers aimed to slip through the strait in time to raise the Golden Gate in the early part of November, but at least one straggler was trapped almost every year. The master of the *Coral* reported in 1882 that the San Francisco fleet had entered the Arctic in May, finding its best luck between 72 degrees 40 minutes and 73 degrees 10 minutes in the open ocean, and had passed southward through the strait on October 11—a typical season.

The *North Star*, of 489 gross tons, the first steam whaler to be lost in the Alaskan Arctic, was William Lewis's third intended for service out of San Francisco. Dispatched from New Bedford on August 2, 1881, directly to the North Pacific, she was reported sunk off Cape Barrow in th following summer. Lewis's fourth steam whaler initiated another aspect of San Francisco's intensive whaling. Prompted by his success with the first *Mary and Helen*, but before he had news of the *Belvedere's* good fortune, he decided to convert his bark *Lucretia*—one of the few square-riggers built as whalers after the Civil War—into a 313-ton steamer: the

Three oil paintings by C. S. Raleigh of ships built for Captain William Lewis, pioneer of steam whaling out of San Francisco. The *North Star* (top), launched in 1881, and the *William Lewis* (center), launched in 1888, were both built as steam barks. The *William Baylies*, portrayed at her launch in 1886 as a conventional whaling bark, was converted to steam eight years later. All fly Lewis's house flag. (See pp. 454, 456, 465–66, 471–72, 499–501.)

first of several such conversions. On her maiden sailing voyage, commenced in 1877, she had made the best catch of sperm in eight years. Her first trial as a steamer, however, was a fiasco. She sailed late for a Cape Horn passage, on December 15, 1881. Her qualities as a sailer had been disturbed by her machinery. In equinoctial weather she was unable to buck her way into the Pacific. Her skipper acknowledged the wind's will and stood eastward for what amounted almost to a circumnavigation south of Australia to San Francisco, having collected when he arrived on November 24, 1882, only 30 barrels of sperm. The *Lucretia's* luck improved slowly on annual voyages out of her new home port until she was lost at Herald Island, about 400 miles north and a bit west of Bering Strait, on September 5, 1889.

Lewis named his fifth steam whaler after his first, destroyed while in the service of the government. The *Mary and Helen II* measured 409 tons and was sent as usual directly to the Arctic from New Bedford, but when on November 14, 1883, she brought her first modest catch into San Francisco, her owner's resources were overextended. Bad luck had marked his recent ventures: the prompt loss of his third steamer was compounded by that of his favorite sailing whaler, the *Sappho,* both while the *Lucretia* was making her costly wrong-way voyage. He consequently wired instructions for the sale of his *Mary and Helen II* to the newly incorporated Pacific Steam Whaling Company, to which he had already lost his personal San Francisco representative, Captain Josiah Nickerson Knowles, a commission merchant who was to have managed the vessel in Lewis's interest and who carried the task of her management with him when he joined the new concern. Her sale seems to have been negotiated while she was still at sea because when she arrived her catch—950 barrels of whale oil, 15,000 pounds of bone, 1,000 pounds of ivory—was consigned to the Pacific Steam Whaling Company, which had not yet come into existence when she was sailing southward for San Francisco through Bering Strait.

JOSIAH N. KNOWLES AND THE PACIFIC STEAM WHALING COMPANY

When Goodall, Perkins & Company assumed an ambitious new corporate guise on October 30, 1883, the firm owned four or perhaps five steam whalers that were bound for San Francisco from their summer's fishing in the Arctic. The Pacific Steam Whaling Company was consequently a consolidation of existing and planned enterprises, anticipating by two decades the kind of bid for domination of a nautical activity that Crowley and Lawson were to attempt in the case of the coal schooners. Lewis's demonstration that ships owned in New Bedford could operate more profitably out of San Francisco had spurred the western city's merchants to the next logical conclusion: that they could be operated more profitably still if all phases of the industry were concentrated in their port of registry. The new company consequently was provided with a wholly owned subsidiary, the Arctic Oil Works. Here too the location of San Francisco afforded an advantage. Oil received in New England at the end of long voyages through tropical seas was graded at three levels, that bringing the lowest price described as "black and stinking." Oil from Arctic fisheries was kept in automatically refrigerated hulls for all but the last two or three weeks of a voyage to San Francisco. Processors ashore had less corruption to eliminate, and the refined oil could be kept indefinitely in huge tanks to stabilize a formerly capricious market.

In 1882 Goodall and Perkins had added to their original *Bowhead* the *Orca*, of 462 tons. She sailed in the favorable season, on December 15. During that winter the Dickie yard rushed two more steam whalers to completion, the externally identical *Narwhal* and *Balaena*, measuring 390 tons each. They got to sea on April 11 and 26, respectively. The *Narwhal* contained below decks San Francisco's major innovation in whaling technology: as the *Alta California* phrased it, she was "fully tanked with iron tanks" to carry more oil in less space than either predecessor. The *Bowhead* and *Orca* both had had screws that could be unshipped; the *Narwhal's* was of the sturdier fixed variety. Her 26 tanks held 3,000 barrels of oil, but their number must have been soon reduced as bone became the more valuable component of a whale's carcass. The cooper in a classic whaler could set up casks as needed, allowing for a more flexible use of space. The original tanker-whaler carried home less than 600 barrels of oil from most of her voyages, and never half as much as her rated 3,000 barrels.

When the *Narwhal* had a trial run in the bay on April 10, 1883, the notables on board included Josiah N. Knowles, who was to have responsibility for her management. William Lewis had consigned the original *Mary and Helen* to himself, at San Francisco, but his *Belvedere* on her first two voyages had been consigned to J. N. Knowles, who also appears as consignee of the Lewis barks *Thomas Pope, Sappho,* and *Mabel.* Knowles was the famous Lazarus of the San Francisco waterfront: in his twenty-eighth year he had sailed from that port on February 9, 1858, in command of the medium clipper *Wild Wave,* of 1,547 tons, bound for Valparaiso. After several months, when no news of her had come north in the fast coastal steamers, she was presumed to have foundered with all hands lost; but on September 29 the bay boatman who had rowed him off to his ship in February saw the missing skipper standing at the rail of the bark *Yankee,* just in from Honolulu. Describing their encounter, Knowles wrote in his diary, "He looked at me in perfect amazement and exclaimed, 'My God! is that you, Captain Knowles?' . . . This was a gala day to me, meeting, as I did, so many of my old friends." A letter from the east informed him that his daughter had been born at about the time he sailed out of knowledge, news that made him "wish above all things that there was an overland telegraph that I might at once communicate with my friends." Knowles had returned from a demonstration of exemplary seamanship and ingenuity in the art of survival. This is what happened.

In 1824 the master of the whaleship *Oeno* brought home to Nantucket news of an atoll south and east of the Tuamotus, where his chart showed only open ocean. A small dot was thereupon added to future charts of eastern Polynesia in 24 degrees 1 minute south, 130 degrees 37 minutes west and named Oeno Island. Although this looks like a typical transliteration of a cluster of separately pronounced Polynesian vowels, it comes from the Greek and may have been spelled on the whaler's stern with a diphthong: *Œno.* At the noontime beginning of nautical day March 5, 1858, Captain Knowles, close-hauled against the southeast trades, was still working his way southward from San Francisco to the latitude where he could get the westerlies astern to push him crosswise to Chile. Prevailing winds made two sides of a right-angled triangle a speedier course than a straightaway slant down the hypotenuse. He was nearer the 131st than the 130th meridian, and thus should have been passing Oeno on his port side at a prudent distance of 20 miles in the darkness. At midnight a cast of the log gave the speed of the *Wild Wave* as 13 knots. An hour later the lookout saw breakers under her starboard bow. Efforts to maneuver came too late. She struck hard on the reef and in five minutes her hold was full of water, while the combers dashed across her decks. In this fashion Captain Knowles gathered for future cartographers the information that the true longitude of Oeno is 130 degrees 54 minutes west.

Daylight revealed a protected lagoon beyond the reef, into which it proved possible to launch the ship's boats. All persons aboard—3 officers, 25 seamen, and 10 male passengers—were got ashore by nightfall with supplies that Knowles estimated as adequate for five months. He had feared a greeting by cannibals, but the atoll at this time was without Polynesian inhabitants. The captain, a Cape Cod schoolboy when *Typee* was published, probably had in mind the phrase "long pig." On the day following, the ship's livestock—sheep, pigs, fowl—was landed. Knowles found by observation that the atoll was "twenty miles out of the way, as laid down on my chart." He estimated that "Pitcairn's Island, lying about one hundred miles South," would be a likelier spot for a rescue because "whalers often touched there for supplies," furnished by descendants of the *Bounty* mutineers and their Tahitian wives. He decided to try for it in one of the ship's boats, but high surf prevented an offing until March 13. With him he "took several setting seabirds from their nests, intending to use them, on my arrival at Pitcairn's Island, as bearers of dispatches to my men left behind." Less than two days' sailing had brought Knowles, his mate, five seamen, and two boxes containing $18,000 in gold coin within sight of their objective when the wind became a gale and they were obliged to row the last 30 miles. At nightfall they had the usual difficulties in finding a possible landing place on the steep, harborless island and had to lie to, offshore, until daylight. "Having myself done but little manual labor for many years," Knowles wrote, "my hands were in such a condition that blood ran from my fingers' ends." On the fifteenth they got ashore and with difficulty climbed a steep mountain, only to find in the remains of a settlement some notices that the inhabitants—grown too numerous—had all been taken two years earlier to larger Norfolk Island, more than 3,000 miles to the west.

Knowles had left his second mate with instructions to follow him to Pitcairn's if not otherwise rescued within 30 days, and so advised him again by bird post. At the end of a week on the island, however, it seemed to him that he should have tried to reach Tahiti in the first place; but on March 24, when he went to the landing place to repair the boat and put to sea again, he discovered that a high surge of the surf had smashed it and washed the fragments away. After a few more days spent in trying to establish a reasonable social community for what might be a long exile, Knowles wrote on April 1, "We decided today to build a boat and sail for Tahiti, as we almost despaired of ever being found here." He had found a few discarded tools. For his first adventure in shipbuilding he chose the classic, all-purpose American model: a two-masted schooner. A sloop or lugger would have been simpler, but less handy.

The hull, with timbers and plank hand-hewn for want of a saw, took about five weeks to complete. In the meanwhile Knowles devised a ropewalk, had his men pick to shreds the fragments of cordage left in the settlement, and laid up nearly 300 feet of newly twisted rigging. He even made a respectable ensign "from the red hangings of the church pulpit, an old white shirt, and blue overalls." The schooner, when finished, measured 30 feet long, 8 feet wide, 4 feet deep. She was launched on July 23 and got to sea with the captain, the mate, and two of the five seamen. The other three preferred the hazards of remaining on Pitcairn's. Laying a course for Tahiti, distant about a thousand miles west-northwest, Knowles discovered that he had indeed got himself south into the westerlies when the wreck of the *Wild Wave* occurred. After head winds all night, he steered northward for the Marquesas instead, hoping to touch at Oeno, but was held downwind of it by relentless gales. Making more than a hundred miles a day, on August 3, the ninth day out, Knowles sighted the southernmost of the major islands, Tahuata. He called his landfall Ohitahoo, for Vaitahu Valley, where he spoke with "very savage and warlike" natives and declined their urgent invitation to come ashore.

At Melville's Nukuhiva, another hundred miles or so northwest, he found on August 4 the United States sloop of war *Vandalia* as well as a missionary who proved to be in the market for a schooner and was sufficiently impressed by the quality of

Knowles's first attempt at marine construction to pay him $250 for her. The old *Vandalia*—designed by Samuel Humphreys at Philadelphia in 1825—was the first American ship to visit the Marquesas in five years and had paused for only a two-day visit when Knowles arrived. To compound luck with coincidence, the ship's boat that met him contained a man who had sailed with him in the *Wild Wave* a year earlier. The *Vandalia* took him to her next intended port of call, Tahiti, then returned to pick up the castaways on Oeno and Pitcairn's. Knowles, with his boxes of gold, went in a French sloop of war to Honolulu, and thence to San Francisco in the *Yankee.*

During the Civil War he dodged Rebel raiders in the Boston ships *Expounder*, of 1,176 tons, and *Charger*, of 1,169 tons, the latter a Portsmouth-built medium clipper of technical interest because, remeasured under the Moorsom system, she gained 3 per cent in registered capacity when almost all the other medium clippers ended up with reduced registry figures.

On August 19, 1871, Knowles took his departure from Boston in McKay's last major vessel, the *Glory of the Seas*, then less than two years old. He brought her to a San Francisco berth 120 days later. His family had gone out by a shorter route to greet him in the city that was to be thereafter their residence on shore. His New Bedford second wife had made voyages with him in the *Charger*. She had others to look forward to in the *Glory of the Seas*. Her husband had deepened his commitment to the ship by buying a one-sixteenth share. He continued to command her in the grain races of the next several years, maintaining a fine average of speed in competition with such vessels as the extreme clipper *Young America* and the sharp ex-steamers *Ericsson* and *Three Brothers*, even though the *Glory of the Seas* was a solidly built transitional type. Often called a medium clipper, she was nearer in concept to the full-bodied down easters that emerged as a class eight or ten years after her launch. Beginning with Knowles himself, a series of excellent commanders helped her to attain high repute. She made no remarkable day's run or maximum speed. Even during her 95-day dash out to San Francisco in the winter of 1873–74—previously bettered only by eight more heavily sparred clippers and never since equaled—Knowles logged no single day's work of more than 300 miles; instead, hour by hour, he relentlessly kept her moving.

Two views of Donald McKay's shipyard at East Boston. The daguerreotype above was made in 1855, the launching year of the medium clippers *Zephyr* and *Defender*, either of which might be the one still incompletely framed. The photograph below was taken just before the launch of McKay's last large vessel, the *Glory of the Seas*, in 1869. Note the vestigial trail boards, which Griffiths had eliminated from his clippers more than 20 years earlier. (See pp. 196, 255ff., 461, 463–64.)

He was not always in such a hurry. Twice in the four and a half years when the ship was his family's home, Captain Knowles backed his main yards off Pitcairn's Island for visits with the group of former residents who had tired of Norfolk and had returned to the place of their birth. On February 20, 1873, he was met by women and children "inclosed in rather scanty wardrobe. . . . I took the hand of one buxom lass and sprang on the rocks dry-shod, and on the very rock which I built my boat on. . . . 'And is this really Captain Knowles?' I expect they would have kissed me if I had made an advance, but, you know, I am a diffident youth in the presence of ladies."

Another aspect of his diffidence emerges from the response he published when the master of the British ship *Langdale*, with which he had sailed in company from Liverpool, objected that her velocity had been insufficiently celebrated in the San Francisco papers. Knowles published this reply:

If it will satisfy the captain of the Langdale, *I will say that whenever I raised his ship, she was astern of the* Glory *but came up and passed her. When I got to San Francisco there was no* Langdale, *but as the passages of the ships were 131 and 132 days respectively, I think that is sufficiently long to prevent any discussion of the great speed of either.*

The captain's character concerns us because, when he swallowed the anchor in 1876, he began a second career that soon made him the central figure guiding San Francisco to pre-eminence as the primary whaling port of the world. On September 18 of that year he agreed to represent the Boston shipping firm of J. Henry Sears & Company, principal owners of the *Glory of the Seas,* as West Coast agent and as a general shipping and comission merchant. In the original arrangement, Sears was to pay the expenses of his office and the profits would be shared equally. Knowles's name is to be found thereafter in the shipping columns as consignee of cargoes from the western Pacific as well as from various North Atlantic ports. He operated in the fashion that flourished on all busy waterfronts until about 50 years ago, selling the cargoes of incoming ships and buying goods for those that were up for foreign ports, earning a commission in either case of 1 per cent, which distant shippers and purchasers were willing to pay to one who knew the state of the local market. Knowles also chartered ships for particular voyages, as for example, in 1877, his own former command the *Glory of the Seas,* in which he continued to hold an investment of a one-sixteenth share.

On the day when news arrived that Lewis's first steam whaler had put in at Drake's Bay, a few hours' sail northwest of the Golden Gate, Knowles was considering bids for the cargoes of two newly arrived ships consigned to him by merchants in Hong Kong. The *Alta California* of the day following took little notice of the arrival that was to revolutionize the activities not only of Knowles himself but of San Francisco as the ultimate focus of the Pacific whaling industry. Referring to the *Belvedere* it merely said that it was the "intention to put this vessel into the Honolulu trade for the winter." Lewis's sale of her instead to the government was another indication of the importance of having a trusted negotiator on the spot, to respond in an emergency. The impression given in another account—that Knowles switched jobs, leaving the employment of Lewis in 1883 for that of the Pacific Steam Whaling Company—fails to reflect the function of a commission merchant, whose success depended upon a reputation for independent probity. On one day he might be exacting the highest price for a commodity from the same firm in behalf of which he would be seeking the lowest price for a different commodity on the day following.

Consequently, when Knowles gave up the management of West Coast affairs for Lewis and others, to become general manager of the Pacific Steam Whaling Company and the Arctic Oil Works, he provided an early instance of an evolutionary shift in mercantile organization. The expert commission merchant, who would buy or sell to best advantage for any reputable client, was to be gradually replaced by buyers and salesmen who specialized in only one of these functions for a single employer. Since Knowles, unlike Lewis, had never been a whaling master himself, it seems clear that the flexibility of his competence in the management of a variety of vessels carrying many kinds of products was what impressed the partners who asked him to take charge of their unprecedented whaling enterprise, which quickly became known as the corporation.

Goodall, Perkins, Knowles, and a fourth associate—Millen Griffith, who controlled most of the tugboat business on the bay —began by simplifying the ancient complexities of maritime finance. Their Pacific Steam Whaling Company, with a capital of $2,000,000 for offshore operations and $1,000,000 more for its refinery, could afford to own its vessels outright. The intricate pattern of investment that survived into the Crowley-Lawson schooner trust was replaced by the holding of shares in one corporation, with an annual accounting of dividends regardless of the fortunes of particular vessels or voyages. Crowley's later but more primitive managerial organization, operating vessels for many distinct clusters of shareholders, was in a poor position to dictate that some vessels be tied up at a loss in order that others might command higher freights; but the San Francisco corporation could attune the frequency of sailings to expectations of the economy. Even in the generally prosperous days of Nantucket and New Bedford, profits had been made seriously uncertain by intermittent investors who on the heels of a good year would send out too many whalers, with overproduction and falling prices, or small catches for most, resulting. The San Francisco corporation was able to divert vessels to other uses in a period when the total market for whale products was steadily decreasing. The chief instance was the Alaskan gold rush, which coincided with a temporary slump in the market for bone. Several steam whalers then earned their keep as improvised passenger ships.

Steam was not a guarantee of safety. Twelve steam whalers, half of San Francisco's total count, were destroyed in the Arctic between 1881 and 1906. During that quarter century, three times as many sailing whalers were lost there, but the proportion of losses in the ice for both fleets was about the same. Their replacements differed. Between 1879 and 1904, vessels newly built or rebuilt as steam whalers numbered 24, while the old sailing whalers were simply being used up, or moored to rot in Oakland Creek. Lewis's *William Baylies*, a bark built in 1886, was an exception, and she too became a steamer. Once in a while a retired whaler was hove down and caulked for another try. For precedent there was the veteran bark *Coral*, which in 1875 at the age of 56 had brought into New Bedford 630 barrels of sperm, 1,320 of whale, and 12,000 pounds of bone—only to be condemned as unfit for her business. Cobbled together again and sent out to San Francisco, she began a notable twilight career by delivering in 1880, from her first voyage out of that port, 3,850 barrels of whale and 37,000 pounds of bone—a catch never equaled afterward by a sailing vessel and bettered by only a few steamers. She had been out three summer seasons. In 1882 she did almost as well in a single season, with 34,000 pounds of bone. She proved to have six more successful voyages in her before the 1889 entry of 1,200 whale and 13,000 bone was followed by the laconic "Withdrawn." She had been at sea for 70 years, as a ship until 1858, when she was converted to bark rig. In both home ports she was known as a lucky vessel—lucky in retirement too, when such veterans as the perhaps even older *Triton* are remembered, which were pushed into the ice for one last voyage too many. New Bedford still had in 1888 ten sailing whalers left to send out to the Pacific Arctic, with orders to return to San Francisco, before the older port settled in 1893 for fishing solely on the Atlantic side of the continent. These ten, however, were over-matched by subtraction in the same years of twenty San Francisco sailing whalers lost in the ice, or condemned, or withdrawn.

Lewis, its originator from afar, and Knowles, its central developer, were hardly challenged during the rise of San Francisco's steam whaling. James McKenna attained notice in 1881, both by reaching the whalers' farthest north so far, the seventy-fourth parallel, and by his comment that he "could have gone much farther, but it was coming on night, and his business was hunting whales, not glory." He made voyages in 1885 and 1886 as master and manager of the converted steamer *Alliance*, of 214 tons, and tried again a decade later in a converted Norwegian steamer, the *Fearless*, of about 400 gross tons, owned by San Franciscans but flying the Panamanian flag. On her third voyage in 1901 McKenna lost her at Dutch Harbor. Losses and replacements kept competition with the Pacific Steam Whaling Company's growing fleet at a token level. There were only three seasons when Lewis had as many as three steamers out fishing. Now and then he had only one. A few other competitors were briefly active. In 1892 Knowles sent all eight of his steamers north; Lewis, as usual, dispatched two. That year's interloper was the *Karluk*, converted for whaling by the meat packers Roth, Blum & Company.

A somewhat more meaningful challenge was presented by sailing whalers as they adjusted their operations to one-season voyages. The steamers were consistently more successful, but the sailers represented less than one-third of the investment hazarded in steamers of equivalent capacity. The Pacific Steam Whaling Company continued, until the middle nineties, to send out two sailing barks, the durable *Wanderer*, of 288 tons—destined long afterward to be the last square-rigger to go whaling in the Atlantic—and the *John and Winthrop*, of 321 tons. Lewis, by the middle eighties, had shifted all but two of his sailers to San Francisco. His modest brig *Alexander*, of 136 tons, tried Hudson Bay in 1886; when she brought him only 25 barrels of whale he sent her too around the Horn and sold her. That left him with only one schooner for a last Atlantic voyage. Her sale in 1889 marked the complete transfer of vessels he then owned or managed to the West Coast.

By testimony of two of his captains, Bodfish and George Fred Tilton, William Lewis was the exemplar of the close-fisted, calculating owners of nautical legend. Tilton, hero of a fabulous trek in midwinter from the north coast of Alaska to Kodiak Island to summon help for ships caught in the ice without adequate provisions, made the point in his memoirs that when he was settling accounts with the Lewis agency in San Francisco, the large differential between East Coast and West Coast prices always worked in his disfavor. The contrast between Lewis and Knowles in their manipulation of steam whalers is particularly revealing of a transition in commercial method. New Bedford was diversifying its endeavors in a fashion parallel to that of San Francisco: local manufacturing in the 1880's had become much more important than whaling. Lewis should have had no trouble in organizing a corporation similar to that managed by Knowles, but he balanced his innovations with a preference for the old, closely held, personal kind of supervision and kept his commitments to an appropriate size. In 1889, at the end of his operations in the adjacent ocean, he is listed in a New Bedford promotional document as a director of the Board of Trade, of which both he and his son Edgar R. Lewis were members. The father served also on the board's committee of three on "shipping interests." An account of him in the document credits him with having originated the idea of steam whaling. It describes with some particularity his latest steam whaler, the *William Lewis*, of 460 gross tons, her dimensions given as 145 by 30 by 16½. She was built entirely of live and white oak with a two-inch

A popular impression that the bazooka was a weapon first used in World War II is dispelled by the advertisement above from a Civil War newspaper of March 28, 1865. What appears to be a field of sawgrass or perhaps pineapples *(below)* is nothing of the sort. It is whalebone, drying at San Francisco. The steam whaler *Orca* is moored at the left. The whaling schooner *Amelia* of New Bedford, drawn by C. S. Raleigh for the United States Fish Commission *(upper right)*, was of the rig that antedated and outlasted New England's square-rigged whalers. (See pp. 470, 476–77.)

sheathing of hickory. Her stem was protected by heavy "composition plates." Her cabin, steerage, and fo'c's'le were steam heated. She was provided with two iron tanks between decks, each holding 100 barrels of oil received from the cooler, to be piped when convenient into casks below.

Lewis did buy two more sailers, in 1890 the ship *Horatio*, of 332 tons, and in 1891 the 49-year-old bark *California*, of 348 tons, but each sailed promptly for the North Pacific, to be based thereafter at San Francisco. The final dispatch of a Lewis whaler from New Bedford occurred on July 6, 1892, when the *Navarch*, of 254 tons, his seventh steamer, took her departure via Cape Horn.

Knowles sometimes would charter large sailing vessels to carry coal from Vancouver, the nearest efficient producing area, west-northwest two thousand miles to fuel the corporation's whalers at Dutch Harbor in the Aleutians. Bodfish tells in his memoirs of occasions when he went ashore near Port Clarence and Cape Parry in the Arctic to dig coal from surface veins. "We blasted it out with powder, sacked it up and boated it aboard." In 1892, the year when the old *Ericsson*, for want of her caloric engine, was blown ashore near the Vancouver coal chutes and wrecked, Knowles diverted another coal ship—his former command the *Glory of the Seas*—from her customary run down to San Pedro and sent her to Unalaska instead.

The development of coaling stations on the Bering Sea was a response to the cresting activity of San Francisco's formerly seasonal fleet. Knowles, in his quest for efficiency, sent two of his steam whalers north in 1890 with orders to winter in the Arctic on purpose. These were the *Grampus*, of 250 tons, built at San Francisco in 1886, and the *Mary D. Hume*, a small Oregon steamer of 108 tons, hastily refitted to participate in the rising market for whalebone. Bodfish, first mate in the latter, said, "It was planned to fill the ships with stores, and to do no whaling on the way north, which would have been impractical with the cargo we should have to carry. We were to take no oil, nothing but whalebone." A warehouse was to be built ashore and stocked to sustain the adventurers, who could then afford to extend the fishing season into the fall and would be ready to begin again several weeks ahead of the vessels that would have to hold off until the opening of Bering Strait. The *Grampus* returned at the end of her second summer above the Arctic Circle to deliver 30,000 pounds of bone, just as the market reached the highest average figure it was ever to attain: $5.38 a pound. The *Orca,* of 462 tons, which also had been built at San Francisco, and Lewis's *Belvedere* arrived a few days later. Their catches, 23,000 and 20,000 respectively, were even more impressive because they were the results of a single season's fishing.

It remained for the *Mary D. Hume*—which had spent ten years as an ocean freighter before being adapted as a brig-rigged steam whaler with davits for only three boats—to shatter all precedents. Knowles kept her in the north throughout a second winter. While she was away, Bodfish began to establish his repute as "the surgeon of the north," amputating a smashed toe of his own on the sudden decision that it would be better to do so while his foot was still numb than to wait for the captain to find time to do it. When the little whaler arrived at San Francisco on September 29, 1892, she carried what was by far the largest and most valuable catch to date—70,000 pounds of bone—for sale in a market that had fallen only three cents from the preceding year's all-time high. One of the smallest vessels ever to adventure into the fisheries farthest north, the *Mary D. Hume* was remarkable in other ways. Her second and last whaling voyage was probably the longest ever made, from April 13, 1893, to September 30, 1899. By this time shore facilities that even provided some social life in the dark months of winter had been established on the northern coasts of Alaska and of Canada's northwest territory. During her six years away from her home port, the *Mary D. Hume* spent most of her time frozen in, under the lee of ice-breaking islands in the boreal ports of refuge. Her original skipper was relieved midway by Captain William H. Hegarty, who had had the 77-year-old bark *Triton* go wearily to pieces under him in August of 1895 near Herschel Island. He seems to have had on his mind the loss in her of a sizable accumulation of bone; at any rate, he stayed out long enough to match exactly his new command's phenomenal performance on her only previous voyage. She again brought home 70,000 pounds of bone, an amount never equaled or surpassed by any other vessel except Bodfish's *Beluga,* which arrived five days later with 106,000 pounds taken in three seasons. Unlike Bodfish, Hegarty did not have to be excused by the press for lack of time "to spade out fat." Although the *Mary*

D. Hume had come home clean of oil on her first voyage, she carried 1,085 barrels of whale on her last one—all she could hold.

In 1894–95 the masters of 15 vessels with crews totaling 500 had set out to winter at Herschel Island. The chief reason for this practice was the observation, by whalers caught by the ice north of Alaska, that Eskimo hunters took many whales in stripes of dark water long before the ice-locked door of Bering Strait cracked open. Most of the whales had gone mysteriously elsewhere before the first whaleships arrived. To be ready at Herschel Island for the opening of rifts in the Arctic was the excuse for enduring a sometimes ferocious winter in ships with temporary houses built over them. Several captains' wives shared the experience. Its charms were not so evident to foremasthands. Some tried to trek southward and froze to death. Others mutinied. When three steamers were crushed in the ice in the winter of 1897–98, the lure of profit from "wintering over" dwindled. After three more were lost in the same manner in 1901–2 the practice was almost abandoned.

With the last transfer of a New Bedford sailing whaler to San Francisco, in 1892, the test of relative merit between steamers and sailers became straightforward. It has its clearest reflection in the operations of the Lewis fleet rather than in the lopsided concentration of engine-powered vessels in Knowles's contest against the field. Lewis evidently balanced higher returns from the more costly kind of vessel against the modest earnings of his barks. In the late 1880's he sent out six or seven barks each season to supplement his pair of steamers. In the middle nineties the two types in his fleet briefly evened up. This resulted in part from his significant decision at the end of the 1893 season to subtract one sailer and add one steamer by installing an engine in his strongest bark, the relatively new *William Baylies*. He had had her built in 1886 when seasonal voyages out of San Francisco seemed to offer a renewal of hope for the classical sailing whaler.

The changes in the Lewis fleet reflected those of the entire enterprise. Shortly before corsets brought West Coast whaling to its profitable zenith, three or four times as many sailing whalers as steamers cleared for a summer season in the north. In 1889–90 the count was 40 and 10. Five years later it was 11 sailers and 7 steamers. At the turn of the century it was 7 of each.

With a little annual seesawing, this even division between sailers and steamers was maintained as owners attempted to match the size of the San Francisco fleet to the dwindling of demand for its products until, in 1914, no whaler of any sort put to sea through the Golden Gate.

In these uncertain years the management altered. The Pacific Steam Whaling Company in 1896 lost its particular guiding genius. Knowles at the beginning of that year's summer season departed in the tender *Jeanie* for a tour of inspection of the corporation's floating salmon canneries in the north. A cold that he had taken to sea with him developed into pneumonia. The steamer put back, but on the morning of June 9 he died suddenly, at home. The cause given was the same as in the case of Pook: apoplexy. The corporation might have continued successfully with further diversification in the salmon fishery, in colliers, and in other nautical enterprises, but when Knowles died at the age of 66, whaling out of San Francisco had already entered a decline from which no-one could have saved it because its problems centered inland.

George Fred Tilton got his first command in 1903, when the captain of the ship in which he was serving as first mate— Lewis's *Belvedere*—died at sea. "But when I got to Frisco," Tilton wrote, without revealing any sorrow, "I found that Old Man Lewis was dead and his son Edgar was running the business." The younger Lewis confirmed Tilton in command for another voyage. There is a comparative interest in his comment at the end of it: "We got nine whales, which gave us a good voyage." His catch is listed as 200 barrels of whale oil and 2,000 pounds of bone. Five years earlier, Bodfish had brought home the all-time record cargo of no oil and 106,000 pounds of bone, having killed exactly seven times as many whales to do so. Luck seesawed even for him. In 1905, in the *William Baylies*, Bodfish got 35,000 pounds of bone, but in the year following the best he could manage was 3,000.

Edgar Lewis continued to send out the veteran bark *California* and one or two steamers, but when Bodfish lost him the *William Baylies* off Siberia in 1908, he wound up his affairs and transferred the *Belvedere* to another San Francisco owner. After a vacation, she was one of four steamers that joined two barks and a schooner to constitute the fleet of 1911. The steamers brought home a remarkable average catch of nearly 28,000 pounds of bone—but into a market that within a year or two had plunged from $3.75 a pound to 21 cents. The *Belvedere,* by staying out an extra season, fared even worse than the others. When she arrived in the fall of 1912, bone was worth 7½ cents. Why she was tried again, a few months later, is hard to understand. Up until this point she had always been registered at her original home port, New Bedford. When she completed her 1913–14 voyage at Seattle, her registry was shifted to that port, where she was made into a motorship rigged as a schooner. Her occupation for the rest of her days was described as "whaling and trading."

After the blank year 1914, one member of the whaling fleet returned to her task: the steamer *Herman,* of 229 tons. Built at Bath in 1884 as the *Morning Star,* of 290 tons, she had made under that name a first whaling-trading voyage in 1903, returning with a substantial cargo of furs and whalebone. During the following winter her owners, H. Liebes & Company, furriers, refitted her more adequately to operate in the ice. Renamed, she made 15 more voyages out of San Francisco, including the last four sailed by Bodfish. Her ambivalent use both as fur trader and as whaler explains her active survival during the five bleak years from 1915 to 1919, when she alone constituted San Francisco's entire whaling fleet. In those years she did have for intermittent companionship the Seattle-based *Belvedere,* but at age 39 that longest-lived of the Pacific steam whaler fleet met the fate she was designed to avoid and was crushed in a Siberian ice pack.

WHALING IN THE TWENTIETH CENTURY

While classical barks and transitional steamers intensified a witless slaughter of bowheads in the Pacific Arctic, wholly canvas-powered fleets in the Atlantic were operating at a rate that permitted sperm whales to increase their numbers somewhat. This, with the skittishness of the prey off Alaska, persuaded New Bedford owners to recall into their first ocean some barks that had been based for a time at San Francisco. The price of sperm, which by old rule of thumb should be double that of whale oil, had fallen in 1896 almost to parity with it. Improved technology in the applications of illuminating gas, particularly the incandescent Welsbach mantle, had greatly diminished the luxury market for spermaceti and other fine candles. A few years later, with the improvement of lubricants made from ground oil, a major market for whale oil in the bearings of heavy industry similarly collapsed. Whale oil then dropped to about two-thirds the value of sperm, a ratio that persisted with little fluctuation until after the First World War. During this period of about two decades, although the total market for whale products continued to shrink, the Atlantic sperm fishery was relatively the more important again.

There had been a hiatus of about six years, commencing at the height of San Francisco's whaling activity, between the sailing from New Bedford of her last bark that carried orders to stay in the Pacific and the arrival in New England of the first one to be shifted back to the Atlantic side. This was the *Josephine*, of 365 tons. Since 1881 she had been carrying all her catches, mostly of whale, into San Francisco, but in 1897 she entered Boston harbor with nothing but sperm aboard. On February 19, 1903, the *Wanderer* cleared for a cruise from the Golden Gate with orders to proceed to her first home. John P. Knowles of New Bedford had committed her to the care of Josiah N. Knowles in 1883. During her 20 years of hunting out of San Francisco she had taken not a barrel of sperm. The 620 barrels that she discharged at her New Bedford wharf upon her arrival on September 4, 1904, an indifferent catch, were all sperm.

The old whaling port, which had tried to turn San Francisco into a colony and had created instead a dominant competitor, continued to recall its own. In 1904 the *Charles W. Morgan*, then in 1906 the *Alice Knowles* and the *Andrew Hicks*, followed the track of the *Wanderer* back to New Bedford. These transferences, together with heavy losses in the Arctic and the settling of many antiquated sailers into the Oakland mud, narrowed San Francisco's lead in the number of vessels cleared annually for whaling voyages. If we ignore the year of the great earthquake and fire, which disorganized everything, it was between the sailings of 1908 and 1909 that primacy returned to the East Coast city. During the two years of American involvement in World War I, a period of abnormal scarcities and demands, the price of whale oil whizzed from eight or nine cents to 75 cents, while sperm rose from 32 cents to almost a dollar. New Bedford responded with 29 wartime sailings, but San Francisco had lost interest. Her lonely *Herman* went out twice.

Except for a single cruise to the Indian Ocean in 1905, whalers out of New England's ports did their fishing after 1891 entirely on the Atlantic side. With most of her finest barks on the West Coast, New Bedford had kept a few for the small mixed fleet she continued to employ in nearer waters. In 1905 she cleared only square-riggers, five of them; in 1908 eight schooners comprised her entire departing fleet. Despite Lewis's steam auxiliaries, which made their maiden voyages out of New Bedford, never to return, and one steamer sent directly from Bath, where she was built to join the fleet of Knowles's corporation, the New England ports put only sailing whalers to their own uses up to the very end. San Francisco sent out a scattering of modest sailers in the early twenties, but her last notable whalers were motorships. Brief notes on both sorts are included in Appendix C. Sailings were so few from either coast in the postwar decade that a pressing of comparisons becomes silly. No-one knew in 1928 that the last whaling voyage of the motorship *Patterson* concluded the American phase of an ancient deep-water enterprise. In the annual *List of Merchant Vessels of the United States* the *Patterson* was identified as a whaler throughout another decade, as if to keep open the possibility that the traditional far-ranging fishery might again be revived. Then she receded into the vast anonymity of the designation "ocean freight carrier." After 1928 the freight carried by American vessels registered as whalers was oil from whales caught by Alaskan and Californian shore-based hunters or by the harpooners in vessels of another nationality.

In the 15 closing years of San Francisco's whaling era, all her whalers were vessels originally built for other uses. New Bedford's last two were appropriately representative of classical types. Her final working square-rigger was the *Wanderer*, launched at neighboring Mattapoisett in 1878. Except for her appearances in the film *Down to the Sea in Ships*, she served throughout her 46 years as a whaling bark exclusively. On August 25, 1924, she began her twenty-third voyage. When she dropped her hook near Cuttyhunk to pick up some foremast-hands, a hurricane was twisting northeastward off Hatteras. One liner that brought a load of damaged passengers into New York reported being swept by 100-foot waves. The great whirl of wind reached the chops of Buzzard's Bay in time to convert a prudent anchorage suddenly into a lee shore. The *Wanderer* dragged and struck, and was beyond saving.

New Bedford's last working whaler of any sort, the *John R. Manta*, a 98-ton schooner built at Essex in 1904, was a nearer reflection of pre-Revolutionary origins of her art. In that year she made the first of her seven whaling voyages out of Provincetown. In 1922, after she had been transferred to New Bedford, she was the base for actual harpooning scenes in the same picture that starred the *Wanderer*. The *John R. Manta's* eighteenth whaling voyage, in the summer of 1925, was the last to be successfully completed out of a New England port. Her two boats' crews, which had taken 15 small whales apiece, may not have had the same sense of accomplishment as her owners. The men, signed on under the ancient lay system, got an average of $30 apiece when earnings were calculated, but all had larger amounts charged against them for slop chest items. In deference to New Bedford custom, each received anyhow a fine five dollar bill for three months' labor. At San Francisco, where prices were lower, the equivalent magnanimity was known as the iron dollar.

After a year's vacation, the *John R. Manta* was patched up for one more try. She got to sea on June 22, 1927, but a hard blow chewed most of her aged sails to shreds and opened her seams. She drifted back into port again on July 14—and that was the end of New England's vast adventure in search of leviathan.

It was not the end of whaling far from home. A different sort of venture had taken shape in 1905 when the Norwegians rebuilt their *Admiralen* to be moored as a factory ship in a harbor of South Georgia, not far from the Antarctic Circle. Smaller steam-powered hunters fished the surrounding waters and towed their catches to the processing vessel. Shore stations, mostly in the northern Pacific region, continued to boil out a little oil from local catches. The Eskimos as always killed whales for their own uses—but the once great northern enterprises diminished as those to the southward grew. It was an informal collaboration between Norway and Great Britain that produced the final logical extension of Nantucket's concept: the self-sufficient, far-wandering hamlet afloat—the combination of hunter, processor, freighter, and dwelling place. This time, however, the resulting creation was somewhat nearer to a mobile industrial town. The first example was the Brocklebank liner *Mahronda*, built in 1905 and converted into a floating factory of 4,921 tons in time to head southward in 1923, registered as the *Sir James Clark Ross,* the first of that name. The old practice of carrying 28-foot whaleboats on davits was supplanted by a fleet of self-powered hunting vessels developed from those that had dragged their kill into harbor to be processed in an anchored ship. The trouble with that earlier arrangement had been the quick reduction, by efficient steam hunters, of the whale population within feasible towing distance of South Georgia. The *Sir James Clark Ross* could follow her hunters anywhere. These small steamers actually had about the same measurements as those of classical sailing whalers, typical examples being registered at 250 to 400 tons. They were equipped with cannon that made the old heroic approach within touching distance of the prey unnecessary, and they fired special harpoons with explosive heads. Some eventually were equipped with missiles that dragged wire-cored lines through which the whales could be killed by high voltage, but these were never perfected to the point of popularity with the harpooner-commanders of the hunting vessels. Smaller bombs to kill whales had been in use for more than a century, preferred by some mates, disliked by others. Bodfish's penny-scouring owners once supplied him with cheap ones that sometimes failed to explode or did so too soon, blowing the gun to bits.

Hunters in the Antarctic adapted two practices of the North American aborigines. The last great reserve of whales still existed there because they were "sinkers," which could not be saved if killed from cedar boats. The new pelagic whalers consequently kept them afloat after death by injecting air into the body cavities and by plugging the vents: practices akin to the use of inflated walrus hides in Bering Strait and blowhole plugs off Florida. The small hunting vessels either towed their taken whales back to the factory ship or left them to be gathered up by a specializing ocean tug. The first *Sir James Clark Ross* cut up her whales alongside, into pieces that could be handled on deck, but the next floating factory, the rebuilt liner *Flackwell,* of 7,866 tons, was equipped with a slipway through which the whales could be hauled aboard whole and subjected to a seagoing production-line procedure.

The shift of the whaling industry toward Antarctica appears in the fact that the first free-sailing factory ship measured seven

times the combined capacity of all four of the surviving United
States whalers still operating out of San Francisco and New
Bedford. Yet this original *Sir James Clark Ross* was only a primitive forerunner of a fleet that soon numbered 41, almost all with
slipways and some much larger than she was. The average size
of the floating factory whalers was something like 12,000 net
tons. At the height of the business they were accompanied by
eight or nine hunters apiece—each as large as a classical whaler.
These had no space for barrels or trypots. Instead they had powerful steam engines to drive them quietly in pursuit of a sounding
and reappearing whale, at its own pace, which generally was
much faster than a cedar boat could be sailed or rowed. When
it was necessary they could tow half a dozen whales back to the
mother ship, three at each side.

The earlier floating factories were reconstructed liners that
had been superseded in the booming tourist traffic of the twenties. Beginning in 1930, the southern fleet was joined by many
newly built vessels, designed with slipways between starboard
and port funnels and otherwise constructed for their special
function—responses to a brisk European demand for whale oil
that followed the development of chemical processes for its
conversion into margarine. The new vessels carried few sailors
by comparison with the number of steamfitters, electricians,
chemists, machine operators, and expert butchers—often more
than 400 persons to form an intricately organized social group.
The vessels had a variety of steam digesters operating at different
temperatures, with centrifuges and other subtle mechanisms to
derive such products as vitamins and hormones from parts of the
whale that formerly had been wasted. The notable saving, however, was in the almost complete elimination of low-grade oils.
The average carcass was fully processed on the day it was killed.
Other aspects of the new efficiency were the provision, first of
seaplanes, then of helicopters, finally of radar, to locate and
follow the prey, which from the air were usually visible under
water. The hunting vessels, having inflated and flagged a whale,
were able after World War II to attach to the flagstaff an elec-
tronic beacon, which made its recovery certain even in the dense,
high-latitude fogs. They could hunt for many hours in the long
daylight of southern summer and return to gather up the catch

at their convenience, or leave the task to a following tug attuned to beacons spiked into the carcasses.

Prior references to the end of United States whaling, except from a few shore stations, may have seemed to suggest that Americans took no part at all in the developing Antarctic fishery. It is literally true that the foremost whaling nation of the nineteenth century made no creative contribution to the new technology of pelagic whaling from factory ships—true also that it has left the actual whale hunt in Antarctica entirely to other countries. There was, however, a dubious American involvement with factory ships that has made it proper, in a book so much concerned with the nature of whaling vessels and craft, to give some attention in conclusion to these vessels, their way of operating, and the result.

The decline of whaling in the United States was closely related to the general stagnation of the American merchant marine, brought about chiefly by protective legislation that forbade United States registry of foreign-built vessels and assured comparatively high salaries to American seamen. The mixture of merits and flaws in such a policy invites differing evaluations, but it should be noted again that the business of whaling could not be brought back to prosperity by decisions taken in New Bedford or San Francisco because its problems centered inland. As southern pelagic whaling attained a new importance in the latter 1920's, the failure of United States shipowners to participate was related to mounting surpluses of agricultural products. When a devastating depression struck at the end of the decade, vegetable oils were so abundantly available that American capital was not lured toward a competitive material for the making of margarine. The dairy lobby, furthermore, kept legal obstacles in the way of any cheaper substitute for butter.

It was just as well. The rapid production of still larger factory ships resulted in such an assault upon the whales in the 1930–31 season that prices plummeted. Sailings for the next season were drastically curtailed and world production was only one-quarter that of the extravagant preceding year, which, as it has turned out, was the all-time peak for world production of whale oil. The idea that New England, in the 1840's and 1850's, had brought whaling to its quantitative apex slumps under examination.

The earlier statistics—usually given in barrels or tuns—represent uncertain amounts at different times and in different countries, but rough equivalents suggest a maximum of 10,000 tons a year for the great days of the Dutch fishery in the seventeenth century, with considerably smaller yields the rule until New England, just before the American Revolution, began to bring in about 7,000 or 8,000 tons annually of sperm alone to add to the Greenland product. The British southern fishery, in the middle 1830's, was producing about 12,000 or 13,000 tons of sperm, an amount that declined rapidly as the Nantucketers and New Bedford men almost usurped the business in the forties and fifties, when they brought home 40,000 tons a year. It is therefore unlikely that in the heyday of the classical whaler, recorded and unrecorded catches ever represented a world total of much more than 50,000 tons a year. In the middle of the nineteenth century Americans produced about three-quarters of the world's whale oil, primarily because Quaker frugality had shown the way to a higher operating efficiency in long voyages than could be achieved under traditional maritime practices. The British fishery diminished chiefly as a result of the adding of unnecessary costs to keep aristocracy going.

Norway's intensive entry into the southern fishery was aided by national traits akin to the old Quaker frugality. Shore whaling off the fjords, moreover, had been made difficult—as it once had been for the messy New Englanders off Newfoundland—by regulations in the interest of shore dwellers and of the fishermen, who insisted (maybe they were right) that there was a positive relationship between the presence of whales and the abundance of smaller marine creatures. A shift toward the Antarctic, facilitated by Scottish builders and City of London investors, consequently began. When assessing the new pelagic whaling methods, there is no need to be parsimonious in estimating nineteenth-century production figures, which simply fade out of range. The precisely accounted-for world production in 1930–31 was 614,496 tons of oil, somewhere in the order of ten times the maximum for the best nineteenth-century year. This did not mean anything like so large a proportionate slaughter of whales because nearly all that were struck with explosive weapons were taken and because efficient use of the whole carcass rendered a great deal more oil than the old practice of blanket stripping.

The maximum kill of whales annually, at the peak of production in the last century, probably was 20,000. The actual highest total of whales killed in any year of record was a little under 55,000—in 1937–38. At that time unchecked competition was threatening the once-abundant blue whales with the near extinction already visited upon more vulnerable varieties elsewhere. Except for the summer of 1931–32, when world production dropped to 152,640 tons, the Antarctic fishery alone produced throughout the 1930's more than 400,000 tons annually, a yield that continued through the first season of the Second World War. Then, as in prior conflicts, man gave the whales a respite while he turned his ferocity upon his own kind.

The reason for saying that America played no creative part in developing the Antarctic whaling industry will appear more from the nature than from the extent of United States involvement. A vessel variously traceable as the *Golaa,* the *Frango,* the *Clifford,* and the *Hakko Maru,* measuring 4,547 tons, built at Chester, Pennsylvania, in 1917, was sold to Norway when the war was over. She was fitted to carry petroleum in cylindrical tanks, and consequently was not too difficult to convert into a factory ship. The American Whaling Company of New York repurchased her about a decade later for use in the Indian and Antarctic oceans, under United States registry. However, to circumvent laws that had been devised to protect the American shipbuilding industry as well as the wages of seamen, she was accompanied by three foreign-built, foreign-manned killer vessels flying Panamanian colors. Thus the *Frango,* 80 per cent owned by a United States corporation, acted as processing plant and freighter of whales caught under the authority of a different country.

The *Ulysses,* of 6,801 tons, another petroleum tanker converted into a factory ship in 1937, was similarly employed by the Western Operating Company of New York. Her seven hunters, named *Kos I, Kos IV, Kos V, Kos VI, Kos VII, Kos IX,* and *Kos XIV,* all were Norwegian. Under this arrangement, everything produced could be entered duty-free at United States ports. Noticing particularly that foreign stockholders controlled the Western Operating Company, Congress bunged up the loophole with a provision of the Revenue Act of 1938, requiring that duty-free whale products must be derived from animals "taken and captured by vessels of the United States." Both of the improvised American factory ships consequently reverted to the carrying of petroleum. The involvement of United States owners in the most productive of whaling eras was belated, minor, incomplete in nature, and concerned with innovation only through the devising of an international formula for tax evasion.

Should we be mortified or relieved over such a sleazy end to our country's once undisputed leadership in an enterprise no longer heroic? The question invites an attempt in conclusion to summarize the qualities by which any vessel's success may fairly be judged. Speed, size, capacity, have merit only in relation to the task; these and other narrow factors are elements in the composite test of a vessel's durable rightness within all the surrounding circumstances of its intended use. A changing economy, as in the case of the clippers, may cancel the outstanding virtue of a particular design for which too much else has been sacrificed. But what if the physical surroundings for which a marine structure has been explicitly devised are changed in a drastic measure by the operation of the vessel itself?

When overproduction in the 1930–31 season got the old-fashioned rebuke of a ruinous slide in oil prices, attempts were made to limit the size of the combined annual catches of participating countries with a sort of unacknowledged cartel. Basic long-range considerations were publicized, but immediate profit appears to have been the compelling object. Even so, the neediest participants were those whose economies had been starved for fats. Japan resisted all restraints, but pioneering Norway passed in 1929 a stringent law of her own that prohibited the taking of calves, of cows with sucking calves, and of any right whales.

One difficulty was that it took a Norwegian to make such judgments during the chase. Norway had expertly succeeded to a function that Nantucketers had taken over from the Basques: she had become supplier of whaling skills to the world and had trained up an abundance of harpooner-commanders for the relatively quiet, free-questing hunter steamers by which the whaleboats of James Beetle had at last been superseded. Norwegians commanded the ten hunters that supplied two United States floating factories. They served the other participating countries without subterfuge. Until the middle 1930's they commanded nearly all of the several hundred killer steamers and supplied

a preponderance of crewmen for the entire pelagic whaling enterprise. Echoing the great years of small Nantucket, the northern
country farthest from the southern ice still had enough skilled
men left over to operate her own dominant fleet, which, for the
1938–39 season, consisted of 14 floating factories. The British
then had 13. Six other countries lifted the world total at that
time to 44, of which 39 had built-in slipways. The active killer
steamers numbered more than 400.

Between casualties and conversions, only nine floating factories survived the war in usable condition. When these went
back to work it quickly became evident that the long respite
during hostilities had not brought the ravaged herds up to normal again. With less than half the number of hunters competing,
the average catch by each was only three-quarters of what it had
been ten years earlier. The whales were smaller. The most dis-
quieting evidence implied that the reproductive process had been
somehow upset: there was a much reduced proportion of preg-
nant females in the kill. An editorial in the *Spectator* of London
suggested in 1947 that the dumping of oil sludge and spent processing chemicals might have affected the health, not only of
the whales, but even more importantly of the underwater clouds
of tiny shrimp upon which the whales, after the long starvation
of mating, came south to feed. Factory whaling was not only
responsible for excessive direct slaughter of whales that could
no longer outdistance their pursuers; it seemed to be upsetting
the normal biological restoration of the herds by poisoning the
ocean with industrial wastes never emitted by the old sailing
whalers.

An international convention in 1946 at last had found the
formula for securing general if not total compliance in measures
to restrict the fishery: a system of "blue whale units" authorizing
substitutions in each nation's account, such as six sei whales
for one blue. But at the same time new radar-equipped factory
ships were being built to replace the war losses. The 16,000-unit
limit for a seven-month season proved too high. By 1965 it had
been worked down to 4,500, still not low enough. At that point
Japanese participation was accounting for about 40 per cent of
the world's whale oil production. If this seems disproportionate,
the Japanese had in memory the period about a century earlier
when scores of barks from New England had almost eliminated

the whales that for ages had been caught by shore-based craft of Japan. The reversal was dramatic. The United States share in the world's whale oil production, all from shore stations, stood in 1965 at less than one-half of 1 per cent, and for many years had not been higher than that figure.

In 1968 biologists who regularly accompanied the other specialists in factory ships announced that by their estimates the entire Antarctic population of blue whales, once in the vicinity of 100,000, had fallen to no more than 600. The number of floating factories was down to eight. Norway, creator of the modern fishery, trainer of harpooner-commanders, announced her withdrawal from the contest.

In the fall of 1970, Walter Hickel, suddenly jettisoned as United States Secretary of the Interior for the political sin of having learned a great deal that he did not know when he took the job, decreed in celebration of his departure a complete embargo upon whale products. The southern season was about to begin. Hickel's was a sharp warning that the United States stood with Norway in refusing at last to assist in the hunting to death of a desperately endangered species. The dullest cattleman, in the Kirghiz Soviet Republic or in Texas, has the wit to maintain an optimum productive herd; but on the high seas, technology has provided disorganized international man—at a time of widespread and desperate need for fats—with a marvelous device for the elimination from his planet of a major source of fats.

Man, the remorseful predator, the beast that grieves, has done this in the worst of ways. The floating factory whaler is a secretive extrusion, working with such efficiency in the loneliest waters that its very existence—when called to notice by Hickel's embargo—was a surprise to an American public that at least had heard of *Moby Dick* as a book someday, proudly, to be read. Shall we then regret that the most technological of nations developed no superb innovation of its own for this ultimate kind of whale hunt?—that our lawmakers for once had the sense, even if for the wrong reasons, to prevent our doing what we so cleverly could have done? Wait and see. My guess is that the factory whaler will end up along with other lunacies of a glib technology uncontrolled by humanistic purpose that has devastated our ethically primitive century.

Many professional whalers have expressed personal remorse

and grief over their own activities, but a sense of wider social concern is at least a century old. The *Alta California*, on November 4, 1882, in greeting some steam whaleboats that recently had arrived by transcontinental rail to be tried out by Knowles's *Bowhead* and *Orca*, foresaw "a melancholy outlook for the poor whale, every year they have more and more to contend with, and it would not be astonishing if they soon gave up 'blowing' altogether." For a more emphatic recent example, here is the apologia of W. D. R. McLaughlin, who identifies himself as "senior deck executive officer of a modern whale factory ship."

> . . . in the battle of man versus whale, man's part is not worthy of his superior intelligence. . . . commercial interests . . . in a race for profits have wantonly over-exploited the rich resources of Antarctica for many years. . . . No whaling man is made so callous . . . that he cannot spare a pang of pity or remorse for his prey, the whale.
>   The death of this defenseless mammal in all its horror is, in fact, a load on the minds of many whaling men. . . . Man is a killer, but a killer with a conscience. . . . This is why I tell, not only of the thrill of the chase, the wild excitement of the kill, but also the grim facts of the whale's fight for life and his inevitable, cruel death.
>   . . . there is no longer any comparison between Melville's highly imaginative saga of Moby Dick in the eighteen-fifties and the scientific slaughter of whales in the nineteen-sixties. . . . It is a sordid hunt. The whale becomes the helpless victim of the floating abattoir. . . .
>   There is no doubt that the animal suffers. How few people realize the cruelty, the brutality, that is involved in chasing, harpooning, and killing the whale. How few people realize the despairing fight it puts up before dying of convulsions with an explosive shrapnel grenade tearing at its vitals. It has to be seen to be believed.

McLaughlin, whose book *Call to the South* (1962) is prefaced as "a plea by a whaling man who has spent many seasons in Antarctica for action to save the whale before it is too late," disposes of the soothing notion that the grenade-tipped harpoon kills quickly to save the whale from the long, slow anguish witnessed in many accounts of old-style whaling. He says that "the first harpoon rarely kills. Two, three, up to six harpoons have to be used before some animals die." Bodfish described a difficult contest when he was serving as third mate in Lewis's *Lucre-*

tia: "I used up all the bombs from my gun without any effect and finally killed him with the darting-gun."

Is there a relationship between man's hardness of heart, in pressing for brief advantages, and the long view of his own welfare? I think so, and that the problem applies in all his activities, as in the shaping of ships to serve that welfare.

THE ULTIMATE WHALER

Can one kind of vessel be singled out in which shipbuilders of the American hemisphere, taking into account the surroundings and conditions of its use, have solved the complex puzzles of design better than in any other? The kayak, perhaps? The schooner? The clipper? The submarine? The first of these, which may have fulfilled its exacting function longer than any other distinctive American vessel, was so limited in useful range that its superb qualities are not comparative. The fishing schooner had a wider range, but it never attained general dominance over other watercraft put to the same uses alongside it by other countries. Either as fishermen or as freighters, small-to-middling schooners could cope with all weathers everywhere, but lacked carrying capacity to dominate any competitive distant trade, while schooners large enough to do so were dangerous failures in long voyages. The Yankee clipper, crafted to its ultimate shape with unparalleled swiftness within the customarily slow progression of marine developments, had as short a period of successful fulfillment of a task in which it so suddenly attained world dominance. It was a superb answer to transient, distorted conditions. The submarine, although its basic problems were solved by Americans, was first perfected and put to wide use by Europeans.

The case for the whaler is muddled by the variety, from first to last, of vessels hastily adapted from other employments. At times it has seemed that almost anything would do if it could carry a boat or two within sight of a whale's spout and bring home some oil, but this was true only when the chase did not have to be conducted in remote waters. After 1789, when two ships of 172 and 200 tons headed across the Nantucket bar for dubious Woolwich Bay—some 8,000 sailing miles southeastward—a reliable, specializing vessel began to emerge. The last steam whalers built at Bath a hundred years later were closely related in size, form, and rig, as well as in structural materials, to the sailing whaleship perfected by Nantucket early in the nineteenth century. Amid all the fortuitous whalers—preceding the mechanical monsters that still put in at Woolwich, or Walvis, Bay—a purposeful, classical whaleship can be identified. A good example, fortunately, is the *Charles W. Morgan,* built at New Bedford in 1841 under the eyes of innumerable experienced whalemen and still visible to the curious at Mystic Seaport in Connecticut. Perhaps the best, somewhat more fully developed type is symbolized by the *James Arnold,* of 346 tons, also built at New Bedford, eleven years later, as the clipper ship era was lifting toward its crest.

The *James Arnold* and a few of her contemporaries, designed in an age of high confidence, in the early 1850's, expressed the full experience of a tremendous thrust of energy and imagination that engaged two New England towns in a single, world-ranging purpose. Many fine and long-lived whalers had begun life earlier as packet ships. The design of the *James Arnold* undoubtedly profited from experience with those remarkable compromises between ruggedness and speed. The notion that whalers were made bluff and broad bottomed, when built on purpose as such, is refuted by the dimensions of these two and others built at about the same time. They were identical in depth: 17 feet 6 inches. The *James Arnold,* with a breadth of 27 feet 6 inches, was one inch the narrower; but at 115 feet 2 inches she was about 10 feet longer than the *Charles W. Morgan.* Having slightly the smaller capacity, by five tons, the later and longer vessel must have been substantially the sharper in her lines. Their length-to-breadth ratios, 3.8 to 1 and 4.2 to 1, reflect closely the narrowing of packet ships over the same decade. It was not until midway in the 1840's, with the famous early clippers, that this ratio for deep-water sailing ships occasionally rose to 5 to 1. The designer of a whaling bark at midcentury had three- or four-year voyages in mind, but this was not an excuse for capacity at the expense of speed. It was rather a spur to produce a vessel that would waste no time coming and going through fished-out waters.

When New Bedford's last square-rigger went aground in 1924 the *James Arnold* was still a working whaler. Transferred belatedly to San Francisco in 1891, she had been sold to Chile

four years later. The excellence of her original design and construction was demonstrated by her persistence at her specific
task through more than seven decades of good and bad fortune
under two flags. Technicians of 1852 could have made her much
larger—it was the year of McKay's *Sovereign of the Seas* with
seven times her tonnage—but her dimensions reflect a calculated
choice of the optimum size for a purpose that we seem to have
lost the knack for attaining amid our teeming numbers and
our condoning of vast dimensions—as if size had a merit in itself. Judged for its negative aspect, the New England whaleship
was also a "floating abattoir," functioning at a low level of efficiency—but efficient enough, even so, to alter persistently over
an ever-widening range the oceanic environment in which it
had been designed to operate. Its own normal activity consequently made the successful original aspects of its design more
and more obsolescent. The old loitering through many possible
whaling grounds—a factor to be taken into account in designing
and equipping a ship—became uneconomic. As profitable
grounds were erased, the need to get from one to another as
rapidly as possible was obvious. If the fishing was poor off the
west coast of South America, a try at the Sea of Okhotsk might
seem a hopeful alternative, but there were ten thousand miles
to sail in order even to find out.

The square-rigged whalers, mostly barks, were either a little
too numerous, or not quite inefficient enough, in the middle
of the nineteenth century. One control or the other could have
maintained a relationship between men and whales to the merely
physical advantage of both mammals, but the statesmen since
then have proved incompetent and the shipbuilders too clever
by far. Is this to say that we should return on purpose, if the
whales survive, to the more wasteful but more valiant methods
of an earlier time, seeking danger and inefficiency on purpose
to rebuke a false cleverness that has outdone itself? No. The
task is to employ man's innovative faculties to his advantage
rather than to his ruin, which would follow quickly upon the
ruin of oceans that are not his. The latest technological possibility was never necessarily the best; that point is made with
melancholy emphasis by the evolution of the slightly too efficient
sailing whaler into the fully mechanized floating factory. Man's
great achievements are those that fit the hand and delight the

eye, rather than the huge extensions that thrust too many human
beings aside with nothing left for their hands to do. It becomes
clear as we look backward upon a preposterous era of overex-
ploitation that a very few factory whalers, prudently used, could
have supplied man with all of the whales that it was to his physical advantage to put to death. And the question arises, is such a
vessel, of which so few can be prudently used at all, in any sense
a triumph of the nautical arts? The problem extends far beyond
the possibility of controlling the impulse to mechanize. The
remoteness of the factory whaler at work, beyond the average
person's realization that it exists, is its most sinister aspect.
Hardly anyone has been aware of it while it so efficiently proceeded with its insane accomplishments.

That, perhaps, is the most important point. A good ship always
has had a symbolic life of its own into which the lives of its
people can meaningfully—if not always willingly—blend. Great
examples—such as the Viking long ship or the Micronesian
outrigger—have been expressions of the whole life of a people,
not necessarily a numerous people. A self-sufficient whaleship,
epitomizing qualities of the place, made the spindling community of Nantucket more famous throughout the world than many
contemporary nations were. New Bedford's whaling bark was
fastened by invisible ligatures to the conscious life of New England, expressing its virtues along with its canny greed. Far inland from a broken chain of rock-chopped harbors, everyone who
lit a spermaceti candle was aware of the whaler. Pride, felt sometimes for dubious reasons, was a general response to the printed
or carved or painted representations in miniature of the whaler
herself. The whatnot shelves in a multitude of New England
parlors displayed the intimate reminder of an industrious bit
of scrimshaw. The head of a prosperous gentleman's cane was
likely to be a whale's tooth, and every female midriff was caged
in feather-light whalebone—the kindest substance, at least, for
an unkind confinement. Before the great trek west began, a run-
away farm boy's name was logically looked for in the files of
customhouses where whalers had got their clearances.

Whatever was once ennobling in the community's respect
for hunters, who served it at mortal peril, has vanished in the
use of the factory whaler, vanished even in the case of its heli-
copter pilots, who follow a submerged whale that cannot retali-

ate, although the ocean sometimes can. "Mortality among the pilots," McLaughlin tersely admits, "has been high, but there is no dearth of competent airmen." Harpooners who are thus guided to the kill no longer stand braced in the pitching bows of a shell of thin wood, weapon at shoulder or in upraised fist, ready to quicken with unbearable agony a sensitive colossus a yard or so away. They train cannon that are firmly mounted on broad steel fo'c's'les. If heroic competence can be thought in some measure to have offset the cruelty of old-fashioned whaling, nothing but the competence now remains.

It was not much more than a century ago, and largely through the efforts of Griffiths and Pook, that American ships began to get in advance a sophisticated mathematical determination of their probable hydrostatic qualities: a really new dimension, by comparison with rough calculations and enlightened hunches that previously had produced good ships which could all have been better. Have we been as indifferent as their predecessors were to the possibility of a really new dimension, waiting to be understood? Sometimes, taking the long view, it is possible to perceive a virtue that has crested and diminished and to wonder why mankind cannot hang on a little longer to the best moments that hover between advancement and decline. The creation of one ship such as the *James Arnold* can be at best a symbol of the passing of an optimum moment. Another vessel might do as well, and the time be shifted, as we seek to symbolize the event; but in the huge, mixed adventure of whaling, everything developed since about the time of the *James Arnold*'s launch has tipped a balance further against the long welfare of the living earth of which man's destiny is only a part.

Perhaps it is a dimension that has been present all along, unnoticed, during the dark age of our belief in the bracing assurances of Sophocles and the Book of Genesis that man is master of the natural world. If we are lucky, man's greatest achievement of the next few years may be his realization at last that everything he makes and uses—not forgetting his ships—should be designed to work no injury upon the natural world, within which his own survival is linked more than symbolically to the long survival of leviathan.

Appendixes

APPENDIX A.
THE PROBLEM OF SIZE
AS REFLECTED IN TONNAGE

As noted in the Foreword, capacity tonnage is generally the fairest basis for comparison of the merits of different vessels, but the means of arriving at this indication of size has varied so much at different times and in different places that an approximation is the best to be hoped for except when the methods of measurement are known to have been the same—and applied with similar care and skill. Nowadays three different methods are in common use for different purposes. For simplicity's sake I have settled for two, gross and net, and whenever possible have used only the latter.

Prior to the nineteenth century most measurements were taken by a relatively simple calculation of volume through the multiplication of length, breadth, and depth, as if the vessel actually were a rectangular box. The fact that ships were not overgrown shoe boxes was recognized in various ways. The United States method early in the nineteenth century assumed that subtraction of about three-fifths of a vessel's breadth from its length would compensate for the portions faired away at the bows and the stern. Thus, if a ship was 100 feet long, 25 feet broad, and 12½ feet deep, three-fifths of 25 feet—or 15 feet—was first subtracted from 100. The cubic content was then calculated at 85 × 25 × 12½, or 26,562.5, and finally divided by 95, on the assumption that a ton of freight occupied 95 cubic feet: result, 279.6 tons register.

The initial subtraction of three-fifths of the breadth, no more no less, without regard to the true shape fore and aft, meant that a clumsy, blunt ship with great capacity for freight was taxed the same amount levied upon an extremely sharp ship of the same major dimensions. It consequently had discouraged the building of ships designed for speed and had invited the modeling of stodgy ones that could stow more freight than the average, at the expense of safety as well as speed.

In 1865 all American ships were re-registered under the Moorsom system of measurement. This involved a complicated exercise in solid geometry to determine the actual content of the hull. When the new measurements were completed, most ships had a higher tonnage for taxes than before, but the surviving clippers had fallen. The excessive sharpness of the *Challenge* is revealed by the fact that her tonnage measurement fell from 2,006 to 1,375. This was partly due to her sharp ends, but even more to the extreme wedge shape of her bottom. Measurement tonnage is at best only an approximate calculation of a vessel's capacity for stowage, and was far from accurate in most cases under the old rule, but it is obvious from the above pair of figures that if the *Challenge* had been built with a flat floor, she would have stowed almost one-third more cargo inside the same major dimensions. It is curious to realize that she would probably then have been an even faster ship than she proved herself to be. The most successful California clippers reversed a trend that she had pushed to the ultimate extreme. Few were as flat-floored as the *Natchez,* but they were nearer to her in this respect than to the *Challenge.* One reason was the mere increase in size. A deep keel was needed in a small vessel to combat leeway, or sideslip. A large and heavy-laden vessel rode deep in the water anyhow.

In the second volume of his *Monthly Nautical Magazine,* Griffiths published a letter he had received from George Moorsom which acknowledged that a tonnage measurement reflecting displacement might be thought a better system for America if she should want to be rid of the old Custom House rules, but that everyone in England now supported a proper calculation of capacity as the taxable base. He said the new system associated with his name would go into effect on May 1, 1855. After that, all space "which may be made available for profit" would be measured by "tons" of 100 cubic feet. Deck houses, which could endanger the handling of a ship, would no longer be insisted upon by parsimonious owners because of the tax saving.

The *Sea Witch* did not survive to be measured under the new system, but her displacement tonnage has been calculated by

Chapelle at 37 per cent more than her registered tonnage. Displacement tonnage of the *Flying Cloud* was 33 per cent above the registry figure, but that of the *Challenge* was raised by only 9 per cent. These figures simply provide another kind of criticism of the old rule-of-thumb mathematics. They indicate that the two smaller vessels, by the rules in use at the time of launching of all of them, could carry something like a third more dead weight tonnage than their measurement tonnage might suggest, whereas the largest, the *Challenge,* could carry less than a tenth more. To put it another way, the *Flying Cloud* displaced 172 tons more than the supposedly larger *Challenge* displaced. Actually the leaner and sharper *Challenge* was only a foot and a half longer. Each at launching was "the largest merchant ship in the world," but the second was really larger only in length.

In the list of clippers that follows, when only one tonnage figure is given it represents the original registered tonnage. The Moorsom figure, if available, follows in parenthesis.

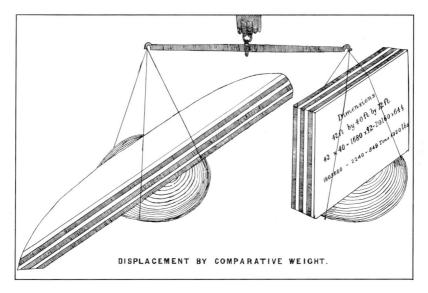

DISPLACEMENT BY COMPARATIVE WEIGHT.

John Willis Griffiths in his treatises on naval architecture did his best to provide rule-of-thumb, old-fashioned shipbuilders with devices for exact calculation that they could comprehend. In this illustration the displacement tonnage of an irregularly shaped body—the lift or slip model representing half of a ship—is brought to a balance against the same number, kind, and thickness of "lifts" of a precisely measurable rectangular shape. One edge of the latter could be planed to achieve an equivalent weight, and the displacement calculated in saltwater cubic feet of 64⅔ pounds each. The lamentable fact that the calculation as shown above displays a mathematical error does not diminish the convenience of the principle. (See pp. 191-93.)

APPENDIX B.
CLIPPER SHIPS ASCRIBED TO SAMUEL HARTT POOK

The following list is intended to be inclusive of persuasive claims made in several previous compilations, although the extent of Pook's contribution in some instances is difficult to determine and in others has not been convincingly verified.

Race Horse. Launched June, 1850, by Samuel Hall at East Boston; 530 tons. Made on her maiden voyage to San Francisco the third swiftest dash of the year. Arrived at the Dardanelles March 19, 1855, in 29 days from Boston, the fastest passage recorded between these points. At sea 15 years. Vanished early in 1865; perhaps a war casualty.

Surprise. Launched October 5, 1850, by Samuel Hall at East Boston; 1,261 tons (1,101 Moorsom). Arrived at San Francisco March 18, 1851, in 96 days 15 hours from New York, breaking the record of the *Sea Witch.* Arrived at Shanghai from San Francisco August 30, 1853, in 38 days, the record at that date. Arrived at New York January 20, 1854, in 39 days from the Cape of Good Hope, in company with the *Stag Hound* at start and finish, both ships three days short of the record set in 1847 by the *Sea Witch.* Arrived at New York March 24, 1857, in 82 days from Shanghai and 17 days from the equator; the former the record at that date, bettered only once, in 1859, by the *Sword Fish.* At sea 26 years.

Witchcraft. Launched December 21, 1850, by Paul Curtis at Chelsea, Massachusetts; 1,310 tons. (The Boston *Post* reported that on the previous day "an unsuccessful attempt was made to launch this vessel, aided by the R. B. Forbes.") Arrived at San Francisco August 11, 1851, in 62 days from Rio de Janeiro—and at Callao September 27, 1854, in 32 days from San Francisco, both records still unequaled. At sea ten years. Wrecked near Cape Hatteras.

Game Cock. Launched December 21, 1850, by Samuel Hall at East Boston; 1,391 tons (1,119 Moorsom). Arrived at Hong Kong December 12, 1850, in 19 days from Honolulu, still the unsurpassed record between these ports. (The *Memnon* had reported the same time a year earlier from a position "off Honolulu."

The *Red Gauntlet* equaled the passage five years later.) Arrived at Bombay January 17, 1851, in 68 days from San Francisco, via Honolulu and Hong Kong, the record. At sea 30 years.

Telegraph. Launched May, 1851, by J. O. Curtis at Medford, Massachusetts; 1,069 tons. Arrived at Boston August 19, 1853, in 58 days from Valparaiso, still the record. Arrived at San Francisco April 16, 1854, in 36 days from Valparaiso, next to the fastest passage on record and a few hours better than the best time of the *Sea Witch.* An unlucky ship, she persisted through several calamities for 17 years until burned at sea.

Northern Light. Launched on September 25, 1851, by E. & H. O. Briggs at South Boston; 1,021 tons. Arrived at Boston May 28, 1853, in 76 days 6 hours from San Francisco, 38 days from Cape Horn, 16 days from the equator, three still unequaled records. Arrived at Manila on June 17, 1856, in 89 days from Boston, still the record. Returned to Boston from this voyage after 7 months 20 days away, including 35 days in port, still the round-voyage record. Lost in a collision after ten years at sea.

Defiance. Launched March 8, 1852, by George Thomas at Rockland, Maine; 1,900 tons (1,691 Moorsom). The first flat-floored Down East clipper, and the first vessel to attain, according to a plausible contemporary report, a speed of 20 knots. As this occurred off Sandy Hook, on her shakedown cruise, and was publicized in the New York press, her flat-floored model had an impressive effect upon ships to come. Arrived at Hampton Roads April 20, 1855, 52 days from Callao, still the unapproached record. Sold to Spanish owners after five years. End uncertain.

Rattler. Launched October 15, 1852, by George Thomas at Rockland, Maine; 1,121 tons (853 Moorsom). Contemporary evidence of her designer uncertain. Thomas quoted later as saying that he had bought the model from Pook, but it has been alleged that he followed the lines of the *Defiance,* earlier designed for him by Pook. Cutler credits her with the record, in 1878, of 28 days from Callao to San Francisco. At sea 38 years.

Belle of the West. Launched March 25, 1853, by Shiverick Brothers, East Dennis, Massachusetts; 936 tons. The smallest of Pook's outright clippers. Equipped with Forbes's rig, topmasts fidded abaft, doublings 9 feet longer than those of the much larger *Flying Cloud.* See page 300 above. Foundered 1868.

Fearless. Launched July 28, 1853, by A. & G. T. Sampson at East Boston; 1,184 tons (909 Moorsom). Arrived at Manila December 26, 1856, in 36 days from San Francisco, equaling the *Winged Arrow's* previous record. Sold to Norway in 1878. Last report, 1892. End uncertain.

Red Jacket. Launched November 2, 1853, by George Thomas at Rockland, Maine; 2,435 tons (2,305 Moorsom). Arrived at Liverpool's Bell Buoy at 2:30 P.M., January 23, 1854, in 12 days from New York; dock-to-dock time 13 days, 1 hour, 25 minutes, having completed at noon on January 19 a day's work of 417 miles. Her time across the Atlantic is still the sailing ship record; her best day's mileage was the record for the North Atlantic, unsurpassed at the time anywhere except by the *Marco Polo,* 12 days earlier, in the Southern Ocean, and bettered on the Liverpool run afterward by only one ship, McKay's *Lightning,* six weeks later. The *Red Jacket* arrived at Melbourne July 12, 1854, in 67 days 13 hours from Liverpool, 44 days from the Atlantic equator, 19 days 15 hours from the Cape of Good Hope; all three being records at that date, the first bettered only three times, and I find no report that the others were ever equaled. Arrived at 26 degrees 25 minutes west longitude on September 2, 1854, in 63 sailing days from her outward crossing of the same meridian, still the record for a circumnavigation in high southern latitudes. Except for her first transatlantic crossing, the *Red Jacket* spent her life under British charter or registry. At sea more than 28 years; after that a coal hulk.

Challenger. Launched December 19, 1853, by Robert E. Jackson at East Boston; 1,334 tons. Made seven California voyages in reliable good time, in and out of season, the two best in 111 and 112 days. Sold to Peru, midway in the Civil War, for a coolie ship. At sea 22 years.

Herald of the Morning. Launched in December, 1853, by Hayden & Cudworth at Medford, Massachusetts; 1,294 tons (1,108 Moorsom). Arrived at San Francisco May 16, 1855, in 100 days from New York, anchorage to anchorage, the fastest passage of any vessel in a year of unusual weather. In her 18 westward

Cape Horn voyages she made reliably fast time even when under the reduced sail plans that followed those of the extravagant climax of the clipper ship era. Particularly noted for her speed in rounding the Horn. Sold to Norway in 1879. At sea for at least 36 years. End uncertain.

Ocean Chief. Launched by J. and C. Morton in 1854 at Thomaston, Maine; 1,228 tons. Arrived at Melbourne August 8, 1854, in 71 days from Liverpool, a passage bettered at that date only by Pook's *Red Jacket* of twice her tonnage and by the slightly smaller *Rip Van Winkle.* Burned at sea after a relatively short career, date uncertain.

Ocean Telegraph. Launched March 29, 1854, by J. O. Curtis at Medford, Massachusetts; 1,495 tons (1,244 Moorsom). Arrived at New York June 25, 1855, in 58 days from Callao, still the unequaled record. Unusually reliable for fast passages: seven from New York to San Francisco in an average time of 117 days, five from San Francisco to New York averaging 97 days. Sold midway in the Civil War to the British Black Ball Line. At sea for about 30 years, thereafter a coal hulk.

Blue Jacket. Launched by Robert E. Jackson August 27, 1854, at East Boston; 1,791 tons (1,403 Moorsom). Her ascription to Pook is uncertain, although her lines were reported to be derived from those of the *Red Jacket.* Griffiths printed a report of one of her sailing masters that she ran at from 20 to 23 knots by patent log, but in a later issue of his magazine this was retracted for lack of proof. A very fast ship nevertheless—once crossed the Atlantic, land to land, in 12 days 10 hours. Burned at sea in 1869.

APPENDIX C.
THE STEAM WHALERS OF SAN FRANCISCO

Although the enterprise of American steam whaling originated in New England, the first vessel to complete a voyage had orders to discharge at San Francisco and did so on October 10, 1880. Some others that sailed on their maiden voyages out of New Bedford followed the same procedure. The lists that follow are arranged by date, to suggest the sizes of vessels that seemed most suitable to the function year by year, whether they were built specifically for the purpose or were adapted to it after serving originally in another trade. In the latter instances, the marginal date is that of a vessel's first departure upon a whaling voyage, after conversion. Tonnage is net unless otherwise noted.

STEAM WHALERS, DESIGNED AS SUCH, BUILT AT
BATH, MAINE:

1879 *Mary and Helen,* 420 gross tons, bought by the United States in 1880 after the completion of one whaling voyage.

1880 *Belvedere,* 339 tons, made 27 whaling voyages out of the Golden Gate, more than any other member of the San Francisco steam fleet—the last in 1913. Registry then transferred to Seattle. Lost in 1919 on a whaling-trading voyage off Siberia.

1881 *North Star,* 489 gross tons. Sailed from New Bedford for the Pacific Arctic, where she was lost on her first voyage. Intended for registry at San Francisco, which she never reached.

1882 *Mary and Helen II,* 409 tons, burned 1886 at San Francisco, rebuilt there promptly as the *Beluga,* of 409 tons; last whaling voyage in 1908.

1883 *Thrasher,* 343 tons. Her service as a whaler interrupted by a period of carrying passengers to the Alaska gold rush in 1900–1901. Later registered at 502 tons, perhaps as a result of alterations then made. Last whaling voyage in 1908.

1888 *William Lewis,* 332 tons. Lost in the Arctic in 1891.

1892 *Navarch,* 254 tons. Lost in the Arctic in 1897.

VESSELS BUILT AT BATH, MAINE, LATER ADAPTED
TO STEAM WHALING:

1881   *Lucretia*, 313 tons. Built in 1877 as a sailing whaler. After
       one four-year voyage rebuilt at San Francisco as a whaling
       steamer of 350 gross tons. Lost in the Arctic in 1889.

1888   *Jesse H. Freeman*, 360 tons. Launched in 1883 as a steamer
       owned in Boston. Refitted for whaling in 1888. Lost in
       the Arctic in 1897.

1894   *William Baylies*, 291 tons. Built in 1886 as a whaling bark.
       Sailed out of San Francisco under canvas until her con-
       version to steam in 1894. Lost in Siberian Arctic in 1908.

1904   *Herman*, 229 tons. Launched in 1884 as the steamer *Morn-
       ing Star*, of 290 tons. Made one whaling voyage in 1903
       before full conversion in 1904 into a whaler. Converted
       to diesel power in 1915–16. Last voyage in 1924.

STEAM WHALERS, DESIGNED AS SUCH, BUILT AT
SAN FRANCISCO:

1882   *Bowhead*, tonnage uncertain. Fitted with a retractable
       screw, the shaft of which could be replaced by a skeg to
       improve weatherliness under sail. Lost in the Arctic in
       1884.

1882   *Orca*, 462 tons. Lost in the Arctic in 1897.

1883   *Balaena*, 390 tons. Lost in the Arctic in 1901.

1883   *Narwhal*, 390 tons. Probably the first tanker whaler. Last
       whaling voyage in 1908. Laid up 1910; afterward used
       as a salmon packer. Following a stint in the movies, sold
       to Mexico in 1931.

1886   *Grampus*, 250 tons. Lost in the Arctic in 1901.

VESSELS BUILT AT BENICIA, ON SAN FRANCISCO BAY:

1892   *Karluk*, 247 tons. Launched in 1884 as a steamer owned
       in San Francisco. Refitted for whaling in 1892. Last whal-
       ing voyage in 1911. Lost some years later during an ex-
       ploring expedition in the Arctic.

1893   *Jeannette*, 217 tons. Built as a steam whaler. Last whaling
       voyage 1911.

VESSELS OF VARIOUS ORIGINS THAT SERVED AS
STEAM WHALERS:

1885   *Alliance*, 214 tons. Launched at Astoria, Oregon, in 1884 as the steamer *Emma Hume*. Went whaling out of San Francisco in 1885 and 1886.

1887   *Beluga*, 409 tons. The *Mary and Helen II*, rebuilt. See above.

1890   *Mary D. Hume*, 108 tons. Launched in 1881 at Ellenburgh, Oregon. One of the first two whalers to winter by intention in the Arctic. Her second and last whaling voyage was probably the longest. It began April 13, 1893, and ended September 30, 1899, thus including seven summer seasons. At the time of the Alaska gold rush she entered the ocean passenger service, but was still listed as a whaler in 1913; then the entry was changed to "Fsh."

1892   *Newport*, 218 tons. Launched at San Francisco in 1875. Her one whaling voyage, from June 1, 1892, to September 26, 1898, was almost as long as the *Mary D. Hume*'s longest. It required the dispatch of three relief captains, the second being the whale-waster, Bodfish. Still listed as an ocean freighter in 1916.

1894   *Alexander*, 159 tons. Built by William H. Webb at New York in 1855 as the steamship *Astoria* of 500 tons, old measurement. Sailed under the Russian flag as the steamship *Alexander*. On her first whaling voyage, of 1894, she stayed out through three summer seasons. Thereafter she sailed annually until wrecked in the Arctic in 1906.

1894   *Fearless*, 400 tons, probably gross. Formerly the Norwegian ship *Elida*. Discharged at San Francisco November 25, 1898, flying the Nicaraguan flag, from a four-year voyage of uncertain origin. Made one fairly successful two-season voyage out of San Francisco, 1899–1900. Still under the Nicaraguan flag, she was lost in the Arctic in 1901.

1899   *Bowhead II*, 243 tons. Built at Christiania, Norway, in 1871 as the steamship *Haardraade*. Sailed out of San Francisco under the Chilean flag for a successful seasonal voyage in 1899. Transferred to United States registry in 1900 for a two-year voyage. Sailed again in 1903 for a voyage of four summer seasons, suffering a consequent mutiny. Made one-season voyages in 1907 and 1908. No further whaling voyages although registered as a whaler at New Bedford when she was burned in 1915.

In the winter of 1915–16, when the *Herman* was converted to diesel power, steam whaling out of San Francisco was abandoned to the historians. There had been earlier portents of a change in the devices of propulsion. The *Monterey,* a schooner of 119 tons, was equipped in 1903 with a gasoline engine by Lewis, Anderson, Foard & Company, which had been partly financed by William Lewis to operate the bark *Alaska,* lost in 1900. The first voyage of the *Monterey* was moderately successful. With a heavier engine she made three more. The second time out she had for explicit competition the larger motor schooner *Barbara Hernster,* of 140 tons, which returned to Seattle. After both of the substantial San Francisco operators had disposed of their fleets, two more oddities turned up: in the 1912 season the little Japanese-built gasoline schooner *Elvira,* of 60 tons, and in 1913 the fishing steamer *Polar Bear,* which measured only 18. In the postwar years the persistent *Herman* had for competition the larger motor schooners *Carolyn Frances,* of 422 tons, *Arctic,* of 418 tons, and *Ottilie Fjord,* of 197. The *Arctic* became in 1924 the last San Francisco whaler lost in the ocean for which she was named. In that year the *Herman,* following her second season of idleness in two decades, made her final voyage. One motorless vessel went whaling out of San Francisco in the postwar years: the schooner *Fox,* of 266 tons, which made voyages in 1920, 1921, and 1922. The *Ottilie Fjord* was refitted for the 1924 season with her horsepower doubled, her crew increased, her tonnage diminished to 160, and her name changed to *Nanuk.* She made one additional voyage, to Herschel Island and thereabouts, in 1925.

San Francisco's final whaling fleet in the Arctic consisted of two sudden latecomers, converted motorships. The *Charles Brower,* built at Alameda in 1918 and measuring 325 tons, made three successive summer-season voyages beginning in 1925. The somewhat larger *Patterson,* of 580 gross tons, a Brooklyn product of 1882, had long served under the same name in the Coast and Geodetic Survey; she went whaling in 1926, 1927, and 1928.

A List of Readings

A book that offers samplings from a large theme has to exclude much that seems as important as what survives in its pages. How can one bear to give only a paragraph or so to the inspired spadework of J. Louis Giddings as he turns up evidence of Arctic whaling almost 4,000 years ago? Giddings, envied by fellow archaeologists for his unteachable knack of "knowing where to dig," and envied just as much by me for his lucid prose. The book he finished shortly before his recent death comes first upon the list that follows.

As *American Ships* was headed for the printer I suggested that an obtrusive encumbrance of footnotes, which might have served the interests of a few specialists while impeding everyone else, be jettisoned with a happy splash. My publishers agreed, making only the condition that a list of readings be excerpted, from the bibliography of sources, for the guidance of general readers who might want to look further into some of the subjects broached in the foregoing chapters. Authority for a number of disputatious judgments has already been given in the text. I shall try to provide by mail the origins of any others that seem bothersome.

The titles that follow have been chosen rather more to supplement than to justify passages in this book. They have been arranged under the headings of subchapters to which they are relevant, here also identified by numerals to permit abbreviated references to them under later subchapters to which they have an additional relationship.

CHAPTER I:1 EARLY AMERICAN WHALE HUNTERS

Giddings, James Louis, *Ancient Men of the Arctic*. New York, 1967.

CHAPTER I:2 DUGOUTS OF THE CARIBBEAN

Columbus, Christopher, *The Voyages of Christopher Columbus, being the journals of the first and third, and the letters concerning the first and last, voyages. . . .* London, 1930.

Martínez-Hidalgo, José Maria, *Columbus' Ships*, Howard I. Chapelle, ed. Barre, Massachusetts, 1966.

CHAPTER I:3 THE GUARA RAFT

Benzoni, Girolamo, *History of the New World . . . travels in America . . . 1541–1556.* London, 1857.

Edwards, Clinton R., *Aboriginal Watercraft on the Pacific Coast of South America.* University of California, 1965.

Heyerdahl, Thor, *American Indians in the Pacific.* London, 1952.

——— *The Kon-Tiki Expedition; by Raft Across the South Seas.* London, 1950.

CHAPTER I:4 THE NORTH AMERICAN BARK CANOE

Chapelle, Howard I., *The Bark Canoes and Skin Boats of North America.* Washington, 1964.

Rosier, James, *A True Relation of the Most Prosperous Voyage made this present yeer 1605, by Captain George Waymouth. . . .* London, 1605.

CHAPTER I:5 THE WHALERS' SHALLOP

Baffin, William, *Voyages of William Baffin, 1612–1622,* Clements R. Markham, ed. London, 1881.

Baker, William A., *Sloops & Shallops.* Barre, Massachusetts, 1966.

Davis, John, *The voyages and works of John Davis,* Albert H. Markham, ed. London, 1880.

Rosier (See I:4, above.)

CHAPTER I:6 SKIN BOATS: THE KAYAK AND THE UMIAK

Chapelle (See I:4, above.)

Davis (See I:5, above.)

Egede, Hans P., *A description of Greenland . . . .* London, 1745.

Frobisher, Martin, *The Three Voyages of Martin Frobisher,* R. Collison, ed. London, 1867.

CHAPTER I:7 EUROPEAN OBSERVERS

Egede (See I:6, above.)

White, John, *The American Drawings of John White, 1577–1590.* London, 1964.

CHAPTER I:8 THE EXPLORER'S SHIP

Martínez-Hidalgo (See I:2, above.)

White (See I:7, above.)

CHAPTER I: GENERAL REFERENCES

Bry, Theodore de, *Collectio Navigationum in Indiam Occidentalem.*

Frankfurt, 1590–1602. (There are many other early editions, some with portions of the text in English. Consult a reference librarian.)

Hakluyt, Richard, *The Principal Navigations, Voiages, Traffiques and Discoueries of the English Nation . . .* , enlarged edition. London, 1598–1600. (The best modern edition was published at Glasgow, 1903–5, in 12 volumes. There is a version in print in the Modern Library.)

Purchas, Samuel, *Hakluytus posthumus or Purchas his Pilgrimes . . . .* London, 1625. (Reprinted at Glasgow, 1905–7, in 20 volumes. Less reliable than Hakluyt, but the only source of many accounts of voyaging.)

CHAPTER II:1 BEACH-BASED WHALING CRAFT AND THE CEDAR WHALEBOAT

Baker (See I:5, above.)

Starbuck, Alexander, *A History of the American Whale Fishery from its Earliest Inception to the year 1876.* Washington, 1878. (If unavailable separately, this volume may be shelved in some libraries as Senate Miscellaneous Document 107, 44th Congress, First Session, Document No. 1666.)

CHAPTER II:2 THE WHALING SLOOP

Albion, Robert G., *Forests and Sea Power . . . .* Cambridge, Massachusetts, 1926.

Ashley, Clifford W., *The Yankee Whaler.* Boston, 1926.

Blanckley, Thomas Riley, *A Naval Expositor . . . .* London, 1750. (An illustrated nautical dictionary from which something can be gathered about many vessels in use in the 1740's.)

Starbuck (See II:1, above.)

CHAPTER II:3 TRYWORKS OFFSHORE

Ashley (See II:2, above.)

Baffin (See I:5, above.)

Scoresby, William, *An account of the Arctic Regions, with a history and description of the northern whalefishery.* Edinburgh, 1820.

Martens, Friedrich, *De Noordsche Wereld.* Amsterdam, 1685. (An edition in English was published in 1694, bound up with Sir John Narborough's *An Account of Several Late Voyages . . . .*)

Stackpole, Edouard A., *The Sea Hunters; the New England Whalemen . . . 1635–1835.* Philadelphia, 1953.

CHAPTER III:1 DAVID BUSHNELL'S SCREW-DRIVEN SUBMARINE

The American Journal of Sciences and Arts (Silliman's Journal). New Haven, November, 1820. (Contains on pp. 94–100 Charles Griswold's communication to Professor Benjamin Silliman regarding his interview with Ezra Lee, first combat operator of Bushnell's submersible.)

American Philosophical Society, *Transactions,* IV:303 ff., 1799. (Contains David Bushnell's letter to Thomas Jefferson describing the Connecticut turtle.)

CHAPTER III:2 BUSHNELL AT WAR

Except for the two documents cited under III:1, above, material on Bushnell is too fragmentary, scattered, and unreliable to invite references beyond those excerpted in the text.

CHAPTER III:3 ROBERT FULTON'S SCREW-DRIVEN SUBMARINE

Delpeuch, Yves Maurice, . . . *La Navigation Sous-Marine à travers les siecles* . . . . Paris, 1902.

Dickinson, Henry W., *Robert Fulton, Engineer and Artist.* London, 1913.

Pesce, G.-L., *La Navigation Sous-Marine.* Paris, 1906.

Papers turned up in France by Emile Duboc in 1896 add importantly to the scope of the three works listed above, which therefore supersede previous accounts. The only substantial American work of later date is, as noted in the text, unreliable. Dickinson is sadly in error on Bushnell.

CHAPTER III:4 SCREW PROPELLERS OR PADDLE WHEELS?

Chapelle, Howard I., *Fulton's "Steam Battery": block ship and catamaran.* Washington, 1964.

Flexner, James T., *Steamboats Come True.* New York, 1944.

Tyler, David B., *Steam Conquers the Atlantic.* New York, 1939.

CHAPTER IV:1 DETACHABLE HAMLETS OF NANTUCKET

Coggeshall, George, *History of the American Privateers.* New York, 1856.

Scoresby (See II:3, above.)

Stackpole (See II:3, above.)

Starbuck (See II:1, above.)

CHAPTER IV:2 THE ADAPTED NANTUCKET WHALESHIP

Ashley (See II:2, above.)

Starbuck (See II:1, above.)

CHAPTER V:1 THE UNFAIR FRIGATES

Albion (See II:2, above.)

Chapelle, Howard I., *The History of the American Sailing Navy, the Ships and their Development.* New York, 1949.

Falconer, William, *An Universal Dictionary of the Marine.* London, 1769. (Chiefly for the sections concerned with naval ordnance, rates, and tactics.)

CHAPTER V:2 THE PILOT SCHOONERS

Albion, Robert G., *The Rise of New York Port (1815–1860)*. New York, 1939.

Chapelle, Howard I., *The Baltimore Clipper*. Salem, Massachusetts, 1930.

————*The History of American Sailing Ships*. New York, 1935.

Eastman, Ralph M., *Pilots and Pilot Boats of Boston Harbor*. Boston, 1956.

CHAPTER V:3 THE LINER PACKETS

Albion (See V:2, above.)

————*Square Riggers on Schedule*. New York, 1938.

Cutler, Carl C., *Queens of the Western Ocean*. Annapolis, 1961.

Morrison, John H., *History of New York Shipyards*. New York, 1909.

Webb, William H., *Plans of Wooden Vessels . . . built by . . . from the year 1840 to the year 1869*. N. P. or D.

CHAPTER VI:1 BRIG INTO WHALESHIP—THE *LEO*

Coggeshall (See IV:1, above.)

Stackpole (See II:3, above.)

Starbuck (See II:1, above.)

CHAPTER VI:2 THE PERFECTED WHALEBOAT

Ashley (See II:2, above.)

Davis, William M., *Nimrod of the Sea*. New York, 1874.

Stackpole, Edouard A., *Small Craft at Mystic Seaport*. Mystic, Connecticut, 1959. (Illustrations and descriptions of whaleboats.)

CHAPTER VI:3 NANTUCKET YIELDS TO NEW BEDFORD AND THE BARK RIG

Ashley (See II:2, above.)

Davis (See VI:2, above.)

Starbuck (See II:1, above.)

CHAPTER VI:4 TRADITION AND EXPERIMENT AT THE WHALING PORTS

Browne, John Ross, *Etchings of a Whaling Cruise . . . .* New York, 1846.

Hegarty, Reginald B., *Birth of a Whaleship*. New Bedford, c. 1964.

Starbuck (See II:1, above.)

Turner, Harry B., *The Story of the Island Steamers*. Nantucket, 1910. ("The Story of the Camels," pp. 102–13.)

CHAPTER VII:1 HABIT AND CONCEPT IN THE SHAPING OF SHIPS

Beaufoy, Mark, *Nautical and Hydraulic Experiments.* London, 1834.

Charnock, John, *An History of Marine Architecture . . . .* London, 1800–1802.

Petty, Sir William, *Treatise of Naval Philosophy.* London, 1691.

CHAPTER VII:2 JOHN WILLIS GRIFFITHS AND HIS COMPLICATED ART

Albion (See V:2, above.)

Chapelle, Howard I., *The Search for Speed Under Sail.* New York, 1967.

Cutler, Carl C., *Greyhounds of the Sea.* New York, 1930.

Griffiths, John W., *Marine and Naval Architecture, or the Science of Ship Building, Condensed Into a Single Lecture. . . .* New York, 1844.

———— *The Ship-builder's Manual and Nautical Referee.* New York, 1853.

———— *Treatise on Marine and Naval Architecture. . . .* New York, 1850.

Morrison (See V:3, above.)

CHAPTER VII:3 ROBERT H. WATERMAN AND THE COTTON CARRIER

Chapelle (See VII:2, above.)

Clark, Arthur H., *The Clipper Ship Era.* New York, 1910.

Cutler (See VII:2, above.)

CHAPTER VII:4 THE CHINA PACKETS

Clark (See VII:3, above.)

Cutler (See VII:2, above.)

Low, Charles P., *Some Recollections of Captain Charles Porter Low, Commanding the Clipper Ships "HOUQUA," "JACOB BELL," "SAMUEL RUSSELL," and "N. B. PALMER" in the China Trade 1847–1873.* New York, 1905.

CHAPTER VII:5 NATHANIEL B. PALMER AND THE FLAT FLOOR

Clark (See VII:3, above.)

Cutler (See VII:2, above.)

Low (See VII:4, above.)

CHAPTER VII:6 SHIPS FOR THE GOLD RUSH

Chapelle (See VII:2, above.)

Clark (See VII:3, above.)

Cutler (See VII:2, above.)

Griffiths (See VII:2, above, third entry.)

Maury, Matthew F., *Explanations and Sailing Directions to Accompany the Wind and Current Charts.* Philadelphia, 1854.

Webb (See V:3, above.)

CHAPTER VII:7 THE YACHT *AMERICA*

Lawson, Thomas W., and Thompson, Winfield M., *The Lawson History of the America's Cup.* Boston, 1902.

Stone, Herbert L., *The America's Cup Races.* New York, 1930.

CHAPTER VIII:1 MATERIALS AND PROPELLANTS

Multiplicity of sources for this subject makes it impractical to cite particular works.

CHAPTER VIII:2 THE FORBES-ERICSSON AUXILIARIES

Church, William C., *The Life of John Ericsson.* New York, 1890.

Forbes, Robert Bennet, *The Forbes Papers,* Frederick S. Allis, ed. (This important collection at the Massachusetts Historical Society in Boston, embracing the papers of several members of the Forbes family, was made generally available in 1969 on 47 reels of microfilm.)

————*Notes on Navigation.* Boston, 1884.

————*Personal Reminiscences.* Boston, 1882.

CHAPTER VIII:3 DOUBLE TOPSAILS

Forbes, Robert Bennet, *An Appeal to Merchants and Ship Owners, on the Subject of Seamen.* Boston, 1854.

————*The Forbes Rig.* Boston, 1862.

————*A New Rig for Ships and Other Vessels, Combining Economy, Safety and Convenience.* Boston, 1844.

Underhill, Harold A., *Masting and Rigging the Clipper Ship & Ocean Carrier . . . .* Glasgow, 1946.

CHAPTER VIII:4 THE PUZZLE OF DONALD McKAY

Chapelle (See VII:2, above.)

Clark (See VII:3, above.)

Cutler, Carl C., *500 Sailing Ship Records.* Mystic, Connecticut, 1952.

———— (See VII:2, above.)

Fairburn, William A., *Merchant Sail.* Center Lovell, Maine, 1945–55. (Many scattered references, some extensive, indexed throughout all six volumes. See note on this work in the last section below.)

McKay, Richard C., *Some Famous Sailing Ships and their Builder, Donald McKay*. New York, 1928.

Mjelde, Michael J., *The Glory of the Seas*. Middletown, Connecticut, 1970.

CHAPTER VIII:5 THE *MARCO POLO*, "A VERY ORDINARY WOODEN SHIP"

Lubbock, Basil, *The Colonial Clippers*. Glasgow, 1921.

Wallace, Frederick W., *In the Wake of the Wind Ships . . . the square-rigged merchant marine of British North America*. Toronto, 1927.

CHAPTER VIII:6 SAMUEL HARTT POOK, NAVAL ARCHITECT

Clark (See VII:3, above.)

Cutler (See VII:2, above.)

Fairburn (See VIII:4, above. Again, many references throughout the six volumes.)

CHAPTER VIII:7 THE FAST BARK *RACE HORSE*

Clark (See VII:3, above.)

Cutler (See VII:2 and VIII:4, above.)

CHAPTER VIII:8 POOK'S CLIPPERS: A CONSISTENT EXCELLENCE

Chapelle (See VII:2, above.)

Clark (See VII:3, above.)

Cutler (See VII:2 and VIII:4, above.)

Howe, Octavius T., and Matthews, Frederick C., *American Clipper Ships 1833–1858*. Salem, Massachusetts, 1926–27.

CHAPTER VIII:9 THE YEAR 1853

Bates, William W., *American Navigation . . . its rise and ruin . . . .* Boston, 1902.

Church (See VIII:2, above.)

Eastern Steam Navigation Company, *The Great Eastern Steam-ship*. London, 1861.

Forbes, Robert B., *Remarks on Ocean Steam Navigation*. Boston, 1855.

Tyler (See III:4, above.)

CHAPTER IX:1 THE TURN TOWARD IRON AND STEAM

Hall, Henry, *American Navigation, the Cause of its Recent Decay, and the Means by which its Prosperity May be Restored*. New York, 1880.

—— *The Shipbuilding Industry in the United States*. Washington, 1884.

(If this work is not shelved separately it may be found in the eighth volume of *Reports* of the tenth census of the United States, same date.)

Tyler (See III:4, above.)

CHAPTER IX:2 THE 90-DAY GUNBOATS

Bennett, Frank M., *The Steam Navy of the United States.* Pittsburgh, 1896.

Osbon, Bradley S., *Handbook of the U.S. Navy.* New York, 1864.

Porter, Admiral David, *The Naval History of the Civil War.* New York, 1886.

Executive Documents, House of Representatives, 37th Congress, 3rd Session, Volume 3. (Contains reports from the commanders of several 90-day gunboats of actions in which they participated. This document appears as Serial Set No. 1158.)

CHAPTER IX:3 THE COASTAL IRONCLADS

Baxter, James P. III, *The Introduction of the Ironclad Warship.* Cambridge, Massachusetts, 1932.

Bennett, Frank M., *The Monitor and the Navy Under Steam.* Boston, 1900.

————(See IX:2, above.)

Church (See VIII:2, above.)

Forbes (See VIII:2, all three entries.)

MacBride, Robert, *Civil War Ironclads; the Dawn of Naval Armor.* Philadelphia, 1962.

Osbon (See IX:2, above.)

Porter (See IX:2, above.)

CHAPTER IX:4 WAR UNDER WATER

Lake, Simon, *The Submarine in War and Peace.* Philadelphia, 1918.

Pesce (See III:3, above.)

CHAPTER IX:5 SAMUEL HARTT POOK, NAVAL CONSTRUCTOR

Bates, William W., *The American Marine, the Shipping Question in History and Politics.* Boston, 1893.

————(See VIII:9, above.)

Bennett (See IX:2, above.)

Dalzell, George W., *The Flight from the Flag.* Chapel Hill, 1940.

Forbes (See VIII:2, all three entries.)

Hall (See IX:1, above, both entries.)

CHAPTER X:1 WHALING: THE SHIFT TO SAN FRANCISCO

Hare, Lloyd, *Salted Tories; the Story of the Whaling Fleets of San Francisco.* Mystic, Connecticut, 1960.

Hegarty, Reginald, *Returns of Whaling Vessels Sailing from American Ports, 1876–1928.* New Bedord, 1959. (An extension, with a slight overlap, of Starbuck's compilation.)

Hunt, Cornelius E., *The Shenandoah; or, the Last Confederate Cruiser.* New York, 1867.

Starbuck (See II:1, above.)

CHAPTER X:2 THE DOWN EASTERS

Bates, William W., *The Comparative Performances of American and Foreign Ships—our Superiority.* Boston, 1893.

Hennessy, Mark W., *The Sewall Ships of Steel.* Augusta, Maine, 1937.

Lubbock, Basil, *The Down Easters.* Boston, 1929.

Matthews, Frederick C., *American Merchant Ships 1850–1900.* Salem, Massachusetts, 1930.

Mjelde (See VIII:4, above.)

CHAPTER X:3 THE MULTIMASTED WOODEN SCHOONERS

Crowninshield, Bowdoin B., *Fore-and-Afters.* Boston, 1940.

Marvin, Winthrop L., *The American Merchant Marine.* New York, 1902.

Parker, William J. Lewis, *The Great Coal Schooners.* Mystic, Connecticut, 1948.

CHAPTER X:4 THE BRONZE SKIMMING DISH *INDEPENDENCE* OF 1901

Crowninshield (See X:3, above.)

Lawson and Thompson (See VII:7, above.)

Stone (See VII:7, above.)

CHAPTER X:5 THE STEEL SCHOONERS

Crowninshield (See X:3, above.)

Parker (See X:3, above.)

CHAPTER X:6 THE *THOMAS W. LAWSON*

American Neptune, April, 1969, pp. 133–38. (Reprint of "Wreck of Thomas W. Lawson," Western *Weekly News,* December 21, 1907.)

Crowninshield (See X:3, above.)

Parker (See X:3, above.)

CHAPTER X:7 WILLIAM LEWIS AND
THE SAN FRANCISCO STEAM WHALERS

Bodfish, Hartson H., *Chasing the Bowhead*. Cambridge, Massachusetts, 1936. (An autobiography broadly interesting beyond its specific relevance to this book. On page 267 Bodfish sails through the tail of Halley's comet.)

Hare (See X:1, above.)

Hegarty (See X:1, above.)

Lubbock, Basil, *The Arctic Whalers*. Glasgow, 1937.

Tilton, George Fred, *"Cap'n George Fred" Himself*. New York, 1929. (A highly personal account which parallels and corroborates that of Bodfish from the standpoint of a very different kind of man.)

CHAPTER X:8 JOSIAH N. KNOWLES AND
THE PACIFIC STEAM WHALING COMPANY

Bodfish (See X:7, above.)

Hare (See X:1, above.)

Hegarty (See X:1, above.)

Mjelde (See VIII:4, above.)

Tilton (See X:7, above.)

CHAPTER X:9 WHALING IN THE TWENTIETH CENTURY

Bodfish (See X:7, above.)

Brandt, Karl, *Whaling and Whale Oil During World War II*. Stanford University, 1948.

———*Whale Oil: an Economic Analysis*. Stanford University, 1940.

Grierson, John, *Air Whaler*. London, 1949.

McLaughlin, William R. D., *Call to the South*. London, 1962.

Tripp, William H., *"There Goes Flukes"; the Story of New Bedford's Last Whaler . . . .* New Bedford, 1938.

CHAPTER X:10 THE ULTIMATE WHALER

Hegarty (See VI:4, above.)

Hirshson, G. Warren, *The Whaleship* Charles W. Morgan. New Bedford, 1938.

From the numerous appearances of some books under different headings, above, it should be evident that the writings of several authors provide rich extensions of topics that have been restricted, in the foregoing text, only by the tyranny of available space. The most comprehensive of these works, William Armstrong Fairburn's 4,179-page *Merchant Sail*, could have been cited much more often. One reason for placing a limitation upon it is the vexatiously repetitive mixture it contains of generally accurate data and discursive—I think often dubious—opinion. As a monumental bundle of references to information that should be checked elsewhere it is an invaluable resource. Its best virtues begin at the end, with an index of 13,278 vessels, and with a separate general index of more than 150 tall columns of type, both prepared under the direction of Ethel M. Ritchie, who managed to put the huge, chaotic work into some kind of order after its compiler-author's death. Everyone concerned with the record of American shipping is vastly indebted both to Mr. Fairburn and to Miss Ritchie, but the nature of the work should be borne in mind by its users.

Three periodicals, among the many consulted during the preparation of *American Ships*, are particularly suited to further browsing. John Willis Griffiths and William W. Bates, whose individual books appear frequently in the list above, began to publish in 1854 their *United States Nautical Magazine and Naval Journal*, usually referred to under its later title, *The Monthly Nautical Magazine and Quarterly Review*. Conceived of as the clipper ship era was at its crest of activity, this journal during the slightly less than four years of its publication reveals the state of the art of shipbuilding at its imaginative height in America, as well as some reasons for a swift decline. Complete sets are hard to locate, but they are well worth the seeking.

The Mariner's Mirror, The Quarterly Journal of the Society for Nautical Research, published at Cambridge, England, continuously over sixty years of war and partial peace, is full of riches for the general reader with a marine bent as well as an indispensable argosy of treasures for the researcher. Much of its contents is concerned with exploration of the Americas and with ships of the United States.

The American Neptune: A Quarterly of Maritime History, this year exactly half as old as its British predecessor, has been preponderantly concerned with the American record. It has had the great advantage of being edited and issued at the Peabody Museum of Salem. Both of these journals are well indexed. I have consulted one or both with a combination of awe and profit during the composition of almost every page of this book, and am grateful.

—A. L.

Index of Vessels

Page references to pictures appear in bold type. When more than one vessel of the same name is indexed, the dates of launchings are given in parentheses. Naval vessels are identified by the usual abbreviations. The reading list is not indexed.

Index of Persons

Page references to a few portraits of persons appear in bold type. Firms are indexed only when they include the full name of an individual. Thus A. A. Low & Brother is indexed under "Low, Abiel Abbot." The reading list is not indexed.

PICTURE CREDITS

Salem: title page, pp. 112 (bottom), 122 (bottom), 139 (top, right), 152 (middle), 161 (bottom), 172 (top), 179 (middle), 194 (middle), 203 (top), 206 (bottom), 226 (top), 235 (top), 244 (top), 251 (bottom), 257 (bottom), 269 (top), 276 (bottom), 294 (bottom), 304 (top), 315 (top), 323 (bottom), 376 (top, left), 379 (top; bottom), 399 (all), 405 (top), 421 (top), 462 (bottom). Pepysian Library, Magdalene College, Cambridge: p. 189 (bottom). Public Archives of Canada: p. 16 (middle). Franklin Delano Roosevelt Library: pp. 348 (top), 363. Royal Photographic Society, London: p. 304 (bottom). San Francisco Maritime Museum: pp. 173 (top), 405 (bottom), 451, 452 (top, center and right), 468 (bottom). Seamens Bank for Savings: p. 211. Smithsonian Institution, Division of Transportation: pp. 46 (bottom, right), 104 (bottom), 109 (bottom), 112 (top), 113 (top), 194 (bottom), 212 (top), 235 (bottom, left; bottom, right), 276 (middle), 397 (top), 406 (bottom, left), 439 (top), 452 (top, left); Harry T. Peters Collection: p. 216 (top). Society for the Preservation of New England Antiquities: p. 420 (top). State Street Bank and Trust Company: pp. 226–27. Universitetets Oldsaksamlung, Oslo: p. 31 (bottom). University Library, Ghent: p. 30 (top, right). United States Naval Academy Museum: pp. 250 (top), 251 (top). United States Navy: pp. 227 (top), 337 (top), 339, 341 (bottom), 345 (bottom), 348 (bottom), 353 (top), 357 (bottom), 362 (middle), 368, 369 (bottom), 376 (top, right), 380 (all). Wells Fargo Bank and Union Trust Company, San Francisco: p. 212 (bottom). West Point Museum: p. 16 (bottom). Henry Francis Du Pont Winterthur Museum: p. 139 (bottom). Yale University Library: pp. 30 (middle, left), 38 (bottom, left), 82 (top, left), 269 (bottom); Coe Collection: p. 38 (top).
Drawings by Joseph Phelan: pp. 82–83.
Drawing by Alexander Laing: p. 123 (bottom, right).

American Heritage Press gratefully acknowledges the generous help of the following persons:

M. V. Brewington, Kendall Whaling Museum, Sharon, Massachusetts
William Geohegan, Division of Transportation, Smithsonian Institution
Charles Morgan, Boston, Massachusetts
Philip Chadwick Foster Smith, Peabody Museum, Salem, Massachusetts